T0135170

Lecture Notes in Computer Science   **14731**

Founding Editors

Gerhard Goos
Juris Hartmanis

The series Lecture Notes in Computer Science (LNCS), including its subseries Lecture Notes in Artificial Intelligence (LNAI) and Lecture Notes in Bioinformatics (LNBI), has established itself as a medium for the publication of new developments in computer science and information technology research, teaching, and education.

LNCS enjoys close cooperation with the computer science R & D community, the series counts many renowned academics among its volume editors and paper authors, and collaborates with prestigious societies. Its mission is to serve this international community by providing an invaluable service, mainly focused on the publication of conference and workshop proceedings and postproceedings. LNCS commenced publication in 1973.

Xiaowen Fang

Editor

HCI in Games

6th International Conference, HCI-Games 2024
Held as Part of the 26th HCI International Conference, HCII 2024
Washington, DC, USA, June 29 – July 4, 2024
Proceedings, Part II

 Springer

Editor
Xiaowen Fang
DePaul University
Chicago, IL, USA

ISSN 0302-9743   ISSN 1611-3349 (electronic)
Lecture Notes in Computer Science
ISBN 978-3-031-60694-6   ISBN 978-3-031-60695-3 (eBook)
https://doi.org/10.1007/978-3-031-60695-3

Foreword

This year we celebrate 40 years since the establishment of the HCI International (HCII) Conference, which has been a hub for presenting groundbreaking research and novel ideas and collaboration for people from all over the world.

The HCII conference was founded in 1984 by Prof. Gavriel Salvendy (Purdue University, USA, Tsinghua University, P.R. China, and University of Central Florida, USA) and the first event of the series, "1st USA-Japan Conference on Human-Computer Interaction", was held in Honolulu, Hawaii, USA, 18–20 August. Since then, HCI International is held jointly with several Thematic Areas and Affiliated Conferences, with each one under the auspices of a distinguished international Program Board and under one management and one registration. Twenty-six HCI International Conferences have been organized so far (every two years until 2013, and annually thereafter).

Over the years, this conference has served as a platform for scholars, researchers, industry experts and students to exchange ideas, connect, and address challenges in the ever-evolving HCI field. Throughout these 40 years, the conference has evolved itself, adapting to new technologies and emerging trends, while staying committed to its core mission of advancing knowledge and driving change.

As we celebrate this milestone anniversary, we reflect on the contributions of its founding members and appreciate the commitment of its current and past Affiliated Conference Program Board Chairs and members. We are also thankful to all past conference attendees who have shaped this community into what it is today.

The 26th International Conference on Human-Computer Interaction, HCI International 2024 (HCII 2024), was held as a 'hybrid' event at the Washington Hilton Hotel, Washington, DC, USA, during 29 June – 4 July 2024. It incorporated the 21 thematic areas and affiliated conferences listed below.

A total of 5108 individuals from academia, research institutes, industry, and government agencies from 85 countries submitted contributions, and 1271 papers and 309 posters were included in the volumes of the proceedings that were published just before the start of the conference, these are listed below. The contributions thoroughly cover the entire field of human-computer interaction, addressing major advances in knowledge and effective use of computers in a variety of application areas. These papers provide academics, researchers, engineers, scientists, practitioners and students with state-of-the-art information on the most recent advances in HCI.

The HCI International (HCII) conference also offers the option of presenting 'Late Breaking Work', and this applies both for papers and posters, with corresponding volumes of proceedings that will be published after the conference. Full papers will be included in the 'HCII 2024 - Late Breaking Papers' volumes of the proceedings to be published in the Springer LNCS series, while 'Poster Extended Abstracts' will be included as short research papers in the 'HCII 2024 - Late Breaking Posters' volumes to be published in the Springer CCIS series.

I would like to thank the Program Board Chairs and the members of the Program Boards of all thematic areas and affiliated conferences for their contribution towards the high scientific quality and overall success of the HCI International 2024 conference. Their manifold support in terms of paper reviewing (single-blind review process, with a minimum of two reviews per submission), session organization and their willingness to act as goodwill ambassadors for the conference is most highly appreciated.

This conference would not have been possible without the continuous and unwavering support and advice of Gavriel Salvendy, founder, General Chair Emeritus, and Scientific Advisor. For his outstanding efforts, I would like to express my sincere appreciation to Abbas Moallem, Communications Chair and Editor of HCI International News.

July 2024   Constantine Stephanidis

HCI International 2024 Thematic Areas
and Affiliated Conferences

- HCI: Human-Computer Interaction Thematic Area
- HIMI: Human Interface and the Management of Information Thematic Area
- EPCE: 21st International Conference on Engineering Psychology and Cognitive Ergonomics
- AC: 18th International Conference on Augmented Cognition
- UAHCI: 18th International Conference on Universal Access in Human-Computer Interaction
- CCD: 16th International Conference on Cross-Cultural Design
- SCSM: 16th International Conference on Social Computing and Social Media
- VAMR: 16th International Conference on Virtual, Augmented and Mixed Reality
- DHM: 15th International Conference on Digital Human Modeling & Applications in Health, Safety, Ergonomics & Risk Management
- DUXU: 13th International Conference on Design, User Experience and Usability
- C&C: 12th International Conference on Culture and Computing
- DAPI: 12th International Conference on Distributed, Ambient and Pervasive Interactions
- HCIBGO: 11th International Conference on HCI in Business, Government and Organizations
- LCT: 11th International Conference on Learning and Collaboration Technologies
- ITAP: 10th International Conference on Human Aspects of IT for the Aged Population
- AIS: 6th International Conference on Adaptive Instructional Systems
- HCI-CPT: 6th International Conference on HCI for Cybersecurity, Privacy and Trust
- HCI-Games: 6th International Conference on HCI in Games
- MobiTAS: 6th International Conference on HCI in Mobility, Transport and Automotive Systems
- AI-HCI: 5th International Conference on Artificial Intelligence in HCI
- MOBILE: 5th International Conference on Human-Centered Design, Operation and Evaluation of Mobile Communications

List of Conference Proceedings Volumes Appearing Before the Conference

1. LNCS 14684, Human-Computer Interaction: Part I, edited by Masaaki Kurosu and Ayako Hashizume
2. LNCS 14685, Human-Computer Interaction: Part II, edited by Masaaki Kurosu and Ayako Hashizume
3. LNCS 14686, Human-Computer Interaction: Part III, edited by Masaaki Kurosu and Ayako Hashizume
4. LNCS 14687, Human-Computer Interaction: Part IV, edited by Masaaki Kurosu and Ayako Hashizume
5. LNCS 14688, Human-Computer Interaction: Part V, edited by Masaaki Kurosu and Ayako Hashizume
6. LNCS 14689, Human Interface and the Management of Information: Part I, edited by Hirohiko Mori and Yumi Asahi
7. LNCS 14690, Human Interface and the Management of Information: Part II, edited by Hirohiko Mori and Yumi Asahi
8. LNCS 14691, Human Interface and the Management of Information: Part III, edited by Hirohiko Mori and Yumi Asahi
9. LNAI 14692, Engineering Psychology and Cognitive Ergonomics: Part I, edited by Don Harris and Wen-Chin Li
10. LNAI 14693, Engineering Psychology and Cognitive Ergonomics: Part II, edited by Don Harris and Wen-Chin Li
11. LNAI 14694, Augmented Cognition, Part I, edited by Dylan D. Schmorrow and Cali M. Fidopiastis
12. LNAI 14695, Augmented Cognition, Part II, edited by Dylan D. Schmorrow and Cali M. Fidopiastis
13. LNCS 14696, Universal Access in Human-Computer Interaction: Part I, edited by Margherita Antona and Constantine Stephanidis
14. LNCS 14697, Universal Access in Human-Computer Interaction: Part II, edited by Margherita Antona and Constantine Stephanidis
15. LNCS 14698, Universal Access in Human-Computer Interaction: Part III, edited by Margherita Antona and Constantine Stephanidis
16. LNCS 14699, Cross-Cultural Design: Part I, edited by Pei-Luen Patrick Rau
17. LNCS 14700, Cross-Cultural Design: Part II, edited by Pei-Luen Patrick Rau
18. LNCS 14701, Cross-Cultural Design: Part III, edited by Pei-Luen Patrick Rau
19. LNCS 14702, Cross-Cultural Design: Part IV, edited by Pei-Luen Patrick Rau
20. LNCS 14703, Social Computing and Social Media: Part I, edited by Adela Coman and Simona Vasilache
21. LNCS 14704, Social Computing and Social Media: Part II, edited by Adela Coman and Simona Vasilache
22. LNCS 14705, Social Computing and Social Media: Part III, edited by Adela Coman and Simona Vasilache

47. LNCS 14730, HCI in Games: Part I, edited by Xiaowen Fang
48. LNCS 14731, HCI in Games: Part II, edited by Xiaowen Fang
49. LNCS 14732, HCI in Mobility, Transport and Automotive Systems: Part I, edited by Heidi Krömker
50. LNCS 14733, HCI in Mobility, Transport and Automotive Systems: Part II, edited by Heidi Krömker
51. LNAI 14734, Artificial Intelligence in HCI: Part I, edited by Helmut Degen and Stavroula Ntoa
52. LNAI 14735, Artificial Intelligence in HCI: Part II, edited by Helmut Degen and Stavroula Ntoa
53. LNAI 14736, Artificial Intelligence in HCI: Part III, edited by Helmut Degen and Stavroula Ntoa
54. LNCS 14737, Design, Operation and Evaluation of Mobile Communications: Part I, edited by June Wei and George Margetis
55. LNCS 14738, Design, Operation and Evaluation of Mobile Communications: Part II, edited by June Wei and George Margetis
56. CCIS 2114, HCI International 2024 Posters - Part I, edited by Constantine Stephanidis, Margherita Antona, Stavroula Ntoa and Gavriel Salvendy
57. CCIS 2115, HCI International 2024 Posters - Part II, edited by Constantine Stephanidis, Margherita Antona, Stavroula Ntoa and Gavriel Salvendy
58. CCIS 2116, HCI International 2024 Posters - Part III, edited by Constantine Stephanidis, Margherita Antona, Stavroula Ntoa and Gavriel Salvendy
59. CCIS 2117, HCI International 2024 Posters - Part IV, edited by Constantine Stephanidis, Margherita Antona, Stavroula Ntoa and Gavriel Salvendy
60. CCIS 2118, HCI International 2024 Posters - Part V, edited by Constantine Stephanidis, Margherita Antona, Stavroula Ntoa and Gavriel Salvendy
61. CCIS 2119, HCI International 2024 Posters - Part VI, edited by Constantine Stephanidis, Margherita Antona, Stavroula Ntoa and Gavriel Salvendy
62. CCIS 2120, HCI International 2024 Posters - Part VII, edited by Constantine Stephanidis, Margherita Antona, Stavroula Ntoa and Gavriel Salvendy

https://2024.hci.international/proceedings

Preface

Computer games have grown beyond simple entertainment activities. Researchers and practitioners have attempted to utilize games in many innovative ways, such as educational games, therapeutic games, simulation games, and gamification of utilitarian applications. Although a lot of attention has been given to investigate the positive impact of games in recent years, prior research has only studied isolated fragments of a game system. More research on games is needed to develop and utilize games for the benefit of society.

At a high level, a game system has three basic elements: system input, process, and system output. System input concerns the external factors impacting the game system. It may include but is not limited to, player personalities and motivations to play games. The process is about game mechanism and play experience. System output includes the effects of gameplay. There is no doubt that users are involved in all three elements. Human-Computer Interaction (HCI) plays a critical role in the study of games. By examining player characteristics, interactions during gameplay, and behavioral implications of gameplay, HCI professionals can help design and develop better games for society.

The 6th International Conference on HCI in Games (HCI-Games 2024), an affiliated conference of the HCI International Conference, was intended to help, promote, and encourage research in this field by providing a forum for interaction and exchanges among researchers, academics, and practitioners in the fields of HCI and games. The conference addressed HCI principles, methods, and tools for better games. Papers included in the proceedings have actively explored the area of game design from various viewpoints including gamification, empathy, playfulness, affordances, mobile gaming, and tutorial design. Furthermore, papers have contributed state-of-the-art research on player experience and engagement, addressing attainable game experiences, aesthetics, meaning, and toxicity, as well as user studies on player behavior and perspectives. The impact of games in learning and education has also been actively explored, with research focusing on the user experience of immersive games and embodied experiences and exploring various application domains of serious games such as language learning, environmental awareness, physical therapy and rehabilitation, cultural heritage, and art. Finally, as AI technologies continue to advance, their transformative impact on game experience has been studied, from producing game content with natural language to designing game characters and intelligent agents or creating adaptive games and evaluating game experiences.

Two volumes of the HCII 2024 proceedings are dedicated to this year's edition of the HCI-Games Conference. The first focuses on topics related to Game Design and Gamification, Game-Based Learning, and Games and Artificial Intelligence, while the second focuses on topics related to Advancing Education Through Serious Games, and Player Experience and Engagement.

The papers in these volumes were accepted for publication after a minimum of two single-blind reviews from the members of the HCI-Games Program Board or, in some cases, from members of the Program Boards of other affiliated conferences. I would like to thank all of them for their invaluable contribution, support, and efforts.

July 2024   Xiaowen Fang

6th International Conference on HCI in Games
(HCI-Games 2024)

Program Board Chair: **Xiaowen Fang**, *DePaul University, USA*

- Amir Zaib Abbasi, *King Fahd University of Petroleum & Minerals, Saudi Arabia*
- Saeed Abo-oleet, *Najran University, Saudi Arabia*
- Barbara Caci, *University of Palermo, Italy*
- Benjamin Ultan Cowley, *University of Helsinki, Finland*
- Khaldoon Dhou, *Texas A&M University-Central Texas, USA*
- Reza Hadi Mogavi, *University of Waterloo, Canada*
- Kevin Keeker, *Sony Interactive Entertainment Europe, USA*
- Daniel Riha, *Charles University, Czech Republic*
- Owen Schaffer, *Elmhurst University, USA*
- Jason Schklar, *UX is Fine, USA*
- Chaoguang Wang, *Bournemouth University, UK*
- Hanan Makki Zakari, *Ministry of Communications and Information Technology, Saudi Arabia*
- Fan Zhao, *Florida Gulf Coast University, USA*
- Miaoqi Zhu, *Sony Pictures Entertainment, USA*

The full list with the Program Board Chairs and the members of the Program Boards of all thematic areas and affiliated conferences of HCII 2024 is available online at:

http://www.hci.international/board-members-2024.php

HCI International 2025 Conference

The 27th International Conference on Human-Computer Interaction, HCI International 2025, will be held jointly with the affiliated conferences at the Swedish Exhibition & Congress Centre and Gothia Towers Hotel, Gothenburg, Sweden, June 22–27, 2025. It will cover a broad spectrum of themes related to Human-Computer Interaction, including theoretical issues, methods, tools, processes, and case studies in HCI design, as well as novel interaction techniques, interfaces, and applications. The proceedings will be published by Springer. More information will become available on the conference website: https://2025.hci.international/.

General Chair
Prof. Constantine Stephanidis
University of Crete and ICS-FORTH
Heraklion, Crete, Greece
Email: general_chair@2025.hci.international

https://2025.hci.international/

Contents – Part II

Player Experience and Engagement

Contents – Part I

Advancing Education Through Serious Games

LEGO® for Professional Development: A Systematic Literature Review

Dimitra Chasanidou[1,2(✉)] [iD] and Natassa Raikou[2,3] [iD]

[1] Norwegian University of Science and Technology, 7491 Trondheim, Norway
dimitra.chasanidou@ntnu.no
[2] Hellenic Open University, 26335 Patras, Greece
{std146411,raikou.anastasia}@ac.eap.gr
[3] University of Thessaly, 38221 Volos, Greece
araikou@uth.gr

Abstract. The purpose of this systematic literature review is to map how LEGO® is currently utilised within formal and non-formal education to support professional development of adults. The review process encapsulates a wide range of evidence related to LEGO use® in diverse educational practices and settings. A total of 43 articles were thoroughly reviewed to answer three research questions and explore the use of diverse LEGO® types and its effect in professional development. The SLR identified a number of applications in both formal and non-formal education, methodological approaches and a number of benefits related to the use of LEGO® in professional development, particularly in supporting diverse skills, such as teamwork, learning, and creativity. Finally, the paper suggests a taxonomy of professional skills in adult education with LEGO®, organised in personal, social and methodological skills.

Keywords: LEGO® · Adult education · Higher education · Professional development · Systematic Literature Review

1 Introduction

Since the dawn of the 21st century, the landscape of employability and professional competencies has undergone a significant transformation, with a growing focus on fostering creativity, alongside the mastery of design and engineering processes [9]. Emphasis has been placed on employability to address the needs of prospective employers and increase students' chances of succeeding in the job market [3]. An increased emphasis on diverse skills over the last 5-10 years targets to fulfil the needs of a continuously changing work environment. Experts point out that various skills (e.g., personal, social, methodological) are closely connected with employability, particularly for young graduates [43]. Higher Education Institutions (HEI) and companies need to work together to guide students' awareness on professional skills adapt to the changing labour market and improve their employability [43]. This is inline with lifelong learning which is adequately

© The Author(s), under exclusive license to Springer Nature Switzerland AG 2024
X. Fang (Ed.): HCII 2024, LNCS 14731, pp. 3–21, 2024.
https://doi.org/10.1007/978-3-031-60695-3_1

incorporated as an important part of the Sustainable Development Goals (SDG) that calls for "adult up-skilling and reskilling in fast changing labor markets" [32]. In order to address these challenges, new skills and methods are necessary. LEGO® bricks and its method LEGO® Serious Play applied in many different educational settings and fields. LEGO® could be applied in adult learning with constructivist activities, where learners try to associate meanings to learning from active inquiry of their life experiences [28]. Rooted to the essence of experiential learning and constructivism, learning with LEGO® can be achieved through own experiences and reflective practices [19, 28].

Several works explored the pedagogical and technological potential that LEGO® can offer in education, focusing on a specific type of LEGO®, or its impact on a specific profession. A review on the use of LEGO® bricks in education and training identified 26 articles and proposed a typology to help educators introduce LEGO® providing four types of LEGO® brick applications in education, namely learning facilitation, thinking facilitation, individual application, and group application [21]. Another review focused on the education of new nurses and explored the use of LEGO® Serious Play across a broad range of disciplines including nursing, play therapy, occupational therapy and marketing [47]. By analysing 11 relevant texts, a number of benefits from LEGO® are underscored by the review, in relation to supporting reflection, formation of professional identity and the development of resilience. Additionally, a third review explored LEGO® Robotics in an holistic research context and identified 36 studies [42]. Main findings discuss environments and programming languages adopted in the LEGO® Robotics context, educational practices applied in classes, as well as the educational levels in which robotics has been applied with positive results.

However, there is still very little understanding of the impacts and contributions of LEGO® in adult education for professional development. Inspired by previous work and to fill this gap in the field, we conducted a systematic literature review with the purpose of mapping how LEGO® is currently utilised within formal and non-formal education to support the professional development of adults. To the best of our knowledge, there are no literature reviews focused on surveying the adult education within formal or non-formal education, focusing on the impact of LEGO®on professional development. The remainder of this paper is organized as follows. Section 2 describes the methodology for the review process adopted in this study. Section 3 provides the results according to the research questions. Specifically, educational practices, LEGO® types and educational settings are explained in the context of professional development. The paper also presents a taxonomy of the identified professional skills. Finally, Sect. 4 concludes this SLR, discussing limitations and further research directions.

2   Methodology

The SLR follows the guidelines of Kitchenham [17, 18] in order to encapsulate a broad range of evidence relating to the use of LEGO® within a variety of educational settings. This SRL methodology has been gaining attention in the

Software Engineering community because it follows a rigorous and auditable protocol allowing to evaluate available studies relevant to a particular field and answer research questions. In addition, it enables the identification of gaps in current researches, thereby opening possibilities for future work [17]. The detailed procedure is described in the following subsections.

2.1   Research Questions

The central research question of this review is to explore how LEGO® is being used to support the professional development of adults within educational settings. We expanded the search and explored three specific questions:

- **RQ1:** How is LEGO® being used in adult education for professional development?
- **RQ2:** Which LEGO® types and research settings have been used in adult education for professional development?
- **RQ3:** What are the identified benefits of LEGO® in various educational settings for adults?

2.2   Conducted Search

We followed a five-step approach to identify relevant literature to the review question. First, the main keywords were identified according to the RQs. The main keywords were "LEGO" and "adult education" and "profession" or "industry" or "business". The retrieved articles enabled the initial search terms to be expanded based on their associated keywords. This revised list of search terms was then used in the second step to undertake a wider and more rigorous search. Databases searched included ACM Digital Library, ScienceDirect, and Scopus. Furthermore, we used Google Scholar in the forward and backward snowballing step. Retrieved articles were screened for relevance and compiled in a file to summarise the key components and findings of each source. At the final steps of this process, we searched the reference lists of all selected articles. The search process is summarised in Fig. 1.

2.3   Inclusion and Exclusion Criteria

The selection of the studies considered inclusion and exclusion criteria. The inclusion criteria refer to: a) adult education, either formal or non-formal educational context, b) use of any type of LEGO® or an adaptation of it, c) focus on professional development of adults, d) include any type of study with LEGO®, e) be available in English and full-text, and f) be published in a peer reviewed journal. The exclusion criteria refer to: a) secondary studies, i.e., reviews in the field, b) studies that are outside the field of research, c) studies that are published in conference proceedings, or non-peer reviewed studies, such as abstracts, posters, reports, keynotes, etc., d) studies in other languages than English, or not accessible electronically.

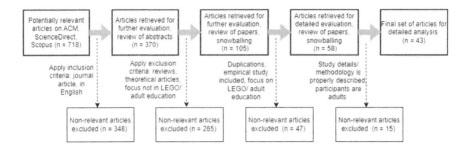

Fig. 1. Search process of the systematic literature review.

Initially, we excluded conference papers, and articles not written in English. Then, based on the titles and abstracts, we selected 370 articles where some exclusion criteria were applied, such as we excluded review articles, theoretical articles, and those with focus other than in LEGO or adult education. Furthermore, remaining articles were read through and snowballing method was applied to fulfill the dataset with missing articles. These were checked for duplications, empirical study, and proper research focus. In the next step, the methodology and results sections of 58 selected studies were read and excluded those without study details or adults as study participants. In this phase, 43 studies fit the research context with information capable of answering the research questions. These studies were read and carefully analyzed in order to extract the information. Based on the coding schemes, one author coded the dataset individually. To ensure interrater reliability and reduce individual coding biases, the coding scheme was negotiated between authors; subsequently, any necessary changes were made in the coding scheme. This approach allowed the researchers to better understand the content of articles. After coding a sample of 10% of the dataset and receiving a satisfactory interrater agreement (K = 0.81), the remaining data were coded by one researcher.

3   Results and Discussion

3.1   Demographics

We will first give an overview of the selected publications and present the general results. The distribution of articles per year is shown in Fig. 2(on the left) together with the country of study (on the right). There is a notable peak of publications in 2018 which could be explained by the inclusion of papers (11 out of 12) from a special issue in International Journal for Management and Applied Research, dedicated to LEGO® and LEGO® Serious Play applications in diverse contexts. In addition, the increasing number of articles per year demonstrates a growing interest of the scientific community in studies for the use of LEGO®. Regarding the publication venues, the analysis shows that 43 papers have been published in 31 different journals. The top publication venue is the International Journal for Management and Applied Research, due to the special issue.

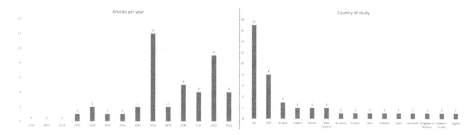

Fig. 2. Left: Number of articles per year. Right: Country of study for LEGO® applications.

Two journals, namely Journal of Further & Higher Education and International Journal of Research & Method in Education, have two articles each published with relevant focus. The rest of the journals have one article each. Overall, we noticed a diverse group of publication venues, including 10 education-oriented journals (e.g. Journal of Further and Higher Education, Journal of Learning Development in Higher Education), 7 management- oriented journals (e.g., International Journal of Innovation and Technology Management, Journal of Organizational Change Management), 3 medical-oriented journals (e.g., Journal of Surgical Education, American Journal of Pharmaceutical Education) while the rest are in diverse areas (e.g., Journal of Sport Psychology in Action, Journal of Play in Adulthood). Furthermore, the country of study presents the various places where LEGO® studies were implemented. The majority of studies presented empirical evidence from a single country. However, there is one article with empirical work in two countries, and one other study was conducted online. UK is by far the country with most implementations, which suggests a systematic interest in conducting studies for LEGO®. In addition, USA was the second most popular place where studies for LEGO® were conducted, while the following four countries (Austria, Ireland, Taiwan and New Zealand) have 2 or 3 studies each. The rest of the countries have single studies.

3.2 How Is LEGO® Being Used in Adult Education for Professional Development?

To answer the first RQ, we identified two separate educational types for LEGO® applications in professional development: within formal education (in HEIs) and non-formal education (beyond HEIs).

Applications of LEGO® Within Formal Education. Table 1 presents 19 educational practices within formal education, which correspond to 44% of total studies of our examined articles. Overall, the results support that, through the application of LEGO®, many HEIs strive to strengthen students' professional skills to adapt to the changing labour market and improve their employability. One observation relates to the diverse HEIs where LEGO® studies are implemented. Disciplines in medicine, business, computer science, economics, education, fashion and others, consist the educational context which LEGO® implementations target to enhance. Out of 19 practices, 12 refer to implementations linked to specific courses, where LEGO® is embedded as part of the course. Specifically, examples of LEGO® applications in university courses aim to:

- explain complex theoretical concepts and combine theoretical and practical learning in Optometry lectures prior to 'lab' sessions [10],
- expand and deepen students' knowledge about leadership theory and practice, in shared leadership [36],
- offer an engaging active learning experience and to promote a deeper understanding of the basic, technical knowledge in nanotechnology ethics together with social, ethical, and environmental issues [16],
- reflect around students' hopes and fears for their future in medicine [46],
- train young professionals to work in globally distributed projects and to reflect about challenges and problems associated with global environments in global software engineering(GSE) [40].

The rest of educational practices expand courses' boundaries and contribute to students' professional development with a future-oriented view, an assessment experience or emotional support among others. More in detail, examples of LEGO® applications in such educational practices aim to:

- to gain a deeper understanding and knowledge of the realities and experiences of the students and panel members involved in the context of the professional assessment [31],
- to help students articulate their thoughts about their practice of their chosen profession in an engaged manner [38],
- to explore doctoral students' emotions, as a first step towards wellbeing [5], and
- to evaluate a nontraditional method of evaluating urology residency applicants' ability to communicate and work in teams [4].

Applications of LEGO® in Non-formal Education. Table 2 presents 24 educational practices of non-formal education, which corresponds to 56% of the total studies of our examined articles. The results indicate a wide variety of LEGO® applications in non-formal education. In fact, there are five subcategories to describe the context of educational practices, namely the experimental setting, the organizational setting, the project work, the career seminars and the summer schools/ conferences. The majority of studies refer to organizational settings (6 studies) or career seminars (6 studies). Examples of LEGO® applications in these contexts aim to:

- to promote psychological health in the workplace by constructing a workplace stress reduction model in an Employee Assistance Program [11],
- to achieve real-time evaluation and self-feedback in a strength-based career counselling in career guidance centres [12],
- to foster resilience capabilities in a strategic management seminar [7],

Table 1. Educational practices for professional development within formal, higher education.

No	Education Type	Educational practice	Study
1.1	Within formal	Personal and Professional Development study - International Preparation for Fashion course, undergraduate programme	[15]
1.2	Within formal	Assessment strategy for "Learning and Teaching in Higher Education" module, Postgraduate Certificate in Academic Practice, University of Salford	[31]
1.3	Within formal	'Reflective Practitioner' course, graduate level, public university	[35]
1.4	Within formal	Lab course in Optometry, undergraduate level, University of Manchester	[10]
1.5	Within formal	Project work, postgraduate community, University of Kent Graduate School	[5]
1.6	Within formal	A leadership course, graduate level, public university	[36]
1.7	Within formal	Nano Ethics At Play (NEAP) workshop series, undergraduate level, public university	[16]
1.8	Within formal	Doctoral supervision, postgraduate level, Manchester Metropolitan University	[30]
1.9	Within formal	Undergraduate medical program, public university	[46]
1.10	Within formal	Extra-occupational master program	[52]
1.11	Within formal	Global software engineering course and seminar, public university	[40]
1.12	Within formal	Youth and Community Work course, undergraduate level	[38]
1.13	Within formal	"Teaching Learning and Leadership" module, postgraduate level, University of Sunderland	[13]
1.14	Within formal	Quality improvement measure, postgraduate level, Urology residency interviews	[4]
1.15	Within formal	Experiment/ research with students, undergraduate level, Bachelor of Pharmacy program	[20]
1.16	Within formal	Intensive course for Introductory Accounting, undergraduate level, public university	[44]
1.17	Within formal	A revision exercise in Cell Biology, part of a four-year undergraduate biological sciences honors degree	[8]
1.18	Within formal	A teaching activity, first-year undergraduate students in a business school	[23]
1.19	Within formal	Intervention for one academic semester, undergraduate level, in a business school	[27]

Table 2. Educational practices for professional development with non-formal education.

No	Education Type	Educational practice	Study
2.1	Non-formal	European Union Lifelong Learning Programme (LLP) Leonardo Da Vinci, Transfer of Innovation scheme	[24]
2.2	Non-formal	Play therapist professional identity in individual and group supervision - Workshops with play therapy supervisors	[34]
2.3	Non-formal	LeGOMAKE project in US libraries, by Rutgers University Art Library Lego Playing Station	[22]
2.4	Non-formal	Experiment/ research, a coaching approach within organisational setting	[50]
2.5	Non-formal	Professional Development Planning (PDP) seminar, Intercultural Practice module	[6]
2.6	Non-formal	Summer school for Entrepreneurship	[29]
2.7	Non-formal	Brainstorming session on strategy of an Education department/ wider University strategy	[26]
2.8	Non-formal	Employee assistance program (EAP)	[11]
2.9	Non-formal	Strength career counselling in career guidance centres	[12]
2.10	Non-formal	Volunteer tourism exchange programme	[48]
2.11	Non-formal	The Scottish Design Relay activity, in V&A Dundee museum	[14]
2.12	Non-formal	Workshop in an innovation laboratory	[1]
2.13	Non-formal	Comparative and International Education conference in North America	[25]
2.14	Non-formal	Experimental setting, innovation workshop	[51]
2.15	Non-formal	Experimental setting, offsite interventions	[37]
2.16	Non-formal	UK Research and Innovation-funded initiative	[45]
2.17	Non-formal	Extra-occupational master program	[53]
2.18	Non-formal	Coaching session	[39]
2.19	Non-formal	World Wide Opportunities on Organic Farms (WWOOF) programme	[49]
2.20	Non-formal	UK Research and Innovation project	[41]
2.21	Non-formal	Carpentries workshops hosted at University of Kansas (KU) Libraries	[2]
2.22	Non-formal	Leeds International Summer School	[3]
2.23	Non-formal	Strategic management seminar	[7]
2.24	Non-formal	Workshop in Gaelic Athletic Association	[33]

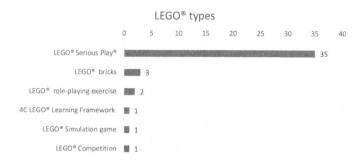

Fig. 3. Applied LEGO types across studies.

– to help an athlete identify instances of growth mindset in his play and to overcome fix mindset thinking (Gaelic Athletic Association) [33].

In other subcategories, many studies refer to diverse project work (5) or experimental settings (4) as an educational practice to apply LEGO®. Such LEGO® applications aim to:

– to understand how hosts (farmers) and guests (WWOOFers) construct the 'ideal' WWOOFing experience to ensure a mutually beneficial encounter for both farmers and volunteers [49],
– to identify whether representatives of different sectors could collaborate and work together on urban planning issues (UK Research and Innovation-funded initiative) [45],
– to study collaborative innovation processes with the aim of collaboratively developing new ideas for open data strategies [51],
– to embody and expand the understanding of co-design, creativity and play on three-dimensional form in V&A Dundee museum during the Scottish Design Relay activity [14].

The remaining 3 studies refer to educational practices of summer schools or conferences, where LEGO® applications aim, e.g.:

– to understand the importance of teamwork in a multicultural context in summer school for entrepreneurship [29], and
– to elicit ideas of International Education and combine these ideas into a single shared narrative during the Comparative and International Education conference in North America [25], and
– to introduce the contemporary business environment and challenges that managers and organisations face [3].

3.3 Which LEGO® Types and Research Settings Have Been Used in Adult Education for Professional Development?

LEGO® applications presented positive results for diverse professional skills, in non-formal and within formal education. The use of LEGO® offers several advantages, including enhancing creativity and problem-solving skills, facilitating experiential learning and engagement, promoting teamwork and communication, and providing a hands-on approach to learning complex concepts, that are essential in developing 'soft skills' for professional development.

The majority of the examined studies reported on cases with the LEGO® Serious Play method or modification of it (81%). The rest of the studies applied only bricks (e.g., [5]), a role-playing exercise (e.g., [4]), the 4C Learning Framework [31], a simulation game [44], and a competition [10] based on LEGO® (Fig. 3). Regardless the type of use, almost all studies discuss theoretical background of LSP method or LEGO® in general, and few studies discuss theoretical underpinnings, in relation with the examined field. Overall, articles with LSP-focus explore the use of LSP as an unconventional means of developing student learning (e.g., [15]), if it could be used as a tool for reflective practice within a specif profession (social care practitioners, [6]), as a mechanism for sharing conceptual metaphors to support collaborative activity in strategic planning [26] and other diverse objectives.

Based on 43 articles, we created a taxonomy of the professional skills in adult education, that were extracted from research designs and results by applying LEGO® (Table 3). To better organise the findings, this review adopted categories of soft skills, as they are described by C. Succi and M. Canovi [43]. Specifically, we found that categories of personal, social and methodological skills fit to our findings, while some subcategories are new and represent the results of LEGO® applications. Specifically, Table 3 presents an overview of the skills expected to be improved through the application of LEGO® across various settings. Hereafter, selected examples per category will be mentioned. In personal skills, reflectivity is a desired skill described in fields, such as urban planning, medicine, and tourism. Psychological health/safety seems to support collaboration, shared vision, group flow among others, in fields, such as doctoral supervision, sports, coaching, and organisational settings. In social skills, teamwork skills consist favorable skills in fields like in medical education, organisations, and software engineering. Additionally, co-creation is seen as attractive skill for multilingual students, in tourism and organizational settings. Lastly, methodological skills were identified in studies with LEGO® to describe problem-solving, management, and strategic planning skills. For example, problem-solving is seen as skill to teach complex concepts in optometry mechanics, learning software and management education.

We also present methodological approaches in Tables 4 and 5. Table 3 could be read in relation with the following two tables to gain better overview of examined articles. Based on Tables 4 and 5, a summary of methodological considerations is discussed hereafter. These considerations include aligning educational activities with learning outcomes, ensuring participant engagement through the process of workshops or activities with LEGO®, adapting the complexity of tasks to the group's skill level, and incorporating reflective sessions to deepen learning. Additionally, facilitators should be trained to guide LSP process in workshops, encourage collaboration and help participants to draw connections

Table 3. Taxonomy of professional skills in adult education with LEGO®.

Category of skills	Subcategory	Description
Personal skills	Reflectivity	critical reflection [45], reflective practice [35, 46], reflection [6, 31], reflection for ideation with stakeholders [1], reflection on personal experiences [49], self-reflection [20]
	Learning skills	experiential learning [36], kinesthetic learning [35], peer learning [6], independent learning [8], reflection on learning [15], creative learning/ complex learning [14], learning how to apply technical knowledge [44], professional learning [2]
	Professional identity	explore own professional identity [24, 34], establishing, framing and articulating professional identity [13], 'professional love' [38], professional discussion [31], explore career options, positions, and action plans [12], resident selection, resident interview, core competency [4]
	Creativity/ Innovation skills	creativity [8, 14, 22, 25, 38, 46, 49, 52], creative thinking skills [20], creativity techniques in organizations [53], creativity and learning journeys [31], innovation [25, 45], innovation process [51]
	Psychological health/safety	psychological health in the workplace, workplace stress reduction [12], psychological safety [39, 50], positive psychology [33, 39, 50], growth mindset [33], coaching [39, 50], positive psychology coaching [39], play therapy [34], empowerment/ play [8], emotion work/ emotional labour/ wellbeing [5], affective experience [30]
Social skills	Teamwork skills	teamwork skills [7, 22, 23, 40, 46], team building [29], organisational team-building [22], team resilience capabilities [7], team learning/ team cohesion [50], team confidence and trust [40], collaboration/group collaboration [10, 22, 29, 45, 50], group involvement [12], individual /group skills building [3], inter-disciplinary cross-sectoral thinking [45]
	Communication skills	communication [4, 20, 29, 36], cross-disciplinary communication [16], informal communication and improvisation skills, ability to communicate effectively using a common terminology and language [40], computer-mediated communication [40], social interaction [8], human-robot interaction in social care [41]
	Co-creation	co-creation skills [27, 48, 53], co-creative learning [1], co-construction/ co-design [14]
	Leadership skills	leadership skills [40], shared leadership/ leadership education/ shared leadership development [36]
	Conflict management	conflict resolution [40]
Methodo-logical skills	Problem-solving skills	problem-solving [2, 10], complex problem solving [52], creative approaches to problem-solving [3], professional judgment in unstructured problems [44]
	Management skills	business management [3], education management [3, 26], management thinking [3], time management skills [40], managing ambiguity and uncertainty [40]
	Strategic planning skills	strategic planning [26, 37, 51], organisational change [37, 51], organizational learning [1]

between LEGO® activities and professional scenarios. Effective integration of LEGO® requires thoughtful planning and a clear understanding of the tool's potential to enhance learning through hands-on, creative problem-solving exercises.

3.4 What Are the Identified Benefits of LEGO® in Various Educational Settings for Adults?

Findings of this review align with results from previous reviews, such as [47] and [21], and therefore confirm the benefits of using LEGO® in the examined context. Specifically, the benefits of using LEGO® for professional development include the ability to gain a deep understanding of complex concepts and diverse perspectives, to foster creativity, innovation and problem-solving skills, to enhance communication and collaboration among participants, to promote active and engaged learning, and to provide a hands-on approach to understand complex concepts [3,4,10,24]. A key benefit of LEGO® is the creation of metaphors during workshops, as a means of communication and interpretation, that allows multiple realities of a phenomenon. Metaphors also allow to enhance the understanding of a concept, and through LEGO® to create physical representations of these understandings. LEGO® activities encourage learners to think creatively and work together, making it an effective tool for improving professional and soft skills in various educational practices, methodological settings, and fields.

Table 4. Methodological approaches in (within formal) adult education with LEGO®.

No	LEGO® types	Study focus	Methods	Participants	Ref
1.1	LSP	Student learning, reflection on learning	workshop, Critical Incident Questionnaire	48 undergraduate students	[15]
1.2	4C LEGO® Learning Framework	Professional discussion assessment, academic development	workshop, individual interviews	20 teachers in higher education	[31]
1.3	LSP	Reflective practice, kinesthetic learning	phenomenological approach, interviews	29 occupational therapy graduate students and one faculty member	[35]
1.4	LSP/ competition	interactive learning, Optometry	workshop, questionnaire	80–90 s year Optometry students	[10]
1.5	LEGO® bricks	Emotion Work, Doctoral students	workshop, observations	8 doctoral students	[5]
1.6	LSP	Shared leadership, Leadership Education	phenomenological approach, observations	11 leadership graduate students	[36]
1.7	LSP	active learning, cross-disciplinary communication, Undergraduate Education	Workshops, surveys, focus groups, observations	19 class participants, diversified class population	[16]
1.8	LSP	Affective Experience, Doctoral Supervision	phenomenographic study, semi-structured interviews	5 LSP facilitators/ doctoral supervisors	[30]

continued

Table 4. continued

No	LEGO® types	Study focus	Methods	Participants	Ref
1.9	LSP	Reflective Practice, Medical Education	27 workshops, observations	30–35 undergraduate students, three years, more than 800 participants	[46]
1.10	LSP	innovation course, digital entrepreneurship education	qualitative approach with two open questions	all the MSc students who attended the course	[52]
1.11	LEGO® bricks	global and distributed environments, communication and coordination	workshop, survey, group interviews	104 students from five different courses in two different universities	[40]
1.12	LSP	"professional love", creativity	workshops, reflections, questionnaire	37 undergraduate students	[38]
1.13	LSP	professional identities, epistemic cognition	workshop, reflections, data analysis with situational mapping	16 postgraduate nursing students	[13]
1.14	LEGO® exercise, role-playing	resident interview, urology residency	workshop, qualitative notes, observations, applicants' scores	176 applicants	[4]
1.15	LEGO® exercise, role-playing	reflective practice, problem-based learning in pharmacy	qualitative study rooted in grounded theory	all undergraduate students from first pharmacy year	[20]
1.16	LEGO® simulation game	active learning, perceptions of accounting	team-based simulation game, experimental and control group, survey	59 (experimental group) and 87 (control group) undergraduate accounting students	[44]
1.17	LSP	active learning, cellular biology	workshop, field notes, survey, semi-structured interview	26 undergraduate four-year students	[8]
1.18	LSP	teamwork, higher education	workshop, observations	346 undergraduate students and teachers formed 64 groups	[23]
1.19	LSP	post-COVID-19 well-being, multilingual students	mixed-methods approach: workshop, experiment, pre-and post-tests, students' feedback, reflective report, instructor's field notes	50 final-year international management students	[27]

Table 5. Methodological approaches in (non-formal) adult education with LEGO®.

No	LEGO® types	Study focus	Methods	Participants	Ref
2.1	LSP	professional identity, teaching and learning	3 workshops	pre-service primary school teachers, pre-service secondary school teachers, employees in engineering department	[24]
2.2	LSP	play therapy, professional identity	2 cases in individual and group supervision	a new supervisee, a group of community mental health clinicians	[34]
2.3	LSP	creativity, academic libraries	20 workshops, survey, observations	245 participants (workshops), 235 surveys from academic library faculty and staff employees in 20 academic libraries	[22]

continued

Table 5. continued

No	LEGO® types	Study focus	Methods	Participants	Ref
2.4	LSP	team learning, psychological safety	IPA, workshop, interviews after 6 weeks	6 participants from organisations	[50]
2.5	LSP	reflective practice, social care practitioners	action research, 5 workshops, interviews	71 social care practitioners and students	[6]
2.6	LSP	team building, soft skills	2 workshops	undergraduate and postgraduate students from a business school and a faculty of Engineering	[29]
2.7	LSP	strategic planning, higher education	workshop, video-, audio-recorded	18 participants from an academic department	[26]
2.8	LSP	workplace stress reduction, group cohesion	workshop, Workplace stress scale, feedback questionnaire	7 employed individuals	[11]
2.9	LSP	career counselling, college students	experimental design, workshop, pre-test, post-test, Career Hope Scale	29 college students	[12]
2.10	LSP	co-construction, host-guests' experience	interviews, observations, reflexive notes, workshops, video- and audio- recorded	32 participants, farmers and volunteers	[48]
2.11	LSP	creative learning, co-design	workshop, observations	participants from Abertay University and other universities, and members of museum staff.	[14]
2.12	LSP-inspired	co-creative learning, innovation laboratories	inductive case study design, observations	15 participants	[1]
2.13	LSP	metaphor, international education	workshop, video-, audio-recorded	9 participants, diverse group of professionals	[25]
2.14	LSP	innovation process, organisational change	workshop, questionnaire, ethnographic observation	80 top managers in public sector	[51]
2.15	LSP	Organizational management, change intervention	2 workshops, participant observation, interviews	26 participants of an advertising agency, top and middle management and managers from a non-profit organization in science education	[37]
2.16	LSP	co-design, interdisciplinary cross-sectoral thinking	8 workshops	40 participants, senior managers or new managers	[45]

continued

Table 5. continued

No	LEGO® types	Study focus	Methods	Participants	Ref
2.17	LSP	cocreation, material-mediated individ-ual/group flow	quasi-experimental, 3-h cocreative settings, questionnaire before and after each phase, in total 5 times	39 attendants in extra-occupational master program	[53]
2.18	LSP	coaching, positive psychology	qualitative research methodology, IPA, interviews, comparison between coaching with and without LEGO	5 participants	[39]
2.19	LSP	host-guests' experience, co-creation	workshop, video- and audio-recorded	13 participants on three farms in New Zealand, farmers/ WWOOFers	[49]
2.20	LSP	human-robot interaction, social care	digital workshops	85 care users, care commissioners, roboticists/designers, HRI academics, care/disability academics, professional carers, and social workers	[41]
2.21	LEGO kits, modified	professional learning, collaborative intervention	3 workshops, pre- and post-workshop survey	56 participants in pre-workshop survey, 52 in post-workshop survey from KU faculty, staff, postdoctoral researchers, graduate students, and community and regional learners	[2]
2.22	LSP	management education, higher education	qualitative study: 3 LSP Workshops, diary, written reflections from students	over 20 level-2 undergraduate students with different academical and cultural background	[3]
2.23	LSP	resilience capabilities, student resilience	qualitative observation study, video recorded, qualitative content analysis approach, visual mapping strategy	7 teams from 5 to 6 students each, overall 36 students, randomly assigned to one of three experimental conditions	[7]
2.24	LSP	growth mindset in athletes, positive psychology	workshop, questions afterwards with Clean Language questioning style	7 members of a university hurling team who had just won the Fitzgibbon Cup, data were collected from 1	[33]

4   Conclusions, Limitations and Future Work

The aim of this review paper was to explore how LEGO® was used to support professional development of adults in various educational settings. Our review paper has at least three shortcomings. First, we have focused on journal articles, ignoring other types of publication that might fulfill inclusion criteria. Future research could also investigate other types of publications, like conference papers, as well as could focus on a particular category of professional skills (e.g., social skills, Table 3). Second, we have disregarded studies that don't include any empirical study of LEGO® and explore only the topic conceptually. Future research should analyse theoretical work in the field, as well as discuss theoretical underpinnings of LEGO® applications. Third, the final search was conducted during the last period of 2023 (Nov-Dec.). Although we included the year 2023 in database searches, there might be more articles appearing in later time for 2023. Whilst the examined literature supported the use of LEGO® as an educational tool and presented several common advantages, these findings were largely non comparative and self-reported. Only four articles demonstrated comparative studies with LEGO® ([7,39,51,53]). However, this review mapped the findings into a taxonomy of professional skills in adult education with LEGO®. This in turn will serve as an effective point of departure for further exploration and study. We hope that this SRL can assist the educational and research community on how to use LEGO® for professional development in adult education. The taxonomy of professional skills, educational practices and methodological approaches within formal, and non-formal education identified here can help to provide an overview of the field. Finally, we suggest that the educational and research community should conduct long-term and comparative studies to allow rich results when applying LEGO® for professional development.

References

1. Al-Jayyousi, O.R., Durugbo, C.M.: Co-creative learning in innovation laboratories using lego serious play workshops. Int. J. Innov. Technol. Manag. **17**(07), 2050051 (2020)
2. Albin, T., Brooks-Kieffer, J.: Git going with LEGO: a playful partnership for making sense of technology. J. Play Adulthood **4**(2), 177–204 (2022)
3. Benesova, N.: Lego® serious play® in management education. Cogent Educ. **10**(2), 2262284 (2023)
4. Bethel, E.C., et al.: The LEGO™ exercise: an assessment of core competencies in urology residency interviews. J. Surg. Educ. **78**(6), 2063–2069 (2021)
5. Brown, N., Collins, J.: Using lego® to understand emotion work in doctoral education. Int. J. Manag. Appl. Res. **5**(4), 193–209 (2018)
6. Cavaliero, T.: 'creative blocs': action research study on the implementation of LEGO as a tool for reflective practice with social care practitioners. J. Furth. High. Educ. **41**(2), 133–142 (2017)
7. Duchek, S., Geithner, S., Roth, T.: Mastering team crises: a play-oriented approach to foster resilience capabilities in student teams. Teach. High. Educ. **28**(8), 1937–1956 (2023)
8. Garden, C.L.P.: Lego serious play: building engagement with cell biology. Biochem. Mol. Biol. Educ. **50**(2), 216–228 (2022)
9. Gratani, F., Giannandrea, L.: Towards 2030. enhancing 21st century skills through educational robotics. Front. Educ. **7**, 955285 (2022)
10. Gridley, A.: Building LEGO® models to teach three-dimensional, mechanical concepts in optometry. Int. J. Manag. Appl. Res. **5**(4), 238–244 (2018)
11. Harn, P.L., Hsiao, C.C.: A preliminary study on LEGO®-based workplace stress reduction with six bricks and LEGO® serious play® in taiwan. World J. Res. Rev. **6**(1), 64–67 (2018)

12. Harn, P., Hsiao, C.: Strength-4d career model with lego® serious play and six bricks. Int. J. Manag. Appl. Res. **5**(4), 157–172 (2018)
13. Hayes, C., Graham, Y.: Understanding the building of professional identities with the LEGO® serious play® method using situational mapping and analysis. Higher Educ. Skills Work-Based Learn. **10**(1), 99–112 (2020)
14. James, A.: Co-design and co-construction: LEGO®-based approaches for complex, creative learning. Int. J. Manag. Appl. Res. **5**(4), 304–312 (2018)
15. James, A.R.: Lego serious play: a three-dimensional approach to learning development. J. Learn. Devel. Higher Educ. (6) (2013)
16. Jensen, C.N., Seager, T.P., Cook-Davis, A.: LEGO® serious play® in multidisciplinary student teams. Int. J. Manag. Appl. Res. **5**(4), 264–280 (2018)
17. Keele, S., et al.: Guidelines for performing systematic literature reviews in software engineering (2007)
18. Kitchenham, B.: Procedures for performing systematic reviews. Keele, UK, Keele University **33**(2004), 1–26 (2004)
19. Kolb, D.A.: Experiential Learning: Experience as the Source of Learning and Development. FT Press (2014)
20. Lee, S.W.H., San Saw, P.: The use of building blocks to teach communication and social skills to first-year pharmacy students. Am. J. Pharmaceut. Educ. **85**(8), 8464 (2021)
21. Liang, D.N.Y., Yun, F.N.J., Minato, N.: Investigating the use of LEGO® bricks in education and training: a systematic literature review. J. Appl. Learn. Teach. **4**(1), 107–113 (2021)
22. Lotts, M.: On the road, playing with LEGOS®, and learning about the library: the Rutgers university art library LEGO playing station, part two. J. Libr. Adm. **56**(5), 499–525 (2016)
23. Martin-Cruz, N., Martin-Gutierrez, A., Rojo-Revenga, M.: A LEGO® serious play activity to help teamwork skills development amongst business students. Int. J. Res. Meth. Educ. **45**(5), 479–494 (2022)
24. McCusker, S.: LEGO®, serious play TM: thinking about teaching and learning. Int. J. Knowl. Innov. Entrepreneursh. **2**(1), 27–37 (2014)
25. McCusker, S.: Everybody's monkey is important: LEGO® serious play® as a methodology for enabling equality of voice within diverse groups. Int. J. Res. Meth. Educ. **43**(2), 146–162 (2020)
26. McCusker, S., Swan, J.C.: The use of metaphors with LEGO® serious play® for harmony and innovation. Int. J. Manag. Appl. Res. **5**(4), 174–192 (2018)
27. Meletiadou, E., et al.: Transforming multilingual students' learning experience through the use of LEGO serious play. IAFOR J. Educ. **11**(1), 1–24 (2023)
28. Merriam, S.B., Baumgartner, L.M.: Learning in Adulthood: a Comprehensive Guide. Wiley, Hoboken (2020)
29. Mouratoglou, N.: LEGO®, learning and facilitation: a reflective approach. Int. J. Manag. Appl. Res. **5**(4), 281–289 (2018)
30. Nerantzi, C.: LEGO® serious play® as an affective experience in doctoral researchers' support: Tensions and new freedoms. Int. J. Manag. Appl. Res. **5**(4), 290–303 (2018)
31. Nerantzi, C., Despard, C.: Do LEGO® models aid reflection in learning and teaching practice? J. Perspect. Appl. Acad. Pract. **2**(2), 31–36 (2014)
32. Orlović Lovren, V., Popović, K.: Lifelong learning for sustainable development-is adult education left behind? In: Handbook of Lifelong Learning for Sustainable Development, pp. 1–17 (2018)

33. O'Sullivan, D., Baxter, E.: Using LEGO® bricks to build a growth mindset: a case study. J. Sport Psychol. Action **14**(2), 86–96 (2023)
34. Peabody, M.A.: Building with purpose: using LEGO serious play in play therapy supervision. Int. J. Play Therapy **24**(1), 30 (2015)
35. Peabody, M.A., Noyes, S.: Reflective boot camp: adapting LEGO® serious play® in higher education. Reflective Pract. **18**(2), 232–243 (2017)
36. Peabody, M.A., Turesky, E.F.: Shared leadership lessons: adapting LEGO® serious play® in higher education. Int. J. Manag. Appl. Res. **5**(4), 210–223 (2018)
37. Piironen, S.: Producing liminal spaces for change interventions: the case of LEGO serious play workshops. J. Organ. Chang. Manag. **35**(8), 39–53 (2022)
38. Purcell, M.E.: Hubris, revelations and creative pedagogy: transformation, dialogue and modelling 'professional love' with LEGO®. J. Furth. High. Educ. **43**(10), 1391–1403 (2019)
39. Quinn, T., Trinh, S.H., Passmore, J.: An exploration into using LEGO® serious play®(LSP) within a positive psychology framework in individual coaching: an interpretative phenomenological analysis (IPA). Coaching: Int. J. Theory, Res. Pract. **15**(1), 102–116 (2022)
40. Šāblis, A., Gonzalez-Huerta, J., Zabardast, E., Šmite, D.: Building LEGO towers: an exercise for teaching the challenges of global work. ACM Trans. Comput. Educ. (TOCE) **19**(2), 1–32 (2019)
41. de Saille, S., et al.: Using LEGO® serious® play with stakeholders for RRI. J. Respons. Technol. **12**, 100055 (2022)
42. Souza, I.M., Andrade, W.L., Sampaio, L.M., Araujo, A.L.S.O.: A systematic review on the use of LEGO® robotics in education. In: 2018 IEEE Frontiers in Education Conference (FIE), pp. 1–9. IEEE (2018)
43. Succi, C., Canovi, M.: Soft skills to enhance graduate employability: comparing students and employers' perceptions. Stud. High. Educ. **45**(9), 1834–1847 (2020)
44. Sugahara, S., Cilloni, A.: Mediation effect of students' perception of accounting on the relationship between game-based learning and learning approaches. J. Account. Educ. **56**, 100730 (2021)
45. Tewdwr-Jones, M., Wilson, A.: Co-designing urban planning engagement and innovation: using LEGO® to facilitate collaboration, participation and ideas. Urban Plann. **7**(2), 229–238 (2022)
46. Thomson, C., Johnston, J.L., Reid, H.: Rich stories: embedding LEGO® serious play® into undergraduate medical education. Int. J. Manag. Appl. Res. **4**, 313–325 (2018)
47. Warburton, T., Brown, J., Sandars, J.: The use of LEGO® serious play® within nurse education: a scoping review. Nurse Educ. Today **118**, 105528 (2022)
48. Wengel, Y.: LEGO® serious play® in multi-method tourism research. Int. J. Contemp. Hosp. Manag. **32**(4), 1605–1623 (2020)
49. Wengel, Y., McIntosh, A., Cockburn-Wootten, C.: A critical consideration of LEGO® serious play® methodology for tourism studies. In: Qualitative Methodologies in Tourism Studies, pp. 169–191. Routledge (2022)
50. Wheeler, S., Passmore, J., Gold, R.: All to play for: LEGO® serious play® and its impact on team cohesion, collaboration and psychological safety in organisational settings using a coaching approach. J. Work-Appl. Manag. **12**(2), 141–157 (2020)
51. Zenk, L., Hynek, N., Krawinkler, S.A., Peschl, M.F., Schreder, G.: Supporting innovation processes using material artefacts: comparing the use of LEGO bricks and moderation cards as boundary objects. Creat. Innovation Manag. **30**(4), 845–859 (2021)

52. Zenk, L., Hynek, N., Schreder, G., Zenk, A., Pausits, A., Steiner, G.: Designing innovation courses in higher education using LEGO® serious play®. Int. J. Manag. Appl. Res. **5**(4), 245–263 (2018)
53. Zenk, L., Primus, D.J., Sonnenburg, S.: Alone but together: flow experience and its impact on creative output in LEGO® serious play®. Eur. J. Innov. Manag. **25**(6), 340–364 (2022)

Motion-Control Video Games to Train and Assess the Articular Range of Motion in Physical Therapy Sessions

Eric Contreras[1], Matías Orellana Silva[2], Maria Gabriela Hidalgo[2,3], Jorge A. Gutiérrez[2,3], and Francisco J. Gutierrez[1(✉)]

[1] Department of Computer Science, University of Chile, Beauchef 851, North Building, Santiago, Chile
{ercontre,frgutier}@dcc.uchile.cl
[2] Instituto Teletón de Santiago, Avenue Libertador Bernardo O'Higgins, 4620 Estación Central, Santiago, Chile
morellana@teleton.cl
[3] Corporación de Ayuda al Niño Quemado – COANIQUEM, Avenue San Francisco, 8586 Pudahuel, Santiago, Chile
{ghidalgo,jgutierrez}@coaniquem.org

Abstract. Physical therapy sessions are usually long, repetitive, and painful. As a way to increase adherence to this kind of treatment, video games have emerged as a valuable asset due to their ability to foster engaging and flow experiences. However, the design of assistive video games requires integrating multiple layers of art and practice, ranging from game design to specialized domain-specific knowledge. In this paper, we report the design of a prototype video game aiming to train and assess the articular range of motion in physical therapy sessions, i.e., the extent or limit to which a part of the body can be moved around a joint or a fixed point. Such a video game explicitly uses Nintendo Switch Joy-Cons, state-of-the-art, and readily available off-the-shelf motion-based video game controls. As a case study, we sought to provide alternative ways to exercise the range of motion in burned children in a way that they could find engaging, yielding results that could be comparable to those obtained by more traditional means, such as with a goniometer. We conducted a proof-of-concept study involving a sample of domain experts working with patients from this population (e.g., physiatrists and therapists) as well as with a sample of potential end-users to gauge the perceived usefulness and adoption potential of the conceived solution. Our results are highly encouraging, providing more evidence of the effectiveness of (serious) video games for rehabilitation.

Keywords: Rehabilitation · Children · Video games · Physical therapy

X. Fang (Ed.): HCII 2024, LNCS 14731, pp. 22–33, 2024.
https://doi.org/10.1007/978-3-031-60695-3_2

1   Introduction

Physical therapy requires a strong commitment from patients, given that recovery sessions are usually long, tedious, repetitive, and painful. This is even more stressed in younger patients, who tend to lose focus more easily. In fact, according to Lohse et al. [10], patient nonadherence with therapy is a significant barrier to rehabilitation: recovery is often limited and requires prolonged, intensive rehabilitation that is time-consuming, expensive, and difficult.

Furthermore, according to Vygotsky [15], play can be considered one of the most critical enablers for developing children's social, affective, and intellectual skills. Therefore, it is unsurprising that play finds its place in rehabilitation, particularly in physical therapy. Recent advances in the development of video games have shown that they promote flow experiences [2], which motivate players and have the potential to cause a stronger adherence to the recovery process [10].

Video game rehabilitation [16] allows patients to improve their physical and mental recovery through active adherence to playful interactive activities. More precisely, video games are used as a source of motivation to ensure engagement and commitment in the therapeutic process, where the patient shifts their focus from pain and distraction to engagement, flow, and immersion. In addition, video game controls can passively track patient data, such as biometrics and complex movements that can be difficult to measure with conventional methods. For instance, motion controllers (such as PlayStation Move, Microsoft Kinect, and Nintendo Switch Joy-Cons) can practice rehabilitation-relevant movements [10], where well-designed game mechanics can improve patient engagement and motivation in physical rehabilitation. In physical therapy, the range of motion (i.e., the extent or limit to which a part of the body can be moved around a joint or a fixed point [11]) is one of the critical measures that must be trained and assessed. To do so, a goniometer is one of the most common tools for measuring the range of motion. However, this instrument requires significant training to yield reliable results [5].

In this paper, we explore how to design motion-control video games to support young patients in their physical therapy sessions, namely in training and assessing the articular range of motion. As a particular case study, we worked with young children recovering from burned injuries at COANIQUEM[1], a Chilean not-for-profit organization that provides support for burned children in Latin America and the Caribbean. As hardware support, the games were designed around Nintendo Switch Joy-Cons, state-of-the-art controls that come in pairs (one for each hand) and can detect a user's natural movements through an embedded gyroscope and accelerometer. We argue that this interaction paradigm can potentially attract patients' attention during their rehabilitation. In addition, the developed video games have the potential to assist physiatrists and physical therapists in acquiring reliable range of motion measurements comparable to those obtained with a goniometer.

---

[1] https://coaniquem.cl/en.

We conceived two motion-controlled video games. The first one focuses on the shoulder joints, relating the patient's physical movement with that of a bird flapping their wings, which has to traverse through a route (akin to a forest), avoiding randomly placed hazards. The second video game focuses on the elbow joints, explicitly addressing the extension movement through actions such as running, jumping, and shooting enemies in a progressive runner stage.

The rest of this paper is structured as follows. Section 2 reviews and discusses prior work. Section 3 reports the design rationale and key components of the motion-controlled video game. Section 4 presents the results of a proof-of-concept study aiming to validate the developed software's usability, perceived usefulness, and adoption potential. Finally, Sect. 5 concludes and provides perspectives on future work.

2   Related Work

Video game rehabilitation aims, at its core, to use off-the-shelf video game mechanics, controls, and consoles to design novel strategies to improve physical and mental recovery through a supervised therapeutic process. As such, these video games are increasingly gaining the interest of therapists in a wide range of fields [9].

In the particular case of physical therapy and rehabilitation, recovery sessions usually require a strict commitment from patients, involving lengthy periods where they have to endure pain and other negative feelings such as frustration. Therefore, it is not strange that patients often drop out of these treatments, posing a challenge to rehabilitation programs. Furthermore, according to Hall et al. [6], video games allow for a closer and more positive relationship between patient and therapist in video game rehabilitation.

The effectiveness of video games in rehabilitation has been explored in several domains. For instance, Fernández-González et al. [3] studied how non-immersive serious video games could be used to treat Parkinson's disease. Their results show that games not only increased satisfaction and compliance with treatment but also showcased increased performance rehabilitation measures, such as coordination, speed of movement, and fine dexterity in the upper limbs.

Likewise, Unnikrishnan et al. [14] developed a software toolkit that allows physiotherapists to integrate physical therapy exercises through video games. This toolkit comprises various motion-tracking sensors that could help therapists monitor the progression of their patients and adjust the program accordingly. In particular, the promise of embedding these techniques into popular video games may help in improving motivation and engagement with the rehabilitation process.

Active video games (also known as exergames) can also help promote physical activity in rehabilitation. This technique has proven to have comparable—and even greater—effects than traditional approaches, was considered acceptable and enjoyable [13]. For example, Wii Fit (i.e., a commercial video game published by Nintendo for the previous generation of consoles) provided impressive support in physical rehabilitation due to the use of motion controls and a dedicated balance board, displaying positive results in reducing and controlling pain, improving patient satisfaction, and being a support in managing balance confidence, lower extremity function, and knee range of motion [4]. Likewise, Wii Bowling coupled with standard exercise improved functional capacity among long-term care patients [8]. Finally, video game rehabilitation also showed positive results among children and adolescents with lower limb amputation, who displayed improved postural control [1].

All in all, we are faced with a scenario where video games in rehabilitation are thriving. As such, we still require further empirical evidence (e.g., through blind randomized controlled trials) to understand better what factors trigger patient adherence and improved performance. To bridge such a gap, in this paper, we explore the perceived usefulness and adoption potential of physical therapy video games in the particular domain of burned children actively involved in a recovery program.

3   Video Game Design

We developed two independent video games covering the training of two different joints: shoulder and elbow. These applications were designed in collaboration with a team of expert domains (i.e., physical therapists and physiatrists) from COANIQUEM, who work closely in assisting young children in their recovery. In that respect, expert domains supported this work in informing and validating the design of the prototyped video games. That way, perceived usefulness and adoption potential by end-users can be reached more easily.

Both video games were initially conceived as endless experiences, allowing the medical team to progressively and continuously monitor the range of motion in the target joint (i.e., shoulder or elbow). To do so, each video game comprises two complementary sessions: one for the player, which sustains the main interactivity and navigation with motion controls, and one for the physiatrist, which allows them to keep track of the movements and monitor the evolution of the recovery program. In this paper, we focus on the design rationale of the conceived game mechanics and their potential acceptance across the different stakeholders involved in the rehabilitation process.

The design process followed a participatory approach involving professionals from the physical recovery team within COANIQUEM (particularly, physiatrists). These informants validated the incremental design artifacts, providing and stressing the domain-expert knowledge required to produce a potentially acceptable software solution. In particular, regarding ergonomy, the key restriction consisted of how the game controls would allow for smooth interaction and simultaneously provide the best data possible. In that respect, in this first step, the approach focused on working with upper limbs (i.e., shoulder and elbow joints) and promoting separation and approximation movements for the former, while extension and flexion movements for the latter.

3.1   Game Mechanics

In the first video game (Fig. 1), the player assumes the role of a bird who has to bat their wings to traverse a forest trying to reach fruit targets (that award points) and avoid tree branches (obstacles). More precisely, this game's main mechanic is allowing the patient to exercise the shoulder joint range of movement, which is mapped to the motion controls mediated by the Joy-Cons. To keep the player engaged, the game progressively increases its difficulty, for instance, by displaying more random hazards on the stage or increasing the speed of obstacles. Difficulty is also managed by the gravity physics in the game scene, which means that the player would have to exercise more physical effort to achieve their goals. The physical therapist controls all these variables in-game, supports the player, and monitors their actions. In particular, the key metrics that are captured by this game are: (1) rotation angles of the left and right shoulder joints, (2) variations of these angles, (3) player performance (i.e., score), and (4) timestamps.

Fig. 1. Game #1: Shoulder Joint Training

The second video game is a runner (i.e., an automatic scrolling scene where the player continuously traverses) aiming to support the elbow range of motion (Fig. 2). The effort is mapped to an energy bar loaded depending on the running movements the Joy-Cons captured. In addition, by computing the variation in the accelerator sensing data captured by the controls, the game maps this value to the strength in which every movement is executed. The player must avoid obstacles that randomly appear in the game scene and are fixated on the screen borders. The game also has ice physics as a way to increase the difficulty in controlling the interaction of the main character with their surroundings. Similar to the first game, the difficulty is adjusted dynamically and in control of the physical therapist controlling the experience. The key metrics that are captured by this game are: (1) extension angles of the left and right elbow joints, (2) variation of these angles, (3) player performance (i.e., score), and (4) timestamps.

Fig. 2. Game #2: Elbow Joint Training

3.2 Motion Controls

Given that in physical therapy, the treating team needs to count with accurate and precise data regarding the patient's interaction with the game, we need to integrate several sources of motion sensors as well as controlling as much as possible the incremental noise that naturally happens when capturing data with these instruments. In this work, we used Nintendo Switch Joy-Cons, state-of-the-art motion controls integrating gyroscope and accelerometer, with reasonable accuracy and precision. However, given that these controls do not integrate a magnetometer, angle detection and their variation will not be completely accurate. In particular, Joy-Cons come in pairs (one for each hand), measuring 4.1 in. wide, 6.8 in. tall, and 2.12 in. deep. Therefore, they are quite ergonomic (at least, for the hands of a child) and allow for a smooth and reliable connection through Bluetooth 3.0.

To map natural movements to a computer-mediated scene, we referred to Euler angles. These constructs, widely used in computational geometry and rigid-solid physics, aim to describe the orientation of a 3D object in space. These angles are: (1) roll, which represents the rotation on the X-axis, i.e., movements forward or backward; (2) pitch, which represents the rotation on the Y-axis, i.e., movements to the left or right; and (3) yaw, which represents the rotation on the Z-axis, i.e., clock-wise or counter clock-wise movements.

The composition of these three angles allow to completely describe the physical orientation of an object in a 3D space. In particular, the Unity game engine provides support to manipulate these values and simplifies the development of these game physics. However, given that computing these angles in every time-frame is quite resource-consuming, there is an inevitable error propagation that needs to be accounted for and properly adjusted.

3.3 Solving the Orientation Problem

An orientation problem in the Joy-Con emerges when they are constantly shaken for a while. This increases the error when computing the angle orientation in the XZ plane in Unity. In other words, the error is captured in the vertical rotation of the Joy-Cons, which, if not corrected, might yield different valid rotation configurations in the virtual scene for a particular real-world manipulation (e.g., Figs. 3 and 4). Naturally, this is an undesired effect that needs to be corrected throughout the player interaction with the game scene.

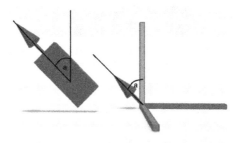

Fig. 3. Posible posición del vector en la posición superior.

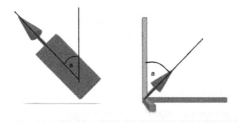

Fig. 4. Otra posible posición

The only angle that remains constant despite the error described above is the angle formed between the vertical axis (i.e., Y-axis) and the tip of the Joy-Con (which maps the orientation). Given that we expect that the movements to perform actions and interact with the game elements are only situated on a single axis, we then restricted the movement alongside the Y-axis and used it as a frame of reference. Therefore, to correct the orientation and compute the adjusted rotation angle, we devised the following procedure: (1) *Define the primitive orientation:* The first step in the game scene is to map the Joy-Con orientation to every interactive object. This step is only executed at the beginning of the scene; (2) *Rotation:* The object has to be rotated 90° along the X-axis, following the respective Euler angles; and (3) *Computing the resulting angles:* The adjusted angle then needs to be calculated between the Y-axis vector (in the Unity space) and the vector that represents the tip of the Joy-Con, according to the rotation of the interactive object.

Once these steps are performed, we have a more accurate representation of the angle at which the Joy-Con is rotated. These values are then used to compute the dynamic placement of game elements in the interactive scene, game actions, and data logging.

4   Proof of Concept

We conducted a proof-of-concept study with both prototypes to explore the perceived usefulness and adoption potential of the conceived video games for physical therapy. In this section, we describe the followed empirical setup and discuss the obtained results.

We recruited a sample of $N = 54$ participants to play with one of the two prototyped video games. Furthermore, in each group, we randomly split participants into one of three groups of equal size ($N = 9$): (1) with no restrictions during the gameplay session (i.e., control condition); (2) limiting the movement of the shoulder; and (3) limiting the movement of the elbow. Complying with ethical standards when conducting empirical research with human subjects, all study participants had to provide explicit, free, and informed consent. The study was approved on ethical grounds by the Institutional Review Board at the University of Chile.

Once the video games were developed, a team of domain experts inspected the produced software regarding functionality and perceived usefulness. These domain experts actively work in physical rehabilitation (e.g., physiatrists and physiotherapists). Having reached a satisfactory level for all assessment dimensions, we ran a proof of concept study to formally measure usability, playability, and adoption potential.

Once the players completed their assigned game, we asked them to complete the NASA Task-Load Index (NASA-TLX) questionnaire [7]. This is a valid and reliable instrument to quantify the effort that took every participant to complete each game across several dimensions, namely: mental demand, physical demand, temporal demand, performance, effort, and frustration. To control for hardware conditions, all participants interacted with their assigned game using the same background equipment: a Gaming PC and paired Joy-Cons via Bluetooth.

4.1 Shoulder Joint Training

Figure 5 shows the distribution of NASA-TLX scores along each dimension for the game.

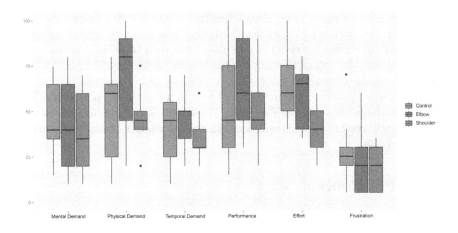

Fig. 5. Results of Game #1: Shoulder Joint Training

For the shoulder joint training video game, the task-load dimensions that yielded the highest average results were performance and perceived effort. This means that participants who interacted with this video game felt quite comfortable about how well they achieved the required tasks (i.e., collecting apples while avoiding getting stuck or colliding with tree branches). However, a high perception of effort can be linked to increased difficulty in achieving those tasks. In practical terms, this opens up the opportunity to design difficulty adjustments (e.g., dynamically) to help players with their onboarding while simultaneously keeping a steady learning curve and progressive exercises of the range of motion for these articulations. This should be addressed jointly with the rehabilitation and physical therapy specialists to promote regulated and potentially effective training.

It is also worth noting that the frustration levels were perceived as the lowest among all measured task loads. This means that the game successfully engages participants in a way that may trigger—and boost—motivation. In that respect, further design considerations (for instance, based on the intrinsic motivation constructs of the self-determination theory [12]) could improve these results even more.

4.2   Elbow Joint Training

Figure 6 shows the distribution of NASA-TLX scores along each dimension for the game.

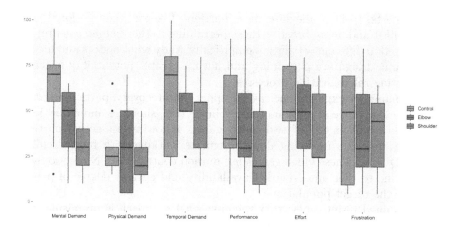

Fig. 6. Results of Game #2: Elbow Joint Training

For the elbow joint training video game, the task load dimension that yielded the highest score was temporal demand. This could be due to the challenge posed by the game, where players have to react continuously to the random hazards that appear on the screen (i.e., obstacles that must be avoided while the game character is in permanent movement due to the game being of the runner genre). This poses a challenge to the physical therapy component of the treatment, given that a high level of demand might be challenging, hence increasing the possibility of patients quitting the program or being frustrated by being unable to properly complete the proposed goals. This is stressed by similar values in the mental demand, performance, and effort dimensions: players might feel satisfied with their performance during the game, but its learning curve might be somewhat steep and more difficult to master than the shoulder joint training video game. Regarding performance, although the game might be effective in proposing a concrete goal, given that the speed at which the runner progresses through the scene increases, it might pose more difficulty in managing reaction times, hence reducing the potential scores that players could achieve. This might impact the perceived levels of frustration, so there are open opportunities for redesigning the game balance, providing a more affordable challenge in line with the rehabilitation goals of the physical therapy that supports the program.

5   Conclusion and Future Work

Training the articular range of motion of upper limb joints is crucial for correctly and effortlessly performing daily live activities. However, patients who are in physical therapy rehabilitation programs (such as burned children in recovery), might be burdened or feel progressive demotivation in completing them. Among the most common reasons for this, we can cite lack of motivation, pain, and prolonged time and effort. To bridge this gap, video game designers have increasingly been proposing alternative mechanisms (e.g., serious games), co-designed with domain experts, to help alleviate these barriers. Likewise, conventional games (such as WiiFit and, more broadly, those pertaining to the exergame genre) have been deployed in different settings to empirically study what factors and mechanics from game design are pertaining and have a greater potential of success in complementing rehabilitation processes.

In this paper we explored the case of upper limb recovery, particularly training the articular range of motion of upper limbs (i.e., shoulder and elbow joints) through the development of two video games following an active participatory design approach involving domain experts working with burned children at COANIQUEM. These video games use motion controls, i.e., Nintendo Switch Joy-Cons, due to their mass-market availability and current degree of penetration within the target population.

The obtained results show that the envisaged approach is promising, when measuring different task-load dimensions using the NASA-TLX scale. However, we also observed some areas of improvement, involving the design of some game mechanics, smoothing entry barriers and learning curve, and dynamically adjusting the proposed level of challenge in the games, which has to be in line with the therapeutical goals of the rehabilitation program.

Although the games were developed with video game console controls in mind, there were also technical challenges that needed to be overcome. In particular, the accuracy and precision of the embedded sensors in the Joy-Cons yielded error propagation when mapping real-world movements to virtual-screen pointing. This opens up the opportunity to redesign the games but with controls mediated by mid-to-high-end smartphones, which also are integrated with reliable sensors to gauge 3D movements (i.e., accelerometer, gyroscope, and magnetometer). As future work, we envisage running a summative A/B experimental study comparing the performance, playability, usability, perceived usefulness, and adoption potential of the presented video games, controlled either with Joy-Cons on the one hand and with mid-end and high-end smartphones, on the other hand.

References

1. Andrysek, J., et al.: Preliminary evaluation of a commercially available videogame system as an adjunct therapeutic intervention for improving balance among children and adolescents with lower limb amputations. Arch. Phys. Med. Rehabil. **93**(2), 358–366 (2012). https://doi.org/10.1016/j.apmr.2011.08.031
2. Csikszentmihalyi, M.: The Flow Experience and Its Significance for Human Psychology, pp. 15–35. Cambridge University Press (1988). https://doi.org/10.1017/CBO9780511621956.002

3. Fernández-González, P., et al.: Leap motion controlled video game-based therapy for upper limb rehabilitation in patients with parkinson's disease: a feasibility study. J. NeuroEng. Rehabil. **16**(1) (2019). https://doi.org/10.1186/s12984-019-0593-x

4. Fung, V., Ho, A., Shaffer, J., Chung, E., Gomez, M.: Use of Nintendo WII fit in the rehabilitation of outpatients following total knee replacement: a preliminary randomised controlled trial. Physiotherapy **98**, 183–188 (2012). https://doi.org/10.1016/j.physio.2012.04.001

5. Gajdosik, R.L., Bohannon, R.W.: Clinical measurement of range of motion: review of goniometry emphasizing reliability and validity. Phys. Ther. **67**(12), 1867–1872 (1987)

6. Hall, A.M., Ferreira, P.H., Maher, C.G., Latimer, J., Ferreira, M.L.: The influence of the therapist-patient relationship on treatment outcome in physical rehabilitation: a systematic review. Phys. Therapy **90**(8), 1099–1110 (2010). https://doi.org/10.2522/ptj.20090245

7. Hart, S.G.: Nasa-task load index (nasa-tlx); 20 years later. In: Proceedings of the Human Factors and Ergonomics Society Annual Meeting, vol. 50, no. 9, pp. 904–908 (2006). https://doi.org/10.1177/154193120605000909

8. Hsu, J.K., Thibodeau, R., Wong, S.J., Zukiwsky, D., Cecile, S., Walton, D.M.: A WII bit of fun: the effects of adding Nintendo WII bowling to a standard exercise regimen for residents of long-term care with upper extremity dysfunction. Physiother. Theory Pract. **27**(3), 185–193 (2011). https://doi.org/10.3109/09593985.2010.483267

9. Kamkarhaghighi, M., Mirza-Babaei, P., El-Khatib, K.: Game-Based Stroke Rehabilitation, pp. 147–162. Springer, Cham (2017). https://doi.org/10.1007/978-3-319-49879-9

10. Lohse, K., Shirzad, N., Verster, A., Hodges, N., Van der Loos, H.F.M.: Video games and rehabilitation: using design principles to enhance engagement in physical therapy. J. Neurol. Phys. Ther. **37**(4), 166–175 (2017)

11. Physiopedia: Range of motion. https://www.physio-pedia.com/Range_of_Motion. Accessed 27 Oct 2023

12. Ryan, R.M., Deci, E.L.: Self-determination theory and the facilitation of intrinsic motivation, social development, and well-being. Am. Psychol. **55**(1), 68–78 (2000). https://doi.org/10.1037/0003-066X.55.1.68

13. Staiano, A.E., Flynn, R.: Therapeutic uses of active videogames: a systematic review. Games Health J. 351–365 (2014). https://doi.org/10.1089/g4h.2013.0100

14. Unnikrishnan, R., Moawad, K., Bhavani, R.R.: A physiotherapy toolkit using video games and motion tracking technologies. In: 2013 IEEE Global Humanitarian Technology Conference: South Asia Satellite (GHTC-SAS), pp. 90–95 (2013). https://doi.org/10.1109/GHTC-SAS.2013.6629895

15. Vygotsky, L.S., Veresov, N., Barrs, M.: Play and its role in the mental development of the child. Int. Res. Early Childhood Educ. **7**(2), 3–25 (2016)

16. Webster, J.G., Cook, A.M., Tompkins, W.J., Vanderheiden, G.C.: Electronic devices for rehabilitation. Am. J. Occup. Ther. **40**(4), 298 (1986)

Tommi - A Web-Based Serious Game for Children Incentivizing a Healthy Lifestyle Combined with Environmental Awareness

Christian Eichhorn[1]([✉]), Christian Schepers[3], David A. Plecher[1], Atsushi Hiyama[2], Andreas Butz[3], and Gudrun Klinker[1]

[1] Chair for Computer Aided Medical Procedures and Augmented Reality, The Technical University of Munich, Munich, Germany
christian.eichhorn@tum.de, {plecher,klinker}@in.tum.de
[2] Graduate School of Social Data Science, Hitotsubashi University, Kunitachi, Japan
hiyama@imaginics.sds.hit-u.ac.jp
[3] Chair for Human-Computer-Interaction, Ludwig Maximilian University of Munich, Munich, Germany
c.schepers@campus.lmu.de, andreas.butz@ifi.lmu.de

Abstract. Healthy food alternatives, as well as the impact of food items on the environment, are often overlooked when grocery shopping. The lack of education and missing early contact with these topics in childhood are major contributing factors. We want to take a closer look at a balanced diet and the environmental impact of food production based on the literature and an interview conducted with a representative of German farmers. This will lay the foundation for a Serious Game targeting children between 9 and 12 years old. As teaching content, the Nutri-Score and healthy recipes combined with topics such as regionality, seasonality as well as water and CO2-eq. Footprint will be included in a child-friendly representation in the form of a farming simulation called 'Tommi'. Game mechanics include scanning real food items via barcodes and physical game cards describing recipes, which are presented as traditional trading cards. This connects virtuality with physicality and allows the children to engage with food products outside of the farming simulation by linking to the child's personal food choices. Additionally, eye-tracking for attention analysis to adapt to the difficulty of the game is included. The project is evaluated in two user studies with positive outcomes, such as the age group being appropriately chosen, as well as findings, such as the learning content being accepted with an impact on consumer behavior.

Keywords: Serious Game · Education · Children · Healthcare · Food Production · Environmental Awareness · Carbon Footprint · Cooking · School · Nudging · Card Game · Eye-Tracking · Study

© The Author(s), under exclusive license to Springer Nature Switzerland AG 2024
X. Fang (Ed.): HCII 2024, LNCS 14731, pp. 34–53, 2024.
https://doi.org/10.1007/978-3-031-60695-3_3

1   Introduction

Teaching children about a healthy diet is becoming increasingly important to reduce obesity and other diseases. However, since cooking and eating take place at home, this topic should be introduced to the family environment to achieve changes in nutritional behavior. Therefore, making children more aware can influence the parents responsible for buying food and for cooking. Our Serious Game 'Tommi' directly targets children who are in the age range of 9–12 years old, where they start to comprehend such a subject. Therefore, one part of the teaching content focuses on their health and the influences of food on it.

Additionally, we target the understanding of the complex interrelationships of environmental influences that arise in food production. This impact on the environment is often not considered when choosing products in the supermarket. Food production impacts the ecosystem through greenhouse gas emissions and water consumption. Forming a foundation, an interview was conducted with the chairwoman of UNSER LAND GmbH, who represents a community of German farmers. Furthermore, environmental impacts have been investigated based on literature, including aspects such as Water and CO_2-eq. Footprint.

Up until now, the link between food production and a healthy diet has been neglected when looking at education for children. Through an analysis of both topics, a child-friendly representation is developed in the form of a web-based farming simulator called 'Tommi'. By utilizing the proven approach of Serious Games (SGs), educating about a healthy diet as well as conveying environmental awareness can have long-reaching benefits. Additionally, we include useful game mechanics such as storytelling and goal-oriented learning by encouraging personal solutions to target a healthy diet. Auxiliary game mechanics include dynamically adapting the difficulty level to keep the player in the flow zone [42]. In the web-based SG 'Tommi', eye-tracking is utilized to determine the focus of the children combined with in-game analyses to then adapt to the difficulty of the game. To further enrich the experience, mini-games are available, and a connection between the virtual and real world is created by, on the one hand, including real scanned food items via barcodes and, on the other hand, physical game cards describing recipes in the style of traditional trading cards. This allows engagement with food and its environmental impact outside of the central farming simulation by providing a link to the child's personal food choices.

To acquire an understanding of how 'Tommi' and its serious content is received by the target group, two user studies with children aged 9–12 have been conducted. For the first study with 21 children lasting over four weeks (allowing for flexibility to play), an online setting has been chosen. An understanding of the teaching content was visible, and in part, a change in food consumption could be detected. In the second study with 3 participants under lab conditions, the focus was placed on adapting the difficulty level based on the attention and skill of a user. The user's gaze was used in order to detect attention loss. If such a phase was detected, attention should be returned to the game by a difficulty adjustment. A series of tests showed that a loss of attention with a subsequent adjustment of the difficulty could lead to improved flow.

2   Fundamentals for Serious Game Development

An important difference exists between an SG and gamified teaching content (gamification). While in both cases, the goal is to teach serious content by using reward systems and game elements, the approach differs greatly. Gamification uses game techniques to modify existing serious content in order to enhance the incentive to learn [23]. A simple example from the field of nutrition education targets obesity in children. In order to improve the diet, two dishes (one unhealthy and one healthier alternative) are presented and compared. After guessing the healthier alternative with a time limit, points can be collected, and a leaderboard is available combined with rewards [5]. In contrast to gamified elements, in an SG (also known as an educational game), the teaching content is integrated, and passive learning is enforced through fun and emotions [14,15,17,38]. Advantages of such an approach include and are not limited to:

1. **'Fun Factor'**: Playing games includes aspects such as: 'agency, immersion, challenge, reward, immediacy, a dialect of repetition and variety, physical and mental engagement, and multi-sensory stimulation' [22]. These are seen as strong incentives for players to engage with a topic and thus allow for an easier foundation to impart knowledge.
2. **The Interplay of Intrinsic and Extrinsic Motivation:** 'Especially intrinsic motivation which separates from extrinsic motivation in that people conduct an activity for inherent satisfaction and enjoyment is important for behavioral changes' [7]. As intrinsic motivation needs time to grow, an SG provides the necessary playtime with engagement to do so. While extrinsic motivation can be directly used through, e.g., rewards, it can help keep the player in the flow and motivate further contact with the topic to build a bridge towards intrinsic motivation.
3. **Flow and Storytelling:** There is the need for a balance between challenge and boredom to keep a player in the flow zone [8]. This narrow channel describes an optimal engagement and difficulty level. Educational content needs to be represented in an understandable and appealing form: 'Hugo Gernsback saw the genre [Games] as encouraging popular science education by communicating innovative theories or compelling research results in a language that is more accessible' [36]. Many techniques can be used in games to convey complex topics by introducing step-by-step plots and integrating individual elements into a storyline. Feedback is given on actions, correct or incorrect, and it is encouraged to explore a topic through trial and error. With SG in particular, it is important that the players are in a state of flow with regard to both the gaming challenge and the learning challenge posed by the serious content [30].

SG design, however, has a number of challenges that influence its success, e.g., the choice of a game genre that fits the theme. Furthermore, the creation of an SG requires competencies [22]:

1. **Interface Design:** The User Interface (UI) must be adapted to the target group. This includes the graphic style, the complexity, and the number of elements. If the game is aimed at children, graphics should be colorful and recognizable, and characters should be presented in an approachable manner.
2. **Domain Expertise:** Knowledge of the educational content is a basic requirement for creating the story in the game, as well as the challenges a player is confronted with. This expertise can significantly improve the flow and feel and intellectually stimulate the player to the right degree.
3. **Pedagogical Knowledge:** It 'not only dwells on the content of a subject but also how it is to be presented in a form that will reach the learner in an effective and entertaining way without any 'noise' creeping into the communication and without any vital information getting lost' [22]. If these points are not fulfilled, it can happen that the SG becomes 'edutainment'. Also, neglect of rules and objectives to guarantee a better storyline can lead to edutainment. Edutainment 'is a hybrid genre that relies heavily on visual material, on narrative or game-like formats, and on more informal, less didactic styles of address. The purpose of edutainment is to attract and hold the attention of the learners by engaging their emotions through a computer monitor full of vividly colored animations' [6]. The problem with edutainment, however, is that it 'often fails in transmitting nontrivial [...] knowledge, calling again and again the same action patterns and not throwing the learning curve into relief' [12].

3   Related Work

In this chapter, we want to introduce important topics such as existing SGs for children targeting a healthy diet and a fundamental understanding of the topics associated with environmental factors of food items.

3.1   Serious Games for Children - A Healthy Diet

With the advance of digitalization, play among children and young people is shifting further into the digital realm. According to the report, more than 90% of children aged 6–7 already play video games every day [34]. This can be utilized to capture the attention of young target groups through digital educational games [25]. To achieve a health intervention, adequate difficulty, trial and error [26], and the learning progress adapted to one's own abilities need to be incorporated [24]. In the SG 'NoGo' [5], children and adolescents are targeted through educational measures in the form of puzzles to avoid obesity. The game challenges the player through the time needed to differentiate healthy food from unhealthy ones. The aim is to create a positive association with healthy alternatives through repetition and to internalize them in such a way that no reflection is necessary when confronted with food. Another example SG in the form of a physical board game, 'The Kingdom of Taste' [35], allows children to explore and taste fruits and vegetables. In this story-based game, children have to help a cook and come into contact with food that is available in the real world. The game is a series of different missions that have to be fulfilled, and the integration of real food items is a rarely used design element. In a game designed by children for children in the project by Baytak and Land's [4], children were asked to develop their own educational games. One example result was a racing game to consume less unhealthy food by avoiding unhealthy items. In another game concept by Lieberman [25], a multiplayer approach has been explored. The game aims to teach about diabetes through a simulation with a question segment, and the players are supposed to learn about the challenges a diabetic faces.

3.2   Impact of Food Production on the Environment

Various factors influence resources needed, e.g., the amount of water used for watering plants or used as drinking water for farm animals is associated with the product and results in the Water Footprint (WF) [21].

Water Footprint of the Food Production. Rockström et al. [32] have defined WF with worldwide recognition to have uniform, comparable values. They differentiate three types of water consumption [9]:

- **The Green Water Footprint:** This part of the footprint describes the amount of water that is taken naturally from the environment and not extracted by humans from the natural water cycle. This includes, for example, the water that plants withdraw from the soil or groundwater or, in the case of animal products, the water that animals take in through grazing.
- **The Blue Water Footprint:** This part of the footprint describes the amount of water used in production that is actively withdrawn by humans from the natural water cycle. This includes any activity where water comes out of the tap or is taken from rivers, lakes, or groundwater.
- **The grey Water Footprint:** This part of the footprint describes the amount of water needed to dilute contaminated water to the extent that it meets ambient water quality standards, e.g., for chemicals or fertilizers.

The production process can be divided into steps: inputs, farming, processing, and outputs. The calculation is thus highly complex and requires a precise analysis of the cultivation forms and measurement of water consumption. Products of the category 'Animal Products' have, on average, a much higher WF compared to the average of vegetables and fruits. This leads to the fact that even the small portion of 15% of non-vegetable products of the daily average calorie intake accounts for more than 50% of the WF resulting from nutrition. Based on calculations by Falkenmark [19], the average person consumes up to 2700 kcal per day, of which 2300 kcal is from plant-based products and 400 kcal from animal products. Although these values vary greatly, especially regionally and based on the development of a country [43], e.g., North America: 98.5 kg meat/p/y vs. Africa: 12.7kg meat/p/y [37], the proportion calculated can be used as a global average. According to Vanham et al. [41], the average food footprint per person is 4265 l/cap/d, 53% of which is attributable to animal products. It can be concluded that a reduction in meat consumption, as well as in the consumption of animal products in general, has a noticeably positive impact on global water consumption. However, since the WF is not apparent to the consumer in the supermarket, educational work is required in order to change consumption behavior in the long term and thus achieve a reduction in personal water consumption.

Carbon Footprint of the Food Production. Additionally to the WF, the CO_2-eq. Footprint (CF) of food needs to be communicated to improve the impact on the environment. Similar to the WF, the calculation is a complex interaction of many factors. The total greenhouse gas released in the food life cycle must, therefore, be calculated. However, the definition of 'total life cycle' varies in the literature [31], which leads to complications in comparing footprints. In particular, there is disagreement about the end of the cycle: (1) the end is reached with the sale to the customer, or (2) that the purchase, processing, and disposal of the food scraps and packaging materials are included. For our understanding of CF, we decided on variant (2), mainly due to the consideration of the packaging waste. The calculation of the CF can be divided into 5 main areas [31,33]: pre-farm emissions, on-farm emissions, indirect emissions, post-farm emissions, and End-of-Life (EoL). Important are the many extra components, such as emissions generated before the production, such as the production of agricultural machinery or fuel processing. Additionally, on-farm emissions can be subdivided into many other aspects, e.g., field preparation, emissions from machinery, or emissions by farming animals. Also, before the farm is even created, e.g., deforestation and the initial cultivation of fields are necessary. After leaving the farm, transport, storage, and packaging are standard aspects that contribute to the overall CF. In EoL, aspects close to the final consumer are looked at, such as the preparation of food or disposal of packaging. In general, animal products in all forms have a noticeably higher CF. This is based on the emissions from feed production and those directly related to the animal. This is also reflected in the breakdown of the food footprint of an average diet. Here, meat products account for more than half of all emissions, and dairy products an additional 18.3%. Fruits and vegetables make up only 1.6% and 2.6% of the total dietary footprint, respectively [39]. Also, waste disposal leads to major problems for wildlife (especially that of the oceans). The Life Cycle Assessment (LCA) is a good basis for comparing the environmental impact of food products, but has limitations. According to Elin Röös [33], the LCA is a 'limited representation of reality built on several choices regarding functional unit, system boundaries, allocation principles, etc., introducing scenario uncertainty'. In order to be able to draw a meaningful comparison between different products, it is therefore important that the same calculation scheme is used, taking into account the same influencing factors. Since the delivery routes contribute to a large extent to the CF, how much the footprint of imported goods and regionally produced food differs will be discussed in more detail.

4   Implementation

For the SG 'Tommi', we first present an additional foundation for our learning content in the form of an interview targeting environmental topics.

4.1   Interview About Regionality and Seasonality

In order to gain a more detailed insight into the local production methods and educational approaches with regard to the emission of greenhouse gases and the waste of water, an interview was conducted with the chairwoman of the umbrella organization UNSER LAND GmbH. The UNSER LAND network is a complex union of a GmbH, an umbrella association, and 10 non-profit solidarity communities. Each part of this network has the same goal, the 'preservation of the livelihoods of people, animals, and plants in the region', which is transported with different approaches. The following excerpts from this interview, conducted in German, have been translated into English and summarized:

As pointed out: 'the network is not about making the biggest possible profit, but about carrying the ideology forward'. Here, the focus is not on marketing for products but on real insights into regional production processes with their advantages and disadvantages. The environmental impact of food is a high priority because preserving diversity and strengthening the region can only be achieved through well-thought-out and goal-oriented production methods. The producers in the network contribute to the awareness of the impact of food production. Some of them explicitly have their farms' footprints calculated to improve production with regard to the environment. The idea of sustainable food production is also to be conveyed through solidarity community projects. Since all UNSER LAND foods are produced in the network area, regionality is seen as important: 'Buying regional food creates a direct link between the buyer and the ecosystem in which he lives'. Food is valued more, and transparency in production makes it easier to create changes in consumer behavior than with imported goods. 'An important point here is the short delivery routes', while importing goods means that foodstuffs have to travel much longer distances, which is directly linked to increased emissions. As an example, imported apples transported by ship from New Zealand to Germany have a footprint over 1.5 times higher than regional apples [10]. For asparagus shipped by air from Peru, the CF value can increase up to 16 times that of regionally grown [28].

The seasons are another important influencing factor regarding the environmental impact of food items. Buying fruits and vegetables outside of the actual harvest season is usually associated with growing the food in greenhouses. This artificial creation of ideal growing conditions pollutes the environment. In addition, green water cannot be used to irrigate the plants; blue water is used instead. The greatest environmental impact of out-of-season produce is greenhouse heating. A calculation by the University of Gießen [40] shows that tomatoes grown in greenhouses emit up to 11 times as much CF as conventional, seasonally, and regionally grown. 'The big problem with seasonality is that many people no longer have any idea when what grows and which foods are in season. This requires a lot of awareness work to impart this knowledge'.

In response to the question of when children or young people are at an age to be brought into contact with the topic of nutrition, reference is made to the children's cooking courses offered by the UNSER LAND network. The age is less important than the approach. The goal should be to interest children in nutritional backgrounds in a playful way and with enjoyment.

4.2 A Game Concept to Teach About Water/Carbon Footprint

The target group (children, 9–12 years old) and choice of learning content based on cognitive abilities need to be defined. Due to the fact that nourishment is a topic that most often appears at home and in combination with the children's parents, the game also addresses them. Additionally, conveying the WF and CF of food products and creating awareness of the environmental impacts of foods were chosen (e.g., regionality and seasonality).

The title of the SG is 'Tommi - The Web-based Food Game' and belongs to the category of simulation games with a central reward mechanism based around collectible cards, which the players can unlock throughout the game. 100 food products were manually selected to be included and represent different product categories: meat and seafood (16), livestock products (14), fruits (24), vegetables (33), nuts (6), and processed food products (7). A dataset consisting of the product name, the season it can be harvested (if applicable), the typical growing region, the emission of CF in grams per 100g, and the water consumption in liters per 100g was created. All information except the emission of the CF and the water consumption can easily be researched. For the water footprint of food items, a report of the UNESCO-IHE Institute for Water Education based on the method of green, blue, and grey water formed the foundation [27]. For the remaining gaps, a combination of data found in the 'Water Footprint of Food Guide' [2] and data provided by the 'Water Footprint Network' [1] was used. For the CF, the majority of information was taken from calculations by the Institute for Energy and Environmental Science Heidelberg[1]. For the CF, it is important to consider the region that is used as the origin point. Otherwise, transportation would vary and distort the result. Due to the fact that the SG was released in Bavaria, Germany, a Heidelberg dataset represents the CF appropriately.

4.3 Adapting the Serious Content for Children

Raw WF/CF numbers are hardly comprehensible, even for adults. To confront a 9–12-year-old with these numbers needs adoption, and it is important to have some kind of reference or scale by which these numbers can be interpreted. A simple medal system, including theme-referencing pictograms, was chosen (see Fig. 5a). At this juncture, a high footprint corresponds to a high medal count. Furthermore, to avoid the association of a high medal count with a positive

---

[1] https://www.ifeu.de/en/ (last access 02/02/2024).

influence, a color scale that is based on a common traffic light scheme with green representing low, yellow representing middle, and red representing high values is added to the medal background. To index the foods, a scale of half and full points is introduced. Therefore, a gradation of 10 levels exists. When analyzing the sorted representation of all the CF values as a curve function, a similarity to a power or exponential function is given. Because the initial conversion function is linear, manipulating the CF equation in such a way that the result would also be closer to a linear function would lead to a more even distribution of medals among the foods. This can be achieved by applying the inverted function to the curve, meaning a logarithmic or root function. A distributed final result for the 100 food items can be seen in Fig. 1a.

(a) Final distribution of the carbon medals for 100 foods

(b) Final distribution of the water medals for 100 foods

Fig. 1. Final distributions

For the water footprint, the updated function projects the initial range of values of [19;1728] onto [0;6.11]. Therefore, the same conversion method that is used for the carbon values (Formula 3.3) can be applied. This then results in the following distribution of the water medals for the 100 food items in Fig. 1b.

4.4 Building Blocks of the Serious Game Tommi

The components of the game can be split into three sections:

- **Farming Simulation:** This is the central game used to convey most of the learning content. It is also the part in which the player can unlock new collectibles of food products.
- **Recipe Crafter:** In this section, the players can combine their earned ingredients into real recipes that can be cooked in real life.
- **Week Planner:** This section helps to plan the week by using unlocked recipes and receiving feedback on their environmental impacts.

The game is designed to run on a browser (cross-platform), with the optimal system being a PC at home. On the other hand, the game can be played on mobile in different places like the kitchen, while traveling, or in school, which again favors the use of a mobile application for a smartphone or tablet. Interacting with the SG through touch or with a mouse and keyboard is working for our game. The most limiting factor in terms of performance is the integrated eye-tracking feature. 'Tommi' is developed from scratch using HTML5, JavaScript, CSS3, and a node.js back-end server. As for the graphics, most were created using Adobe Photoshop and Adobe Animate.

 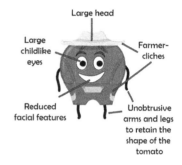

(a) Design of the level-overview-page with showing the linear level structure

(b) Design elements of the main character Tommi

Fig. 2. Designs of the farming simulation

Farming Simulation. Here, the majority of the knowledge transfer happens. Also, this is the main way to earn new collectible cards with food products. Texts have been carefully written, combining information and fun dialogues. The game consists of 24 individual levels that the player can play in chronological order (see Fig. 2a). In each of these levels, the production cycle of a food item is represented. This enables the player to experience at which points in the production process a food item has an impact on the environment and how damaging these effects are.

The player's progress is shown by the coloring of levels already played and the display of stars earned. Levels that have already been played can be repeated at any time in order to possibly achieve a better score. As emerged from the interview with the chairwoman from UNSER LAND, the food should also revolve around regional products but also represent a variety of cultivation methods and product categories. We included all major categories: meat and seafood, livestock products, fruits, vegetables, Nuts, and processed food products. The player is guided through this simulation by the main character, Tommi, who is visually based on a tomato. The character was designed in such a way that it is accessible due to its childlike appearance and can be associated with the theme due to its cliché-like accessories (see Fig. 2b).

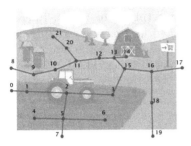
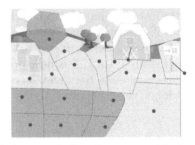

(a) Movement graph excluding connections between points that are out of frame

(b) A map of all action areas with the according movement graph position

Fig. 3. Movement graph and map

In order to understand why a product has an impact on the ecosystem, the entire production process is to be re-enacted. For this purpose, a game world is created, adapted for each level, but sharing the same basic elements. These level-overarching basics include a background (reflecting all 4 seasons) consisting of a simple hilly landscape, some interactable farming elements, which are present in each level, and a movement graph. This graph, over which the character can move, consists of 21 points and 21 unweighted edges (see Fig. 3a).

Fig. 4. Cylinders next to the playing field that indicate the carbon emission and water consumption of the current game state

A large part of the gameplay takes place in the lower left quarter of the playing field (colored red in Fig. 3b). Here, depending on the food, an individually designed overlay is displayed on which most of the steps of the development take place. For vegetables, this is usually a field, for fruit bushes or trees, and for animal products, an enclosure/stable. A second important area is located at the end of the path leading to the left hill for processing buildings (colored blue in

Fig. 3b). Here, depending on the product, a suitable building for e.g., cleaning, packing, slaughtering, mills, or similar, is displayed. Next to the central game area, two cylinders representing the current CF and WF are visible at all times on the right and left sides (see Fig. 4). These fill up in the course of the play process based on the environmental influences of the respective production steps. Each mark corresponds to half a medal of the food medals. For a product that contains 3 CF medals and 1.5 water medals, the cylinders will fill up to a level of 6 and 3 lines, respectively, in the course of the game.

(a) Medal system with theme-referencing pictograms

(b) The level progress bar includes three stars as milestones that show the score

Fig. 5. Medal system and progress bar

In the course of each level, the player receives a golden puzzle piece. Clicking on this puzzle piece opens a mini-game that the player can play as an interlude to the regular gameplay to collect bonus points. There are three basic mini-game modes implemented that are customized to the particular production process: puzzle of a product picture, memory with different pictures of products, and a single-choice quiz for a specific product. The score bar fills up over the course of a level and is displayed at the top of the screen. This gives the player a guideline for the progress he has already made in this level, how much is still ahead of him, and how many of the three possible stars he has earned (see Fig. 5b). The bar serves as a visual representation of the underlying point system that ranges from 0 to 100 and can be increased in two ways: (1) Earning points by correctly performing the required game actions. A perfect game earns the player 75 points. In the worst case (the player needs more than 2 hints), he gets 40 points. It is important to note that the scoring system is not based on the speed of the player but a trial-and-error concept to achieve real learning effects. (2) Through mini-games, which are solved voluntarily. Independent of the actual number of stars but linked to the successful completion of the level is the unlocking of a trading card. After the player has had a chance to look closely at the unlocked card, more cards are presented based on the number of stars earned. These are random product cards that are selected from the 100 implemented food products. Apart from the reward mechanism and the progress visualization, the player's score has another central role in the gameplay. The player's score is used as the basis for in-game skill analysis.

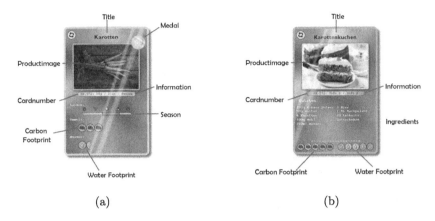

Fig. 6. Design elements and displayed information of the collectable ingredient (a) and recipe cards (b)

Collectables in the Form of Trading Cards. In 'Tommi', collectible cards are used as a reward mechanism. Trading cards come in two basic types: trading cards with food product information and recipe cards with information about dishes, including the recipe for cooking. They feature an appealing design trying to bridge from extrinsic to intrinsic motivation. Inspiration has been taken from well-known collectible card games such as Pokémon, Yu-Gi-Oh, or Magic: The Gathering. A cross-card scoring system for better comparability is included, and in some cases, symbols or medals are used to categorize cards. For the learning content, the cards contain important information, which includes the calculated CF and WF, as well as the season of the food (see Fig. 6). In the online version, the design principle of information on demand is incorporated, and players can obtain more detailed information on the visualized values. On the back side, more information is presented through a short block of text. This includes interesting or exciting information about food items and the beginning of the recipe for recipe cards. In addition, for recipe cards, there is a button with the inscription 'Cook now', which directs the player to a subpage where the complete recipe with ingredients, procedure, recipe picture, and the title is shown. All cards are equipped with an individual barcode (CODE128 format) on the back so that printed cards can be scanned into the game. The players can print out cards and trade them with others. These exchanged cards can then be scanned to be added to the collection folder. This takes the teaching content out of the game and into the real world and is intended to lead to an exchange of the product/recipe cards, thereby both spreading and deepening knowledge.

Recipe Crafter. This section is all about creating recipes from ingredients:

– Unlocked food cards are displayed at the edge of the window, divided into five categories such as meat & fish or vegetables.

– The second option targets preventing food waste and integrating reality more into the game by allowing to scan real existing products using a barcode on their packaging with a camera. If successful, it is transmitted to the connected OpenFoodFacts database[2], which returns a JSON file with a number of product information. Most important is the Nutri-Score. All the information is then analyzed, and an attempt is made to find one of the 100 implemented products that can represent the scanned ingredient. The mapped in-game card equivalent and the product's Nutri-Score are then shown. 'The NutriScore is a tool that can be used to identify the nutritional quality of a product. With the NutriScore, products can be compared easily and quickly' [18].

The player has the possibility to select up to five cards via these two options. For the recipe database, an existing Kaggle database was used as the foundation.

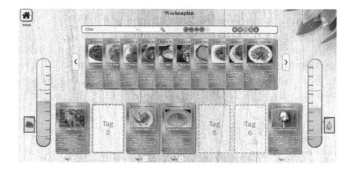

Fig. 7. The week planning page consists of a list of owned recipe cards with filter options, seven planning placeholders, of which 4 are filled in this scenario, and cylinders indicating the week's performance in regard to the footprints.

Week Planning. The last implemented subpage allows players to plan their week (see Fig. 7). The goal of this part is to influence consumption behavior in the long term and to reduce the WF and CF of the players in terms of food consumption. In the center of the playing field, the player has an overview of all the recipe cards that have already been unlocked. At the bottom of the board, there are seven placeholders, representative of seven days of the week, which the player has to fill with recipes.

4.5   Adapting the Difficulty Level with Eye-Tracking

Being overwhelmed or bored can make teaching content less effective. A central element to keep the player in the flow channel is progressing. However, this design principle has limitations, as it often cannot cover all skill groups. This is an issue

---

[2] www.OpenFoodFacts.org (last access 02/02/2024).

with the target group of children as they have varying levels of skills, even when being the same age [42]. Thus, the difficulty needs to adapt more dynamically:

- **Level Design:** As seen with the flow zone, the option to change the difficulty throughout the gameplay is necessary. 'Flow is achieved by increasing the level of challenge as the individual's skill level increases' [3]. Challenges must be chosen to be easier initially and increase in complexity as they progress.
- **In-Game Analysis:** Another option is to adjust the difficulty of the game individually by incorporating previous interactions. One difficulty that arises in this approach is to estimate the skill of the player [13, 20].
- **Tracking the Attention Span:** Although a break in attention does not yet indicate whether it is over- or under-challenging, it is an option to measure whether a player is in flow [16]. In combination with a rudimentary pre-analysis of the in-game gameplay, it is possible to determine the point at which the difficulty needs to be individually adjusted. In order to identify the player's attentional break, eye-tracking can be used [11].

To bring all three aspects together, our SG 'Tommi' is built on variable difficulty adjustment options, remembering previous progress, and we target the measurement of the attention span through eye-tracking. Only a conventional webcam is required.

 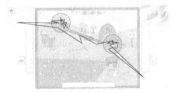

(a) Determining the Area of Inattention (AoI) with (1) being the coordinate-origin of the eye-tracking coordinates and (2) being the area for which the Inattention is assumed

(b) Measured eye-tracking points with a high measuring rate for a user looking at the barn and then at the hill with two wrong measurements being inside the AoI

Fig. 8. Area of Inattention (AoI) and measured eye-tracking points

The eye-tracking software WebGazer.js [29] is used as it is optimized for the browser. By calculating the data locally, intransparent and uncontrollable processing on a server can be avoided, and the privacy of the users can be protected. The result of the eye-tracking software is the coordinates of the point that the software has calculated as a prediction for the direction of gaze relative to the upper left corner of the window. Based on this, the active play area is defined, and an Area of Inattention (AoI) is set (see Fig. 8a). If the gaze remains in this AoI for a longer period of time, this is interpreted as a loss of attention.

The AoI must be adjusted depending on the window size for each scaling. A weighting function is used to measure the activity progression. If the player's gaze is in the AoI, the weighting is increased; if the eye-tracking position is within the game area, the weighting is decreased. If the weighting is above a threshold, adequate adaptations are made in the game, on the one hand, to draw attention back to the game and, on the other hand, to adjust the difficulty so that the player does not lose attention further. In Fig. 8b, the raw output of the eye-tracking is visible, and an algorithm for smoothing is used on it.

At the first loss of attention, a visual indicator is used to try to draw the user's attention back to the screen. If unsuccessful, or if a repeated loss of attention is detected, the difficulty of the game is adjusted. The stars already earned in previous levels serve as an indicator of over- or under-challenge, whereby 2 stars corresponds to an adequate challenge, 1 star is an indicator of over-challenge, and 3 stars is an indicator of under-challenge. If an over-challenge is detected, the player receives assistance that does not negatively affect the current level score. In addition, the bonus levels are simplified. If an under-challenge is detected, e.g., hints are reduced.

5 Evaluation

Two user studies have been conducted: (1) Evaluating whether the game appeals to the selected target group and whether the teaching content is conveyed. (2) Serves to evaluate the feature of difficulty adjustment through eye-tracking.

5.1 User Study Evaluating the Teaching Content

21 children who were reached through youth groups and schools were participating. The test persons received a link that gave them the opportunity to access the game online in a PC browser and another link that asked them to complete an online survey in the form of a questionnaire (with school grade-like system 1 to 6, 1 being the best). By handing out links and the resulting uncontrollable game conditions, the survey could be conducted in a realistic environment. Consent forms were discussed with the groups and schools, and consent forms targeting the parents were handed out. The game was explained first, and younger children were advised to do the final survey together with their parents. There were no deliberately set goals and time limits (study duration: 4 weeks). Results were saved in an anonymized user database, which allows for detailed insights into the in-game progress of the users. After initial demographic data, questions targeted the favorite food items in the game, as well as questions about their activities in the farming simulation. In the next part of the questionnaire, attention and difficulty were checked. Also, the comprehensibility of the learning content was included by asking them about foods/recipes and the weekly planning feature via pictures. The distribution of the 21 pupils was 71.4% high school, while 'Realschule' and elementary school are represented by 14.3% each. The age distribution showed a 57.1% share of 11–12-year-old testers, 19%

are 9–10 years old, and 19% are older than 12. Only 1 participant was under 9 years old. Some noticeable results of the questionnaire include: Two-thirds of the respondents gave the appearance of the trading cards a grade of 1 (very good), and the average score was 1.43 ($\sigma = 0.68$). The design of 'Tommi' was also very well received, and 52.4% of the testers gave it a grade of 1, with an average of 1.52 ($\sigma = 0.60$). The design of the game world scored lowest, with an average of 1.90 ($\sigma = 0.83$), with criticism given about its childlike appearance. In terms of difficulty, with an average score of 1.60 ($\sigma = 0.82$), the area of combining ingredient cards into recipe cards scored best. The farming simulation feature received an average score of 1.65 ($\sigma = 0.74$), and the bonus puzzles were the least fun for testers, with a score of 1.71 ($\sigma = 0.85$). A mean of 3.5 was scored for the overall difficulty, and with increasing age, a drop in perceived difficulty was recognizable. 100% of the respondents said they had played bonus puzzles as well as tried out the combining products to recipe section. 90% said they had tested the weekly planning feature. All users stated that they played more than 3 of the farming levels. The scanning of cards or products was tested by 30% of the participants and was well received. In the image-based questions to check the learning success, about 85% of the respondents chose the correct answer.

5.2   User Study Evaluating the Adjusting Difficulty Settings

The eye-tracking feature for attention recognition was part of the second study, with a small tester group of 3 volunteers, and was conducted at their homes to minimize distraction. After the parents and children had given their consent, a mobile setup consisting of a laptop with an integrated webcam and an external mouse was introduced. Before the test began, the eye-tracking was explained, and the tests were carried out under supervision. The children were given the goal of playing 3 levels of the game (35 min needed) without a time limit. The recovery of attention when a loss of attention is detected is investigated. After the end of the game phase, further questions about the game content were asked in a dialogue. The interviewees were a 9-year-old primary school pupil and a 10- and 12-year-old secondary school pupil. The eye-tracking software recognized all participants' eyes. The task of playing three of the implemented levels did not pose a challenge to any of the respondents in terms of attention span. Only in the case of the 9-year-old did motivation wane slightly at the end of the game process and in the subsequent interview. In order to evaluate the quality of the tracking, a red dot was displayed at the beginning of the game and at the end of the last level played, visualizing the gaze prediction of the eye tracking. According to the testers, this was no distraction. The cause of three of the five unrecognized lapses of attention was a rotation of the head and the associated stop of the trackability of the eyes. Based on correctly detected attentional lapses, it was also possible to examine the attentional retrieval and adaptation of the assistance. With regard to the recovery of attention through game elements, attention retrieval proved to be a challenge, as the test subjects did not recognize the gentle visual stimuli well enough. The stimuli need to be reinforced in order to redirect the focus. The skill-dependent difficulty of the mini-games was chosen appropriately for the users in all cases. One issue with eye-tracking software was to detect the eyes when they were facing away from the camera. In this situation, the loss of attention can't be detected.

6   Conclusion and Outlook

With positive results of the user study, especially on the understanding of the teaching content with a potential change in the consumption behavior, some aspects can be summarized. An important part of purposeful teaching can be to include real objects as visible through features such as collectible cards. Besides being inspired by trading card games, another connection to the children's game Quartet, allows us to indirectly categorize the use of CF and WF to be comparable with each other. The reward of winning a game with a card that has a low footprint is positively associated. This can indirectly address the consumer behavior of the next generation (today's children) and improve it. Another advantage of printed cards is that they can be exchanged among each other. By introducing the regionality medal (gold color), regional foodstuffs stand out, usually having a number of advantages over imported goods in the area of environmental footprint or healthy aspects (measured with the Nutri-Score). All cards are equipped with an individual barcode with which they and real-world food products can be brought into the game. This enables the collector of the cards to convert newly acquired ingredients directly into recipes. Improving healthy nutrition is a challenge with the target group as it depends on considering additional diseases and dieting behavior over time, where our weekly planning feature lays a foundation. Looking at the eye-tracking feature, further testing will be necessary to improve its effectiveness to support the player. Another future goal would be to perform a long-term test series with a detailed analysis of consumption behavior. Our study with 21 participants only provides an initial indication of a possible change. When looking at schools, a concept for integration into the curriculum would be a major step to bring the topics into the classroom. Another option would be to distribute the trading cards in grocery shops.

References

1. Water Footprint Network water needed for the production of different foods and products. http://tinyurl.com/h7rbwzca. Accessed 01 Oct 2022
2. Water Footprint of Food Guide water needed for the production of different foods. http://tinyurl.com/mr37cbc9. Accessed 01 Oct 2022
3. Annetta, L.A.: The "i's" have it: a framework for serious educational game design. Rev. Gen. Psychol. **14**(2), 105–113 (2010)
4. Baytak, A., Land, S.M.: A case study of educational game design by kids and for kids. Procedia. Soc. Behav. Sci. **2**(2), 5242–5246 (2010)
5. Blackburne, T., Rodriguez, A., Johnstone, S.J., et al.: A serious game to increase healthy food consumption in overweight or obese adults: randomized controlled trial. JMIR Serious Games **4**(2), e5708 (2016)

6. Buckingham, D., Scanlon, M.: That is edutainment: media, pedagogy and the market place. In: International Forum of Researchers on Young People and the Media, Sydney (2000)

7. Chow, C.Y., Riantiningtyas, R.R., Kanstrup, M.B., Papavasileiou, M., Liem, G.D., Olsen, A.: Can games change children's eating behaviour? A review of gamification and serious games. Food Qual. Prefer. **80**, 103823 (2020)

8. Csikszentmihalyi, M., Abuhamdeh, S., Nakamura, J.: Flow. In: Handbook of Competence and Motivation, pp. 598–608 (2005)

9. Čuček, L., Klemeš, J.J., Kravanja, Z.: Overview of environmental footprints. In: Assessing and Measuring Environmental Impact and Sustainability, pp. 131–193. Elsevier (2015)

10. Dallmus, A.: Was ist besser für die umwelt: Bodensee- oder neuseelandapfel? (2018). http://tinyurl.com/3pzvp3ty. Accessed 20 Dec 2022

11. Dohan, M., Mu, M.: Understanding user attention in VR using gaze controlled games. In: Proceedings of the 2019 ACM International Conference on Interactive Experiences for TV and Online Video, pp. 167–173 (2019)

12. Dondlinger, M.J.: Educational video game design: a review of the literature. J. Appl. Educ. Technol. **4**(1), 21–31 (2007)

13. Duersch, P., Lambrecht, M., Oechssler, J.: Measuring skill and chance in games. Eur. Econ. Rev. **127**, 103472 (2020)

14. Eichhorn, C., et al.: A framework to incentivize the use of augmented reality in daily lives of older adults. In: Gao, Q., Zhou, J. (eds.) HCII 2023. LNCS, vol. 14042, pp. 531–551. Springer, Cham (2023). https://doi.org/10.1007/978-3-031-34866-2_38

15. Eichhorn, C., Plecher, D.A., Golovnya, O., Volkert, D., Hiyama, A., Klinker, G.: Tangible chess for dementia patients – playing with conductive 3d printed figures on a touchscreen. In: Gao, Q., Zhou, J. (eds.) HCII 2021. LNCS, vol. 12787, pp. 38–57. Springer, Cham (2021). https://doi.org/10.1007/978-3-030-78111-8_3

16. Eichhorn, C., Plecher, D.A., Klinker, G., Lurz, M., Leipold, N., Böhm, M., Krcmar, H., Ott, A., Volkert, D., Hiyama, A.: Innovative game concepts for Alzheimer patients. In: Zhou, J., Salvendy, G. (eds.) ITAP 2018. LNCS, vol. 10927, pp. 526–545. Springer, Cham (2018). https://doi.org/10.1007/978-3-319-92037-5_37

17. Eichhorn, C., Plecher, D.A., Trilk, A., Hiyama, A., Klinker, G.: Guessingcarbs-a serious game about healthy nutrition in old age combining virtual and tangible components. In: Stephanidis, C., Antona, M., Ntoa, S. (eds.) HCII 2022. LNCS, vol. 1583, pp. 407–415. Springer, Cham (2022)

18. Facts, O.F.: Vergleichen sie die nährwertqualität von lebensmitteln mit dem nutriscore! (2023). https://de.openfoodfacts.org/nutriscore. Accessed 10 Jan 2023

19. Falkenmark, M.: Meeting water requirements of an expanding world population. Philosoph. Trans. Roy. Soc. Lond. Ser. B: Biol. Sci. **352**(1356), 929–936 (1997)

20. Glickman, M.E.: The Glicko system. Boston Univ. **16**, 16–17 (1995)

21. Hoekstra, A.Y.: The water footprint of food. The Swedisch Research Council for Environment, Agricultural Sciences and Spatial Planning (Formas) (2008)

22. Jayakanthan, R.: Application of computer games in the field of education. Electron. Libr. **20**(2), 98–102 (2002)

23. Kim, S., Song, K., Lockee, B., Burton, J.: What is gamification in learning and education? In: Gamification in Learning and Education. AGL, pp. 25–38. Springer, Cham (2018). https://doi.org/10.1007/978-3-319-47283-6_4

24. Kozma, R.B.: Learning with media. Rev. Educ. Res. **61**(2), 179–211 (1991)

25. Lieberman, D.A.: Health education video games for children and adolescents: theory, design, and research findings (1998)

26. Malone, T.W., Lepper, M.R.: Making learning fun: a taxonomy of intrinsic motivations for learning. In: Aptitude, learning, and instruction, pp. 223–254. Routledge (2021)
27. Mekonnen, M., Hoekstra, A.Y.: The green, blue and grey water footprint of crops and derived crops products. volume 2: Appendices (2010)
28. Nordrhein-Westfalen, V.: Saisonale ernährung - warum eigentlich? (2023). http://tinyurl.com/yknmt3cz. Accessed 10 Jan 2023
29. Papoutsaki, A., Sangkloy, P., Laskey, J., Daskalova, N., Huang, J., Hays, J.: Webgazer: scalable webcam eye tracking using user interactions. In: Proceedings of the 25th International Joint Conference on Artificial Intelligence (IJCAI), pp. 3839–3845. AAAI (2016)
30. Plecher, D.A.: Impacts of Serious Games for Cultural Heritage. Ph.D. thesis, Technische Universität München (2021)
31. Ribal, J., Estruch, V., Clemente, G., Fenollosa, M.L., Sanjuán, N.: Assessing variability in carbon footprint throughout the food supply chain: a case study of valencian oranges. Int. J. Life Cycle Assess. **24**(8), 1515–1532 (2019)
32. Rockström, J., Falkenmark, M., Karlberg, L., Hoff, H., Rost, S., Gerten, D.: Future water availability for global food production: the potential of green water for increasing resilience to global change. Water Resour. Res. **45**(7) (2009)
33. Röös, E.: Analysing the carbon footprint of food, vol. 2013 (2013)
34. Saad, S., Al-Sager, M.O., Al-Maadeed, N., AlJa'am, J.M.: Play, learn and eat healthy food: a mobile game for children to fight obesity. In: 2018 International Conference on Computer and Applications (ICCA), pp. 369–376. IEEE (2018)
35. Skouw, S., Suldrup, A., Olsen, A.: A serious game approach to improve food behavior in families-a pilot study. Nutrients **12**(5), 1415 (2020)
36. Squire, K., Jenkins, H.: Harnessing the power of games in education. Insight **3**(1), 5–33 (2003)
37. Statista: Per capita consumption of meat worldwide from 2019 to 2021, with a forecast for 2031, by region (2022). http://tinyurl.com/tz2atj32. Accessed 01 Dec 2022
38. Strahringer, S., Leyh, C.: Gamification und serious games. Vorgehen und Anwendungen. Wiesbaden, Grundlagen (2017)
39. Center for Sustainable Systems, U.o.M.: Carbon footprint factsheet (2021). http://tinyurl.com/ytchb83y. Accessed 03 Jan 2023
40. Universität Gießen: Co2 ausstoß von tomaten bei unterschiedlichen produktionsarten (2015). http://tinyurl.com/5n7xtdzz. Accessed 20 Dec 2022
41. Vanham, D., Bidoglio, G.: A review on the indicator water footprint for the EU28. Ecol. Ind. **26**, 61–75 (2013)
42. Vinter, A., Perruchet, P.: Implicit learning in children is not related to age: evidence from drawing behavior. Child Dev. **71**(5), 1223–1240 (2000)
43. Wallace, J.S., Gregory, P.J.: Water resources and their use in food production systems. Aquat. Sci. **64**(4), 363–375 (2002)

An Interactive Game Design for Children's Bird Watching Based on Flow Experience Theory

Zhuofen He[1] , Langqing Chen[1] , ZhuKe Wu[2] , and Ao Qi[3(✉)]

[1] Guangdong University of Technology, No. 729, Dongfeng East Road, Yuexiu District, Guangzhou, China
[2] The Guangzhou Academy of Fine Arts, No. 257, Changgang East Road, Haizhu District, Guangzhou, China
[3] South China Normal University, No. 55, West Zhongshan Avenue, Tianhe District, Guangzhou, China
18588456977@163.com

Abstract. With the acceleration of urbanization, the natural environment of cities is becoming increasingly depleted. At the same time, rapid advances in science and technology, as well as increasing pressure to learn, have left children in urban areas with limited opportunities to connect with nature. This results in a significant gap between urban children and the natural environment. Therefore, this study designed a multi-sensory interactive bird watching game based on flow experience theory and developed an experience model for children's bird watching activities. By simulating a real birding environment, children are encouraged to participate in birding activities through multi-sensory interaction of sight, hearing and touch. This approach develops intrinsic motivation, allowing children to independently learn the activity of birding, appreciate the beauty of birding, and ultimately connect with nature. This study invited 20 children aged 6–12 to participate in an experiment to evaluate their gaming experience using the System Usability Scale (SUS). After testing, we also conducted user interviews to obtain further recommendations. The results of SUS scores and interviews showed that most participants had a high level of acceptance of the game and expressed willingness to continue playing this training game.

Keywords: Children · Flow experience · Bird watching interactive game

1 Introduction

With the rapid development of urbanization, the natural environment of cities is decreasing day by day. At the same time, the rapid development of science and technology and the increasing pressure to study have led to limited opportunities for urban children to contact nature, creating a huge gap between urban children and the natural environment. This phenomenon is called nature deficit disorder by Richard Louv [1]. It can lead to a range of behavioral and psychological problems, such as excessive stress, depression and difficulty concentrating, and obesity. The fundamental reason is that electronic media and academic burdens occupy children's time in contact with nature, causing many children to lose their interest in nature and the ability to experience nature.

X. Fang (Ed.): HCII 2024, LNCS 14731, pp. 54–68, 2024.
https://doi.org/10.1007/978-3-031-60695-3_4

Bird watching activities refer to observing wild birds in their natural state with the help of optical tools such as telescopes. Birds are rich creatures that can be observed in urban environments. During bird watching, you need to be quiet and patient, otherwise you will disturb the birds. Encouraging children to participate in bird watching activities helps guide children to observe birds in the natural environment, including better identifying birds, stimulating children's interest in birds, experiencing and enjoying nature, and improving children's cognitive abilities and patience [2].

However, with the process of modernization and urbanization, the natural environment in cities is gradually decreasing. The popularization of the Internet and the development of emerging technologies are inevitable trends. In this study, we used video games as an intermediary for children to connect with the natural world, integrating gamification into learning, which has been proven to create a relaxing, enjoyable and positive environment for children [3]. It plays a huge role in improving children's learning initiative, interest and problem-solving abilities [4, 5].

More and more studies have proven that game-based learning can build a contextualized and immersive learning environment for children. Let it enter the flow experience and improve children's learning interest and cognitive development ability. Chinese scholar Wang Yonggu developed a speech rehabilitation training game "Dr. Miaoyin Paradise" for special children, which combines speech rehabilitation training with games. The learning effect was quantitatively evaluated in the form of a questionnaire, which verified that educational games can effectively stimulate children's learning interest and enthusiasm for language learning. This research is beneficial to cultivating students' social and emotional attitudes and affirms the feasibility of educational games in language learning [6]. Cai Li and Liu Fanghao developed an online educational game for teaching Chinese as a foreign language called "Dongxueji". The game tasks include Chinese listening, reading, communication and grammar exercises. The virtual learning environment and teaching scenes in "Tong Xue Ji" can make it easier for players to immerse themselves in Chinese learning. It can be seen that applying flow theory to game design can effectively improve children's interest in learning and exercise their patience [7].

Among the contradictions between children, electronic games and nature, how to use electronic games as an intermediary to attract children's attention and interest, exercise their cognitive abilities and patience, and promote the connection between children and nature is the most important. Therefore, this study proposes to design a multi-sensory interactive bird watching game based on the flow experience theory, with the orientation of creating an effective learning environment, allowing learners to have a flow experience in an effective gamified learning environment, thereby stimulating learning motivation and promoting learning activities to improve the quality of learning.

This study explores:

1. How to gamify bird watching activities and design its mechanism;
2. How to improve children's cognitive ability and patience through bird watching games;
3. How to connect children with nature through bird watching games;

2 Related Work

With the advancement of urbanization and modernization, nature deficit disorder has become a problem that cannot be ignored in the growth of children. However, in the face of nature-deficit disorder in children, the current types of coping methods are relatively limited and the media are relatively traditional. As a product of modern development, video games have the potential to serve as an intermediary to assist in the cure of nature-deficit disorder in children.

2.1 Traditional Intervention Methods for Nature Deficit Disorder

At present, educational countermeasures for children with nature deficit disorder can be divided into three types: first, guiding children to form a correct view of nature from a conceptual perspective. For example, parents choose leisure methods that are closer to nature for their children, allowing them to walk into nature or visit a natural history museum. The second is to build a public space that is closer to nature, so that the concept of nature can subtly penetrate into all aspects of children's lives. For example, construct an "ecological campus" with a butterfly garden or greenhouse. The last step is to make changes in education methods, construct comprehensive, natural and practical courses, and weaken the problem of boring knowledge caused by the subject system, which makes children indifferent or even tired of learning natural knowledge [8, 9].

2.2 Video Games Help Boost Cognitive Development in Children

Research shows that the content and graphics of electronic games will promote human brain development and sensory organs, and also have a significant impact on cognitive development [10].

For example, Li Hua found in an experimental study on the impact of prosocial video games on the prosocial behavior of 3–6-year-old children that the pictures and content of prosocial games can significantly increase children's prosocial thinking and prosocial behavior. Another study by Liu Xiaocen and others on cooperative games showed that the content and context of cooperative games can promote children's peer interaction and prosocial behavior in both electronic games and traditional games, and there is no difference in the effects between the two [11, 12].

The above research illustrates the possibility of rationally applying electronic games in the field of education to promote children's development. And educational games with different contents and situations can lead to children's cognitive development in different fields.

To sum up, current measures to deal with nature deficit disorder in children are basically based on traditional media, which has problems such as high cost and difficulty in fully activating children's interests. Based on the above issues, this study uses the flow experience theory of AR games in natural situations as a link to connect children with nature deficit disorder and nature, and explores the possibility of electronic games with nature as the background to stimulate children's desire to explore nature.

3   Proposed Solution

The solution proposed in this study consists of two parts: 1. Based on the flow experience, build a bird watching experience model that attracts children's learning interests. 2. Use AR technology to build a card collection mechanism in the game mechanism setting to form a game environment and nature. Environmental interconnection.

3.1   Build a Bird Watching Game Experience Model

Relevant research shows that flow theory can describe students' optimal learning state, and it is believed that students in a flow state can produce efficient learning. How to get players into a flow state so that they can learn and acquire knowledge efficiently. Research by K. Jegers and D. Weibel found that players' game experience during the game is consistent with the dimensions of flow experience, and players often obtain flow experience during the game [13, 14]. Hoffman and Novak defined flow as a state that occurs when navigating the Internet and found that a pleasant online user experience was positively related to "fun, casual, and experienced" experiences and negatively related to work-oriented activities. This suggests that online flow experiences are more associated with games and entertainment activities than with work or task-oriented activities [15]. Kiili applies flow theory and experiential learning theory to educational game design and proposes an experiential educational game model [16]. This model proposes that clear goals, timely feedback and appropriate difficulty play an important role in educational games. The above three elements It is conducive to learners' flow experience and enhances the teaching effect of educational games. It can be seen that the application of flow experience theory to the bird watching game experience model can promote children's interest in bird watching activities and concentration in learning during the game experience, and clear goals, timely feedback and appropriate difficulty will influence children Interest and effectiveness in learning.

Csikszentrnihalyi proposed the flow experience theory, which summarized 9 important characteristics of flow experience [17]. Novak et al. (2000) summarized these nine characteristics into condition, experience and outcome factors based on the process of flow experience [18]. Chen, Wigand and Nilan further divided flow into three stages: pre-event, experience, and effect [19]. "Clear goals", "immediate feedback", and "matching challenges and skills" are necessary conditions for entering the flow state, (see Fig. 1) [16].

- "Clear goals" means that the activities have clear goals, such as chess, painting, sports, etc., which have clear goals, action guidelines and strict evaluation standards [29]; "immediate feedback" means that the activities allow participants to Get timely feedback on results and have a clear understanding of your own behavior; "challenge and skill matching" refers to the balance between personal skills and challenge difficulty. If the difficulty of the challenge is too high, it will cause deep frustration, worry, and even anxiety. If the challenge is too easy and the ability is more than enough, you will feel bored after you get over it. Only when high-difficulty challenges and outstanding abilities match each other can one's full devotion trigger flow and create experiences and feelings that are different from ordinary ones.

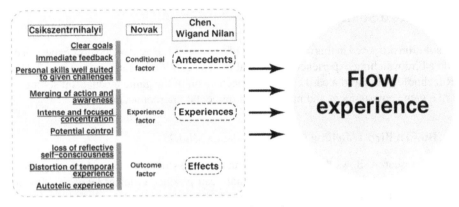

Fig. 1. Flow experience theory

- The three conditional factors of flow experience are applied to the design of the bird watching game experience model and summarized into the following six basic requirements (see Fig. 2):

1. In the bird watching game experience, use voices, pictures, etc. to provide children with clear operational guidance;
2. In the design of the game experience interface, the control interface should be simple and use more visual elements to facilitate children's recognition and experience;
3. Provide accurate, appropriate, multi-sensory interaction and feedback when children experience games;
4. During the game, provide appropriate props and motivating feedback for children to complete tasks, so that they can receive certain help and encouragement without giving up;

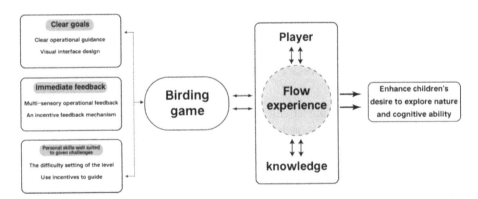

Fig. 2. Bird watching game experience model

5. The popularization of bird watching knowledge is divided into several scenes and levels according to the tools used and regional seasons, and corresponding rules and learning processes are formulated for children;
6. In the game, through the incentive system of collecting level cards, children are provided with goals to strive for level by level.

3.2 AR Card Collection Promotes Children's Connection with Nature

In this study, in order to encourage children to get out of the room and walk into nature, we first determined that this is a game that applies augmented reality (AR) technology and uses a combination of virtual and reality to collect bird cards as the main activity. Sections involving AR include bird knowledge popularization, bird hunting cameras, bird cards, and bird illustrations. Children need to hold a device and go into nature on the basis of mastering certain knowledge about birds, and follow the prompts to find specific birds and observe them. After successful identification, they can see the cartoon image of the corresponding bird in the game and obtain the illustrated card of the bird, and conduct advanced learning about this bird.

At the same time, in order to get children into a state of flow experience faster, the accuracy data of the bird-finding session will be fed back to the backend to evaluate and analyze children's learning results of bird knowledge, push relevant reinforcement

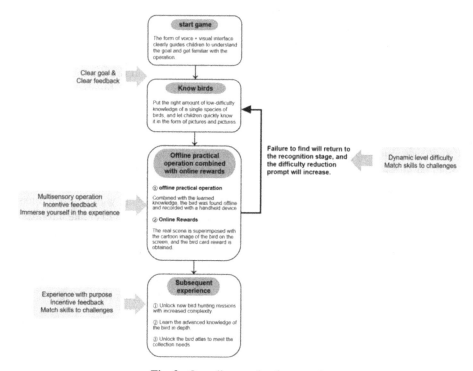

Fig. 3. Overall gameplay framework

information, and adjust the difficulty of delivering content. degree of ease. Make it easier for children to master knowledge; to be more easily motivated to maintain their interest in nature.

The overall framework of its gameplay (see Fig. 3).

4   Game Development

This chapter aims to provide an in-depth explanation of the development process of children's bird watching interactive game. The detailed content involves key aspects such as visual art design, scene design, game mechanics and technical implementation, etc., aiming to apply the flow experience theory to games to promote children's learning and development.

4.1   Visual Design Scene Design

"Quietly" is a bird watching game designed to enhance multi-sensory interaction. It not only excels in the diversity of game modes, but also carefully considers the design of the main menu interface. The main menu interface of this game is mainly divided into two parts: indoor mode and outdoor mode. The indoor mode mainly provides mini program gaming experience, while the outdoor mode incorporates augmented reality (AR) technology to bring users into nature and achieve direct interaction with nature, consistent with the core concepts advocated by this research. This menu integrates the core functions of game progress, points, energy values, announcements, illustrations, rankings, user feedback, sharing functions and setting options to provide an integrated user interaction platform to create a coherent and intuitive operating experience, thereby Promote effective learning and immediate feedback. Players can browse the details of unlocked levels, including the types of birds included in that level, by clicking on the Level option in the main menu. Based on personal preferences, players can select a level and click to enter to start the game, and the corresponding interface will be displayed (See Fig. 4).

In the selection of game elements, the game "Quietly" focuses on creating the environmental atmosphere required for a flow state. Using elements close to nature such as trees, green plants, rocks, and water flows, we increase the realism of the scene and optimize the interactive experience. In terms of visual design, lively yellow-green tones are used as the main color, and natural colors are cleverly combined to create a relaxed and peaceful game atmosphere. This atmosphere is not only conducive to stimulating children's positive emotions, but also deepens their immersion in the game and their motivation to learn. In terms of character design, the team devoted their efforts to creating a variety of bird images, and transformed them into a style more suitable for children through cartoon processing, making the characters more approachable (see Fig. 5).

Fig. 4. Game home page, game main menu bar and game level display

Fig. 5. Character design

4.2 Game Experience Process Design

The experience process design of the game "Quietly" focuses on using mobile phone applets as an intermediary tool for children to participate in bird watching activities. The game design cleverly incorporates augmented reality (AR) technology, with the goal of gradually prompting children to get in touch with and integrate into the natural environment. In the initial stages of the game, players will receive instructive text prompts, which help players quickly understand the game mechanics. Subsequently, players need to select appropriate props according to personal preferences within a limited time to eliminate environmental noise and facilitate entering the next stage of bird watching activities. Using tools such as a magnifying glass or telescope, players can find and appreciate various birds. After successfully identifying a bird, players can unlock the bird and add it to their collection of cards. The main interface of the game allows players to view the cards they have collected so far. With the help of these cards, combined with AR technology, the game guides players to real wild habitats to discover more birds. In order to unlock additional illustrations, players can continue to challenge higher-level levels. In different levels, players will encounter different types of birds and play in scenes that change accordingly (see Fig. 6).

Fig. 6. Successful experience process

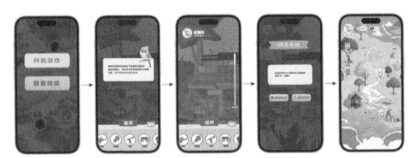

Fig. 7. Failure experience process

If the player fails to select the correct props to eliminate noise within the specified time, he will not be able to pass the level. The game interface will display the corresponding prompt text. The player can then choose to return to the previous interface or challenge the level again. If you choose to restart the game, the system will provide more introductory text to increase the player's pass rate on the next try, thereby improving the game experience (see Fig. 7). Through this coherent design, the game aims to provide children with a path from digital interaction to actual bird watching, hoping to deepen children's understanding and appreciation of the natural world through this method.

4.3 Technical Realization

This research uses augmented reality (AR) technology to create an interactive game experience combined with the real world through the advanced functions of the Unity 3D engine, thereby encouraging children to go to nature. This technology implementation not only provides a multi-dimensional interactive environment, but also ensures that children can enjoy unpretentious natural exploration while being full of challenges through its three core modules - props and character control, scene switching, and game logic processing.

First of all, in terms of props and character control, this game allows children to use AR technology to experience the process of finding and observing birds. For example, when using telescope props, the AR interface blends real-world scenes with virtual elements in the game, giving players a bird watching experience as if they were in the wild. While using C# scripts to improve control accuracy, children can interact with the touch screen of a tablet or mobile phone to accurately navigate the telescope and observe birds in real time. The use of props and the character's feedback mechanism are enabled by touch and physical triggers, such as the OnTriggerEnter2D event, which not only allows children to get immediate and intuitive feedback, but also enhances the fun of learning.

Scene switching is implemented by Unity's SceneManager, which can easily load and switch different pre-designed scenes to provide children with a more stable game transition experience. AR technology plays a key role here. Through the dynamic generation of prefabs, it ensures that children can obtain a seamless visual experience during their interaction with the natural environment. Each ecological environment scene in the game is not only rich in details, but also can respond instantly to children's interactive behaviors, enhancing their awareness and curiosity about the real natural world.

The design of the game system logic processing module focuses on how players can use props to successfully observe birds and obtain points within a limited time. The innovation here is that the game will automatically adjust the challenge difficulty based on the child's birding success rate within a specific period of time, ensuring that the game experience is both appropriate and engaging. AR technology closely combines the interaction between virtual elements and the real world. This method allows children to naturally learn how to observe and appreciate natural creatures in the game, simultaneously improves their enthusiasm for learning and cognitive development, and subtly induces them to Get outside and explore nature in its authentic surroundings.

In short, AR technology provides an innovative method for the "Quiet" game, allowing children to enjoy the fun of natural exploration in the combination of virtuality and reality, and be inspired to personally experience the beauty of the outdoor world. This interactive game experience not only enriches children's learning resources, but also opens a door to the natural beauty of the real world.

5 Evaluation and Results

5.1 Participant

Usability evaluation is an important evaluation method to verify the functionality of a product or system and help it iterate [21]. To assess the game's acceptance among children, the researchers used usability evaluation methods. This study recruited a total of 20 children for usability testing of the game. All participants were from Shantou, Guangdong, with an age range of 6–12 years old (mean = 9.4 and standard deviation = 2.74). There are 10 men and women, all with primary school education background. 13 of them have bird watching experience and 7 have no bird watching experience. They are all participating in an online bird watching game for the first time.

5.2 Usability Evaluation Process

All 20 participants underwent a complete usability evaluation, including: introduction (test purpose, game tasks, game goals), 10 min of game experience (see Fig. 8). Before the test began, the researchers briefly introduced the concept and importance of training cognitive abilities, specific interaction methods and goals to the participants, and provided them with game instructions.

Fig. 8. Children participate in the play experience

The specific testing process is as follows:

1. Introduce the test purpose, interaction methods and goals to the participants;
2. The tester enters the game on the mobile phone to understand the rules of the game;
3. Click the start game button;

4. Start the game operation according to the on-screen prompts and complete the corresponding game tasks;
5. Conduct multiple game tests within 10 min;
6. After the game is over, fill in the evaluation questionnaire.

In order to assess the acceptance of the electronic games developed in this study among Chinese children, we used the SUS (System Usability Scale) questionnaire to verify the usability of the games [22–24]. SUS has become the main measurement tool in many fields and industries. Each participant filled out a questionnaire after finishing the game test. During the actual test, some participants were illiterate or unable to understand the meaning of the questions. Researchers explained and filled in the questions. The SUS System Usability Scale consists of the following 10 questions:

1. I think I would like to play this game often;
2. I think the interaction method of this game is relatively complex;
3. I feel that after experiencing the game, my willingness to get closer to nature will increase;
4. I feel that my willingness to continue playing this game is not high;
5. I think the different content about bird watching in this game can be well combined;
6. I feel that the content of this game is inconsistent;
7. I think I can get started with this game very quickly;
8. I think the equipment used in this game is very complicated and clumsy;
9. I feel very confident while playing the game;
10. I need to have a lot of knowledge about bird watching before playing the game.

The SUS System Usability Questionnaire uses a Likert scale to verify the level of agreement for each question [25]. There are 5 levels in this model: 5 is strongly agree, 4 is agree, 3 is neutral, 2 is disagree, and 1 is strongly disagree. Agree. Scores were given when participants completed the game. Among them, odd-numbered questions are positive statements, and even-numbered questions are negative statements. The scoring method for odd-numbered questions is "original score - 1", and the scoring method for

Table 1. Statistical table

Question	1		2		3		4		5	
	N	%	N	%	N	%	N	%	N	%
Q1	0	0	1	5	2	10	11	55	6	30
Q2	4	20	10	50	4	20	2	10	0	0
Q3	0	0	1	5	6	30	6	30	7	35
Q4	6	30	4	20	8	40	2	10	0	0
Q5	9	45	6	30	4	20	0	0	1	5
Q6	0	0	0	0	3	15	7	35	10	50
Q7	1	5	2	10	3	15	7	35	7	35
Q8	7	35	9	45	2	10	1	5	1	5
Q9	0	0	3	15	3	15	6	30	8	40
Q10	7	35	4	20	2	10	6	30	1	5

even-numbered questions is "5 - original score". After calculating the score for each question, you need to add all the scores and multiply by 2.5 to get the overall score (Fig. 9 and Table 1).

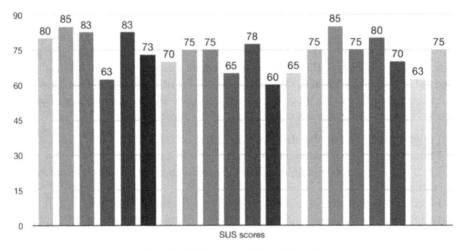

Fig. 9. SUS scores of 20 participants

5.3   Results (SUS Test Results)

The average SUS test result score for this experiment is 74. According to Cunha, a SUS score above 80 points indicates that the tester is satisfied with the system, and a score below 60 indicates dissatisfaction [26]. Overall, participants were generally willing to use the online bird watching game and had a positive attitude toward the game.

6   Conclusion and Future Work

Based on the flow experience theory, this study proposes a bird watching experience model, and designs a bird watching interactive game for children to attract children's interest in bird watching activities. It combines the AR card collection mechanism to attract children's connection with nature and exercise them. Patience and cognitive abilities. Through the Unity 3D engine, it provides children with a multi-dimensional interactive environment, and through its three core modules: props and character control, scene switching, and game logic processing, it ensures that children can enjoy the fun of natural exploration while being full of challenges. According to feedback from children participating in the experiment, most children are willing to use the online bird watching game, have a positive attitude towards electronic games, and are interested and willing to increase their interaction with nature. Future work will improve the problems found in this test, explore more interesting game forms, cooperate with primary schools, nurseries and other institutions, recruit groups of children to participate in game tests multiple times, and improve and optimize the game in a timely manner.

Acknowledgments. This study was funded by Guangzhou Philosophy and Social Science Planning Project, No. 2022GZGJ258; Guangdong Science and Technology Innovation Strategy Special project, No. pdih2023b0170; Guangdong Province philosophy and social science planning project (GD23XLN07).

References

1. Louv, R.: The Last Child in the Woods: Saving Children with Nature Deficit Disorder. China Development Press, Beijing (2014)
2. Zhao, J., et al.: A review of birdwatching tourism research at home and abroad. Tourism Tribune **21**(12), 85–90 (2006)
3. Zhang, J., et al.: Research on flipped classroom teaching model. J. Dist. Educ. **31**(01), 73–78 (2013)
4. Bruner, J.: Play, thought, and language. Peabody J. Educ. **60**(3), 60–69 (1983)
5. Piaget, J.: Play, Dreams, and Imitation in Childhood. Routledge, New York (1999)
6. Wang, Y., et al.: Elements of educational game design framework based on flow theory: a case study of speech learning games for special children. J. Dist. Educ. **32**(3), 97–104 (2014)
7. Cai, L., et al.: Research and application of game design model for teaching Chinese as a foreign language. E-educ. Res. **4**, 91–95 (2011)
8. Fan, Y., et al.: Nature deficit disorder of children and its educational countermeasures. Educ. Sci. Res. **05**, 67–71 (2018)
9. Fu, W.: Study on nature deficit disorder and related problems in children. J. Mudanjiang Univ. **24**(11), 164–175 (2015)
10. Liu, X., et al.: Effects of video games on children's behavior. Chin. Ment. Health J. **16**(1), 64–65 (2002)
11. Fei, G., et al.: Hinder or promote? – A review of research on the effects of video games on children's physical and mental development. Res. Child. Adolesc. **10**, 5–30 (2022)
12. Liu, X., et al.: Effects of short-term exposure to two-person video games on peer interaction and prosocial behavior of young children. Psychol. Sci. **41**(2), 364–370 (2018)
13. Weibel, D., et al.: Pervasive game flow: understanding player enjoyment in pervasive gaming. Comput. Hum. Behav. **24**(5), 2274–2291 (2008)
14. Jegers, K.: Pervasive game flow: understanding player enjoyment in pervasive gaming. Comput. Entertain. **5**(1), 9 (2007). https://doi.org/10.1145/1236224.1236238
15. Chiang, Y.T., et al.: Exploring online game players' flow experiences and positive affect. Turk. Online J. Educ. Technol. **10**(1), 106–114 (2011)
16. Kiili, K.: Digital game-based learning: towards an experiential gaming model. Internet High. Educ. **8**(1), 13–24 (2005). https://doi.org/10.1016/j.iheduc.2004.12.001
17. Csikszentmihalyi, M., Classics, H.P.M., Perennial, H.: Creativity: Flow and the Psychology of Discovery and Invention. Harper Perennial, New York (1996)
18. Hoffman, D.L., et al.: Marketing in hypermedia computer-mediated environments: conceptual foundations. J. Mark. **60**(3), 50–68 (1996)
19. Hsiang Chen, R.T., Wigand, M.S.N.: Optimal experience of web activities. Comput. Hum. Behav. **15**(5), 585–608 (1999). https://doi.org/10.1016/S0747-5632(99)00038-2
20. Csikszentmihalyi, M.: Finding Flow: The Psychology of Engagement with Everyday Life. Basic Books, Hachette (1998)
21. Branaghan, R.J., O'Brian, J.S., Hildebrand, E.A., Foster, L.B.: Usability evaluation. In: Humanizing Healthcare – Human Factors for Medical Device Design, pp. 69–96. Springer, Cham (2021). https://doi.org/10.1007/978-3-030-64433-8_4

22. Brooke, J.: SUS – a quick and dirty usability scale. Usability Eval. Ind. **189**(194), 4–7 (1996)
23. Brooke, J.: SUS: a retrospective. J. Usability Stud. **8**(2), 29–40 (2013)
24. Lewis, J.R.: The system usability scale: past, present, and future. Int. J. Hum. Comput. Interact. **34**(7), 577–590 (2018)
25. Likert, R.: A technique for the measurement of attitudes. Arch. Psychol. **22**(140), 1–55 (1932)
26. Cunha, M.L.C.: Redes sociais dirigidas ao contexto das coisas. Pontifícia Universidade Católica, Rio de Janeiro (2010)

Empowering Female Founders with AI and Play: Integration of a Large Language Model into a Serious Game with Player-Generated Content

Tim Reichert$^{(\boxtimes)}$ⓘ, Mergim Miftariⓘ, Claudia Herlingⓘ,
and Nicola Marsdenⓘ

Heilbronn University, Heilbronn, Germany
{tim.reichert,mergim.miftari,claudia.herling,
nicola.marsden}@hs-heilbronn.de

Abstract. This paper presents a novel approach to empower female founders by integrating a Large Language Model (LLM) into a serious game featuring player-generated content. The game leverages interactive visual novels to enhance resilience and awareness of gender-based discrimination in startup environments. The implementation of generative AI for bias detection in the conversations encountered by founders enables the provision of insightful feedback on discriminatory elements within the visual novels in which players immerse themselves. The game allows players to create personalized visual novels, reflecting their own entrepreneurial experiences. The system selects backgrounds, characters, and dialogue options, transforming players into creators while identifying and providing feedback on discriminatory elements within stories. The game's architecture, designed for modularity, supports the integration of various LLMs, enhancing its adaptability and future-proofing. Preliminary results demonstrate the game's feasibility, with expert evaluations affirming the effectiveness of its bias and discrimination detection mechanisms. This research contributes to the fields of gender equality and entrepreneurship in the digital domain, highlighting the potential of serious games and AI in addressing social challenges.

Keywords: Serious Games · Large Language Models · Visual Novel · Gender Equality · Female Entrepreneurship

1 Introduction

Entrepreneurship is essential for economic growth [1], but women are still underrepresented in startups. Societal norms are slowing down women's startup activity [2] and female founders face unique challenges including discrimination based on gender [3]. Previous work in our project [4] identified interactive visual novels as a tool for empowering founders through role playing difficult situations during the startup process.

© The Author(s), under exclusive license to Springer Nature Switzerland AG 2024
X. Fang (Ed.): HCII 2024, LNCS 14731, pp. 69–83, 2024.
https://doi.org/10.1007/978-3-031-60695-3_5

In this paper, we present the current architecture and prototype of a serious game with interactive visual novels [5], which has been developed to empower female entrepreneurs by bolstering their resilience [6] in the face of typical founding process adversities and fostering awareness of discriminatory situations and biases specific to female entrepreneurship.

Our ongoing research is conducted in cooperation with the National Agency for Women Startup Activities and Services in Germany [7] and the development of the serious game is guided by an advisory board of 18 experts in female entrepreneurship [8]. It should be noted that the visual novels and the serious game we discuss are being developed in German and the prompts for the LLMs are also written in German. For the sake of discussion, we translated some of the examples given in this paper to English.

2   Approach and Overview

We have currently finished a first prototype of our serious game specifically designed for female entrepreneurs. The upcoming sections shed a light on the gender-specific challenges that women founders face, informing the objectives and design of our game. We provide insight into the game design and the visual elements of our current prototype. The architecture of the game is elaborated upon, with a particular emphasis on the integration and application of LLMs.

2.1   Considerations and Goals

Loan negotiations, business registration, and interactions with family, employees, or co-founders are typical scenarios faced by founders. While they are challenging for everybody on their journey to entrepreneurship, there are additional challenges that women face based on their gender [9–13]. We aim to provide a game experience in which players are able to play through typical scenarios in the founding process and experiment with different choices when confronted with gender biases or discriminatory situations. These may include inappropriate questions on family planning as well as implicitly or explicitly discouraging or insulting comments. Our prototype contains a set of eleven pre-constructed novels covering the typical scenarios faced by founders. They were developed within the project with experts on women and entrepreneurship [4]. They allow players to choose responses from a set of possible answers. Based on events in the story and choices taken by players, the game should provides tailored feedback at the end of a play session that puts the specific situation in context of known biases, helps players to contextualize choices taken and encourages experimentation by trying out different choices.

Previous research in game design of visual novels has shown that real-life scenarios and being able to share own experiences enhances reflection [14] more successfully than fictional narratives [15]. It also highlights the importance of experiential fidelity to facilitate transfer [16] and to help players relate the game to their own experiences [17].

Thus, our game aims to provide not only pre-constructed visual novels by the developers, but also to enable players to transform their personal experiences into playable stories. For this approach to be viable, the process of generating or altering visual novels needs to be sufficiently user-friendly to enable individuals lacking specialized technical expertise to perform these tasks effectively. Our ultimate goal is to be able to create interactive visual novels based on a natural language description of real-world experiences and events.

Since every founder has a different background and training needs, different visual novels in our game may be more or less relevant. Thus, the game requires a guidance system - something we call "Game Director" - that matches players with relevant content based on information they provide to the game.

2.2 Game Design and Visual Elements

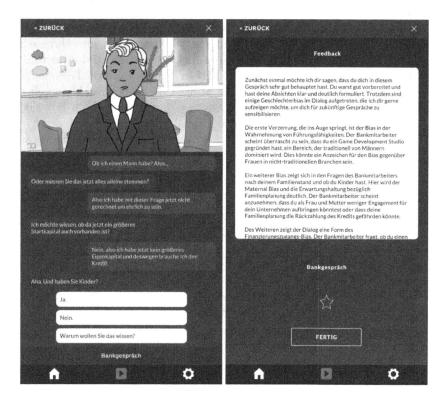

Fig. 1. Prototype screenshots of visual novel and feedback view

Figure 1 (left) shows a screenshot of a visual novel in our current prototype. The visual elements are the representation of non-player characters (NPCs), backgrounds and dialogue between player and NPCs. NPCs have different facial expressions that may change during the progression of the story. Dialogue is conveyed in a format akin to text messaging applications, which offers the benefit of a scrollable history. Players have dialogue choices that may affect the story. For example, they may choose to react to an inappropriate comment by pointing out the wrongdoing or by ignoring it. After playing a session, feedback is provided to players by giving them a) information on which biases were present in the story and b) an analysis of how they reacted to them, as shown in Fig. 1 (right).

2.3   Architecture and LLM Use

Large Language Models (LLMs) like GPT 4 are advanced AI systems capable of processing natural language and generating human-like text [18,19]. In our research, we use LLMs for novel creation, discrimination detection, feedback for players, and content matching players with content. Figure 2 gives an overview of the current architecture of the game with AI-based components implementing the aforementioned features shown in grey.

The central concept is the interactive **visual novel**. A visual novels tells a story in an interactive way. Its creation can be subdivided into three editor components: **character maker**, **environment maker** and **dialogue maker**. While these components can be used manually in a more traditional development approach, they provide an interface to be utilized by generative AI to generate content from natural language descriptions, as shown on the top left side of Fig. 2. The dialogue graph of the resulting visual novel can be analyzed by the LLM for potential biases so that feedback is available throughout the creation process.

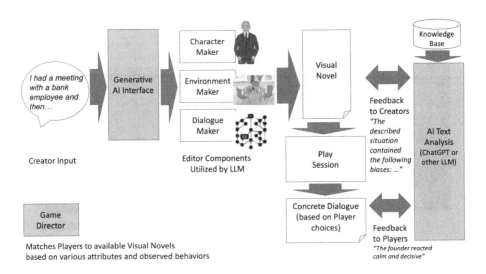

Fig. 2. Architecture overview

In a play session, players have choices that may alter the course of the story, resulting in a log of **concrete dialogue**, i.e. a path through the dialogue graph. Based on this log and a domain specific knowledge base the AI creates feedback for the players. This will be explained in detail in Sect. 3. Finally, the **game director** component analyzes the player's individual situation and training need based on a short entrance interview to match players with appropriate content.

Due to the novelty and rapidly changing capabilities of LLMs, we aim to be independent of a concrete LLM and to be able to replace the GPT 4 model we are currently using with other cloud-based or local LLM-implementations. Thus, we have designed the interfaces in a modular way by abstracting the component that performs the API calls to query the model. The actual natural language query content can thus be understood by different LLMs due to the natural language processing capabilities of these models. The way that the model is queried is described in Sects. 3, 4, and 5.

Our current prototype fully implements playing and analysis of visual novels including the feedback component for which an evaluation is provided in Sect. 6. The generative AI interface is working and can create novels based on natural language input, but is considered experimental with encouraging initial results, see Sect. 5. The game director component is currently being developed with promising initial testing done with GPT 4, see Sect. 4.

To provide a low barrier of entry, the game is created as a mobile application that we aim to distribute through the App Store and Google Play.

3   Bias and Discrimination Detection

Biases and discrimination may be implicit and hard to spot in everyday situations [20]. Nuances in human language and context specificity in discriminatory practices present considerable challenges for recognition even for humans [21]. Advanced AI models can recognize patterns that might suggest bias or discrimination, but their accuracy is dependent on the data they were trained on and the specific instructions and context provided [22,23]. Keeping this in mind, our experience is that GPT 3.5 and GPT 4 are able to spot certain forms of discrimination and identify biases. For example, one of our novels features an employee of a funding information center asking a female founder during negotiations if she plans to have children. When providing the log of such a dialogue to GPT 4, the model will identify the question as potentially inappropriate and discriminatory in the business context.

By providing a domain-specific knowledge base to the LLM we aim for precise feedback that refers to known biases. We also aim to have to rely less on the discrimination-specific dataset a specific model was trained on so that working with different LLMs is possible. The knowledge base we have developed for this purpose covers 25 biases derived from research on female entrepreneurship and gender studies [9–13], giving the name and a short description of e.g. maternal bias, attributional biases regarding performance, biases regarding risk aversion in women, prove-it-again bias.

After playing a visual novel, the session log is analyzed with a focus on problematic situations encountered and players reactions to them so that useful feedback can be provided to players. To utilize an LLM in our game in this way, it is necessary to prepare a prompt for the model and process the text-based result. Our prompt engineering effort has resulted in prompts that are structured into five parts: Role, Assignment, Context, Knowledge Base, Output Format and Target. Table 1 shows an abbreviated example for the visual novel "Talking to my parents" in which the founder experiences biases.

Table 1. Structure of the prompt for discrimination detection and feedback

Section	Example
Role	"You are a gender researcher."
Assignment	"Your assignment is to analyze the log for discrimination and gender biases and give feedback to the player..."
Context	"The founder plans to start a software company and talks to her concerned mother about it."
Knowledge Base	Consisting of a description of 25 biases that women founders are confronted with.
Output Format	"Write an analysis of the dialog..."
Target	This entails the log of dialogue (Mother: "Hello and thank you for coming" Player: "Hi"...)

To ensure that the suggestions of the LLM are appropriate and helpful for players, we have integrated a player-feedback loop into the serious game. After receiving suggestions from the AI system, players can rate the satisfaction with the feedback on a 5-point Likert scale and can comment in a free text field whether the information provided was helpful. Players can also request an expert opinion, in case they have question regarding the AI feedback. As described above, we are developing the game together with an advisory board of experts in the field of female entrepreneurship and gender. The board members are using the app in an "expert mode" and have the ability to provide expert feedback. Feedback of players and experts is stored together with the session log and AI-feedback in a data base. An analysis of initial expert evaluation based on the GPT 4 model and the prompting as described above can be found in Sect. 6.

4   Towards Matching Players with Content

In the current prototype, players manually select novels from a list. We are currently working on a component that connects players with the most suitable built-in or player-generated content automatically. The idea is, that in the on-boarding phase, players engage with an initial visual novel that derives insights such as their startup's field, personal context, perceived strength and weaknesses and challenges they expect in their startup journey. The system then aims to connect players with the most suitable novels based on their provided data. For each novel, the LLM initially creates a title and a short summary that is stored with the novel. To perform the matching a prompt is created consisting of the title and summary of each novel, the player data and the assignment to rank the novels by suitability for a training situation.

Initial testing revealed that GPT 4 is able to rank the novels in a sensible way. For example, in one of our test cases we asked GPT 4 to rank the following novels for a training course based on role playing depending on how well the course content can support training of a founder that has very supportive parents, is good at negotiations and has problems to give negative feedback to people:

– Parental Discussion: The parents doubt the entrepreneurial capabilities.
– Press Interview: The press wants to focus on gender rather than the startup.
– Credit Appointment: The bank employee asks about the desire for children.
– Colleague Conversation: A problematic situation in the founding team is discussed.
– Employee Discussion: An employee has performed poorly. This needs to be addressed.

The following ranking was provided by the model:

1. Employee Discussion
2. Colleague Conversation
3. Press Talk
4. Credit Appointment
5. Parental Discussion

While this data point is not conclusive on its own, it showcases the potential for using advanced AI models to rank training content. In future work, we plan to fully implement the system based on the concepts described in the next chapter and to perform an expert evaluation akin to that in Sect. 6.

5   LLM-Based Visual Novel Creation Process

In this section, we outline how visual novels are represented and edited manually, as well as how we utilize LLMs in their creation. We detail AI's role in the selection of backgrounds and characters, and in generating dialogue. We describe the AI-assisted process and finally present an example of a visual novel produced by our tool, illustrating its capabilities in narrative crafting and dialogue branching.

5.1   Basic Concepts

Creating visual novels comprises creating both the visual representations and the content of the conversation. Visual novels are based on a **directed graph**

of conversation nodes where each node may nest another such graph. Connections between nodes represent dialogue options while each node defines a dialogue message and determines background, visible characters, and their facial expressions and gestures. Figure 3 (left) shows the Dialogue Maker's user interface, featuring a board where users freely position nodes to form a directed graph.

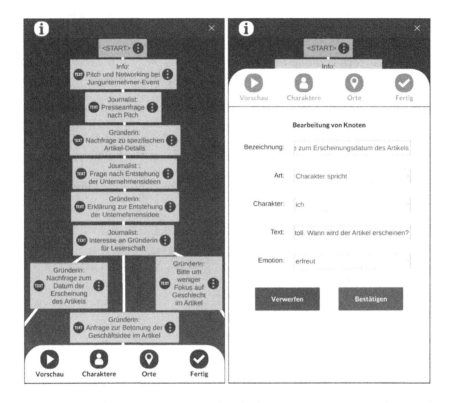

Fig. 3. Creating a visual novel and editing a conversation node

Figure 3 (right) shows the editing process of a conversation node, where users can assign backgrounds, characters, dialogue text, and emotions specific to the situation. Nodes can be named for clarity. The Dialogue Maker includes a preview function for testing the visual novel.

While the tool can be used manually, the next section describes an approach that uses an LLM to convert player narratives from text or voice input into editable, shareable visual novels. Based on the user's input, the AI selects backgrounds and characters for the visual novel and creates dialogues with options.

5.2 Visual Novel Generation Process

Figure 4 outlines the novel generation process, which begins with a natural language description of the visual novel, either through text or voice. To guide users, three questions are provided:

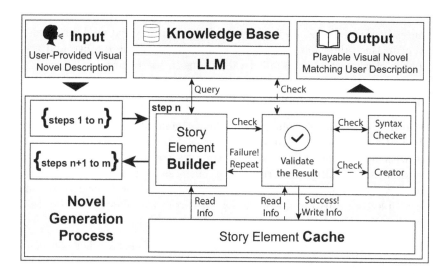

Fig. 4. Structure of the visual novel generation process

1. What are the main events or key moments of your story?
2. Who are the main characters and what roles do they play in your story?
3. What are the important decisions and turning points in your story?

User responses are processed into a complete, editable, and shareable visual novel. The LLM effectively handles colloquial and incomplete sentences. As depicted in Fig. 4, the generation process involves several steps. These steps include character and location determination, dialogue creation, and facial expression assignment for dialogue messages. Story elements are built using an LLM and our domain-specific knowledge base, leveraging a shared cache for information from previous steps. Each story elements is obtained through a response from the LLM and undergoes a validation process. If validation fails, the element can be recreated without disrupting the overall process. Failures are logged for future improvements. The basic form of validation is the syntax checker which ensures output conforms to specifications like JSON format and element count. The system also verifies consistency with existing story elements in the cache, particularly for character consistency in dialogue messages. User-led validation and LLM self-validation are enhancements we are currently experimenting with.

For tasks in which the LLM has to make a choice between different options, it is provided with a description of each option and asked to select the best fit for the situation. This includes the set of available characters, e.g. "casually dressed middle-aged man", "business person in suit", or "young female co-founder" as well as the properties of available backgrounds, e.g. "generic meeting room", "living room", "in front of a computer at night", or "on stage".

Currently, the generation process of a complete novel with 60 nodes using GPT 4 involves roughly 50 LLM requests and takes 12 min. The results are generally usable, but the dialogue sometimes sounds too generic, has inconsistencies, or requires further editing. By improving the prompting and enabling user participation in the validation process we aim to improve the quality and reduce the number of requests due to failed validations in the future.

5.3   Results of the Visual Novel Generation

The following example is from a visual novel generated through the process described above, where the input describes a founder discussing her startup project with her mother. The mother expresses concerns about the founder's ability to start a family while running a business and suggests collaboration with her brother. The LLM chose a private home as the background, one of seven possible locations provided. An excerpt from the dialogue illustrates the coherent linguistic quality:

Info: Your mother looks at you with concern. You sense her concern but also her interest.

Founder: I understand your worries, mom. But I firmly believe that I can do this.

Mother: And what if you're thinking of starting a family? Running a business is a full-time job.

Founder: I'm aware of that, mom. But many women successfully run businesses and have a family at the same time. I can do that too.

Initially, the generated dialogue is linear. The next step involves integrating different dialogue options at various points, either by interrupting and regenerating the dialogue or by inserting gaps to be filled. Different moods can be specified for the LLM, leading to varied answer options:

Mother: Can I help you with this?

Answer opt. 1: I think I can manage on my own. But thanks, Mom.

Answer opt. 2: Sure, Mom. You could help me bake some of your famous chocolate chip cookies. I'll need the energy for the next steps.

Answer opt. 3: Mom, I feel like you're trying to interfere with my startup process. I need to do this on my own.

Answer opt. 4: Um... I'm not sure, mom. I mean, I really appreciate your offer, but I don't know exactly how you could help me.

Finally, the process determines a facial expression for each dialogue option. For instance, the mother reacts with laughter to answer option 2 and with sadness to option 3. The facial expressions are visually reflected when playing the novel through character animations.

6   Evaluation of LLM-Based Feedback

The bias and discrimination detection outlined in Sect. 3 is already implemented in the current prototype of the game: Players receive an analysis of the dialogue as feedback on the novels that they played. To assess the effectiveness of this feedback mechanism, we conducted an expert evaluation. This section outlines the approach employed in the evaluation process and presents an analysis of the findings, encompassing both quantitative and qualitative data. The results offer insights into the feedback's impact on player experience and its overall quality within the game environment.

6.1   Approach

In the evaluation of the discrimination detection integrated in the serious game, the following approach was taken

Participants: Four experts from our project team with knowledge about gender and entrepreneurship and familiarity with issues related to gender bias and discrimination evaluated the app's analysis of the dialogues.

Materials: The study centered around six dialogues, crafted to represent two distinct scenarios. Each scenario was presented in three versions, varying in complexity and context. The dialogues were specifically designed to encompass a range of potential biases, allowing a comprehensive assessment of the app's detection capabilities.

Procedure: The experts were asked to review the dialogues. Each dialogue was analyzed by the app's discrimination detection algorithm employing GPT 4, which then generated a report outlining potential biases. The experts' task was to evaluate these reports in terms of clarity, style, content, and accuracy.

Measures and Data Analysis: The experts provided feedback on 10 items using a five-point Likert scale. The items were developed to capture various aspects of the app's performance, including the accuracy of bias detection, clarity of the reports, relevance of the content, and the overall style of presentation. Descriptive statistics were used to provide an overview. Alongside the Likert-scale items, the experts answered 11 open-ended questions. These questions were designed to gather detailed qualitative feedback, allowing the experts to elaborate on specific aspects of the LLM responses, share observations, and provide suggestions for improvement. The responses to the open-ended questions were subjected to thematic analysis [24].

6.2   Results

The expert evaluations of the app's discrimination detection provided a mix of quantitative and qualitative insights. Quantitative analysis revealed high ratings across various aspects, including clarity, style, content, and accuracy, with scores ranging from 4.73 to 4.95 on a five-point Likert scale with 1 expressing disagreement und 5 agreement. There were no significant differences among the different items assessed. The detailed results for each item can be found in Table 2.

Table 2. Expert evaluation of LLM feedback

Item	Mean	StDev
The language style and structure are appropriate	4.95	0.21
The feedback is thematically relevant	4.95	0.21
The feedback is clear and understandable	4.92	0.28
The feedback is free from incorrect information	4.91	0.29
The feedback covers all essential aspects of the dialogue	4.83	0.38
The tone of the feedback is appreciative and supportive	4.82	0.59
The biases referenced in the feedback are understandable in the context of the conversation	4.75	0.61
The feedback provides a balanced perspective	4.75	0.61
The feedback is free from unnecessary information	4.74	0.75
The feedback is free from prejudices or opinions	4.73	0.63

The qualitative analysis was based on 63 answers to the open ended questions. The thematic analysis of this qualitative feedback resonated with the positive ratings from the quantitative analysis with the experts highlighting the feedback clarity, the friendly and supportive tone, and the high quality of bias identification and interpretation. There were some points that were mentioned for improvement: The experts' opinion varied on the extent of empowering language, with some finding it excessive. Concerns were raised regarding the necessity to mention certain biases - while they were not seen as wrongly applied, some experts felt they did not add to the analysis.

In conclusion, the combined results of quantitative and qualitative analyses affirm the effectiveness of the discrimination detection app in providing feedback that is clear, relevant, and suitably toned. The app received high ratings on the Likert-scale items, and the responses to open-ended questions were predominantly positive. Opportunities for refinement are seen regarding feedback relevance and ensuring not do overdo it on the empowerment messages. The improvement possibilities regarding bias relevance are attributed to the fact that the LLM is "obedient" in the sense that the LLM tries to incorporate as many of the biases as possible from the given prompt, regardless of their exact fit to the specific dialogue under review.

7   Conclusions and Future Work

In conclusion, our research presents the integration of an LLM into a serious game for female founders. The game, leveraging interactive visual novels and an

LLM-based analysis of the conversations, has demonstrated potential in enhancing resilience and awareness of gender-based discrimination in entrepreneurial environments. Our findings indicate the effectiveness of generative AI in creating engaging content and detecting biases, providing meaningful feedback to players. This aligns with our objective to transform players into creators, allowing them to reflect on their experiences through interactive storytelling.

The next step is to systematically evaluate the analyses offered by the LLM with women entrepreneurs as the prime user group. In terms of relating to real-life scenarios, special attention needs to be paid to finding out which elements of the game are able to enhance reflection [14]. Both the role of the content and the role of high- versus low-fidelity needs to be considered. In terms of content, we expect the matching of players with stories and the possibility of creating one's own novel to facilitate transfer [16] and to help players relate the game to their own experiences [17]. In terms of presenting high- versus low-fidelity scenarios via AI, findings from the hyperpersonal model of communication will be integrated [25]. The hyperpersonal model shows that under certain circumstances, low-fidelity communication can actually be helpful to create a setting in which it is easier for a person to open up and engage deeply.

In integrating LLMs into our serious game, we must critically address several ethical implications. The danger of bias in the training materials as well as hallucinations and therefore inadequate answers in LLMs requires vigilant monitoring and continuous refinement. Protecting player-generated data demands strict adherence to privacy standards and explicit user consent protocols. Given the game's focus on gender bias and discrimination, we must be mindful of its emotional impact on players, providing support and a safe environment. Ensuring inclusivity and diverse representation in the game's content is crucial to avoid reinforcing stereotypes and exclusion. Finally, our responsibility extends to considering the long-term societal impact of the game, aiming to contribute positively to social change and gender equality in entrepreneurship.

Future work will focus on refining the AI components and integrating alternative LLMs. While automated novel creation shows promise and works in general, it is currently still experimental and needs more work on quality assurance and optimization before it can be released to end-users. We hope that through testing with the target audience we can find a suitable balance between user control and automation. We plan to expand the game's content and interactivity, enabling a wider range of scenarios and more personalized experiences. Ultimately, our goal is to contribute to the field of gender equality in entrepreneurship, exploring the intersection of AI, serious gaming, and social empowerment.

Acknowledgments. This work has been partially funded by the German Federal Ministry for Family Affairs, Senior Citizens, Women and Youth (Bundesministerium für Familie, Senioren, Frauen und Jugend - BMFSFJ) under Grant Number 3923406K04 as part of the project 'KI-Thinktank Female Entrepreneurship II - KITE II' in the Funding Line 'AI for Public Good (KI für Gemeinwohl)'. The responsibility for all content supplied lies with the authors.

References

1. Stoica, O., Roman, A., Rusu, V.D.: The nexus between entrepreneurship and economic growth: a comparative analysis on groups of countries. Sustainability **12**(3), 1–19 (2020)
2. Sternberg, R., Gorynia-Pfeffer, N., Stolz, L., Schauer, J., Baharian, A., Wallisch, M.: Global entrepreneurship monitor 2021/2022. In: RKW Kompetenzzentrum (2022). https://www.rkw-kompetenzzentrum.de/fileadmin/media/Produkte/2022/Studie/20220527-Studie-GEM-2022.pdf
3. Veckalne, R., Tambovceva, T.: The importance of gender equality in promoting entrepreneurship and innovation. In: Marketing and Management of Innovations, pp. 158–168 (2023). https://doi.org/10.21272/mmi.2023
4. Schirmacher, A., von der Bey, K.: KITE-Thinktank Female Entrepreneurship - Diskriminierungs-Bekämpfung für Gründerinnen durch gezielten Kompetenzaufbau beim Erkennen und Bewältigen von Diskriminierungsmustern - Internal Project Report. In: Project KITE - more info on https://www.kite-bga.de/expertisen/ (2022). (in German)
5. Camingue, J., Carstensdottir, E., Melcer, E.F.: What is a visual novel? In: Proceedings of the ACM on Human-Computer Interaction 5.CHI PLAY, pp. 1–18 (2021). ISSN 2573-0142
6. McGonigal, J.: Reality is Broken: Why Games Make Us Better and How They Can Change the World. Penguin, New York (2011). ISBN 1101475498
7. National Agency for Women Start-Up Activities and Services in Germany. In: Bundesgründerinnenagentur (BGA) (2024). https://innogruenderinnen-bga.de/
8. Advisory Board KITE II. In: Projektbeirat KITE II (2024). https://kite2.de/beirat-kite-ii/
9. Laguía, A., García-Ael, C., Wach, D., Moriano, J.A.: Think entrepreneur-think male": a task and relationship scale to measure gender stereotypes in entrepreneurship. Int. Entrep. Manag. J. **15**, 749–772 (2019). https://doi.org/10.1007/s11365-018-0553-0. ISSN 1554-7191
10. Tonoyan, V., Strohmeyer, R.: Gender role (in-) congruity and resource-provider gender biases: a conceptual model. Int. J. Gend. Entrep. **13**(3), 225–242 (2021). https://doi.org/10.1108/IJGE-12-2020-0201. ISSN 1756-6266
11. Folberg, A., Goering, T., Wetzel, L., Yang, X., Ryan, C.: Viewing entrepreneurship through a goal congruity lens: the roles of dominance and communal goal orientations in women's and men's venture interests. Front. Psychol. **14**(2023). https://doi.org/10.3389/fpsyg.2023.1105550
12. Williams, J.C., Dempsey, R.: What Works for Women at Work: Four Patterns Working Women Need to Know. NYU Press, New York (2018)
13. Mavin, S., Yusupova, M.: Competition and gender: time's up on essentialist knowledge production. Manag. Learn. **52**(1), 86–108 (2021). https://doi.org/10.1177/1350507620950176. ISSN 1350-5076
14. Khaled, R.: Questions over answers: reflective game design. In: Playful Disruption of Digital Media. Gaming Media and Social Effects, pp. 3–27 (2018). https://doi.org/10.1007/978-981-10-1891-6_1. ISSN 9811018898
15. Iacovides, I., Cutting, J., Beeston, J., Cecchinato, M.E., Mekler, E.D., Cairns, P.: Close but not too close: distance and relevance in designing games for reflection. Proc. ACM Hum. Comput. Interact. **6**, 1–24 (2022). https://doi.org/10.1145/3549487

16. Súilleabháin, G.Ó., Sime, J.-A.: Critical design and effective tools for E-learning. In: Donnelly, R., Harvey, J., O'Rourke, K. (ed.) Higher Education: Theory into Practice, pp. 113–126. IGI Global (2010). ISBN 1615208801

17. Hammer, J., To, A., Schrier, K., Bowman, S.L., Kaufman, G.: Learning and role-playing games. In: Deterding, S., Zagal, J. (ed.) Role-Playing Game Studies, pp. 283–299. Routledge (2018). https://doi.org/10.4324/9781315637532

18. Bang, Y., et al.: A multitask, multilingual, multimodal evaluation of ChatGPT on reasoning, hallucination, and interactivity. In: arXiv preprint (2023). https://doi.org/10.48550/arXiv.2302.04023

19. Chang, Y., et al.: A survey on evaluation of large language models. In: arXiv preprint arXiv:2307.03109 (2023). https://doi.org/10.48550/arXiv.2307.03109.

20. Greenwald, A.G., Banaji, M.R.: The implicit revolution: reconceiving the relation between conscious and unconscious. Am. Psychol. **72**(9), 861–871 (2017). https://doi.org/10.1037/amp0000238

21. Greenland, K., West, K., Van Laar, C.: Definitional boundaries of discrimination: tools for deciding what constitutes discrimination (and what doesn't). J. Appl. Soc. Psychol. **52**(10), 945–964 (2022). https://doi.org/10.1111/jasp.12902

22. Gallegos, I.O., et al.: Bias and fairness in large language models: a survey. In: arXiv preprint (2023). https://doi.org/10.48550/arXiv.2309.00770.

23. Mao, R., Tan, L., Moieni, R.: Developing a large-scale language model to unveil and alleviate gender and age biases in Australian job ads. In: 2023 IEEE International Conference on Big Data (BigData), pp. 4176–4185. https://doi.org/10.1109/BigData59044.2023.10386083

24. Braun, V., Clarke, V.: Using thematic analysis in psychology. Qual. Res. Psychol. **3**(2), 77–101 (2006). https://doi.org/10.1191/1478088706qp063oa. ISSN 1478-0887

25. Walther, J.B., Whitty, M.T.: Language, psychology, and new new media: the hyperpersonal model of mediated communication at twenty-five years. J. Lang. Soc. Psychol. **40**(1), 120–135 (2021). https://doi.org/10.1177/0261927X20967703

Learning or Entertaining? A Study on the Acceptance of Serious Games in Chinese Museums

Wennan Wu[1], Ruisi Liu[2], and Junjie Chu[1](✉)

[1] Ocean University of China, Qingdao 266100, China
chujunjie@ouc.edu.cn
[2] Northwestern Polytechnical University, Xi'an 710072, China

Abstract. Currently, serious game activities in Chinese museums are becoming more and more popular and loved by audiences. Serious Games in Museums aims to increase audience engagement and develop their creative thinking and learning skills through online interactions and scenario simulations. Therefore, it is necessary to explore the factors that influence users' acceptance of serious games in the museum field. In addition, an extended TAM for the games with the highest scores were established in order to explore what factors affect users' intention to use the games. The research results show that perceived enjoyment has a significant impact on perceived usefulness and behavioral intention. This means that when designing serious games, designers should consider appropriately optimizing the game experience to make users more willing to accept. In addition, perceived usefulness has a significant impact on users' behavioral intention. This means that designers of serious games in the museum field should still prioritize education nature and focus on adding popular science content to the games. Based on the findings, the article proposes an experiential game model, designs a serious game accordingly, and describes the methodology for game development.

Keywords: Serious Game · Museum · technology acceptance model (TAM) · structural equation modeling (SEM)

1 Introduction

In the past few years, research on serious games has been gradually increasing, and people have given great attention to the development of serious games. The initial definition of serious games in history was limited to "games designed for learning and education" [1]. Nowadays, as an emerging technology, serious games have great potential for promoting educational change: since 2011, the New Media Consortium (NMC) Horizon Report has almost annually listed gaming and game-based learning as new technologies for future educational applications [2]. In 2007, the research on serious games formed a system in the academic community. From 2007 to 2021, serious game research has gradually gained recognition from academia and development companies, and has been expanded to a certain extent [3].

With the development of technology, the contradiction between modern culture and traditional culture has become increasingly prominent. Nowadays, people's understanding of the cultural heritage system is no longer sufficient to support the protection and inheritance of material cultural heritage [4]. A survey has pointed out that applying serious games to museums is a new trend [5]. The widespread dissemination of ICT (Information and Communication Technology) also provides possibilities for education in museum heritage [6].

In 2022, The International Council of Museums (ICOM) defines museums as "a not-for-profit, permanent institution in the service of society that researches, collects, conserves, interprets and exhibits tangible and intangible heritage. Open to the public, accessible and inclusive, museums foster diversity and sustainability. They operate and communicate ethically, professionally and with the participation of communities, offering varied experiences for education, enjoyment, reflection and knowledge sharing" [7]. Serious games serve both educational and entertainment purposes. When serious games are applied to museum environments, the experience of visiting museums becomes more enjoyable and meaningful [8]. At present, serious games have been widely used in the field of museum [1]. However, some researchers have also proposed that there are still some problems in the exploration of the application of serious games in museums [9]. Since serious games are a branch of gaming, people often overlook the knowledge they need to learn and focus on the experience of games [10]. How to achieve a balance between learning and entertainment is an issue that needs to be studied [11–13]. Therefore, this article conducts a comprehensive evaluation of serious games in China's national first-class museums, and adopts TAM to explore users' acceptance of serious games in museum represented by the serious game *Exploring Whale World* from Shanghai Science and Technology Museum.

2 Theorical Background

2.1 The Application of Serious Games in the Field of Museums

The essence of serious games is a combination of self-motivated learning and entertainment [14]. Museum is an environment that combines knowledge and entertainment, which is suitable for practicing this learning method. Research has shown that serious game has a promoting effect on the development of the cultural heritage protection and museum field [10]. Museums that use serious games are more likely to attract young people to visit [14], and the participation and feedback of tourists are generally high [4, 15]. Compared to traditional learning methods, tourists' learning outcomes are better when acquiring cultural heritage knowledge through serious games [16, 17]. The emergence of serious games enables tourists to learn about cultural relics and collections in an interesting and vivid way, thereby deepening their understanding and impression [18], and contributing to the dissemination of culture [4]. And serious games can simulate actual environments for learners to practice, providing a safe and low-cost learning method for museums [19].

In order to better explore the development of serious games in museums, this article adopts the *SEGR Evaluation Scale* [20]. We select 8 expert users with certain gaming experience to rate serious games in 204 national first-class museums in China. The representative research object is *"Exploring Whale World"* from the Shanghai Science and Technology Museum, which has the highest comprehensive scores in terms of gameplay, education, and technology. Table 1 shows the evaluation results of this game.

Table 1. "Exploring whale world" evaluation results.

Category	0	1	2	Score
Prologue	No game description provided	Provided an introduction to the game description, but did not present the goal of the game	Provide a brief introduction to the game and present clear goal of the game	1
Tutorial/ Practice	No tutorials or introductory exercises	There are tutorials or introductory exercises, but there is no situational feedback	There are tutorials or introductory exercises, and players receive clear feedback	1
Interactive	No interaction with objects or non-player characters (NPCs)	There is almost no interaction with objects or non-player characters (NPCs). Or there is no information provided in the interaction to help players succeed	Have a lot of interaction with non-player characters (NPCs) or objects and provide sufficient information to help players succeed. Clear and intuitive interface	1.625
Feedback	Players do not receive feedback on game content or upgrades	There is feedback but it is not timely, and the content or plot is missing or incorrect	Timely and accurate feedback, relevant to the situation at the time	1.875
Identity	Players do not have the right to choose characters	Players have the right to choose characters, but feel that they are not integrated with the characters	Players have the right to choose characters and can explain why they choose a certain character, and feel that they are integrated with the character	0.125
Immersion	The player did not participate in the game	Players have participated in the game but do not have a sense of presence or identity	Players actively participate and reach Flow status	1.875
Pleasurable frustration	The difficulty of the challenge matches the player's ability level	The game did not adjust difficulty or provide feedback, making players feel challenged but still possible to succeed	Players reach the Flow state, which is highly challenging and provides considerable feedback, making them feel like they can achieve success	1.625

(*continued*)

Table 1. (*continued*)

Category	0	1	2	Score
Manipulation	Players cannot control various things in the virtual world	Players can manipulate various things without any impact or outcome	Players can manipulate various things and produce certain effects or outcomes	1.875
Increasing complexity	Achieving game goals does not require incremental skills	The difficulty of the game is increasing, but the most difficult level does not require all skills	The difficulty of the game is increasing, and overcoming the most difficult level requires all skills	1
Rules	There are no rules in the game	There are rules but no corresponding results	There are clear rules and the corresponding consequences after breaking the rules	2
Informed learning	There is no way or method to collect data	Collect user data using one or two methods	Data can be collected using multiple methods	1.125
Learning	The basic mode of the game is invalid for the knowledge and skills taught	The basic model of the game is effective for the knowledge and skills taught, but it is not sufficiently simplified, resulting in more complex content than teaching the same content in traditional classrooms	The basic model of the game is effective and concise for the knowledge and skills taught, making it simpler than teaching the same content in traditional classrooms	1.375
Pedagogical effectiveness	No understandable learning content	Teachers can effectively teach the learning content in games, but it is too simple and does not require human-computer interaction	Teaching the learning content in games can only be achieved through human-computer interaction, and it has a certain level of difficulty	1.25
Reading efficiency	The text content of the game is inconsistent with the reading level of the target audience	The game text content meets the target audience's reading level, but does not serve as a teaching aid	The text content is beneficial for improving the reading level of the target audience and has a certain auxiliary effect on teaching	1.75
Communication (multiplayer games)	No clear channels for dissemination or communication (VOIP or chat rooms)	There are channels for communication and dissemination, but the effect is not significant	Having clear communication channels and playing a good role	0
Gamification learning	The learning content is completely separated from the game tasks, it is completely two skins	Combining learning content with game tasks but not significantly	The learning content is fully integrated into the game tasks, feeling like it's in the game rather than learning	2

2.2 Technology Acceptance Model (TAM) and Its Adapted Model

The Technology Acceptance Model (TAM) developed by Davis and colleagues has been widely used to predict users' intention to accept new technologies and services, and has strong persuasiveness [21]. TAM consists of six structures: external variables, perceived usefulness, perceived ease of use, attitude toward using, behavioral intention to use, and actual system to use. The researchers added some potential factors (e.g., enjoyment) to the original model and proposed an extended model, which helps to deepen the understanding of technology acceptance [22].

Research has found that the Technology Acceptance Model (TAM) is the most widely used model by scholars to predict students' intention to use serious games for learning [23]. In addition, some scholars have shown that factors such as perceived usefulness, perceived ease of use, enjoyment, and attitude can significantly affect users' intention to use technology [23, 24]. Bourgonjon et al. proposed an extended TAM for predicting students' acceptance of video games and confirmed that this model is reliable and valid in understanding students' acceptance of serious games [25].

3 Hypothesis and Research Model

Based on previous research, this study proposes an extended technology acceptance model in order to explore the factors that affect users' intention of using Shanghai Science and Technology Museum's game *"Exploring Whale World"* for assisted learning. The proposed research model is shown in Fig. 1.

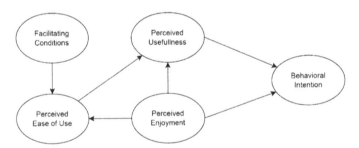

Fig. 1. Research Model

3.1 Perceived Usefulness (PU) and Perceived Ease of Use (PEU)

Perceived Usefulness is the degree to which a person believes that using a particular system would enhance his or her job performance, and Perceived Ease of Use is the degree to which a person believes that using a particular system would be free of effort [26]. Camilleri et al. found that perceived usefulness is a key factor affecting students' intention to use serious games [27]. Park et al. found that perceived usefulness and perceived ease of use have a positive effect on promoting users' use of serious games in learning [22]. In addition, perceived ease of use can also affect users' perceived usefulness in serious game usage [28]. Therefore, we propose the following hypotheses:

H1: Perceived ease of use has a positive impact on perceived usefulness.

H2: Perceived usefulness has a positive impact on behavioral intention.

3.2 Facilitating Conditions (FC)

Facilitating condition refers to objective factors in the environment that observers agree make an act easy to do, including the provision of computer support [29]. In this study, facilitating conditions were defined as resources that can help users experience serious games, such as relevant knowledge, equipment, and external assistance. Wang et al. proposed that facilitating condition, as an environmental factor that promotes or hinders system use, can affect users' intention to use serious games [30]. Therefore, we propose the following hypotheses:

H3: Facilitating condition has a positive impact on perceived ease of use.

3.3 Perceived Enjoyment (PE)

Perceived enjoyment refers to the degree to which a user perceives the use of a technology as enjoyable [31]. Wirani et al. found that enjoyment has a significant impact on students' perceived usefulness when using the game *Kahoot!* [32]. If users have a pleasant experience with a technology, they will develop positive emotions towards the technology, which will influence their intention to use it [33]. For example, research has shown that perceived enjoyment has a positive and significant impact on students' intention to experience serious games [34]. This study suggests that Perceived enjoyment can affect perceived usefulness, perceived ease of use and intention to use. Therefore, we propose the following hypotheses:

H4: Perceived enjoyment has a positive impact on perceived usefulness.

H5: Perceived enjoyment has a positive impact on perceived ease of use.

H6: Perceived enjoyment has a positive impact on behavioral intention.

In Table 2 shows the measurement items corresponding to each factor in the model.

Table 2. *"Exploring whale world"* evaluation results.

Factor	Measurement Items	Source
Perceived Enjoyment	I feel comfortable with the process of *"Exploring Whale World"*	[32]
	When I took the time to experience the game *"Exploring Whale World"*, I felt very happy	
	It is very interesting to experience the game *"Exploring Whale World"*	

(*continued*)

Table 2. (*continued*)

Factor	Measurement Items	Source
Perceived Usefulness	I have found that the game *"Exploring Whale World"* is very useful in learning about whale related science knowledge	[21, 26, 32, 33, 35]
	The game *"Exploring Whale World"* has made me more active in learning popular science knowledge related to whales and dolphins	
	I think if I use the game *"Exploring Whale World"* to learn about whale related science knowledge, I will learn better	
Perceived Ease of Use	I found the game *"Exploring Whale World"* easy to operate	[21, 26, 35]
	It is easy for me to learn the game skills of *"Exploring Whale World"*	
	I found that the usage process of the game *"Exploring Whale World"* is clear and easy to understand	
Facilitating Conditions	I have the necessary resources to use the game *"Exploring Whale World"*	[30, 35]
	I have the necessary knowledge to use the game *"Exploring Whale World"*	
	The game *"Exploring Whale World"* is compatible with other technologies I use	
Behavioral Intention	If possible, I will continue to use the game *"Exploring Whale World"* in the future to learn about whale related science knowledge	[33, 35]
	I am willing to recommend the game *"Exploring Whale World"* to my friends	
	Compared to other learning methods, I would prefer to choose the game *"Exploring Whale World"* to learn about whale related science knowledge	

4   Data Collection and Analysis

4.1   Data Collection

This survey was conducted by using online methods. Before the formal distribution of the questionnaire, a pre-test was conducted on 5 people to determine whether the content of the questionnaire was easy to understand. The results showed that the participants were able to understand the meaning of the questions well and complete the questionnaire independently. A total of 222 questionnaires were collected. According to statistical results, most of the respondents are 19–30 years old, accounting for 60.36% of the total. People aged 18 years old and under, 31–50, 51–70, 71 and above accounted for 6.31%, 19.82%, 10.36% and 3.15% of the total respectively. 80.64% of respondents are undergraduate students, 15.74% are master's students, and 3.62% are doctoral students. More than half of the respondents with bachelor degree education or above, accounting for 56.31% of the total. In addition, women accounted for 54.95% of the total number of respondents, while men accounted for 45.05%. After screening, we deleted (1) Questionnaires with respondents that have not used the game *"Exploring Whale World"*; (2) Questionnaires that took less than 50 s or more than 1,000 s to complete; (3) All but three (or fewer) answers are the same. Finally, 90 valid questionnaires were left. Overall, the questionnaire sample includes students of different genders and educational backgrounds, which is highly representative.

4.2 Data Analysis

Measurement Model. This study used the Likert seven-point scale for data collection. The standardized factor loadings in Table 3 are all greater than 0.6, with most of them exceeding 0.7, reaching the recommended standard. In addition, all R-squared values in Table 3 are greater than 0.36, and most of them are greater than 0.5, which proves that item reliability is up to standard and most items have good reliability.

In Table 4 shows the results of composite reliability, convergent validity, and discriminate validity. The composite reliability (CR) values are all greater than 0.7. In the meantime, the average variance extracted (AVE) values are all greater than 0.5, indicating good composite reliability. In addition, the square root value of most AVE is greater than the corresponding Pearson correlation coefficient, and a few are smaller than but

Table 3. Parameters of the significant test and reliability.

Factor	Items	Estimate	S.E.	Est./S.E.	P-Value	R-square
PE	PE1	0.612	0.093	6.577	***	0.375
	PE2	0.806	0.083	9.699	***	0.650
	PE3	0.913	0.075	12.227	***	0.834
FC	FC1	0.722	0.084	8.567	***	0.521
	FC2	0.662	0.087	7.592	***	0.438
	FC3	0.8	0.081	9.826	***	0.640
PU	PU1	0.628	0.112	5.616	***	0.394
	PU2	0.95	0.063	14.97	***	0.903
	PU3	0.693	0.085	8.17	***	0.480
PEU	PEU1	0.79	0.081	9.788	***	0.624
	PEU2	0.679	0.111	6.102	***	0.461
	PEU3	0.651	0.096	6.804	***	0.424
BI	BI1	0.883	0.05	17.493	***	0.780
	BI2	0.892	0.053	16.821	***	0.796
	BI3	0.608	0.094	6.479	***	0.370

still within the acceptable range, so there is a certain degree of discriminate validity between the dimensions.

Table 4. Composite reliability, convergence validity, and discriminate validity.

	CR	AVE	PE	FC	PU	PEU	BI
PE	0.826	0.619	0.787				
FC	0.773	0.533	0.580	0.730			
PU	0.808	0.592	0.639	0.773	0.769		
PEU	0.751	0.503	0.531	0.820	0.939	0.709	
BI	0.843	0.648	0.726	0.658	0.745	0.665	0.805

Structural Model. The model fitting indicators in this study are shown in Table 5. All the indices meet the recommended values, indicating that the structural model fits well. Table 6 shows the results of the path analysis hypothesized in the proposed structural model. P-value < 0.05 indicates that the influence between constructs is significant, and the hypothesis is supported. There are 6 hypotheses in our research model, of which 5 are supported and 1 are not. The research results are shown in Fig. 2.

Table 5. Model fit.

	Recommended value	Index	.
$\chi 2/df$	$1 < \chi 2/df < 3$	1.532	Matched
CFI	> 0.9	0.935	Matched
TLI	> 0.9	0.918	Matched
RMSEA	< 0.08	0.077	Matched
SRMR	< 0.08	0.063	Matched

Table 6. Hypothesis analysis.

DV	IV	Estimate	S.E	Est./S.E	P-Value	R2	Hypothesis
PU	PEU	0.825	0.075	11.054	***	0.899	Support
	PE	0.202	0.097	2.070	0.038		Support
PEU	PE	0.084	0.131	0.638	0.524	0.665	Not Support
	FC	0.764	0.135	5.658	***		Support
BI	PU	0.481	0.114	4.225	***	0.667	Support
	PE	0.421	0.108	3.883	***		Support

***p<0.001
**p<0.01
*p<0.05

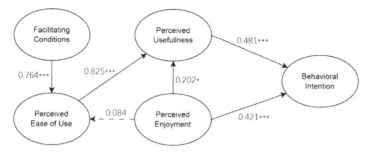

Fig. 2. Research Results

4.3 Discussion

In recent years, issues such as cultural heritage protection and the promotion of traditional culture have been increasingly discussed by people. Major museums have also launched various promotional activities to attract tourists' interest in traditional culture and heritage protection. Serious games, as a learning tool that combines entertainment and learning, are also being adopted and applied by more and more museums. In this study, we first used the *SEGR evaluation scale* to rate the serious games in 204 national first-class museums in China, and the serious game with the highest average score was *"Exploring Whale World"*. And by establishing an extended TAM model, we investigated the factors that affect users' acceptance of the game *"Exploring Whale World"* to learn relevant popular science knowledge. According to the research results, facilitating conditions have a significant impact on perceived ease of use, which means that auxiliary resources and the help of others have a significant impact on users' intention of this game. At the same time, perceived enjoyment has a significant impact on perceived usefulness and behavioral intention. This means that for serious games in the field of museum, entertaining and interesting games can better attract users and enhance their intention to experience them. Consistent with previous studies, perceived usefulness has a significant impact on behavioral intention [32]. This indicates that museums should pay attention to the educational nature of games when designing serious games. When users believe that experiencing the game can effectively learn relevant science knowledge, their intention to use it will significantly increase.

5   Design of Serious Games at the Museum

Based on the results of the analysis, we designed a serious game using the Shanghai Planetarium as an example, to find a way to satisfy the balance between the educational and effective aspects of serious games, and to improve the quality of visitors' visits.

Studies have pointed out that most game types support multiple educational functions, but only two types: simulation and exploration games satisfy all educational needs [36]. To highlight the most important function of serious games in museums: educational, the design of this serious game will combine both exploration and simulation game types.

5.1 Experiential Game Models

To achieve the goal of combining education with entertainment, we designed an experiential gaming model primarily consisting of challenge, player operation, and player experience. Among these, challenge based on learning objectives constitute the core of this model. In overcoming these challenges, on one hand, clear goals focus the player's attention, eliciting positive action. The game should be useable, providing timely feedback to create a positive gaming experience. On the other hand, players are required to explore and manipulate in-game characters, interact with non-player characters (NPCs), and obtain outcome on their actions, adding a level of complexity to player interactions and making the game challenging. Furthermore, as players immerse themselves in the gaming world, they become active participants in the learning process, with their motivation potentially transitioning from external rewards to intrinsic rewards – where the game's rewards transform into knowledge gains (Fig. 3).

Fig. 3. Experiential Game Models

5.2 Game Framework

Following the experiential gaming model, we designed a serious game using the Shanghai Astronomy Museum as an example. "Stardust Revelation" is a serious museum game that combines exploration and simulation game modes. The primary gameplay involves players exploring through a mysterious planet (Ice Fire, named after the "Curious Planet" exhibition at the Shanghai Astronomy Museum) where they must overcome challenges. Only by collecting fragments from the eight planets of the solar system can players return to Earth. Throughout the process of collecting planet fragments, players gain access to educational materials, fulfilling the learning objectives. Thus, this game caters to both the educational needs of players and their desire for an engaging gaming experience.

The framework of this serious game is outlined in Fig. 4.

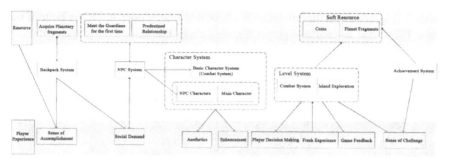

Fig. 4. Game Framework

5.3 Game Prototyping

To achieve game usability, we utilized the Unreal Engine for the design of this game, and the game scene is presented as follows.

Game Interaction. Regarding how player interaction is implemented, in addition to the stylized design of the scenes, we introduced non-Player Characters (NPCs) with dialogue options to enhance the immersive experience. Players can engage in conversations with NPCs by pressing the "E" key when within the trigger distance. We constructed five small islands with buildings, placing NPCs on the second and fifth islands. The first NPC provides essential information for progressing through the game, while the second NPC congratulates the player upon completion (Fig. 5).

Fig. 5. Player gets information about the pass by talking to NPCs.

Collection of Fragments. During the game, the bottom left corner displays the number of fragments collected, allowing players to freely traverse between the five islands and search for glowing planetary fragments. We designed eight planetary fragments based on the eight major planets of the solar system for players to find. Upon collecting a planetary fragment, specific information about that planet pops up in the bottom right corner. The aim is to facilitate player learning about the basic knowledge of the eight planets. However, if a player accidentally falls off an island, they need to re-collect the planetary fragments (Figs. 6 and 7).

Fig. 6. Before the player picks up the planetary fragments.

Fig. 7. Planet-specific information pops up when the player picks up a planetary fragment.

Reward. When collecting the eighth planetary fragment, the system will encourage it, and at the end of the dialogue with the last NPC, the system will automatically pop up the interface to congratulate the player for clearing the level, and provide two options to continue the game or return to the menu (Fig. 8).

Feedback. A channel for feedback is provided on the menu page, with the aim of obtaining feedback on the game from players for later iterative updates (Fig. 9).

Fig. 8. Player Pass Interface.

Fig. 9. The menu page provides a feedback channel.

6   Conclusion

This study investigates the factors influencing users' intention to use serious games in museums by establishing an extended TAM and suggests design directions for serious games in museums. The results show that perceived enjoyment has a significant effect on perceived usefulness and behavioral intention. This means that when designing serious games, museums should consider appropriately increasing the entertainment of the game and optimizing the game experience to make users more willing to accept it. In addition, perceived usefulness has a significant effect on user behavioral intention. This means that serious game de-signers in the museum field should still prioritize education and focus on adding science content to their games.

In the game prototype we designed, gamification was used to make learning more interesting and to stimulate users' interest in learning. This interest makes the audience willing to visit offline museums and learn more about the exhibits, while also promoting reflection and interaction and increasing knowledge absorption. Through serious games, museums are able to absorb a wider audience, including the younger generation, thus promoting the dissemination of culture and history.

References

1. Ullah, M., et al.: Serious games in science education. A systematic literature review. Virtual Reality Intell. Hardware **4**(3), 189–209 (2022)
2. Zeng, J.L., Shang, J.J.: Empirical studies on educational games (2013–2017): a review of literature from WOS databases. Chin. J. Distance Educ. **05**, 1–10 (2019)
3. Wu, Q., Lu, Z.: Knowledge map of serious game research: history, focus and trend. J. Nanjing Arts Inst. (Fine Arts & Design) **2023**(01), 58–65+209–210 (2023)
4. Yang, X.: Research on Serious Games and Digital Protection of Intangible Cultural Heritage——Take Nishan Shaman As an Example. Master, Huazhong University of Science and Technology. (2020)
5. Yang, Y.Y., Ji, T., Zhang, D.D.: Design and application of cultural heritage in serious games. Packag. Eng. **41**(04), 312–317 (2020)
6. Bolognesi, C., Aiello, D.: Learning through serious games: a digital design museum for education. Int. Arch. Photogrammetry, Remote Sens. Spat. Inf. Sci. **43**, 83–90 (2020)
7. https://icom.museum/en/news/icom-approves-a-new-museum-definition/
8. Cordova-Rangel, J., Caro, K.: Designing a serious game to promote visitors' engagement in a science museum exhibition. In: 8th Mexican Conference on Human-Computer Interaction, pp. 1–5 (2021)
9. Xu, H.F.: Research on the Application of Serious Games in Material Cultural Heritage -- A Case Study of Shenyang Imperial Palace in Qing Dynasty. Master, Shenyang Aerospace University (2020)
10. Zhang, Z.H.: Serious games for cultural heritage learning: a discussion based on engagement. Ornamentation **05**, 94–97 (2022)
11. Wang, W.J., Zhao, X.C., Xie, H.X., Xie, Q.K.: A review on the evaluation of digital educational games Abroad. Int. Comp. Educ. **41**(03), 101–108 (2019)
12. Laamarti, F., Eid, M., El Saddik, A.: An overview of serious games. Int. J. Comput. Games Technol. **2014**, 1–15 (2014)
13. Giessen, H.W.: Serious games effects: an overview. Procedia Soc. Behav. Sci. **174**, 2240–2244 (2015)
14. Coenen, T., Mostmans, L., Naessens, K.: MuseUs. J. Comput. Cult. Heritage **6**(2), 1–19 (2013)
15. Rowe, J.P., Lobene, E.V., Mott, B.W., Lester, J.C.: Serious games go informal: a museum-centric perspective on intelligent game-based learning. In: Trausan-Matu, S., Boyer, K.E., Crosby, M., Panourgia, K. (eds.) ITS 2014. LNCS, vol. 8474, pp. 410–415. Springer, Cham (2014). https://doi.org/10.1007/978-3-319-07221-0_51
16. Zilio, D., Orio, N., Zamparo, L.: FakeMuse. J. Comput. Cult. Heritage **14**(2), 1–22 (2021)
17. Kara, N.: A mixed-methods study of cultural heritage learning through playing a serious game. Int. J. Hum. Comput. Interact. **40**(6), 1397–1408 (2022). https://doi.org/10.1080/10447318.2022.2125627
18. Mondou, D., Prigent, A., Revel, A.: A dynamic scenario by remote supervision: a serious game in the museum with a Nao Robot. In: Cheok, A.D., Inami, M., Romão, T. (eds.) ACE 2017. LNCS, vol. 10714, pp. 103–116. Springer, Cham (2018). https://doi.org/10.1007/978-3-319-76270-8_8

19. Lv, Q.Y., Wang, J.Y.: Prospect of international serious games: historical review and category focus. Open Educ. Res. **27**(03), 104–111 (2021)
20. Shen, J., Zhang, Q.J.: A review of educational games assessment at home and Abroad. J. Dist. Educ. **32**(03), 105–112 (2014)
21. Davis, F.D., Warshaw, B.P.R.: User acceptance of computer-technology - a comparison of 2 theoretical-models. Manage. Sci. **35**(8), 982–1003 (1989)
22. Park, E.; Han, J.; Kim, K.J.; Cho, Y.; del Pobil, A.P.: Student acceptance model of educational games in university class. In: Proceedings of the 12th International Conference on Ubiquitous Information Management and Communication, pp. 1–4 (2018)
23. Razami, H.H., Ibrahim, R.: Models and constructs to predict students' digital educational games acceptance: a systematic literature review. Telematics Inform. **73**, 101874 (2022). https://doi.org/10.1016/j.tele.2022.101874
24. Huang, Y.M.: Exploring students' acceptance of educational computer games from the perspective of learning strategy. Australas. J. Educ. Technol. **35**(3), 132–149 (2018)
25. Bourgonjon, J., Valcke, M., Soetaert, R., Schellens, T.: Students' perceptions about the use of video games in the classroom. Comput. Educ. **54**(4), 1145–1156 (2010)
26. Davis, F.D.: Perceived usefulness, perceived ease of use, and user acceptance of information technology. MIS Q. **13**(3), 319–340 (1989)
27. Camilleri, A.C., Camilleri, M.A.: The students' intrinsic and extrinsic motivations to engage with digital learning games. In: Proceedings of the 2019 5th International Conference on Education and Training Technologies, pp. 44–48 (2019)
28. Shiue, Y.M., Hsu, Y.C., Liang, Y.C.: Investigating elementary students' epistemological beliefs, game preference by applying game-based learning to a history course. In: International Conference on Advanced Materials for Science & Engineering (2016)
29. Thompson, R.L., Howell, H.J.M.: Personal computing: toward a conceptual model of utilization. MIS Q. **15**(1), 125–143 (1991)
30. Wang, Y.Y., Wang, Y.S., Jian, S.E.: Investigating the determinants of students' intention to use business simulation games. J. Educ. Comput. Res. **58**(2), 433–458 (2019)
31. Davis, F.D., Bagozzi, R.P., Warshaw, P.R.: Extrinsic and intrinsic motivation to use computers in the workplace1. J. Appl. Soc. Psychol. **22**(14), 1111–1132 (1992)
32. Wirani, Y., Nabarian, T., Romadhon, M.S.: Evaluation of continued use on Kahoot! as a gamification-based learning platform from the perspective of Indonesia students. Procedia Comput. Sci. **197**, 545–556 (2022). https://doi.org/10.1016/j.procs.2021.12.172
33. Huang, Y.M.: Students' continuance intention toward programming games: hedonic and utilitarian aspects. Int. J. Hum. Comput. Interact. **36**(4), 393–402 (2019)
34. Giannakos, M.N., Chorianopoulos, K., Jaccheri, L., Chrisochoides, N.: "This game is girly!" perceived enjoyment and student acceptance of edutainment. In: Göbel, S., Müller, W., Urban, B., Wiemeyer, J. (eds.) Edutainment/GameDays -2012. LNCS, vol. 7516, pp. 89–98. Springer, Heidelberg (2012). https://doi.org/10.1007/978-3-642-33466-5_10
35. Venkatesh, V., Morris, M.G., Davis, G.B., Davis, F.D.: User acceptance of information technology: toward a unified view. MIS Q. **27**(3), 425–478 (2003)
36. Wang, M., Nunes, M.B.: Matching serious games with museum's educational roles: smart education in practice. Interact. Technol. Smart Educ. **16**(4), 319–342 (2019)

The Impact of Alternate Reality Game on the Environmental Cognition for University Freshmen

Shuo Xiong[1], Kun Xie[1], Ruoyu Wen[2]([✉]), Yiyan Zeng[1], and Lingfeng Nie[1]

[1] Huazhong University of Science and Technology, Wuhan, China
{xiongshuo,xiekun}@hust.edu.cn
[2] University of Canterbury, Christchurch, New Zealand
ruoyu.wen@pg.canterbury.ac.nz

Abstract. The application of Alternate Reality Games (ARGs) as a game-based learning tool in educational and commercial settings has been explored in various studies, particularly in regions such as the UK and Australia. Current studies have focused on utilizing ARGs to facilitate student orientation and induction. However, research in this domain is notably sparse within Chinese universities, despite the growing interest in game-based learning in China. This study employed a controlled experimental approach to assess the impact of a puzzle-oriented ARG on the campus experience of 44 students at a Chinese university. The primary objective of the ARG was to encourage comprehensive exploration of the campus and to foster integrative learning opportunities among students. Statistical analysis of the data revealed that players have experienced a knowledge-based increase in their cognition of the objective environment on campus, exhibiting stronger campus exploration behavior and a more positive attitude towards games. The results also indicate that the narrative nature of ARG may play a certain role in helping students alleviate anxiety, but further research is needed.

Keywords: Alternate Reality Game · Serious Games · cognition · University freshman

1 Introduction

An Alternate Reality Game (ARG) is an interactive game that uses the real world as a platform and typically combines multi-media and game elements for storytelling. It often involves puzzles, clues, and community collaboration, with players interacting through various channels like websites, social media, and physical locations, blurring the borderline between the game's world and reality. It used to be widely made for promotional purposes [18,19], Recently, it has also made significant strides in exploring various fields of application in educational contexts. Prior research shows ARG's potential in Education. It can help with

X. Fang (Ed.): HCII 2024, LNCS 14731, pp. 100–113, 2024.
https://doi.org/10.1007/978-3-031-60695-3_7

freshman orientation [39], increase the levels of engagement and participation in learning [35,38], encourage new students' socialization [38], etc.

In China, research in the field of ARG is still in its nascent stage. Although there have been some investigations into ARG mechanics, its application to the educational domain remains largely unexplored, while Chinese freshmen are in demand of a way to support their adapting. As a result of the insufficient provision of relevant education during middle and high school years, Chinese freshmen often experience mild anxiety, feelings of loneliness, and challenges in adapting to university life [26]. During campus forums, it is quite common to come across freshmen expressing their lack of self-confidence and feeling bewildered by the challenges of college life [13,24]. Additionally, as university represents a novel environment, numerous college students experience a profound sense of discomfort upon initially stepping onto campus, and may even grapple with cognitive dissonance.

To solve this problem, this study explored whether ARG can help freshmen in Chinese colleges with the adapting process. The survey was conducted while students playing a location-based ARG on a Chinese campus. The result revealed that in the Chinese context, ARG continues to exert a positive influence on students' comprehension and assimilation into campus life, as well as their exploration of self-worth and attainment of self-identity. Additionally, this research offers valuable insights and suggestions for subsequent design endeavors.

2   Related Work

2.1   Environmental Cognition

Environmental Cognition is a way to "acquire, organize, store, and recall information about locations, distances, and arrangements in the physical environment [34]", plays an important role in people's daily lives. Though there are a lot of traditional ways to enhance environmental cognition, video games, especially Alternate Reality Game (ARG) provide us with a new chance.

Research has shown that "Playing action games—particularly FPS games— produces improvements in sensory, perceptual, and spatial cognitive functions that are different from the expertise acquired in the game [33]." 3D video games can be of great help to blind people's navigation skills. Using a specially made action game, letting blind adolescents explore in a building with the same layout in reality, can dramatically improve the blind adolescents' navigation ability [10]. A 3D sound-based video game called MOVA3D attains blind children's favor and enhances the overall ability of their orientation and mobility skills [31]. Meanwhile, the length of video game experience significantly correlates with adults' performance in virtual navigation tasks [29].

Augmented reality games, like Pokémon Go, motivate players to move around in the real world. It can help tourists navigate in an unfamiliar city. "Playing Pokémon Go is overlaid onto the experience of navigating the city as a tourist [40]." Evidence also shows that Pokémon Go may improve students' spatial orientation skills [8].

Research on the relationship between Alternate Reality Games (ARG) and environmental cognition or spatial navigation skills is still relatively little, and there is nearly no related research in the Chinese context. However, attempts to use ARG in orientation can be found. Alternate Reality Games for Orientation, Socialisation, and Induction (ARGOSI) tried to deploy ARG to "improve students' confidence in navigating the city and university campus" but failed due to multiple reasons [38].

2.2 College Transition

College transition is very important in students' education and life experience, the post-secondary education community believes that the transition from high school to university is a decisive step in the academic path of young people [37]. Tinto quoted Newton's *First Law of Motion* to show that what students experience in the transition period has a persistent effect throughout the next few years [36]. However, for freshmen, the transition period is a difficult time. Some stated that "Many students who are college-ready encounter campus cultures that feel foreign and unfriendly, making college challenging for them to navigate successfully [22]". Researchers have also shown that students during the transition are more vulnerable in academic, social, and emotional adjustment [25, 37].

Nancy K. Schlossberg proposed the transition theory which mainly focuses on how individuals respond to changes that occur. Schlossberg divided transitions into different types, including Anticipated transitions, Unanticipated transitions, and Nonevent transitions. Among them, college transitions belong to Anticipated transitions, which means major life events we usually expect. Transition takes time, and during the transition process, people's reactions will change, whether it's good or bad. For some people, this process occurs easily and quickly, however, many people struggle to find suitable ecological niches, even years later. To cope with transitions, Schlossberg provided a "4S" system namely Situation, Self, supports, and Strategies [32].

2.3 Alternate Reality Games in Transition

The immersive and experiential nature of games allows players to establish meaningful connections with the external world, and the integration of games in the field of education has shown significant traction. ARG can be directly applied in teaching. A study examined the viability of ARG-enhanced education on English foreign language (EFL). "According to the results, both flipped and blended groups receiving ARG-enhanced education performed better than the control group in learning how to give and ask for directions [21]". Another study demonstrated that incorporating ARG into the study of chemistry can also accelerate students' comprehension [30].

Moreover, researches indicate that ARG can enhance students' learning abilities and learning motivation. A study of 10th graders in northern Taiwan showed that while the game did not directly significantly improve students' academic performance, "students in the experimental group showed significant improvement in learning achievement after the game [15]". Another study revealed that it can markedly augment the learning process by amplifying students' motivation to learn [16]. ARG can also foster improvement in students' academic performance through various means, including facilitating socialization among students. "This impacts their sense of connectedness, one of the factors identified as important for success in higher education [12]".

Based on active attempts in the field of education, Alternative reality games can also be a beneficial aid in solving tricky transitional problem strategies. Some ARGs, such as the Universal Student, have made some good attempts to help students smoothly pass through campus orientation [14]. ARG has been proven useful in both physical and mental aspects, including increasing students' physical movement and engagement [20]. Moreover, a research team used ARG in orientation and found that ARG can foster relationships between students in a more economical way than traditional digital games [12].

The relevant work has been done relatively well in countries such as Europe and America, while it is still relatively limited in China. Our research focuses on a similar topic in the Chinese context. Though there are huge differences between Chinese college transition and European or American college transition, We believe there are still a lot of similarities, and research based on the Chinese context can be valuable for research around the globe.

3   Method

3.1   Game Design

My Own Sea is a puzzle-oriented Alternate Reality Game themed around campus landmarks and living guidelines. Designed by the team of Huazhong University of Science and Technology, it aims to stimulate students' and outsiders' desire to explore the campus, enhance its influence, and help people better immerse themselves in various corners of the campus and obtain opportunities for comprehensive learning.

At the beginning of the game, players will be given a story starter on the mobile web, and the story will be interrupted by puzzles in the process of advancing. To solve puzzles and advance the story, Players must follow the prompts on the website to stroll through a 4.6 square kilometer campus and find clues hidden within the campus landmarks, such as search information for corresponding books in the library, numbers on the walls of the school history museum, and information from bus stop signs and cafeteria surveillance.

Based on the characteristics of ARG, this game was also designed to assist social interaction and improve problem-solving abilities to a certain extent. The presentation of character stories can also to some extent regulate students' emotions. The three protagonists are representatives of three personality behaviors among college students, the first person is a person with a firm goal and a focus on oneself, and the second person is an optimist who values freedom as their life creed and tends to have a "three minute enthusiasm" for doing things. The

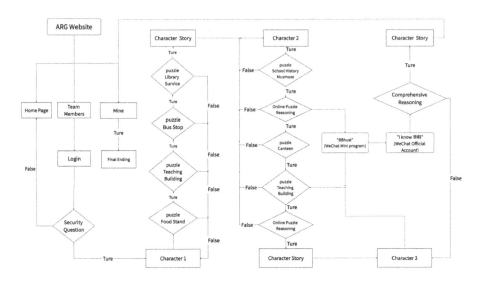

Fig. 1. Game Process

personality of the last person can be understood through the answer "want anything, nothing". The storytelling of three characters may have a certain sensation on students (Fig. 1).

3.2   Theoretical Framework

Bleed. Bleed refers to the interaction between the true life experiences, thoughts, interpersonal relationships, and physical states of the role-playing process, which leads to the blurring of the boundaries between their true selves and roles. Montola et al. view bleed as a design rhetoric that shares similarities with concepts such as character immersion, flow, and engrossment [28]. When the player's thoughts and feelings are influenced by the character, there will be bleed, and vice versa. As the amount of bleeding increases, the boundary between players and characters becomes increasingly transparent.

Bleed is based on a dual consciousness that players both acknowledge and deny the essence of the game and can be divided into two types: bleed-in and bleed-out. Bleed-in occurs when out-of-game factors affect the player's experience, while bleed-out, is the opposite process [4,5]. Another type of bleed is referred to as ego bleed, which occurs when the player's personality content and the character's personality overflow from each other [3].

Mendoza et al.'s literature review on the Viability of Role-Playing Games found that bleed is often framed as something to be handled [27]. Ali et al. view bleed as an "over-abundance of emotion" which facilitates "neither relief nor insight" and over-distanced [1]. Some strategies have been proposed. Leonard et al. believes that a player may be able to reduce bleed-out if they consistently and carefully label their experiences as solely due to in-character dynamics [23].

However, bleed is neither inherently negative nor positive, at its most positive, bleed experiences can produce moments of catharsis and allow players the opportunity to express emotions they might otherwise feel inhibited to share in real life [5].

College Adjustment Scales. The College Adjustment Scales (CAS) offers raw scale scores and linearly transformed McCall T-scores (M = 50, SD = 10) for nine aspects of a student's psychological and adjustment status, including Anxiety, Depression, Suicidal, Ideation, Substance Abuse, self-esteem, interpersonal problems, family problems, academic problems, and occupational problems. The inventory was designed for screening presenting problems, and identifying and classifying the types of psychological maladjustment presented by students at university counseling centers [7].

Campbell et al. provided support for the construct validity of the CAS scale by comparing it with the MMPI college maladjustment scale [6]. The scale has been applied in practice. A study conducted a CAS test on the performance upon entry into a medical school and found that depression, academic problems, substance abuse, and supplementary ideas were associated statistically with low academic performance in the study population [17].

3.3   Procedure and Participants

This study used a control experiment method, and the experimental design was a pre-test Questionnaire-ARG intervention-post-test Questionnaire. Anonymous online surveys were used to collect quantitative data before the game (N = 130) after one month of enrollment. The survey was conducted in the form of a questionnaire, covering five dimensions: campus familiarity and exploration, anxiety, self-esteem, and socialization, to measure their cognitive level and integration into the campus since enrollment. Additionally, the attitude of students towards games was also measured. The questionnaire also surveyed players (N = 52) who had already completed the game through logical design, measuring their attitudes towards puzzles, plot, and art design, as well as their overall perception and suggestions for the game.

Subsequently, 44 students with relatively poor cognitive levels were selected from the remaining 78 students who had not participated in the game, and randomly divided into two groups based on the same gender ratio: the experimental group and the control group. Group A, as the control group, will be prohibited from accessing the ARG works during the experimental period, while Group B will be required to complete the ARG process. Two days after the game ends, both groups will be asked to complete a post-test questionnaire (N = 44) to measure whether and how their behavior and attitudes have changed over a period of time. The post-test questionnaire of Group A is completely consistent with the pre-test questionnaire in terms of question design, while Group B answered several game-related questions at the end of the questionnaire, which were completely consistent with the question design of Group A (or in other words, with the pre-test) questionnaire (Fig. 2).

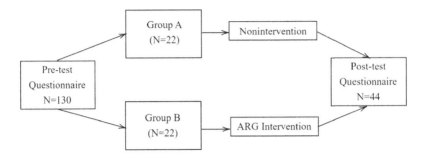

Fig. 2. Study Procedures

Participants were newly enrolled freshmen from Huazhong University of Science and Technology, including first-year undergraduate students and some first-year master's students who are not from the university. All participants were voluntarily recruited one month after enrollment, and certain rewards were provided. Considering that student's sex as an influential moderator variable affects emotion and academic adjustment during transition [12], the gender ratio between Group A and Group B was controlled. The demographics of students in both groups were 31.8% male and 68.2% female.

3.4   Adjustment Categories and Measures

College adaptation is a complex issue that covers a wide range of aspects, however, there is currently substantial agreement among educational researchers as to the structure of the broad adjustment to college construct [11]. According to a literature review by Baker and Siryk [2], students' adjustment to college can be categorized into four dimensions: academic adjustment, social adjustment, personal-emotional adjustment, and institutional attachment.

Guided by the CAS scale and the four dimensions mentioned above, based on *My Own Sea* as a landmark-centered ARG and research objective, our questionnaire ultimately covers five dimensions: campus familiarity and exploration, anxiety, self-esteem, and social interaction. In terms of self-esteem, we pay more attention to academic issues.

Campus familiarity includes campus landmarks and public service facilities familiarity. Participants were presented with key services or locations on campus and were asked if they have learned or knew the location or if they had been there. Anxiety was measured using items such as "I feel lost about college life" and "I feel anxious, worried, or uneasy (in the past month)". Self-esteem was measured using items such as "I am able to keep up with other classmates in my studies" and "I am positive of myself and full of confidence in myself". Socialization was measured using items such as "I made some new friends at school" and "When I encounter problems, I am willing to communicate with my classmates, teachers, and parents". Exploration was measured using items such as "If I have time, I am willing to explore every aspect of the campus as much as possible". Participants provided their responses using a 5-point Likert scale from 1 (strongly agree) to 5 (strongly disagree).

In addition, we also collected data on participants' attitudes towards games through items such as "Playing games can help me acquire some useful skills" and "Playing games is a valuable activity", aiming to explore and analyze whether ARG is helpful in objectively viewing gaming attitudes.

4   Results

This study mainly used Mann Whitney U test and Wilcoxon matched signed rank test to compare and analyze several groups of independent and paired samples, and statistical analysis was conducted using IBM SPSS Statistics 26.

4.1   Campus Familiarity and Exploration

A Wilcoxon-matched signed rank test was conducted between the 44 group B students in the pre-test and post-test. Results showed a significant difference in campus familiarity ($Z = 2.470$, $p = 0.014$). The mean score of campus familiarity in the pre-test (51.364, SD = 3.0635) was significantly lower than the mean in the post-test (54.955, SD = 4.5615). Paired tests were also conducted on Group A as the control group, and the results showed no significant difference ($Z = 1.464$, $p = 0.143$).

Familiarity with campus environment and attitude towards games were implemented through scoring. The higher the score, the more detailed the student's understanding of campus public service facilities, landmarks, and their geographical locations. From the results, Group B had a higher score after ARG intervention, while Group A had no significant changes during this period, indicating that Group B has traveled more landmarks and is more familiar with the campus.

When comparing Group A and Group B, the Mann Whitney U test showed a significant difference in the willingness of middle school students to explore the campus in the post-test ($Z = -2.149$, $p = 0.032$), while there was no significant difference in the pre-test. The exploration dimension is measured through the Likert scale from 1 (strongly agree) to 5 (strongly disagree). According to the U-test results, the mean rank of Group A (26.64) was significantly higher than that of Group B (18.36), indicating that Group B has a more positive attitude towards exploration. Concretely, 45.5% who received ARG intervention strongly agree that "if I have time, I am willing to explore all aspects of the campus", while only 9.1% of students in the non intervention group strongly agree.

4.2   Attitude Towards Challenges and Games

In addition, the Mann Whitney U test showed that there was a significant difference in the attitudes of the two groups of students towards challenges

(Z = 2.342, p = 0.019) and games (Z = 2.175, p = 0.030) in the post-test, while there was no significant difference in the pre-test. In the post-test, Group A students scored higher in their attitude towards challenges, while Group B students scored higher in their attitude towards games. Due to the fact that attitude towards games is measured on a scale of 1 to 10, while attitude towards challenges is also measured on the Likert scale, this result indicates that the attitude of Group B is no different from that of Group A in the pre-test, but became more positive towards challenges and games in the post-test (Table 1).

Table 1. Comparison between Group A and Group B in the post-test

	Explore	Challenges	Games
Mann Wintney U	151.000	144.000	334.500
Z	−2.149	−2.342	2.175
Asymp.Sig.(2-tailed)	0.032	0.019	0.030
Group A Mean Rank	26.64	26.95	18.30
Group B Mean Rank	18.36	18.05	26.70

4.3   Self-esteem, Social Interaction and Anxiety

A Mann-Whitney U test also tested the self-esteem of group A and group B, and the results showed a significant difference (Z = −2.634, p = 0.008). However, the Wilcoxon matched sign rank test showed no significant difference between group B before and after the test (Z = −0.664, p = 0.057). Therefore, this indicates that there are individual differences in self-examination between students in Group A and Group B themselves. In addition, the Mann Whitney U-test and Wilcoxon matching sign rank test both showed no difference in the social interaction of students in groups A, B (Z = −1.703, p = 0.089), and B before and after the test (Z = −0.105, p = 0.916).

An interesting finding is that there was no significant difference in the anxiety dimension between Group A and Group B in the post-test (Z = −1.490, p = 0.136), while they had a significant difference in the pre-test (Z = −2.725, p = 0.006). Comparing the four sets of data before and after the pre-test, it was found that the score of Group A has become slightly lower, the average score of Group A before the pre-test was 14.2273 (SD = 3.23569), while the average score in the post-test was 13.7273 (SD = 3.01080). Meanwhile, Group B scored slightly higher, with an average score of 11.8636 (SD = 2.12234) in the pre-test, while the average score after ARG intervention was 12.2727 (SD = 3.20983).

Since anxiety is also measured using the Likert scale, the lower the score, the more students agree that they are anxious. Therefore, the results indicate that a slightly higher score in Group B during this period indicates a decrease in anxiety, while Group A is the opposite.

5   Discussion

5.1   Summary

This study probes into the impact of an Alternate Reality Game *My Own Sea* on college freshmen, and based on its characteristics, particularly the impact on environmental cognition, made a certain contribution to the literature on environmental cognition and students' transition. The research results show that players report a higher level of familiarity with the campus environment, exhibiting more positive behaviors, including a more positive desire to explore the campus and a more positive attitude towards risk challenges, meanwhile, their attitude towards the game also became more positive after the game compared to the control group, which provide partial support for the impact of ARG on freshmen.

5.2   Campus Familiarity

Márlon et al. believe that ARG Can achieve a diagnosis of student cognitive level and conceptual discussion between students and teachers [30]. The results showed compared with Group A, students in Group B have taken action, visited more campus landmarks, suggesting that ARG played a role in helping students better familiarize themselves with the campus. On the basis of knowledge, students have improved their understanding of the campus environment, which not only demonstrates the impact of ARG on students' objective environmental cognition level but also once again validates existing research results.

The more familiar performance may be due to the puzzle-solving and exploration nature of ARG themed around campus landmarks and living guidelines. For the students in group B, to solve the puzzle, they must go out of the dormitory and look for clues in some places they have been or have never been to, but the members in group A do not have this requirement. The student whose pre-test number was 91 stated: "Thank you for giving me the motivation to leave the dormitory and investigate in places I haven't been to before".

5.3   Attitude Changes

The same goes for changing attitudes towards games. The attitudes of the two groups towards the game were consistent during the pre-test, but after the ARG intervention, things changed. Group B, who completed the ARG, showed a more positive attitude towards the game, while Group A, who prohibited exposure to the ARG, remained unchanged. This indicates that Group B agrees more with the descriptions like "games are a valuable activity", suggesting the positive impact of ARG on attitude change [25]. Similarly, the lower score of Group B in terms of challenges also indicates a more proactive attitude towards responding to challenges after ARG intervention.

Solving puzzles is an interesting and challenging process, which can bring pleasant experience, which can also be seen from the changes in their attitude.

Perhaps it is this pleasure that drives a change in attitude, as well as an increase in the willingness to explore. The Mann Whitney U test results of two groups with no significant changes in the pre-test but significant changes in the post test indicate that students who underwent ARG intervention had an increased desire to explore the campus. ARG provides students with the motivation to go to places they have never been to or do not want to go before, increasing their spirit of exploration, which may have some beneficial effects on their learning and life. The ARG game format is beneficial for cultivating critical thinking skills, information literacy, and collaborative problem-solving abilities [30], and here, various signs indicate that ARG has played a role in improving players' coping abilities and learning literacy.

5.4 Psychological States

Particularly, the anxiety level performance of the A, and B groups in the pre - and post-tests also suggests to some extent that this ARG may help them alleviate their anxiety. After all, Group A and Group B conducted the same questionnaire as the pre-test within the same time interval while Group A scored slightly lower, Group B scored slightly higher. Character stories may have played a certain role to some extent, as stated in pre-test 101, "Everyone's story is very touching and inspiring," but there are also some opposing opinions, what number 113 said, "The plot between the characters is a bit fragmented and not very connected, more like several independent games."

This may be the emergence of ego bleed, in which the persona fits with some of the player's personalities, and the player's feelings and sense of substitution increase. Prompted by the clues of the characters, the player solved the puzzle and the story was finally presented. The characters represent three typical students' personalities. The storytelling and the immersion of puzzles make the players map and reflect on their own lives, and may eventually realize bleed-out, which affects their daily life performance, such as the slight change of anxiety displayed in the results.

5.5 Social Attributes

Meeting people and making friends could assist with the social integration of students and the transition from school to university. However, this study failed to verify the impact of ARG on social connections and self-esteem. This may be due to the lack of more social connections with other students and university staff participating in the game [12] requirements in *My Own Sea*. For example, Pre-test number 91 said "I feel like... there's a lack of teamwork content", and number 101 said, "It seems like they are all single-player tasks. Is it possible to design a level with three or four people working together to come up with a clue". It also may be due to the lack of targeted questionnaire design.

In terms of self-esteem, the questionnaire focuses more on academic self-esteem rather than other scholars studying conscious evaluation of the self [9] and has not used mature scales such as the Rosenberg Self Esteem Scale. Meanwhile, the experimental environment and duration may also be influencing factors. The measurement of self-esteem may require a longer period of observation and a more natural environment.

6   Conclusion

In this research, we conducted a survey with a pre-test/post-test approach. We assess freshman's adaptation to university life by evaluating their familiarity with the campus environment, willingness to explore, attitude toward facing challenges, and psychological state. Our findings suggest that by setting location-based puzzles for players to solve, compared to baseline, ARG can notably encourage freshmen to go out of their dormitories, and play on the campus, which could increase their campus familiarity and willingness for campus exploration, additionally, it could help them alleviate stress to some extent and get a more positive attitude towards challenges. However, the research findings did not support the impact of ARG on the psychological state of social attributes and self-esteem, which may be due to the limitations of the study. The duration of our study was relatively short, which might not suffice to observe the long-term effects on self-esteem and social attributes. Moreover, the presence of an experimental setting, where participants played games, could inadvertently introduce a sense of being observed, potentially influencing their behavior while they are playing ARG. Follow-up experiments may be needed to verify these questions. Overall, our findings offer insights from a Chinese context into the use of Alternate Reality Games (ARG) during freshman orientation, demonstrating ARG's potential within China's educational framework. These results lay a foundational basis for future research in this area.

Acknowledgments. We would like to thank all the students who have designed and put in effort for this campus ARG, and all the students from Huazhong University of Science and Technology who participated in this research.

Disclosure of Interests. The authors have no competing interests to declare that are relevant to the content of this article.

References

1. Ali, A., Wolfert, S., Lam, I., Rahman, T.: Intersecting modes of aesthetic distance and mimetic induction in therapeutic process: examining a drama-based treatment for military-related traumatic stress. Drama Ther. Rev. **4**(2), 153–165 (2018)
2. Baker, R.W., Siryk, B.: Measuring adjustment to college. J. Couns. Psychol. **31**(2), 179 (1984)
3. Beltrán, W.: Yearning for the hero within: live-action role-playing as engagement with mythical archetypes. Wyrd Con Companion 2012, pp. 91–98 (2012)
4. Bowman, S.L.: Social conflict in role-playing communities: an exploratory qualitative study. Int. J. Role-Play. **4**, 4–25 (2013)
5. Bowman, S.: Bleed: Thespilloverbetweenplayerandcharacter. Nordic Larp (2015)

6. Campbell, M.H., Palmieri, M., Lasch, B.: Concurrent validity of the college adjustment scales using comparison with the MMPI college maladjustment scale. Psychol. Rep. **99**(3), 1003–1007 (2006)
7. Campbell, M.H., Prichard, S.T.: Factor structure of the college adjustment scales. Psychol. Rep. **86**(1), 79–84 (2000)
8. Carbonell Carrera, C., Saorín, J.L., Hess Medler, S.: Pokémon go and improvement in spatial orientation skills. J. Geogr. **117**(6), 245–253 (2018)
9. Pereira Santos, C., Hutchinson, K., Khan, V.J., Markopoulos, P.: Measuring self-esteem with games (2017)
10. Connors, E.C., Chrastil, E.R., Sánchez, J., Merabet, L.B.: Action video game play and transfer of navigation and spatial cognition skills in adolescents who are blind. Front. Hum. Neurosci. **8**, 133 (2014)
11. Credé, M., Niehorster, S.: Adjustment to college as measured by the student adaptation to college questionnaire: a quantitative review of its structure and relationships with correlates and consequences. Educ. Psychol. Rev. **24**, 133–165 (2012)
12. Elsom, S., Westacott, M., Stieler-Hunt, C., Glencross, S., Rutter, K.: Finding resources, finding friends: using an alternate reality game for orientation and socialisation in a university enabling program. Interact. Learn. Environ. **31**(5), 2635–2649 (2023)
13. Gao, W., Ping, S., Liu, X.: Gender differences in depression, anxiety, and stress among college students: a longitudinal study from China. J. Affect. Disord. **263**, 292–300 (2020). https://doi.org/10.1016/j.jad.2019.11.121. https://www.sciencedirect.com/science/article/pii/S0165032719320385
14. Glencross, S., Elsom, S., Westacott, M., Stieler-Hunt, C.: Using an alternate reality game to facilitate student engagement during orientation. Student Success **10**(2), 13–22 (2019)
15. Hou, H.T., Fang, Y.S., Tang, J.T.: Designing an alternate reality board game with augmented reality and multi-dimensional scaffolding for promoting spatial and logical ability. Interact. Learn. Environ. **31**(7), 4346–4366 (2023)
16. Kim, S., Song, K., Lockee, B., Burton, J. (eds.): Gamification in Learning and Education: Enjoy Learning Like Gaming. Springer, Cham (2018). pp 159, pp 138. £ 55.16 (hbk). ISBN 978-3-319-47282-9 (hbk) (2020)
17. Iglesias-Benavides, J., Blum-Valenzuela, E., Lopez-Tovar, A., Espinosa-Galindo, A., Rivas-Estilla, A.: The college adjustment scale (CAS) test and recent students' school performance upon entry into a medical school. Medicina Universitaria **18**(73), 201–204 (2017)
18. Janes, S.: Promotional alternate reality games–more than "just" marketing. Arts Market **5**(2), 183–196 (2015)
19. Janes, S.: Alternate Reality Games: Promotion and Participatory Culture. Routledge, New York (2019)
20. Johnston, J.D., Massey, A.P., Marker-Hoffman, R.L.: Using an alternate reality game to increase physical activity and decrease obesity risk of college students (2012)
21. Khodabandeh, F.: Exploring the viability of augmented reality game-enhanced education in whatsapp flipped and blended classes versus the face-to-face classes. Educ. Inf. Technol. **28**(1), 617–646 (2023)
22. Kuh, G.D., Kinzie, J., Schuh, J.H., Whitt, E.J.: Fostering student success in hard times. Change Mag. Higher Learning **43**(4), 13–19 (2011)
23. Leonard, D.J., Thurman, T.: Bleed-out on the brain: the neuroscience of character-to-player spillover in larp. Int. J. Role-Playing **9**, 9–15 (2018)

24. Li, J.B., Wang, Y.S., Sun, Y., Liang, Y., Dou, K.: Individual and interpersonal correlates of changes in college adaptation among Chinese freshmen: a longitudinal study. Curr. Psychol. **42**, 1–13 (2021)
25. Longwell-Grice, R., Longwell-Grice, H.: Testing Tinto: how do retention theories work for first-generation, working-class students? J. Coll. Stud. Retent. Res. Theory Pract. **9**(4), 407–420 (2008)
26. Lu, W., Bian, Q., Song, Y., Ren, J., Xu, X., Zhao, M.: Prevalence and related risk factors of anxiety and depression among Chinese college freshmen. J. Huazhong Univ. Sci. Technol. [Med. Sci.] **35**, 815–822 (2015)
27. Mendoza, J.: Gaming intentionally: a literature review of the viability of role-playing games as drama-therapy-informed interventions (2020)
28. Montola, M.: The positive negative experience in extreme role-playing. The Foundation Stone of Nordic Larp (2010), p. 153 (2010)
29. Murias, K., Kwok, K., Castillejo, A.G., Liu, I., Iaria, G.: The effects of video game use on performance in a virtual navigation task. Comput. Hum. Behav. **58**, 398–406 (2016)
30. Márlon, D.T.S.: O jogo de realidade alternada curto (short arg) como estratégia de discussÃo de conceitos quÍmicos em nÍvel superior. Química Nova (2020)
31. Sánchez, J., Saenz, M., Garrido, J.M.: Usability of a multimodal video game to improve navigation skills for blind children. ACM Trans. Access. Comput. **3**(2) (2010). https://doi.org/10.1145/1857920.1857924
32. Schlossberg, N.K.: The challenge of change: the transition model and its applications. J. Employ. Couns. **48**(4), 159–162 (2011)
33. Spence, I., Feng, J.: Video games and spatial cognition. Rev. Gen. Psychol. **14**(2), 92–104 (2010). https://doi.org/10.1037/a0019491
34. Spencer, C., Gee, K.: Environmental Cognition, pp. 46–53, January 2012. https://doi.org/10.1016/B978-0-12-375000-6.00149-X
35. Stylianidou, N., Sofianidis, A., Manoli, E., Meletiou-Mavrotheris, M.: Helping nemo!"—using augmented reality and alternate reality games in the context of universal design for learning. Educ. Sci. **10**(4) (2020). https://doi.org/10.3390/educsci10040095. https://www.mdpi.com/2227-7102/10/4/95
36. Tinto, V.: Isaac newton and student college completion. J. Coll. Stud. Retent. Res. Theory Pract. **15**(1), 1–7 (2013)
37. Larose, S., Duchesne, S., Litalien, D., Denault, A.S., Boivin, M.: Adjustment trajectories during the college transition: types, personal and family antecedents, and academic outcomes. Res. High. Educ. **60**, 684–710 (2019)
38. Whitton, N.: Alternate reality games for orientation, socialisation and induction (ARGOSI) (2009)
39. Whitton, N., Jones, R., Wilson, S., Whitton, P.: Alternate reality games as learning environments for student induction. Interact. Learn. Environ. **22**(3), 243–252 (2014)
40. Woods, O.: Experiencing the unfamiliar through mobile gameplay: Pokémon go as augmented tourism. Area **53**(1), 183–190 (2021)

Utilizing Party Game Strategies for Language Acquisition: A Novel Approach to Language Learning

Haoqian Yu, Haitao Zheng, Xing Sun[✉], MingYang Su, QiHui Zhou, Yi Wang, Chu Zhang, Kai Zhang, and Fengsen Gao

Tsinghua University, Beijing, Republic of China
`sunxking@sz.tsinghua.edu.cn`, `{sumy22,k-zhang22, gfs22}@mails.tsinghua.edu.cn`

Abstract. This study explores the innovative application of party game strategies in language learning, presenting a novel approach to language acquisition. Party games, known for their interactive and engaging nature, are increasingly recognized in the gaming market. We investigate the integration of these elements into language education, aiming to enhance learning experiences and outcomes. Our research employs the classic SILL model of language learning strategies, combined with game design theories like the social context characteristics model and MDA theory. We developed a multiplayer party game-based language learning (MPGBLL) framework and created "GetBack2Work," an online party game for adolescent language education. The study assesses the effectiveness of MPG-BLL compared to traditional language learning methods and existing language education platforms through knowledge tests and semi-structured interviews. Our findings demonstrate the potential of party games in language education, offering an engaging, interactive, and effective learning alternative.

Keywords: Computer games · Online games · Education games · Multiplayer games · MMORPGs · Party games

1 Introduction

The use of digital games has emerged as a novel instructional approach, aiming to seamlessly integrate education with entertainment. In order to embody the spirit of learning through play, this study explores the utilization of party games as an instructional aid. Party games, as a subset within the multiplayer gaming category, are suitable for social gatherings, designed to foster interaction, provide entertainment, and serve as a leisure activity. Notable party games such as "Among Us," "Party Animals," "Fall Guys," and "Eggy Party" have gained prominence in the market. In early 2023, "Eggy Party" set a historical record with over 30 million daily active users and dominated the iOS download charts in the first quarter.

© The Author(s), under exclusive license to Springer Nature Switzerland AG 2024
X. Fang (Ed.): HCII 2024, LNCS 14731, pp. 114–130, 2024.
https://doi.org/10.1007/978-3-031-60695-3_8

Party games offer diverse modes, varied gameplay, and real-time interactivity. Compared to content that requires rational thinking, they may be better suited for muscle memory-oriented learning. Furthermore, party games exhibit high replayability and extended user retention cycles, offering players enduring training experiences and reliable data analysis results compared to single-player games. This research focuses on language learning, a representative domain of muscle memory-based learning with a prolonged learning cycle. It explores the intersection of party games and language education, with a particular emphasis on their application to language learning.

Drawing from the classic language learning strategy model SILL [1] and integrating game design theories, including the social context characteristics model [2] and MDA (Mechanics, Dynamics, Aesthetics) theory [3], this study constructs a framework for designing multiplayer party game-based language learning (MPGBLL). Based on this framework, a multiplayer online party game for language education named "Get-Back2Work" is developed for adolescents. The research employs knowledge tests and semi-structured interviews to compare and analyze the strengths and weaknesses of traditional language education methods, existing language education platforms, and the proposed approach. Experimental validation and effectiveness assessments are conducted to evaluate the outcomes of this study.

2 Related Works

2.1 Research on Game-Based Learning

In the 1960s, Seymour Papert first proposed the concept of Playful Learning, emphasizing the integration of game elements and entertainment into education with the aim of enhancing student engagement and learning outcomes [4]. Two characteristics contribute to explaining why this pedagogical approach enhances educational value in gaming contexts: intrinsic joy and iteration. Joy, or positive emotion, is associated with improved functional execution and learning achievements [5], and is even correlated with the flexibility of the brain [6]. Iteration, the conscious construction of new knowledge based on hypothesis testing and the ongoing refinement of one's knowledge over time, is a hallmark of both learning and gaming [7]. These two characteristics are inherent in the context of playful learning.

With the rapid development of electronic games, there has been a shift in the entertainment preferences of adolescents. Building on the foundation of playful learning, educational games have emerged as a distinct form of entertainment, gradually attracting attention in the field of education. Educational games, a branch of serious games, are specifically developed for particular educational purposes, characterized by a balance between educational and entertainment aspects. They employ games as a means of education, design games based on mature educational theories, and achieve a balance between educational and gaming elements, thereby realizing the educational process through a gamified approach.

2.2 Research on Game-Based Language Learning

Digital gamified language learning can bring numerous benefits to foreign language learners. Ansteeg contends that digital games can make the process of learning a foreign language more attractive and enjoyable, leading to a more pleasant language learning experience for learners [8]. Hays suggests that foreign language learning is often a long and tedious process, and gamified language learning can reduce the likelihood of users giving up midway [9]. According to Gee, gamified language learning can provide users with highly contextualized interactive environments [10]. Dalton argues that gamified language learning can offer valuable opportunities for cooperation and interaction among users [11]. Cornillie notes that, compared to traditional language learning, gamified language learning provides users with context-based rapid feedback [12]. Furthermore, these benefits have been proven to promote vocabulary learning [8], increase willingness to communicate [13], enhance writing skills [14], and reduce anxiety during foreign language learning [15].

The educational value of gamified language learning has also been extensively validated. Existing research has yielded exploratory and innovative results in areas such as writing norms, pronunciation standards, and enhancing users' motivation in language learning. From a research value perspective, these findings hold significant considerations for language learning.

2.3 Language Learning Dimensions

In the field of language learning, listening, speaking, reading, and writing are widely recognized as the four core dimensions constituting language proficiency. These dimensions represent different language processing methods and skills, encompassing various aspects of language acquisition.

Listen. Listening skills are crucial for understanding both spoken and written language. They are developed through activities such as listening to speech, audio materials, and participating in real or simulated communication. Listening training helps learners enhance their sensitivity to pronunciation, intonation, and context while exercising their ability to comprehend and interpret information in different contexts.

Speak. Speaking proficiency involves the correct and fluent use of language in communication. Learners develop this dimension through engaging in oral practices, role-playing, and actual conversations. Speaking training emphasizes accuracy in pronunciation, grammar usage, and the ability to express thoughts, while also enhancing communication skills and the ability to engage in effective conversations.

Read. Reading is a crucial avenue for acquiring information, understanding texts, and expanding vocabulary. By reading various literary works, articles, and texts, learners can improve their reading comprehension and cultural literacy. Reading training involves aspects such as word recognition, grammar analysis, understanding context, inferencing meaning, and also contributes to the development of critical thinking and analytical skills.

Write. Writing is a key skill for expressing thoughts, constructing grammatical structures, and conveying information. Through engaging in writing exercises, learners can enhance their grammar, vocabulary, and logical thinking abilities. Writing training includes composing essays, papers, diaries, etc., emphasizing grammatical accuracy, clarity of structure, and appropriate language usage.

2.4 Language Learning Strategies SILL

Language learning refers to the individual's process of acquiring the ability to communicate using a language. It involves the recognition, identification, recall, and reproduction of a series of sounds or symbols and their conventionally accepted meanings. Additionally, it encompasses understanding grammar rules and mastering the necessary motor skills for language use, such as pronunciation and writing.

In 1990, Rebecca Oxford classified language learning strategies and proposed the SILL model, categorizing language learning strategies into six modes [1].

Cognitive. Establishing connections between new information and existing knowledge, such as using grammatical inference or analysis as strategies for comprehension.

Mnemonic. Connecting new information with familiar information through the use of formulas, phrases, and poems.

Metacognitive. Optimizing learners' cognition by coordinating planning, organizing, and evaluating methods during the learning process.

Compensatory. Utilizing contextual content to make associations and compensate for missing information in reading and writing.

Affective. Regulating learners' emotions, motivation, and attitudes to maintain a positive learning mindset, facing challenges with optimism, and contributing to the development of good habits.

Social. Interacting with other learners to facilitate cultural understanding and cross-cultural communication, enabling learners to comprehend the cultural implications carried by the target language comprehensively and enhancing their cross-cultural sensitivity.

This study adopts the SILL for the analysis of the learning process, as it is a widely accepted and validated measurement tool in the field of foreign language education [23–25].

2.5 Social Context Characteristics Model

In the realm of multiplayer gaming, the sociability and interactivity components stand as indispensable elements within the context of gamified language learning. A wealth of research underscores the role of multiplayer games in augmenting player experiences and elevating gaming proficiency. Inkpen's investigation discerned disparities in performance between individuals engaged in solitary gameplay and those participating collectively. The outcomes underscored markedly superior performance among players engaged in collaborative play, particularly when sharing a common computing platform [17]. Studies by Mandryk and Ravaja, among others, posit that engaging in in-game battles with friends enhances player immersion and elicits more positive emotions in comparison to encounters with computer-controlled opponents [18, 19]. Ravaja's research reveals that players experience heightened excitement when engaging in battles with unfamiliar counterparts as opposed to computer adversaries, albeit not reaching the level of exhilaration attained when playing against friends [19].

It is apparent that the social interaction facet within multiplayer games plays a pivotal role in advancing both the player's gaming experience and proficiency, with a positive correlation observed in the realms of interaction intensity, social familiarity, and experiential enhancement. Existing research categorizes factors influencing the social gaming experience into three primary classes (see Fig. 1 Players, Game, and Setting [2]. This classification serves as a guiding framework for game designers in structuring social experiences embedded within the gaming environment.

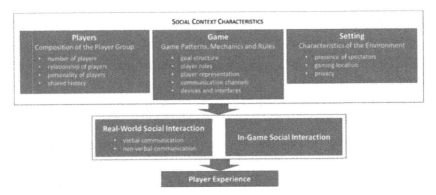

Fig. 1. Emmerich categorized factors influencing the in-game social interaction experience into three distinct classes.

2.6   MDA Game Design Framework

The MDA theory, proposed by Robin et al. in 2004, serves as a theoretical framework for dissecting the game design process. This framework endeavors to establish a bridge between game design, game analysis, and game technology. MDA, as a method, proves beneficial in comprehending game design, allowing designers to strategically plan game design solutions from a macro perspective [3]. As illustrated in Fig. 2 below, MDA stands for Mechanics, Dynamics, and Aesthetics, respectively, representing the components of game design.

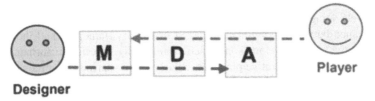

Fig. 2. The designer and player each have a different perspective.

3 The MPGBLL Model

3.1 Model Basic Components Overview

The traditional approach to language learning has long revolved around the four fundamental dimensions of listening, speaking, reading, and writing, each encompassing unique learning techniques and training methods. This study aims to integrate language education with gaming within the framework of traditional language learning. By introducing elements of party games, the study seeks to provide a more engaging and participatory approach to language learning.

In the process of achieving this goal, the study draws on the language learning strategy model SILL, the Game Design Theory (MDA), and the social context characteristics model, constructing an innovative framework for multiplayer language education game design (see Fig. 3). This framework is designed not only to enhance the effectiveness of language learning but also to stimulate learners' interest and motivation through the incorporation of gaming elements.

Firstly, the SILL is employed to assist learners in better understanding and applying learning strategies. By guiding learners to utilize different language learning techniques in a gaming environment, the study aims to deepen their understanding of language knowledge and boost confidence in language application.

Secondly, inspiration is drawn from the Game Design Theory (MDA), the combination of game mechanics, dynamics, and aesthetics to ensure that the game is both entertaining and academically enriching. By incorporating rich aesthetic elements into the game, the study seeks to evoke players' aesthetic experiences. Furthermore, by creating challenging and rewarding feedback systems, the framework aims to enhance learners' enthusiasm and proactivity in language learning.

Finally, the study combines the social context characteristics model, emphasizing the importance of multiplayer interaction. In the framework of multiplayer language

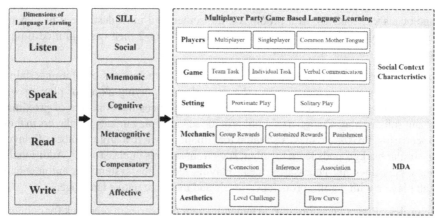

Fig. 3. MPGBLL, based on the MDA (Mechanics, Dynamics, Aesthetics) theory and the social context characteristics model, is constructed as a framework for multiplayer language education game design.

education game design, learners can engage in games with others, improving language communication skills through cooperation and competition. This social experience not only helps break the isolation of language learning but also establishes close connections among learners within the game.

Through this multidimensional language education game design framework, we aim to bring an innovative and dynamic learning approach to the field of language learning, while igniting learners' strong interest in language acquisition. The establishment of this research framework holds the potential to provide new perspectives and methods for advancing the field of language education.

3.2 The Concepts in the MPGBLL Model

Players. According to the characteristics of player groups, the game modes are divided into single-player mode and multiplayer mode to adapt to different learning needs. In single-player games, the pace is generally slower, making it easier for players to focus on the training content itself. This mode is suitable for training scenarios that require careful consideration, such as reading, writing, intensive listening, and intensive reading. In multiplayer games, the pace is faster, and players are more likely to focus on communication and interaction with other players. This mode is suitable for training scenarios that require quick responses, such as describing images or selecting pictures based on auditory prompts. Additionally, grouping players with the same native language into the same game session facilitates communication and interaction.

Game. In terms of the form of game content, the framework primarily provides gameplay objectives in the form of tasks. The task module is divided into single-player tasks and multiplayer tasks. Single-player tasks mainly involve reading and writing training, which players can independently complete. Multiplayer tasks involve listening and speaking training, requiring teamwork to accomplish. Furthermore, through a voice system, various gameplay modes with more diversity and closer interaction can be extended. As shown in Fig. 4 below, Player 1 and Player 2 are teammates. Player 1 receives an image or a short sentence as a prompt on the screen and must describe it to Player 2 through the voice system within a specified time. Player 2 then has a limited time to respond based on what they heard.

Setting. During gameplay, players' environmental characteristics exhibit uncertainty, such as playing with companions on the same device, playing alone, or playing with parental supervision. Therefore, the framework introduces the concepts of proximate play and solitary play. Designers should provide separate play modes for players in these two scenarios. Proximate play is suitable for situations where a large number of players with similar backgrounds learn together, such as in schools or classrooms. Additionally, solitary play does not necessarily mean playing alone; the system can automatically match players with similar proficiency levels and the same native language.

Mechanics. Player decisions during gameplay require a series of feedback for guidance and correction. Positive feedback should be applied when players make correct decisions, while negative feedback should be applied for incorrect decisions. There are various forms of feedback in game design, such as UI, sound effects, animations, and more.

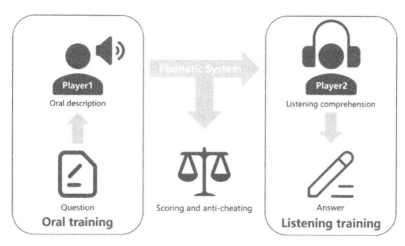

Fig. 4. Listening and speaking collaborative learning.

This framework adopts group rewards and customized rewards as core reward mechanisms, providing positive feedback. It encourages teamwork while requiring individual capabilities. The framework dynamically adjusts the weights and proportions of these rewards based on specific mode requirements. In modes emphasizing individual capability, the weight of customized rewards is higher, while in modes emphasizing teamwork, group rewards carry more weight. Additionally, the punishment mechanism serves as negative feedback to correct players' hasty decisions without thoughtful consideration.

Dynamics. Game dynamics are constructed around the three key elements of connection, inference, and association, guiding the design of core gameplay. Players are presented with numerous asymmetric game elements, including asymmetrical abilities, information asymmetry, challenges asymmetry, goal asymmetry, and more. In situations of asymmetry, players are required to establish information connections to facilitate communication and interaction [20]. Additionally, the game incorporates pre-set gameplay scenarios that assess reasoning abilities, such as grammar inference and vocabulary inference, aiming to enhance logical thinking in the context of second language application. Imaginative settings within the game guide players to engage in associative thinking, for example, playing in the park, on the basketball court, dining in the cafeteria, attending classes in a classroom, or working out in the gym.

Aesthetics. The study evaluates players' memory retention levels using Ebbinghaus' learning curve and the forgetting curve [21]. The Leitner system is employed for spaced repetition [22]. In the Leitner system, the priority of soon-to-be-forgotten knowledge is elevated, and learners are more frequently exposed to this knowledge. Therefore, quantifiable indicators based on the difficulty level of knowledge and learners' proficiency in specific content can be considered. Rational level design is employed, and appropriate training content is arranged for learners according to the Leitner system to maintain the state of flow.

4   Game Design of GetBack2Work

This section systematically introduces the specific gameplay and system design of Get-Back2Work. We will delve into the core mechanics of the game, emphasizing its unique multiplayer collaborative experience and the underlying academic value. GetBack2Work aims to promote close collaboration among players through the gamified form of academic tasks, fostering cognitive, communication, and teamwork skills behind the entertainment. Within this framework, we will elaborate on the game mechanics, room system, skill items, and other aspects of the design to comprehensively understand the academic background and design philosophy of the game.

In the multiplayer mode of GetBack2Work, teams are limited to two players, competing to complete assignments assigned by the teacher using the only laptop available. The team that completes the assignment first wins. In this setting, players can disregard all school rules to achieve higher scores. They can freely jump on tables, snatch others' computers, aggressively confront opponents, or find a corner to secretly work on assignments, aiming to be the first team to finish. This project provides players with a form of close collaboration to complete assignments, promoting communication and interaction among players. When a player earns points by completing assignments on the computer, teammates can choose to lift them to evade enemy pursuit or use fists to guard the teammate finishing the assignment. Visual feedback allows players to clearly understand their teammates' answering situations (see Fig. 5). Frequent incorrect answers add humor to the game and promote interactive communication among teammates.

Fig. 5. Cooperative gameplay and visual feedback.

The project features a common room system in multiplayer games, where players can create or join rooms with friends. In the room, players can freely switch teams and choose their preferred appearance to enter the game (see Fig. 6).

Fig. 6. Room list interface and in-room interface.

Players earn points through the assignment system, where both accuracy and answering speed are crucial (see Fig. 7). When under attack, the panel automatically closes, halting the answering process. Therefore, players should cooperate with teammates to evade enemy pursuit and find suitable opportunities to complete assignments.

Fig. 7. Writing exercise interface.

Furthermore, GetBack2Work provides players with diverse skill items to enhance gameplay (see Fig. 8). For example, the "Melody Disruption" skill can disrupt other players' actions, preventing opponents from completing assignments and testing players' hand-eye coordination.

Fig. 8. Skills and items.

After the player provides an answer, explicit feedback is given regardless of the accuracy of the response. In the case of a correct answer, the player is notified of the specific reward points earned, and the correct answer is highlighted in green. Conversely, when the answer is incorrect, the player's wrong choice is flagged in red, the correct answer is indicated in green, and the player is informed of the penalty points incurred (Fig. 9).

Fig. 9. Rewards and penalties.

5   Experimental Research

5.1   Experimental Design

This study invited high school seniors with diverse backgrounds to participate in a one-week controlled experiment. The participants were divided into three groups, with two being control groups and one being the experimental group. To eliminate the influence of prior knowledge possessed by the subjects, 30 students with the closest rankings in a recent knowledge test were selected for each group, with high school English chosen as the experimental content.

The control groups underwent training using traditional language learning methods and a popular commercial language education platform called "Duolingo." Meanwhile, the experimental group received training through a game developed specifically for this study. Subsequently, an analysis of the learning outcomes of the three groups was conducted to compare the effectiveness of different learning approaches (Table 1).

Table 1. Experimental example.

Group	Language learning approach
Experimental group	GetBack2Work (MPGBLL)
Blank group A	Duolingo
Blank group B	Conventional classroom language learning methods

5.2   Experimental Process

The experimental process in shown in Fig. 10.

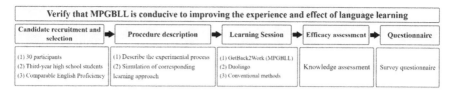

Fig. 10. Experimental process.

5.3 Learning Session

During the learning session, the experimental group engaged in comprehensive language learning using the "GetBack2Work" game developed based on the MPGBLL framework. This game encompassed various aspects of language learning, including listening, speaking, grammar, vocabulary, and writing.

Control group A utilized the widely popular gamified language learning platform, Duolingo, for language acquisition. Similar to the experimental group, the training modules covered pronunciation, listening, vocabulary, and other aspects.

Control group B adopted a traditional teaching approach that combined classroom instruction with homework assignments. Participants in this group followed the standard curriculum within the school environment, attending regular classes and completing assignments at home.

5.4 Experimental Results

In this experiment, the research conducted an analysis of participants' learning strategies to elucidate the most commonly and least frequently employed methods when learning a foreign language. To analyze the qualitative data gathered from interviews, the study employed a microanalysis using the grounded theory approach and conducted open and axial coding [26]. A series of codes were extracted from the interviews and then grouped into similar concepts. Based on these concepts, categories were generated, and their relationships within the qualitative data were analyzed.

This study quantified the participants' proficiency in using the six major language learning strategies through the SILL. Table 2 presents the levels of usage for these six strategy categories, along with the average levels. According to Oxford's definition [1], high usage falls within the average range of 3.5 to 5.0, moderate usage falls within the range of 2.5 to 3.5, and low usage falls within the range of 1.0 to 2.5.

Among the three groups of participants, the experimental group and control group A demonstrated high levels of strategy usage, with scores of 3.83 and 3.72, respectively. In contrast, control group B exhibited a moderate level of strategy usage, with a score of 3.49. Among the six learning strategies, the usage level of social strategies had an average score of only 2.71, indicating a lower usage level. Future development could focus on enhancing social strategies' practicality in gameplay, especially for control group A (2.34) and control group B (2.23), where participants were not actively engaging with other learners. Regarding the use of affective strategies, control group B scored only 1.9, suggesting that learners struggled to maintain a positive emotional state and attitude during the learning process (Tables 3, 4 and 5).

Table 2. The mean (M) scores of participants learning strategies.

	Experimental group	Group A	Group B	Mean
Cognitive strategies	3.78	3.96	3.87	3.87
Mnemonic strategies	3.73	4.65	4.45	4.28
Metacognitive strategies	4.20	4.25	4.51	4.43
Compensatory strategies	4.13	3.25	3.97	3.78
Affective strategies	3.54	3.85	1.90	3.10
Social strategies	3.58	2.34	2.23	2.71
Mean	3.83	3.72	3.49	
Total: n =30				

Data were coded as follows: 'always or almost always use the strategy' as 5, 'generally use the strategy' as 4, 'use the strategy somewhat' as 3, 'generally do not use the strategy as 2, 'never or almost never use the strategy' as 1.

6 Questionnaire Research

All participants involved in knowledge acquisition underwent the same questionnaire survey. Subsequently, the results of the survey were categorized and statistically analyzed based on groups in this study, yielding average scores for participants' evaluations of learning methods. The satisfaction levels with the gaming experience were comparable between the experimental group and control group A, while control group B exhibited a relatively lower satisfaction level in the gaming experience. The scores for the comfort of the learning environment were similar across all groups.

All three learning methods received acknowledgment, with a slight advantage observed in the learning method of the experimental group. Regarding the enjoyment during the learning process, control group B scored the lowest, indicating that participants tended to find traditional learning methods less enjoyable. In terms of the convenience

Table 3. The mean (M) scores and the standard-deviation (SD) scores of the five items measuring participant attitudes towards the program in experimental group.

Question	M	SD
Q1. I am satisfied that I learned from this experience	4.10	1.02
Q2. I felt comfortable in the learning environment	3.92	0.88
Q3. This is a good way to learn English	4.37	0.97
Q4. I enjoy the learning process	4.05	0.70
Q5. It is easy for me to learn English	3.87	1.13
Total: n = 10		

Data were coded as follows: 'strongly agree' as 5, 'agree' as 4, 'neutral' as 3, 'disagree' as 2, 'strongly disagree' as 1.

Table 4. The mean (M) scores and the standard-deviation (SD) scores of the five items measuring participant attitudes towards the program in blank group A.

Question	M	SD
Q1. I am satisfied that I learned from this experience	4.13	0.31
Q2. I felt comfortable in the learning environment	3.90	0.82
Q3. This is a good way to learn English	4.01	1.13
Q4. I enjoy the learning process	4.25	0.98
Q5. It is easy for me to learn English	3.98	1.27
Total: n = 10		

Data were coded as follows: 'strongly agree' as 5, 'agree' as 4, 'neutral' as 3, 'disagree' as 2, 'strongly disagree' as 1.

Table 5. The mean (M) scores and the standard-deviation (SD) scores of the five items measuring participant attitudes towards the program in blank group B

Question	M	SD
Q1. I am satisfied that I learned from this experience	3.20	1.02
Q2. I felt comfortable in the learning environment	3.92	0.88
Q3. This is a good way to learn English	4.10	0.97
Q4. I enjoy the learning process	3.25	0.70
Q5. It is easy for me to learn English	3.77	1.13
Total: n = 10		

Data were coded as follows: 'strongly agree' as 5, 'agree' as 4, 'neutral' as 3, 'disagree' as 2, 'strongly disagree' as 1.

of learning, control group A scored the highest, with the experimental group and control group B scoring close to each other. It is evident that there is a need for simplification and improved clarity in the game mechanism design of this project to reduce the learning costs for players.

7 Discussion and Conclusion

This study integrates experimental and survey methods to collect data from various teaching approaches, validating the positive impact of party games on the learning experience. Furthermore, it conducts a detailed analysis of the correlation among factors influencing the learning experience. During the experimental phase, the primary focus was on measuring and collecting data on users' levels of learning strategy utilization to assess the effectiveness of the learning methods. Utilizing the SILL learning strategy assessment model for analysis, it concludes that party games significantly affect the gamified experience in language education.

In comparison to traditional language teaching methods, the party game instructional approach demonstrates advantages in terms of higher average levels of strategy application and better user evaluations. These advantages manifest in more engaging learning experiences, a more comfortable learning environment, and simpler learning steps. When compared with existing commercialized language education platforms in the market, the party game instructional approach stands out in terms of social experience and the level of social strategy utilization. Additionally, it exhibits a noticeable improvement in the mean value of language learning strategy utilization, indicating a more balanced, professional approach that maximizes the application of strategies.

Among the three groups of subjects, the experimental group exhibited the highest frequency of learning strategy utilization. This is attributed to the game design of GetBack2Work, which aligns with the MPGBLL framework. The game design effectively guides players in applying learning strategies, presenting challenges to players in terms of both the depth and breadth of learning strategies. In contrast, Control Group B, corresponding to traditional classroom teaching methods, demonstrated the lowest level of learning strategy utilization, particularly in emotional and social strategies. This teaching method prioritizes knowledge itself rather than interpersonal connections, leading learners to focus more on their mastery of knowledge and less on their emotions and learning motivation.

Among the six types of strategies, social and emotional strategies were the least utilized. However, even the least utilized level of learning strategies still reached an average range of moderate usage. Introducing elements akin to free discussion segments found in games like Among Us within the gameplay might further enhance the levels of social and emotional strategy utilization. This presents a potential direction for future exploration in this research.

In the survey section, the collected questionnaires exhibit high reliability and validity, making their data suitable for research analysis. However, some questions related to game experience still suffer from broad descriptions and low variability, and they should be optimized in conjunction with actual language learning experiences and game experiences. Based on the results of the questionnaire survey, this study attempts to provide a brief summary analysis.

Participants in Control Group B gave significantly lower scores for Q4 compared to the other two groups, indicating that traditional learning methods still present experiences that learners find difficult to endure. However, the scores for Q3 among the three groups are very close, reflecting the participants' overall acceptance of the learning methods, even though there are still some pain points during the learning process. Participants in Control Group A gave slightly higher scores for Q5 compared to the experimental group and Control Group B. This is attributed to the simple gamification elements incorporated in Duolingo, such as matching, sorting, treasure chests, and scoring.

Introducing game elements and game design into traditional language learning solutions can enhance learning motivation and reduce aversion. Many existing language education platforms primarily adopt single-player quiz-based learning mechanisms involving simple gaming elements such as points, rankings, and treasure chests. However, these platforms often lack substantial cooperative or competitive gameplay between players, resulting in a relatively monotonous and less replayable experience.

In this study, the introduction of multiplayer party games as a teaching aid aims to enhance learning motivation, reduce aversion, and facilitate social interaction among players during the teaching process. During gameplay, players engage in a significant amount of cooperation and competition. The immersive experience allows players to accept the repetition and monotony inherent in the learning process, and the high level of concentration enhances the effectiveness of learning.

The MPGBLL provides a holistic framework for multiplayer game design in language learning. It focuses on basic dimensions of language learning including listening, speaking, reading, and writing. And on this basis, it extends language learning strategies to game design approaches with MDA framework and social context characteristics model. This framework explores the potential integration of educational and party games, offering educational game researchers a more comprehensive design template and presenting a practical new approach for the field of language education.

7.1 Limitations

Due to limitations in experimental conditions, the discussions in this paper are confined to the context of this particular project. Further experiments will be conducted in the future to validate whether similar results can be obtained in other party education games. Additionally, there are still some issues regarding the balance between playing and learning in GetBack2Work. In a multiplayer game session, only one player can be in a learning state at a given time, while the other three players are in a playing state. Although each player has the opportunity to engage in learning, there is an imbalance in the proportion of playing and learning. Subsequent development will consider introducing gameplay that allows multiple players to learn simultaneously to achieve a better balance between the two aspects of playing and learning.

Acknowledgments. GetBack2Work attributes its exceptional level of completion, outstanding playability, and numerous innovative ideas to the year-long, continuous efforts of our seven dedicated team members, coupled with the unwavering support from Professor Sun Xing and Professor Fang Ke. We extend our heartfelt gratitude to each team member for their dedication and contributions, commemorating this wonderful and fulfilling period with this paper.

References

1. Oxford, R.L.: Language Learning Strategies: What Every Teacher Should Know (1990)
2. Emmerich, K., Masuch, M.: The impact of game patterns on player experience and social interaction in co-located multiplayer games. In: Proceedings of the Annual Symposium on Computer-Human Interaction in Play, pp. 411–422 (2017)
3. Hunicke, R., LeBlanc, M., Zubek, R.: MDA: a formal approach to game design and game research. In: Proceedings of the AAAI Workshop on Challenges in Game AI, vol. 4, no. 1, p. 1722 (2004)
4. Stager, G.: Seymour papert-father of educational computing. Nature **537**(7620), 308 (2016)
5. Diamond, A.: Want to optimize executive functions and academic outcomes? Simple, just nourish the human spirit. In: Minnesota Symposia on Child Psychology: Developing cognitive control processes: Mechanisms, implications, and interventions. Hoboken, NJ, USA: John Wiley & Sons, Inc., vol. 37, pp. 203–230 (2013).

6. Betzel, R.F., Satterthwaite, T.D., Gold, J.I., et al.: Positive affect, surprise, and fatigue are correlates of network flexibility. Sci. Rep. **7**(1), 520 (2017)
7. Piaget, J.: Play, Dreams and Imitation in Childhood. Routledge (2013)
8. Ansteeg, L.W.: Incidental lexicon acquisition through playful interaction. Int. J. Emerg. Technol. Learn. **10**(1), 4 (2015). https://doi.org/10.3991/ijet.v10i1.4156
9. Hays, R.T.: Effectiveness of Instructional Games: A Literature Review and Discussion (2005)
10. Gee, J.P.: What video games have to teach us about learning and literacy. Comput. Entertain. **1**(1), 1–4 (2003). https://doi.org/10.1145/950566.950595
11. Dalton, G., Devitt, A.: Irish in a 3D world: engaging primary school children. Lang. Learn. Technol. **20**(1), 21–33 (2016)
12. Cornillie, F., Clarebout, G., Desmet, P.: Between learning and playing? Exploring learners' perceptions of corrective feedback in an immersive game for English pragmatics. ReCALL **24**(3), 257–278 (2012). https://doi.org/10.1017/S0958344012000146
13. Reinders, H., Wattana, S.: Can I say something? The effects of digital game play on willingness to communicate. Lang. Learn. Technol. **18**(2), 101–123 (2014)
14. Palaiogiannis, A.: Using video games to foster strategy development and learner autonomy within a secondary school context. Res. Pap. Lang. Teach. Learn. **5**(1), 259–277 (2014)
15. Hwang, G.J., Hsu, T.C., Lai, C.L., Hsueh, C.J.: Interaction of problem-based gaming and learning anxiety in language students' English listening performance and progressive behavioral patterns. Comput. Educ. **106**, 26–42 (2017). https://doi.org/10.1016/j.compedu.2016.11.010
16. Fan, S., Zou, D., Haoran Xie, F., Wang, L.: A comparative review of mobile and non-mobile games for language learning. SAGE Open **11**(4), 215824402110672 (2021). https://doi.org/10.1177/21582440211067247
17. Inkpen, K., Booth, K.S., Klawe, M., et al.: Playing together beats playing apart, especially for girls. In: The First International Conference on Computer Support for Collaborative Learning, CSCL 1995, Bloomington, IN, USA (1995)
18. Mandryk, R.L., Inkpen, K.M., Calvert, T.W.: Using psychophysiological techniques to measure user experience with entertainment technologies. Behav Inf. Technol. **25**(2), 141–158 (2006)
19. Ravaja, N., Saari, T., Turpeinen, M., et al.: Spatial presence and emotions during video game playing: does it matter with whom you play? Teleoperators Virtual Environ. **15**(4), 381–392 (2006)
20. Harris, J., Hancock, M.: To asymmetry and beyond! Improving social connectedness by increasing designed interdependence in cooperative play. In: Proceedings of the 2019 CHI Conference on Human Factors in Computing Systems, pp. 1–12 (2019).
21. Anzanello, M.J., Fogliatto, F.S.: Learning curve models and applications: literature review and research directions. Int. J. Ind. Ergon. **41**(5), 573–583 (2011)
22. Smolen, P., Zhang, Y., Byrne, J.H.: The right time to learn: mechanisms and optimization of spaced learning. Nat. Rev. Neurosci. **17**(2), 77–88 (2016)
23. Griffiths, C.: Patterns of language learning strategy use. System **31**(3), 367–383 (2003)
24. Hsiao, T.Y., Oxford, R.L.: Comparing theories of language learning strategies: a confirmatory factor analysis. Mod. Lang. J. **86**(3), 368–383 (2002)
25. Oxford, R., Nyikos, M.: Variables affecting choice of language learning strategies by university students. Mod. Lang. J. **73**(3), 291–300 (1989)
26. Strauss, A., Corbin, J.: Basics of Qualitative Research. Sage (1990)

The Challenge of Perception Tower: Fine Art Education Game Design Based on Visual Thinking Strategies

Yuan Zeng, Wei Huang, and Xiaomei Nie[✉]

Shenzhen International Graduate School, Tsinghua University, Beijing, China
zeng-y21@mails.tsinghua.edu.cn, nie.xiaomei@sz.tsinghua.edu.cn

Abstract. Integrating the concept of gamified learning into the field of fine art education is gradually becoming a new trend. However, existing multimedia practices and game applications in design still have shortcomings, such as a lack of clear teaching objectives and rich interactive elements, making it challenging to achieve a balance between educational and gameplay. In light of this, this study developed the Perceptual Tower Challenge—a game for fine art education that combines visual thinking strategies with educational game design methods. The game sets clear and relevant goals, encouraging learners to explore and express themselves through seeing, imagining, and drawing. It balances the transmission of conceptual art knowledge with the promotion of active creative practice, aiming to enhance the performance of art education games in terms of teaching effectiveness and user experience. A pilot study preliminarily verified the positive impact of the game in enhancing learning experiences and initiative.

Keywords: Edutainment/Education games · Art education · Visual thinking

1 Introduction

Fine arts education plays an indispensable role in modern society. It not only promotes exchanges with multiple visual forms but also disseminates culture, inspires creativity, and serves society significantly.

However, current art education faces a series of challenges, such as relying on traditional classroom and community settings, limiting the flexibility of teaching in terms of time and space. Additionally, in China, the prevalence of exam-oriented education emphasizes exam-focused curriculum and skill training in art education, neglecting innovation and personalized development, which may demotivate students [1].

To address these challenges, integrating the concept of gamified learning into art education has become an emerging trend. There are some examples. *Tilt Brush*, a VR painter developed by Google, is applied to art education [2]; *Artsology* a visual arts teaching website, has launched over 100 arts education games for kids [3]; Nintendo released *Art*

Academy[1], which is a series of arts training software; French Ministry of Education proposed that Centre Pompidou and two games companies jointly develop *Prisme-7*[2], an arts education game. With features of dynamic interaction, instant feedback, visual expression, and goal orientation, game-based learning has been proven effective in improving learning motivation and learning effect [4], providing a new perspective for the future development of fine arts education.

Nevertheless, investigation and survey show that the existing multimedia practice and game applications are defective in design. For example, they are short of clear teaching objectives or rich interactive elements, which easily cause students to lose learning motivation. Thus, they are gradually unable to meet the growing demand for fine art education.

In view of this, this research develops an art education game named The Challenge of Perception Tower. The design purpose is to combine the functions of education and gameplay. In terms of education, it takes into account both the imparting of conceptual knowledge of art and the enhancement of initiative creative practice; in terms of gameplay, it provides rich interactive functions and instant feedback on the results of interactions. Advanced real-time visual effects technologies are applied in game development to provide multiple learning activities, including dynamic creation challenges and visual cognition tasks, and build a learning environment that encourages learners to improve their observation, imagination, and drawing skills. Such a colorful and attractive art learning style not only offers a better learning effect and experience for learners but also facilitates the development of the core literacy of fine arts.

2 Related Work

2.1 Fine Art Education Game

Digital games not only provide a new perspective for examining traditional teaching methods but also bring a series of innovative possibilities to educational practice. Crompton et al. [5] point out that although the application of digital games in art education classes is still in a preliminary stage, the potential educational value embedded in their production process, visual characteristics, content, and related processes should not be overlooked. Corrales Serrano [6] designed course content using gamification strategies for art history teaching over three academic years, positively impacting students' learning and fostering favorable views on art and heritage. Furthermore, research by Hwang et al. [7] has shown that employing digital game methods, such as TT-DGA, can effectively enhance students' learning outcomes in recognizing and appreciating art styles.

This article will further analyze the categories of games related to art education and explore how these games impact the practice of art education. Games related to art education are a relatively broad concept, and a clear corresponding category has not yet been formed on mainstream gaming platforms, including Steam and Google Play. Through the research, the following three categories were broadly classified according to the purpose of the design.

---

[1] https://nintendo.fandom.com/wiki/Art_Academy_(series).

[2] https://prisme7.io/.

Category I. Games not designed for art education but applicable to art education practice, such as *The Legend of Zelda*[3], *Gorogoa*[4], and *Monument Valley*[5]. Games as an art form, some are of exquisite and unique visual style, displaying a strong aesthetic attribute, and some are associated with art history in narrative theme or artistic expression. Both can be applied in fine arts education. Martyniuk [8] used games as a tool for art education in his study and designed a teaching guide according to the three phases of visual literacy.

Category II. Games that make drawing the core gameplay. For example, *Passpartout*[6] and *Chicory: A Colorful Tale*[7], all focus on playfulness; *Tilt Brush*, and *Occupy White Walls*[8], focus on the painting experience. Although these games are not designed for art education, their painting operation is a kind of creative activity, able to enhance the artistic expression ability and stimulate the creativity of players to a certain extent. Therefore, they are of a certain function of art education.

Category III. Games designed solely for art education, which is the focus of this paper. Although the visual arts teaching website *Artsology* has launched over 100 arts education games for kids, these various games are relatively homogeneous in gameplay, and the integration of teaching content and game content should be improved. For example, in *Art History Puzzles*, fine artworks are only used as Jigsaw patterns; in *Vermeer Breakout Game*, the painting *Girl with a Pearl Earring* is pixilated to use as materials for breaking bricks. Though incorporating art elements, these games focus only on the external visual features of the artworks, failing to explore their intrinsic meaning and richness. Nintendo also launched *Art Academy*, a series of painting education games, in order to promote the touch screen and stylus features of its game consoles. Presented in the form of drawing skills courses, the game divides the painting process into easily understood tasks. So long as learners follow the steps of the course exactly, they will draw paintings that closely resemble the templates provided in the game. Knowledge about visual elements and principles is interspersed in the process, to train players' image reading and artistic expression ability. Nevertheless, IGN [9] commented that may not be a real game, for it is composed of courses and skill exercises. If players conduct each step correctly all the time, their painting content will not be traced, which reflects the lack of interaction to a certain extent. Similarly, for the art education game *Prisme7*, though containing the wisdom of education experts and game design experts, designers still expressed in an interview that [10], game players encountered problems, indicating that "the content is obscure", "teacher intervention is required", and "the interaction is not strong enough".

In conclusion, the first two categories generally lack clear teaching objectives, for they are not designed for art education, while the third category lacks rich interactive elements, perhaps because they emphasize too much the immersive art experience.

---

[3] https://zelda.nintendo.com/.
[4] https://gorogoa.com/.
[5] https://www.monumentvalleygame.com/mvpc.
[6] https://www.passpartoutgame.com/.
[7] https://chicorygame.com/.
[8] https://www.oww.io/.

Therefore, to balance the educational function and recreational function of art education games, it is necessary to carry out further exploration and in-depth study.

The key to educational game design lies in creating an environment that fosters exploratory learning, where the learning experience is closely intertwined with the gaming experience. The MDA (Mechanics, Dynamics, Aesthetics) framework [11] supports a formal, iterative approach to design and tuning, emphasizing how design decisions impact user experience. Krath's research [4] distilled theoretical principles helpful in explaining gamification, including setting clear and relevant goals, guided paths, providing immediate feedback, positive reinforcement, simplifying the user experience, and others. Successful educational game design requires effectively integrating educational objectives with gameplay to create an engaging, participatory, and effective learning experience.

2.2 Visual Thinking

Visual thinking refers to the ability to process information and think through visual perception, forming the basis for understanding and creating visual artworks. Arnheim has stated that visual perception is strongly identified with creative thinking and precedes language [12]. McKim expanded on Arnheim's concept of visual thinking in his discussion of design thinking and the creative process, describing the interplay between seeing, imagining, and drawing [13]. He proposed a series of methods and strategies to help learners develop and strengthen their visual thinking abilities.

Subsequent researchers, Park and Kim [14] based on theories related to visual thinking, proposed a visual reasoning model (see Fig. 1), elucidating cognitive activities and functioning in the visual thinking process. In this model, the processes of observation, imagination, and drawing are not only closely connected to knowledge and schemas but also form a key component of visual cognition in design. It emphasizes the importance of the iterative steps of observation, imagination, and drawing. Through this cyclical process, designers can refine creative design solutions from initial sketches. Here, the observation process involves perception, analysis, and interpretation, while the imagining process can be classified as generation, transformation, or maintenance. The drawing process enables representation through both ways to internalize and to externalize. Kim et al.'s research [15] showed that this model helps develop design support tools, especially in expressing imagination quickly and accurately.

Visual thinking plays a significant role in art education [16], aiding learners in understanding and interpreting artworks through visual information. Broadly, visual thinking strategies are a series of methods and techniques developed on this basis to enhance an individual's ability to think deeply and innovate through visual elements. For example, Zhang et al.'s research [17] developed a drawing system for children collaborating with artificial intelligence based on visual thinking theories.

Specific Visual Thinking Strategies (VTS), as developed by Housen and Yenawine, is an educational method aimed at enhancing visual literacy [18]. It involves presenting carefully selected art images and guiding students to deeply observe and discuss them, stimulating their thinking and inquiry. The hallmark of VTS is its questioning approach: starting with "What's going on in this picture?" to initiate discussion; followed by "What

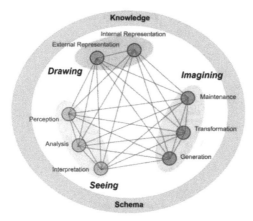

Fig. 1. Visual Reasoning Model (Park and Kim 2007) [14].

do you see that makes you say that?" to encourage students to provide evidence for their observations; and "What more can we find?" to expand and deepen understanding of the artwork. This method encourages students to think critically about art, aiding in the development of their visual literacy.

3 Method

The framework of this game (see Fig. 2) focuses on the concept of visual elements. It combines the three core elements of visual imagery, namely, seeing, imagining and drawing, with game mechanics, dynamics, and aesthetics, aiming to upgrade players' image reading and creative practice ability.

In terms of educational function, the game tasks are designed according to the four core elements of concept-based instruction [19], that is, collaborative thinking, conceptual perspective, guided teaching, and guiding questions. Each sub-task is presented in the form of art practice, disciplinary knowledge and conceptual understanding, to improve players' understanding of conceptual knowledge. For the design of narration, the way of observing and questioning artworks in VTS is adopted to guide players to think.

3.1 Concept

The concepts of seven basic visual elements [20] are made into visual element orbs, serving as the main resource of the game. The core gameplay is to collect and use these element orbs. Players take on the role of an apprentice who can exert visual magic by manipulating a drawing stick and can change the magic with visual element orbs. To become a qualified Mage, players must go to a mysterious continent and take on the challenge of Perception Tower. In this process, players unlock balls of knowledge and power in the tower and complete tasks to gain rewards for element orbs. Collecting crystals can upgrade the drawing stick, unlock new shape brush and color scheme, and

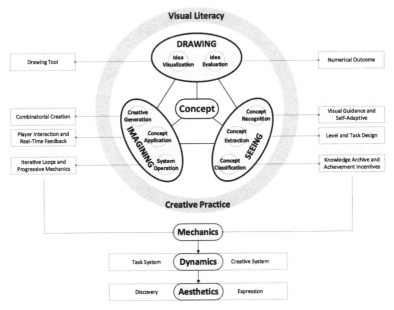

Fig. 2. Game Design Framework

create more personalized powerful magic. Under the guidance of Perception Tower, players will learn the use of various visual elements to explore and fight, and more importantly, to understand and express the deep aesthetics of this world. The detailed design of visual element orbs is shown in the following Table 1.

3.2 Seeing Mechanics

The following mechanics target the three activities involved in seeing, that is, perception, analysis, and interpretation.

Self-adaptive visual guidance mechanics aims to improve the player's perception or concept recognition (see Fig. 3). This mechanism runs throughout the game and adjusts dynamically based on the number of attempts by the player. Starting with weak visual cues, if the player encounters difficulties (such as failing several times or staying too long), it will give strong guidance to help the player get through. It provides a smoother game experience while reducing the cognitive load of players.

The level and task mechanics aims to encourage players to analyze, or concept extraction. Players need to explore the map, to collect various balls scattered in different levels. Each ball represents a task, and finishing the task will be rewarded with visual element orbs and crystals. There are two types of tasks (see Fig. 4). The first is painting matching. To be specific, players, guided by the narration and by clicking buttons, extract visual elements that most match a famous painting; the second is visual perception, that is, to complete tests related to visual perception with operations of click, scroll, and drag, guided by the narration.

Table 1. List of Visual Element Orbs.

Type	Concepts Corresponding to Visual Element Orbs				
Space	Scale	Displacement	Negative Space	Depth Layers	Rotation
Line	Solid-Dotted Change	Thickness Change	Curvature Change	Outline	
Shape	Square	Circle	Triangle	Decorative Pattern	Transformation
Value	Highlight	Shadow	Contrast	Transparency	Grayscale Gradient
Color	Monochrome	Adjacent Colors	Complementary Colors	Triadic Colors	Warm and Cool Colors
Movement	Noise	Jitter	Directionality	Trajectory	Diffusion
Rhythm	Frequency	Establishing Expectation	Ease In and Ease Out	Secondary Action	Acceleration and Deceleration

Fig. 3. In-game Visual Guidance, including Marker Hints, Bubble Tips, and Dialogue Pop-ups.

Fig. 4. Collect Visual Element Orbs through Tasks.

The knowledge archive and achievement incentives aim to encourage players to interpret, or concept classification. The first collection of a new type of visual element orb will open the knowledge archive, and players need to redraw the concept diagram according to their understanding (see Fig. 5). In the knowledge archive, players can classify and organize the visual element orbs they collected, and read related information to deepen their understanding of concepts. Besides, the archive can display the collection progress and provide visual feedback, so that players can see the learning results and missing parts directly. It also offers achievement incentives to players based on their collection progress.

Fig. 5. Obtain and Use the Knowledge Archive.

3.3 Imagining Mechanics

The following mechanics target the three activities involved in imagining, or generation, transformation, and maintenance.

The space provided for players to freely engage in the combinatorial creation of visual elements aims to encourage the generation of creativity. This is facilitated through the use of the drawing board and visual element orbs. Players can create various real-time visual effects, or special effects, composed of a main part and several minor parts. First, players create the main part by drawing a single-color strip on the drawing board, and then adjust it using different visual element orbs. For example, scale orbs can be used to enlarge the strip, or single-color orbs to add color variation. After completing the main part, players adopt the same method to create the minor parts. The interaction between visual element orbs and the drawing content provides players with a rich creative space (see Fig. 6).

Fig. 6. Draw Content and Use Visual Element Orbs.

The interactive operation and instant feedback mechanism encourage players to make further attempts and take full advantage of resources, to conduct transformation. In the course of play, players' creative content is closely tied with real-time visual effects, forming direct and strong feedback and displaying players' creative results. This encourages players to continue to use various resources and techniques to make more diversified works. To increase the interactivity and diversity of resources, there is a shop in the game, where transactions can be made with crystal obtained in tasks. The transactions include a lucky draw to obtain a different type of visual element orb, direct exchange for a given visual element orb, and purchase of a blank element orb, on which custom patterns and color schemes can be drawn and stored (see Fig. 7).

Fig. 7. Shop Transactions and Upgrade the Drawing Wand.

Progressive mechanics and iterative loops are adopted to maintain system operation. The progressive mechanism is a lock-key mechanism, where the design challenge is the lock and the player's ability is the key. Each level is composed of a main challenge and a sub-challenge. The sub-challenge is about drawing tasks related to visual effects, such as drawing a flame or spring for NPC; while the main challenge requests players to complete more complicated design tasks, in order to defeat the boss of the level. Each boss has its weakness, which consists of specific magic (design theme) and tips (design principle). Players create effects with the drawing board and visual element orbs to challenge the boss and trigger the judgment through dialogue with NPC (see Fig. 8). The judgment basis is that the player's design product is in line with the design theme and design principle. Upon the completion of each challenge, players gain more power and can unlock the next level and more complicated challenge. The iterative loop of the main challenge means that players need to constantly innovate the same design content to meet new design themes and principles.

Fig. 8. Use Drawing Tools to Trace the Wand's Path and Display Effects.

3.4 Drawing

Drawing tools can help players to conduct external representation, or idea visualization. There are interactive objects in the game and are available via an intuitive and easy-to-use interface. From the perspective of the player, the left side of the screen is the drawing board and various drawing tools, the right side displays the visual effects generated in real time, and the bottom of the screen is set with a hotkey column and a store bag for visual element orbs available. When selecting an element orb, a value button subject to fine adjustments will appear at the bottom of the screen (see Fig. 6).

The assessment rule displays value results, aiding players in conducting internal representation, or idea evaluation. This rule assesses performance across multiple dimensions, comprehensively valuing player achievements from various aspects. It includes the base attack value, which reflects the degree of matching with the boss's weakness, and the element orbs value, indicative of the player's ability to utilize visual elements. A variable divisor is also employed for balance adjustment. Besides, an extra multiplication bonus is applied, providing a 1.5 times score increase for players who surpass the base level. This forms a positive feedback loop that encourages exploration.

3.5 Dynamics and Aesthetics

Task System and Exploration. The cycle of the task system provides players with goals and motivation to collect resources, bringing an aesthetic experience of exploration.

During task completion, such as solving painting matching and visual perception tests, players continuously collect visual element orbs and crystals. This process sparks players' curiosity, urging them to explore various orb fortresses and environments, fostering their perception and understanding of visual elements. An adaptive visual guidance mechanism, such as providing visual hints and assistance, helps players continually discover new knowledge and challenges during exploration. The process of redrawing concept diagrams in the knowledge archive is not only a consolidation of learned knowledge but also a visual reflection of exploration achievements, enhancing the game's exploratory aesthetics.

Creative System and Expression. The cycle of the creative system encourages players to create content through immediate feedback on real-time visual effects, offering an aesthetic experience of expression.

Players create unique visual effects and magic through a combination of drawing boards and visual element orbs. This process requires not only an understanding of visual elements but also the display of creativity and individuality in real-time creation. Every choice a player makes directly impacts their creative output, thus forming a unique personal imprint in the game. The combat power evaluation rules provide direct feedback on the creative content, further motivating players to explore and experiment in creative expression. Moreover, upgrades to the drawing wand and unlocking new drawing capabilities continuously provide players with a sense of progress and growth in the game, reinforcing the aesthetic experience of expression.

The task and creative systems interweave, forming an organic environment for learning and creation. Exploration and expression together define the emotional and experiential depth of the game, allowing players to discover in exploration and create in expression.

4 Process and Result

This section provides implementation details for the Challenge of Perception Tower game, addressing aspects related to the software architecture and technologies used.

The game project is developed on the Windows 11 system using Unreal Engine 5.2. Unreal Engine offers several advantages: (1) It features the Niagara VFX System[9], a powerful visual effects editing tool with a node-based interface and modular components. This allows developers precise control over particle properties, meeting the core requirements for real-time visual effects and dynamic interaction with game environment data in this project. (2) Unreal Engine provides a third-person template, and the marketplace offers a plethora of models, animations, blueprint tools, and plugin assets, making it user-friendly and significantly reducing development difficulty. Therefore, this game can be independently developed by an artist with basic programming skills. The system architecture is divided into the interaction layer, presentation layer, logic layer, and data layer, and the game implementation approach is briefly described.

4.1 Interaction Layer

The interaction layer records players' basic operations through software and hardware inputs and interactive interfaces. It uses a drawing system based on runtime virtual textures to record player drawing input. In drawing mode, players can select different brush shapes, long-press, and move the mouse within the canvas to draw. The drawing content is recorded in the render target via virtual texture materials, which can be called by the presentation layer and logic layer.

4.2 Presentation Layer

In addition to the basic components like models, materials, rendering, animations, and audio, a real-time visual effects solution within the game is built based on the Niagara system. Render targets and numerical parameters are passed into template materials, processed, and applied to different Niagara particle emitter templates. Multiple emitters form a particle system, allowing real-time modification by the logic layer blueprint using custom and preset parameters. Custom material functions and module scripts were used to achieve specific functionalities required by the project, such as a procedural color matching function for harmonizing colors in color-based visual element orbs and a blur sampling function for achieving a blurred effect on certain line-based visual element orbs. Niagara custom module scripts were developed to optimize the representation of Ribbon effects when players swing the wand and enhance the flexibility of effect asset usage using an adaptive size module.

Post-processing materials were used to achieve different screen representations for different levels, visually presenting the progressive relationship of visual elements within the perceptual tower. Line and space levels use a line outline shader to emphasize the structural boundaries of objects with thick lines, making it easier for players to focus on

---

[9] https://docs.unrealengine.com/5.2/en-US/creating-visual-effects-in-niagara-for-unreal-eng ine/.

key interactive elements in the early stages of the game. The tone level uses a grayscale tone shader to emphasize the grayscale contrast of light and shadow, converting colors into corresponding grayscale values through a weighted average method and adding noise textures to enhance the visual texture. The color and rhythm levels use a colored cartoon shader to enhance the stylized visuals and hand-drawn aesthetics by increasing the blockiness of objects under lighting, minimizing surface normals and micro-normal details, and introducing additional Fresnel edge lighting.

4.3 Logic Layer

In the item interaction logic, the UE5 Inventory and Item System asset[10] is used to swiftly create a basic item interaction system, inventory system, hotkey bar, and currency system for collecting, managing, using, and trading visual element orbs.

For dialogue interaction logic, the Dialogue Plugin asset[11] is utilized to visually create player-NPC dialogue content in a rapid manner. By inserting events and conditional judgments into the dialogue table, players can receive and verify tasks through interactions with NPCs.

In drawing interaction logic, the first step is to obtain the render target input from the interaction layer. Subsequently, by applying techniques such as simplification, pixelation, edge detection, and particle effects in the material, the player's drawing content is stylized. Additionally, through custom functions to compare pixels, the player's drawing range is determined. Finally, by modifying the material parameter sets and Niagara parameter sets in the blueprint, the visual effects of the presentation layer are influenced. The specific design is illustrated in the diagram below.

4.4 Data Layer

In the data layer, we not only record basic in-game data but also capture player behavior data through data tracking points (see Fig. 9).

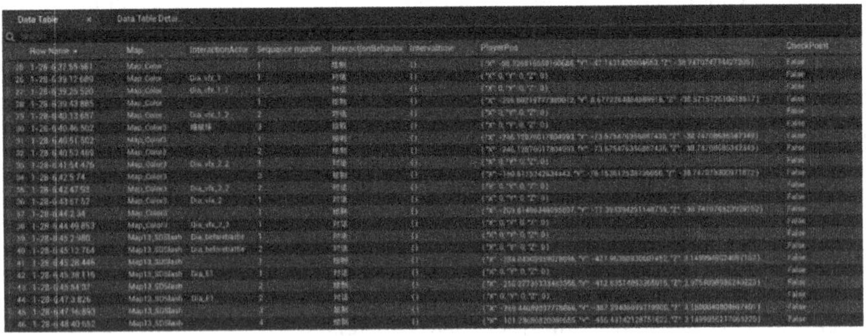

Fig. 9. Partial Player Behavior Data Table.

---

[10] https://www.unrealengine.com/marketplace/en-US/product/inventory-item-system.
[11] https://www.unrealengine.com/marketplace/en-US/product/dialogue-plugin?lang=en-US.

These data points can essentially reconstruct the player's experience of the game, helping to validate whether the player's actual behavior aligns with the design intent. The implementation involves placing markers at key positions where player actions, such as triggering dialogues, tasks, entering drawing mode, and picking up items, can be observed in the game. Then, a data table is created with the current time as the row name, recording information such as the player's current level, interaction actor, interaction behavior, and interval time, which is then entered into the corresponding data table. Particularly, when the player completes a drawing, the render target is exported in PNG format, saving the player's drawn image for populating the in-game catalog and external analysis.

5   Pilot User Study

The main objective of the pilot experiment was, following the completion of prototype development, to assess the realization of game design goals and its impact on participants' learning experiences and motivations through the use of automatically collected player behavior data, survey questionnaires, and interviews.

We recruited 5 players (3 female, 2 male, all aged between 19 and 24 years old) for a pilot test, with each participant undergoing an average of 20 min of testing. During this phase, the game automatically collected behavioral data from the players. Following the experience, players were required to complete a survey and participate in a 5 to 10-min one-on-one interview.

Analysis of the data buried point revealed that, on average, players spent 1 min and 21 s on a single quest, achieving a quest accuracy rate of 69.23%. In the challenge section, players showed an average drawing time of 2 min and 41 s, attempting an average of 3.68 visual element balls. These findings were literally in line with the initial goals of the game design.

The survey, utilizing a 5-point Likert scale, assessed participants' learning experiences and initiative. In terms of learning experiences, the study drew on Fu et al.'s EGameFlow scale [21], based on the game flow theory, evaluating participants across six dimensions: Concentration, Goal Clarity, Feedback, Challenge, Autonomy, and Immersion. For learning initiative, Keller's ARCS learning motivation model and the IMMS scale have proven to be effective tools for studying computer-based learning environments [22]. The study employed the IMMS scale to assess participants in terms of Attention, Relevance, Confidence, and Satisfaction.

Survey analysis (see Table 2) indicated an overwhelming positive evaluation from participants, with an overall average score of 4.02. Participants expressed positive attitudes toward the experience across most aspects, with Feedback receiving the highest satisfaction score of 4.4 on average, reflecting the game's excellent performance in providing timely feedback. Despite a limited sample size, these initial results suggest positive impacts across multiple dimensions, warranting further investigation.

Interviews provided a more nuanced understanding of learners' subjective experiences. The interviews focused on participants' perspectives regarding the game's playability, enjoyment, and ease of learning, recorded with participants' consent. The analysis revealed that four players found the real-time change of visual effects through the brush to be a novel experience, motivating them to make multiple attempts. However, one player noted a delayed understanding of the correspondence between drawing content and visual effect during the second challenge, potentially due to a lack of understanding of the storyline. This underscores the need for more mandatory narrative prompts in the early stages of the game. Additionally, adaptive visual guidance may cause impatience in some players, as one participant preferred obtaining answers without multiple attempts. Nevertheless, some players enjoyed the gradual and autonomous exploration experience, highlighting potential differences in preferences based on game experience and player types. This suggests the need for careful consideration of the presentation format of guidance to appeal to a broader player base.

Table 2. Survey Questionnaire Results on Learning Experiences and Initiative.

Dimension	Indicator	Average	Standard Deviation
Learning Experiences	Immersion	4	1.22
	Challenge	3.8	0.45
	Goal Clarity	4.2	0.84
	Feedback	4.4	0.55
	Concentration	4.2	0.45
	Autonomy	3.6	0.55
Learning Initiative	Attention	3.8	0.84
	Relevance	4.4	0.55
	Confidence	3.6	0.55
	Satisfaction	4.2	0.45
Overall		4.02	0.68

6   Conclusion and Future Work

In this work, we presented the Perceptual Tower Challenge, a novel art education game that integrates visual thinking strategies with educational game design methods. Our approach aimed at bridging the gap between educational efficacy and engaging gameplay, leveraging the strengths of visual thinking to enhance the learning experience in art education. The game's unique integration of real-time visual effects, interactive challenges, and concept-based learning tasks provided a compelling platform for fostering creativity and understanding in art. In particular, our pilot study highlighted the game's potential in enhancing learning motivation and engagement among users. The application of visual thinking strategies not only facilitated a deeper understanding of art concepts but also encouraged players to engage in creative practices.

In future research, insights from the pilot test will inform modifications and improvements to the game design. Given the current requirement for ICT skills in game operations, adjustments to the 3C solution and simplification of operations are necessary. To tackle the issue of players missing vital information, efforts will be made to incorporate persistent hint boards at crucial points in the game. Notably, some players experienced lag issues when combining visual element balls, prompting the need for further performance optimization of textures and particle effects to reduce draw calls.

Acknowledgments. This work was supported by a research grant from the Shenzhen Key Laboratory of Next Generation Interactive Media Innovative Technology (Funding No: ZDSYS20210623092001004), and the Center for Social Governance and Innovation at Tsinghua University, a major research center for Shenzhen Humanities & Social Sciences Key Research Bases.

References

1. Fang, H.: Analysis on the application of invisible class in art curriculum from the perspective of new media. In: Proceedings of the 5th International Conference on Education, Language, Art and Inter-cultural Communication, ICELAIC 2018. Atlantis Press, Moscow, Russia (2018). https://doi.org/10.2991/icelaic-18.2018.54
2. Paatela-Nieminen, M.: Remixing real and imaginary in art education with fully immersive virtual reality. Int. J. Educ. Through Art **17**, 415–431 (2021). https://doi.org/10.1386/eta_000 77_1
3. Wang, T.W.: Open art education: analysis of visual art teaching and learning websites. Vis. Inq. Learn. Teach. Art **6**, 321–333 (2017)
4. Krath, J., Schürmann, L., von Korflesch, H.F.O.: Revealing the theoretical basis of gamification: a systematic review and analysis of theory in research on gamification, serious games and game-based learning. Comput. Hum. Behav. **125**, 106963 (2021). https://doi.org/10.1016/j.chb.2021.106963
5. Crompton, H., Lin, Y.C., Burke, D., Block, A.: Mobile digital games as an educational tool in K-12 schools. In: Shengquan, Y., Ally, M., Tsinakos, A. (eds.) Mobile and Ubiquitous Learning, pp. 3–17. Springer Singapore, Singapore (2018). https://doi.org/10.1007/978-981-10-6144-8_1
6. Corrales Serrano, M.: Gamification and the history of art in secondary education: a didactic intervention. Educ. Sci. **13**, 389 (2023). https://doi.org/10.3390/educsci13040389
7. Hwang, G.-J., Chiu, M.-C., Hsia, L.-H., Chu, H.-C.: Promoting art appreciation performances and behaviors in effective and joyful contexts: a two-tier test-based digital gaming approach. Comput. Educ. **194**, 104706 (2023). https://doi.org/10.1016/j.compedu.2022.104706
8. Martyniuk, S.V.: Game on!—teaching video game studies in the arts classroom. Art Educ. **71**, 14–19 (2018). https://doi.org/10.1080/00043125.2018.1436325
9. Gies, A.: Art Academy Review – IGN. https://www.ign.com/articles/2010/11/12/art-academy-review. Accessed 05 Nov 2023
10. Peyre, N.: Prisme 7: Le premier jeu vidéo du Centre Pompidou. La lettre de l'Ocim, pp. 78–81 (2021)
11. Hunicke, R., LeBlanc, M., Zubek, R.: MDA: a formal approach to game design and game research. In: Proceedings of the AAAI Workshop on Challenges in Game AI, San Jose, CA, p. 1722 (2004)
12. Arnheim, R.: Art and Visual Perception: A Psychology of the Creative Eye. University of California Press (1954)
13. McKim, R.H.: Experiences in Visual Thinking. Brooks/Cole Publishing Company, Belmont (1972)

14. Park, J., Kim, Y.S.: Visual reasoning and design processes. In: DS 42: Proceedings of ICED 2007, The 16th International Conference on Engineering Design, Paris, France, 28–31 July 2007, pp. 333–334 (exec. Summ.) (2007). Full paper no. DS42_P_323

15. Kim, Y.S., Park, J.A.: Design thinking in the framework of visual thinking and characterization of service design ideation methods using visual reasoning model. Des. J. **24**, 931–953 (2021). https://doi.org/10.1080/14606925.2021.1977497

16. Winner, E.: Visual thinking in arts education: homage to Rudolf Arnheim. Psychol. Aesthet. Creat. Arts **1**, 25–31 (2007). https://doi.org/10.1037/1931-3896.1.1.25

17. Zhang, C., et al.: StoryDrawer: a child–AI collaborative drawing system to support children's creative visual storytelling. In: Proceedings of the 2022 CHI Conference on Human Factors in Computing Systems, pp. 1–15. Association for Computing Machinery, New York (2022). https://doi.org/10.1145/3491102.3501914

18. Hailey, D., Miller, A., Yenawine, P.: Understanding visual literacy: the visual thinking strategies approach. In: Baylen, D.M., D'Alba, A. (eds.) Essentials of Teaching and Integrating Visual and Media Literacy: Visualizing Learning, pp. 49–73. Springer International Publishing, Cham (2015). https://doi.org/10.1007/978-3-319-05837-5_3

19. Erickson, H.L.: Concept-Based Curriculum and Instruction: Teaching Beyond the Facts. Corwin Press (2002)

20. Block, B.: The Visual Story: Creating the Visual Structure of Film, TV and Digital Media. Routledge (2013). https://doi.org/10.4324/9780080551692

21. Fu, F.-L., Su, R.-C., Yu, S.-C.: EGameFlow: a scale to measure learners' enjoyment of e-learning games. Comput. Educ. **52**, 101–112 (2009)

22. Li, K., Keller, J.M.: Use of the ARCS model in education: a literature review. Comput. Educ. **122**, 54–62 (2018). https://doi.org/10.1016/j.compedu.2018.03.019

Player Experience and Engagement

The Influence of Game Aesthetics on Game Engagement and Retention in Open-World, Single-Player Games

Chen Chen, Heng Zhang[✉], and Diqiao Liang

Nanyang Technological University, Singapore 639798, Singapore
heng017@e.ntu.edu.sg

Abstract. Studies on game research have gained attention in recent years. Beyond their recreational value, games have been recognized as powerful tools for cultivating creativity, with game aesthetics emerging as an important factor. While a plethora of research has investigated aspects of game engagement and retention, few studies have examined the link between elements of game aesthetics and the enjoyment experienced during gameplay, as well as the subsequent intention to continue playing. Thus, this study introduces a novel approach that examines the influence of game aesthetics on player engagement and retention within the context of open-world single-player games. Through empirical verification, we confirm this approach and identify which factors most significantly impact gaming outcomes. This investigation provide an evaluative paradigm for game aesthetics, enriching the future academic study in this field.

Keywords: Game Aesthetics · Game Engagement · Game Retention · Single-Player Games · Open-World Games

1 Introduction

In the digital age, video games have emerged as a significant form of entertainment. Over their 50-year evolution, they have become a major recreational activity in contemporary society [1]. Going beyond being just mere leisure, video games provide attractive narratives, immersive game worlds, and physical interactive game environments, serving not only as a source of enjoyment but also as a catalyst for creativity and discovery [2,3]. Especially in open-world games which refer to a type of video game that features a large, immersive game environment in which players can explore freely [4]. Open-world games are becoming more and more popular nowadays, and there were numerous open-world games released in 2023, such as *Diablo IV*, *Blue Protocol* and the *The Legend of Zelda: Tears of the Kingdom* (TOTK). Research on open-world games within different domains from education to game design. For example, open-world games have been applied to facilitate the collaborative virtual learning in engineering education [5]. The development of virtual reality(VR) encourage players being more

© The Author(s), under exclusive license to Springer Nature Switzerland AG 2024
X. Fang (Ed.): HCII 2024, LNCS 14731, pp. 149–160, 2024.
https://doi.org/10.1007/978-3-031-60695-3_10

engaged in an open-world games and have more activities in games [6]. Besides that, engagement and retention within video games have emerged as pivotal topics of interest and investigation in the field of game studies. These facets, often interrelated, offer profound insights into player behaviour, motivation, and preferences, serving as critical metrics for evaluating game design effectiveness and player satisfaction. Nonetheless, limited research has been undertaken to examine what factors influencing the engagement and retention in open-world game environments.

The concept of aesthetics traces back to ancient Greek philosophy, yet the concept of game aesthetics has only emerged more recently alongside advancements in the medium of video games. Game aesthetics refers to the emotional reactions evoked in players as they interact with the underlying systems of a game [7]. A renowned game framework known as Mechanics, Dynamics, and Aesthetics (MDA) suggests that game aesthetics can be viewed as the emotional reactions elicited in players as they interact with in-game systems. In other words, game aesthetics encompass how players perceive fun in games and their individual interpretations of it. Various taxonomies of game aesthetics are listed but not limited to fantasy (make-believe), narrative (drama), challenge (obstacle course), fellowship (social framework), discovery (uncharted territory), expression (self-discovery), and submission (pastime). Games can simultaneously embody multiple aesthetics [7]. It encompasses everything from character design, environment graphics, and user interface layout to sound design, music, and even tactile feedback in some games. Game aesthetics play a crucial role in creating immersion, setting the game's mood, and influencing the player's emotional response.

The domain of game aesthetics and how it relates to engagement or retention remains under-investigated in open-world games. Within the purview of this study, two research questions will be addressed: 1) How do game aesthetics influence engagement and retention in the context of open-world single- player games? 2) Which indicators of game aesthetics exert an important influence? TOTK is such a popular open-world action single-player game since its release in May 2023. As a prominent and commercially successful open-world game with a sizable player base, TOTK can serve as an apt object for this study (Fig. 1).

1.1   The Link Between Game Aesthetics and Engagement

Game aesthetics are critical in evoking emotional responses in players during their interaction with a game's underlying systems. It encompasses the subjective experiences, perceptions, and interpretations of fun and enjoyment within a game [7]. Simon Niedenthal's perspective provides a nuanced understanding of game aesthetics, highlighting its sensory, artistic, and humanistic dimensions. Initially, from a fundamental standpoint, game aesthetics pertain to the sensory experiences encountered by players, encompassing visual, aural, haptic, and embodied aspects within games. Subsequently, game aesthetics relate to aspects of video games that they share with other art forms, illustrating the influence of game aesthetics on various arts. Lastly, from a humanistic viewpoint, game aesthetics can be interpreted as a manifestation of pleasure, emotion, sociability,

Fig. 1. The Legend of Zelda: Tears of the Kingdom Interfaces.

and the articulation of expressive forms in games [10]. However, this study does not define specific measures for game aesthetics.

The MDA framework categorizes game aesthetics into elements like fantasy, narrative, challenge, fellowship, discovery, expression, and sensation. For instance, the term 'sensation' can be viewed as representing sense-pleasure in games, while 'fellowship' is indicative of the role games play in facilitating socialization. This framework offers a structured approach to evaluating game aesthetics and exploring related concepts.

In addition, the concept of game engagement is multifaceted, encompassing various aspects such as immersion, presence, flow, and psychological absorption. [9]. These elements contribute to a deeper understanding of a player's involvement in a game.

Firstly, immersion serves as the initial layer of engagement, where players experience a deep connection with the gameplay [9]. It is characterized by a sensory and emotional bond that allows players to feel part of the game's world while still maintaining some awareness of their physical environment. Immersion is not just about being absorbed; it's about the game's narrative, visual and auditory stimuli, and interactivity coming together to create a convincing, engaging experience. When players express feelings like, "I really get into the game," it reflects their level of immersion, indicating how the game successfully captivates their attention and interest. Gamer immersion is influenced by the design of various game elements such as game difficulty, its direction of change, and changing rate [19].

Building on immersion, presence elevates the player's experience by engendering a sense of physical insertion into the game environment [9]. This psychological state transcends mere engagement, making the virtual environment feel almost tangible. Players find themselves engrossed to the point of forgetting their actual physical space, often playing for longer periods than intended. This sensation of presence, where players feel as though they are truly 'in the game,' is crucial in understanding how virtual environments captivate and hold a player's attention, as evidenced by statements like, "I play longer than I meant to."

flow experience is the state that people are entirely focused, engaged, and immersed in a moderately challenging activity [20]. This experience typically leads to higher intrinsic learning motivation, self-efficiency, and achievements [21]. Flow represents the equilibrium between a player's skill and the game's challenge level, a state of profound focus and enjoyment [9]. In this state, players are so engaged that external distractions fade away, resulting in a sense of tranquility and control. This delicate balance ensures that players are neither underwhelmed nor overwhelmed, but instead find themselves in a rewarding and enjoyable state. The feeling of flow is indicative of a game's capacity to offer an engaging and satisfying experience, adjusting challenges in tune with the player's capabilities, as captured by sentiments such as, "Playing makes me feel calm."

At the deepest level of engagement lies psychological absorption, where the player's attention is intensely focused, leading to a loss of self-awareness and a profound immersion in the game's activities [9]. This level of engagement signifies a complete captivation of the player's cognitive and emotional resources, often leading to a disconnection from physical surroundings and the passage of time. Psychological absorption represents a state where the game transcends being an activity and becomes the entirety of the player's experiential reality at that moment, a sentiment echoed in statements like, "I lose track of where I am."

Previous research has explored the impact of game design elements on user engagement, particularly from the perspective of game dynamics. It has been shown that better game dynamics enhance player satisfaction and motivation, leading to increased engagement [12]. While game aesthetics directly influence engagement levels, their relationship has not been empirically tested [12]. Although, there is an alternative research has illustrated that game aesthetics distinctly enhance self-reported engagement during video game play, but this research focuses on the visual aesthetics of games [8].

Focusing on open-world single-player games, which inherently lack robust social elements, allows a concentrated study on design aspects of games [11]. This investigation employs TOTK, an action-adventure game featuring an open-world design, as a case study to examine the relationship between game aesthetics and game engagement. This study aims to fill this gap by hypothesizing that an increase in players' perception of game aesthetics will lead to a higher degree of game engagement. Moreover, the study will examine which types of game aesthetics most significantly affect player engagement. Hence, the following research hypotheses and research questions are proposed:

H1: An increase in players' perception of game aesthetics will correspondingly lead to a higher degree of game engagement.

RQ1: Which specific indicators within game aesthetics hold paramount significance in shaping players' perceptions of aesthetics?

RQ2: What is the influence of game aesthetics in player engagement?

1.2 The Link Between Game Aesthetics and Retention

Game retention is defined as the continued intention to persist in the gameplay(i.e., a player's intention to continue playing a game in the future) [13]. Seven constructs: enjoyment, fantasy, escapism, social interaction, social presence, achievement, self-presentation have been confirmed that having positive influence on continuance intention for Pokémon Go, an augmented reality(AR) mobile game developed by Niantic in 2016. In the measurement definition, enjoyment is considered as a hedonic gratification and fantasy "refers to the themes that engage users in a creative, imaginative, or even fantasized world of play" [13]. Enjoyment can be viewed as a reflection of user engagement and fantasy is a term can be used to describe game aesthetics. Thus, we might propose that there might be a positive relation between game engagement and game retention, game aesthetics and game retention respectively. However, the study is limited on an VR game and have not be tested in an open-world game. Besides that, the other game aesthetics related terms have not been tested. Satisfaction has been showed that can positively affect continuance intention as it plays a crucial role in reinforcing the brand-consumer relationship within the context of branded apps, ultimately influencing users' decisions to continue using the app and maintaining their engagement with the brand [15]. In the measurement of satisfaction, the authors adopted narratives, creative freedom, audio aesthetics and visual aesthetics and etc. In the content of games, we might suppose that the higher the game user experience satisfaction, the higher continuance intention. Thus, the following research hypothesis proposed:

H2: An increase in players' perception of game aesthetics will correspondingly lead to a higher degree of game retention.

RQ3: What is the influence of game aesthetics in game retention?

1.3 The Link Between Engagement and Retention

As discussed earlier, the engagement in video games is a complex, layered phenomenon, comprising immersion, presence, flow, and psychological absorption. Each of these elements plays a pivotal role in shaping a player's gaming experience, ranging from mere engagement to complete absorption. Previous studies have confirmed a positive effect of playing engagement on user retention in different games and contexts. For instance, a questionnaire study found that higher gaming engagement predicted more intense gaming behaviour, such as purchasing in-game items [18]. In addition, a questionnaire study indicated a mediating effect of gaming engagement on the relationship between gamer experience and retention, such that gamer experience (e.g., enjoyment and arousal) enhances retention through increasing gaming engagement [17]. While gamer experience is affected by game elements, no study has examined whether and how the effect of game aesthetics on retention was also mediated by engagement. Understanding these aspects provides valuable insights into how video games captivate and hold the interest of players, offering immersive experiences that are both profound and multifaceted. Thus, the following research hypothesis proposed:

H3: An increase in players' perception of game engagement will correspondingly lead to a higher degree of game retention.
H4: The perception of game engagement among players serves as a moderating factor in the relationship between game aesthetics and the retention of players in the game.

The conceptual model of our study is shown in Fig. 2.

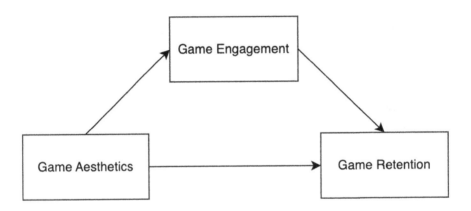

Fig. 2. Aesthetics Model

2   Methods

2.1   Data Collection

A web-based survey was conducted in July 2023 to gather data from the NGA (National Geographic Azeroth) online community, which is dedicated to discussions about video games. The study aimed to investigate the relationship between game aesthetics and player engagement and retention within the context of TOTK. Participants completed the questionnaire on a voluntary basis.

After removing data that did not pass the attention check and eliminating duplicate submissions based on IP addresses, a final sample of 400 respondents was obtained.

Table 1 presents a demographic profile of study respondents. The majority were male (79%). 50.5% of participants is falling between 18 and 25 years old. Marital status showed 66% unmarried and 34% married respondents. TOTK usage predominantly fell at least once a day (63.5%), with 31.5% playing at least once week, 3% playing at least once a month, and 2% less than once a month.

Table 1. Demographic Profile.

Dimension	Characteristic	Statistic (%)
Gender	Male	316 (79%)
	Female	84 (21%)
Age	Less than 18 years old	2 (0.5%)
	Between 18 and 25	202 (50.5%)
	Between 26 and 30	148 (37%)
	Between 31 and 40	44 (11%)
	Above 41	4 (1%)
Marriage status	Unmarried	262 (66%)
	Married	137 (34%)
TOTK use frequency	At least once a day	254 (63.5%)
	At least once a week	126 (31.5%)
	At least once a month	13 (3%)
	Less than once a month	7 (2%)

2.2 Measures

Game aesthetics were assessed using six key components: fantasy, narrative, challenge, discovery, expression, and sensation. These components were selected based on game genres of which aimed to comprehensively capture various aspects of game aesthetics. Game engagement was assessed through four metrics: immersion, presence, flow, and absorption. Retention was evaluated using three factors indicative of continuous intention. All items used a 5-point scale, where participants indicated their responses ranging from "Strongly Disagree" (1) to "Strongly Agree" (5). All measurements exhibited acceptable internal reliability, with Cronbach's alpha exceeding 0.70.

3 Result

The study employed structural equation modeling (SEM) with the Lavaan R package to analyze the data. The SEM model exhibited a strong fit to the observed data with a Normed Fit Index (NFI) of 0.983 and a Comparative

Fit Index (CFI) of 0.988, suggesting that the model adequately represented the relationships between variables. The Root Mean Square Error of Approximation (RMSEA), while slightly larger than 0.05, remained below 0.08, indicating an acceptable model fit.

The latent construct "Game Aesthetics" demonstrated significant and robust positive relationships with all its indicators. Each indicator was a statistically significant predictor of "Game Aesthetics," with p-values below 0.001. This suggests that as the perceived aesthetics of a game increase, there are strong corresponding increases in all the measured indicators. These indicators effectively define the construct of "Game Aesthetics" within the SEM model. It is interesting to note that the importance of certain indicators, such as discovery, sensation, and narrative, exceeded that of others.

In the open-world game TOTK, the expansive game world scenarios captivate players, fostering exploration and discovery in uncharted territories. Players are frequently rewarded for uncovering hidden secrets. Furthermore, the diverse and unexplored maps and equipment offer players a sense of joy, spurring them to continue their exploration. The game's 3D visual effects, alongside rich background and effect music, create an immersive gaming experience, heightening players' sensory delight. Additionally, the game's puzzles are intricately woven with narrative elements, enriching the gameplay. TOTK is celebrated for its intricate plots, memorable characters, and epic quests, with its storytelling and narratives significantly augmenting the overall gaming experience. According to a word cloud analysis reflecting the frequency of terms mentioned by participants when discussing their favorite elements of TOTK, the most commonly cited terms include art style, exploration, freedom, character, role, and scene, aligning with the model's results.

The study also revealed significant positive relationships between aesthetics and both player engagement and retention. Specifically, higher perceived game aesthetics were associated with increased engagement and retention. However, the level of engagement did not significantly associated with retention. This finding underscores the distinct influence of aesthetics on player experiences and suggests that engagement and retention may be influenced by additional factors beyond the scope of this study (Tables 2, 3 and 4) (Fig. 3).

Table 2. Evaluation of Aesthetics Model

RMSEA	CFI	NFI	χ^2	DF
0.058	0.988	0.983	45	19

Table 3. Factor Loadings of Aesthetics Model.

Indicator	β	SE	z-value
Fantasy	0.754***	0.000	–
Mystery	0.799***	0.062	16.637
Discovery	0.868***	0.057	18.316
Sensation	0.857***	0.060	18.053
Expression	0.750***	0.064	15.470
Narrative	0.811***	0.063	16.927

$* \ p < .05, \ ** \ p < .01, \ *** \ p < .001$

Table 4. Regression Coefficients of Aesthetics Model.

Predictor	Outcome	β	SE	z-value
Game Aesthetics	Game Engagement	0.739***	0.064	15.176
	Game Retention	0.736***	0.079	11.629
Game Engagement	Game Retention	0.045	0.050	0.857

$* \ p < .05, \ ** \ p < .01, \ *** \ p < .001$

4 Discussion

In this study, we employed the MDA theoretical framework to delve into the interplay between game aesthetics and player engagement and retention. Our findings unequivocally establish a robust connection between these factors, shedding valuable light on video game design. In the subsequent paragraphs, we will delve deeper into our comprehensive discussion.

Firstly, our research finds that the six delineated indicators for game aesthetics serve as significant factors for player perceptions of aesthetics within TOTK. 'Discovery', 'Narratives', and 'Sensation' rank higher than the others. The observed outcomes may be attributed to the inherent characteristics of TOTK as an open-world game. In such games, the quintessential player experience is rooted in 'discovery,' where individuals are afforded the autonomy to navigate and explore the world freely. Additionally, TOTK's design as a single-player game means that all player actions are intricately tied to the storyline, underscoring the pivotal role of narrative in enriching the player's experience. Furthermore, TOTK elicits a pronounced sensory impact, owing to the tight integration of each game mechanic with visual imagery and interface operations. By engaging in the discovery and narratives of TOTK, players may fulfill their psychological needs and have higher intrinsic playing motivation [22]. Such improvements also have a positive correlation with the enjoyment that players experience, which affects their continued intent to play the game. While the emphasis on fantasy, mystery, and expression in TOTK may be perceived as less dominant compared to the former three indicators, their contribution to player engagement and retention remains significantly positive.

Fig. 3. A word cloud depicting the most favored elements of TOTK.

On the other hand, the single-player nature of TOTK tends to channel player exploration along pre-determined narrative paths, thereby somewhat constraining opportunities for expression. The elements of fantasy and mystery within the game are not as pronounced; while players have the freedom to explore, progression through tasks necessitates adherence to the pre-defined narrative structure. Furthermore, as the fourth installment in TOTK, a substantial portion of the player base, being ardent followers of the series, may find the game's element of mystery somewhat diminished due to their familiarity with the overarching plot. That is why expression, fantasy, and mystery are not as important as the former three.

Even though other studies have demonstrated a connection between engagement and retention [17], games like TOTK can directly affect retention without using engagement as a mediator. This is a significant finding, indicating that the initial aesthetic appeal and the ongoing aesthetic satisfaction may be more critical to player retention than previously thought. However, the absence of a direct link between game engagement and retention does not diminish the importance of engagement. It implies that while engagement is significant, it may operate differently across game genres.

5   Conclusion

This investigation delves into the interplay between game aesthetics, player engagement, and game retention, addressing an unexplored niche within the realm of open-world gaming. It presents two significant contributions. First, it enhances the comprehension of both game designers and researchers regarding the pivotal role of aesthetics in shaping user experiences and the determinants of ongoing game participation. The insights offer developers a novel, aesthetically-informed perspective, bridging the understanding gap between creators and the gaming community. Second, the research introduces an approach for evaluating the influence of aesthetics on player engagement and retention, a model that is applicable across various gaming studies.

There remain limitations that could be addressed by future work. Firstly, the study relied on a single game, which constrains the generalisability of the proposed model. Secondly, incorporating additional factors like players' intention to play could make the model more comprehensive in capturing the value of game aesthetics.

Acknowledgments. This work was not supported by any grants.

References

1. Boyle, E.A., et al.: Engagement in digital entertainment games: a systematic review. Comput. Hum. Behav. **28**(3), 771–780 (2012)
2. Järvinen, A.: Games without frontiers: theories and methods for game studies and design. Tampere University Press (2008)
3. Zhang, H., Chen, V.H.H.: Design consideration of an educational video game through the lens of the metalanguage. In: International Simulation and Gaming Association Conference. Springer International Publishing, Cham (2022). https://doi.org/10.1007/978-3-031-37171-4_5
4. Squire, K.: Open-ended video games: A model for developing learning for the interactive age. MacArthur Foundation Digital Media and Learning Initiative (2007)
5. Schuster, K., et al.: Preparing for industry 4.0-collaborative virtual learning environments in engineering education. Eng. Educ. 4.0: Excellent Teach. Learn. Eng. Sci., 477-487 (2016)
6. Ijaz, K., et al.: Physical activity enjoyment on an immersive VR exergaming platform. In: 2017 IEEE Life Sciences Conference (LSC). IEEE (2017)
7. Hunicke, R., LeBlanc, M., Zubek, R.: MDA: a formal approach to game design and game research. In: Proceedings of the AAAI Workshop on Challenges in Game AI, vol. 4(1) (2004)
8. Wiebe, E.N., et al.: Measuring engagement in video game-based environments: investigation of the user engagement scale. Comput. Hum. Behav. **32**, 123–132 (2014)
9. Brockmyer, J.H., et al.: The development of the game engagement questionnaire: a measure of engagement in video game-playing. J. Exper. Soc. Psychol. **45**(4), 624–634 (2009)
10. Niedenthal, S.: What we talk about when we talk about game aesthetics. Digital Games Research Association (DiGRA), London, UK (2009). DiGRA Online Library
11. Aarseth, E.: I fought the law: Transgressive play and the implied player. Situated Play. Proc, DiGRA (2007)
12. Suh, A., Wagner, C., Liu, L.: The effects of game dynamics on user engagement in gamified systems. In: 2015 48th Hawaii International Conference on System Sciences. IEEE (2015)
13. Bueno, S., Gallego, M.D., Noyes, J.: Uses and gratifications on augmented reality games: an examination of pokémon go. Appli. Sci. **10**(5), 1644 (2020)

14. Andersen, E., et al.: Placing a value on aesthetics in online casual games. In: Proceedings of the SIGCHI Conference on Human Factors in Computing Systems (2011)
15. Li, C.-Y., Fang, Y.-H.: Predicting continuance intention toward mobile branded apps through satisfaction and attachment. Telematics Inform. **43**, 101248 (2019)
16. Krause, M., et al.: A playful game changer: fostering student retention in online education with social gamification. In: Proceedings of the Second (2015) ACM conference on Learning@ Scale (2015)
17. Hermawan, A., Bernarto, I., Antonio, F.: Video game engagement: a passkey to the intentions of continue playing, purchasing virtual items, and player recruitment (3Ps). Inter. J. Comput. Games Technol. **2023** (2023)
18. Jin, W., et al.: Why users purchase virtual products in MMORPG? an integrative perspective of social presence and user engagement. Internet Res. **27**(2), 408–427 (2017)
19. Qin, H., Rau, P.-L.P., Salvendy, G.: Effects of different scenarios of game difficulty on player immersion. Interact. Comput. **22**(3), 230–239 (2010)
20. Mirvis, P.H.: Flow: The psychology of optimal experience, pp. 636-640 (1991)
21. Rachels, J.R., Rockinson-Szapkiw, A.J.: The effects of a mobile gamification app on elementary students' Spanish achievement and self-efficacy. Comput. Assist. Lang. Learn. **31**(1–2), 72–89 (2018)
22. Ryan, R.M., Deci, E.L.: Self-determination theory and the facilitation of intrinsic motivation, social development, and well-being. Am. Psychol. **55**(1), 68 (2000)

Which Exergame Is Better for Older Adults? an Exploratory Study on User Perspectives of Virtual Reality, Exercube, and 2D Exergames

Chao Deng[1]([✉]), Jennifer Hoffman[1], Reza Hadi Mogavi[2], Juhyung Son[3],
Simin Yang[4], and Pan Hui[3,4,5]

[1] Accessible Meta Group, Michigan, USA
{cdeng,jhoffman}@accessiblemeta.org
[2] HCI Games Group, Games Institute, and Stratford School of Interaction Design
and Business, University of Waterloo, Ontario, Canada
rhadimog@uwaterloo.ca
[3] Hong Kong University of Science and Technology (Guangzhou), Guangzhou, China
json120@connect.hkust-gz.edu.cn, panhui@ust.hk
[4] Hong Kong University of Science and Technology, Hong Kong SAR, China
syangcj@connect.ust.hk
[5] Department of Computer Science, University of Helsinki, Helsinki, Finland
pan.hui@helsinki.fi

Abstract. Exergaming, the combination of exercise and gaming, has emerged as a compelling avenue to encourage older adults to remain active. However, there is a notable gap in comparative research on older adults' perspectives and preferences regarding different exergaming platforms. To address this gap, we conducted a survey with 42 East Asian older adults aged 61 to 75 years from China, Japan, and South Korea, aimed at understanding the factors that influence their preferences for Virtual Reality (VR), Exercube, and 2D Exergames. The survey collected initial data on their perspectives, which we then explored in depth through 20 follow-up interviews. Our findings revealed a distinct preference for 2D games, particularly mobile apps, which the older participants found safer, more accessible, cost-effective, and conducive to social engagement. The findings from this study highlight the key factors that are significant to older adults when selecting exergame platforms and point toward future research directions that could improve the desirability and uptake of these interactive technologies for an aging population.

Keywords: Gerontechnology · Exergaming · Older Adults ·
Comparative Study · User Perspectives · HCI · Exploratory Research

1 Introduction

The global demographic shift towards an aging population has brought about numerous challenges and opportunities in various sectors, including healthcare,

X. Fang (Ed.): HCII 2024, LNCS 14731, pp. 161–176, 2024.
https://doi.org/10.1007/978-3-031-60695-3_11

social services, and technology [5, 15, 25]. One prominent challenge is promoting an active and engaged lifestyle among older adults to improve their health and well-being [18, 21]. Physical activity has been shown to play a crucial role in healthy aging by reducing the risk of chronic diseases and maintaining independence [17, 33]. However, traditional methods of encouraging exercise may not always be effective or appealing to the older demographic [1]. This is where the potential of exergaming comes into play, a combination of physical exercise and interactive gaming [21].

Exergaming has emerged as a promising approach to entice older adults into a more active lifestyle by incorporating the motivational elements of gaming with the physical benefits of exercise [4, 21, 34].

Despite the growing interest in exergaming as a tool to facilitate physical activity among older adults, there is a paucity of research comparing the effectiveness and appeal of different exergaming platforms from the user's perspective. This paper seeks to fill this gap by exploring the views and preferences of older adults from East Asian countries regarding various exergaming modalities, namely Virtual Reality (VR), Exercube, and 2D exergames.

A comparative study[1] was carried out among people aged 61 to 75 in China, Japan, and South Korea, who have substantial elderly populations and notable variations in culture and healthcare systems. The main focus of the research was to answer two key inquiries:

- *RQ1:* What criteria do older adults consider most important when selecting between various exergaming platforms, such as Virtual Reality (VR), Exercube, and 2D Exergames?
- *RQ2:* Which exergaming platform (VR, Exercube, or 2D Exergames) is most effective in meeting the needs and preferences of older adults?

To address these questions, we first acquainted our participants with the concept of each exergame type through prototype videos and illustrations (similar to [35]). This approach allowed participants to form an understanding of each platform without the necessity for direct interaction, which could pose challenges for some individuals due to physical or technological constraints.

The research is systematically divided into two distinct phases: an initial survey involving 42 individuals, followed by subsequent in-depth interviews with an additional 20 older adults (apart from those included in the initial survey). This methodological approach was selected in order to obtain a more comprehensive understanding of the participants' inclinations and viewpoints pertaining to exergaming.

---

[1] The comparisons made in this study are not intended to be statistical analyses, due to the presence of numerous confounding factors that can influence the outcomes. These factors include but are not limited to cultural differences, healthcare system variations, and individual health practices, which can all significantly impact the results. Therefore, this study should be viewed as an exploratory investigation aimed at garnering insights and understanding trends rather than establishing statistical correlations or causations.

The results of this study demonstrate that older adults place great importance on independence, safety, efficacy, accessibility, cost, portability, social connection, and durability when considering exergaming platforms/devices. The participants expressed a clear preference for 2D exergames, particularly mobile applications, which were perceived as safer, more accessible, cost-effective, and socially engaging. These findings not only provide insight into the significant factors that drive exergame platform selection among older adults, but also offer guidance for future research efforts aimed at improving adoption and enjoyment of these technologies within an aging population.

2   Related Work

The following section provides an overview of relevant literature in the fields of gerontechnology and human-computer interaction (HCI). Specifically, it discusses studies related to exergaming and its implications for older adults, as well as investigations into technology acceptance and adoption among this population. Such a discussion is essential to provide context for our own research in this area.

2.1   Exergaming and Older Adults

Exergaming has been increasingly recognized as a means to engage older adults in physical activity [21]. The intersection of gaming with exercise provides a unique opportunity to encourage this population to maintain an active lifestyle in an enjoyable manner [21]. Research has consistently shown positive outcomes for older adults who participate in exergaming, including improvements in balance [12,37], strength [28], aerobic fitness [21], and even cognitive function [2,3]. These improvements are crucial for the enhancement of daily living activities and the reduction of fall risk, which is particularly high in this age group [16,21,35].

The positive effects of exergaming on the physical health of older adults have been thoroughly studied, but it is important to note that there are also significant psychological benefits to this form of activity [8,20]. Exergames can contribute to improved mood, greater self-esteem, and a reduction in the feeling of social isolation [8,26]. The interactive and often multiplayer nature of these games can foster a sense of community and connection, which is particularly valuable for older adults who may be at risk of loneliness [6,21].

With these points in mind, it is also important that these games are designed with older users in mind, offering adjustable difficulty levels and providing clear instructions to ensure that the experience is not only beneficial but also enjoyable [21]. Based on the principles of flow theory [30,36], it can be posited that games designed for older adults may be most effective when the challenges presented align with their skill level and abilities. Flow theory, also known as the optimal experience theory, suggests that individuals experience a state of flow when they are fully engaged in an activity that is neither too difficult nor too easy. This state of flow is characterized by a sense of focus, intense concentration, and a feeling of being in control. For older adults, this state of flow can be achieved when the challenges presented in games are tailored to their specific skill level and abilities, promoting a sense of mastery and accomplishment. Therefore, game designers should take into consideration the cognitive and physical abilities of older adults when creating games in order to optimize their gaming experience and promote a state of flow.

The challenges of integrating exergaming into the lives of older adults should not be overlooked [22,32]. Issues such as a lack of familiarity with technology, lack of receiving support, physical limitations, and a fear of injury can act as significant barriers to participation [23,24]. Studies imply that introducing exergames in a supportive environment, such as community centers or assisted living facilities, can help mitigate some of these barriers [7,27]. Moreover, incorporating input from older adults into the design and implementation of exergames can result in more user-friendly interfaces and relevant gaming content, thereby increasing the likelihood of widespread adoption and sustained engagement [21].

2.2 Technology Acceptance and Adoption Among Older Adults

Understanding the factors that contribute to the acceptance and adoption of technology by older adults is critical to the successful implementation of exergaming platforms [9,11,21,35]. The Technology Acceptance Model (TAM) has been adapted to consider the unique circumstances of older adults, recognizing that perceived playfulness, usefulness, and ease of use are primary determinants of technology adoption [10,39]. Research indicates that when older adults believe a technology can enhance their quality of life and is easy to use, they are more likely to adopt it [10].

Cultural factors play a significant role in technology adoption, especially in East Asian contexts where societal and familial expectations can influence individual behavior [11]. For older adults in this region, technologies that facilitate familial obligations, such as maintaining close family ties or engaging in community activities, are more readily embraced [10,11]. This suggests that exergaming systems that can be perceived as supportive of family and social values have a better chance of acceptance in East Asian cultures.

Additionally, intergenerational use of technology further enhances its acceptance among older adults. Studies have shown that when technology is used as a medium for interaction between generations, older adults are more motivated to learn and use it [13,21,41]. For instance, exergaming platforms that allow older adults to connect with their grandchildren through play not only increase physical activity but also strengthen family bonds. This intergenerational aspect highlights the importance of designing technology that caters to the social and emotional needs of older adults, making it more than just a tool for exercise but a bridge to meaningful relationships and enhanced well-being [21,42].

Table 1. Demographic Information of Interviewees

ID	Age	Gender	Country	Tech Literacy	2D Exergame	Exercube	VR
1	61	Female	China	Slightly	Slightly	Slightly	Somewhat
2	67	Female	China	Very	Extremely	Moderately	Quite
3	64	Female	China	Somewhat	Slightly	Somewhat	Somewhat
4	70	Male	China	Somewhat	Moderately	Slightly	Extremely
5	75	Female	China	Moderately	Somewhat	Slightly	Quite
6	65	Male	China	Moderately	Quite	Moderately	Moderately
7	71	Female	China	Moderately	Unfamiliar	Unfamiliar	Quite
8	63	Male	Japan	Somewhat	Moderately	Slightly	Quite
9	69	Female	Japan	Very	Quite	Somewhat	Moderately
10	66	Male	Japan	Very	Moderately	Moderately	Quite
11	72	Female	Japan	Extremely	Extremely	Quite	Extremely
12	61	Female	Japan	Somewhat	Moderately	Slightly	Very
13	67	Female	Japan	Moderately	Moderately	Moderately	Moderately
14	73	Male	Japan	Somewhat	Moderately	Unfamiliar	Moderately
15	65	Female	South Korea	Somewhat	Quite	Unfamiliar	Extremely
16	62	Female	South Korea	Moderately	Moderately	Somewhat	Extremely
17	68	Female	South Korea	Moderately	Quite	Very	Very
18	74	Male	South Korea	Very	Quite	Moderately	Moderately
19	63	Female	South Korea	Very	Extremely	Moderately	Extremely
20	69	Male	South Korea	Very	Extremely	Unfamiliar	Moderately

3 Method

This article presents a preliminary comparative study designed to understand the viewpoints and choices of older individuals when it comes to three types of exergames: Virtual Reality (VR), Exercube, and traditional 2D games. The following sections describe our study's methodology, which includes participant demographics, how the exergames were introduced to participants, data collection and analysis procedures, and ethical considerations.

3.1 Participants

In the survey part of our study, we recruited 42 East Asian participants aged 61 to 75 years from China, Japan, and South Korea through convenience and snowball sampling methods. The demographics of the participants were as follows: China (n = 21), Japan (n = 14), South Korea (n = 7), with an average age of 67.50 (SD = 4.01) and a gender distribution of 25 females (59%). Before participating in the study, all individuals were evaluated for their basic proficiency in technology using a 7 point scale. This was done to ensure that they could provide more accurate responses to the questions.

Fig. 1. An illustrative representation from the introductory presentation, highlighting the game content across the Exercube (left), VR (middle) and 2D Exergame (right) platforms.

Prior to showing each participant introductory videos about each exergame, participants' familiarity with each exergame type was assessed using a Likert scale. For 2D-screen exergames, familiarity levels were reported as: 2 unfamiliar, 12 slightly, 9 somewhat, 6 moderately, 4 quite, 6 very, and 3 extremely familiar. For Exercube, the distribution was: 10 unfamiliar, 11 slightly, 10 somewhat, 5 moderately, 4 quite, 1 very, and 1 extremely familiar. VR exergames familiarity was as follows: 8 unfamiliar, 12 slightly, 10 somewhat, 8 moderately, 2 quite, 1 very, and 1 extremely familiar.

In the interview component of our research, we employed an identical methodology to recruit 20 new participants from the same geographical area. A comprehensive breakdown of the demographics and pertinent information is presented in Table 1.

3.2   Exergame Introduction to Participants

To ensure a basic understanding of the three exergames observed in this study among all participants, an introductory presentation was given. This presentation consisted of a prototype video and relevant illustrations (also see [35]), providing a standardized overview of the VR, Exercube, and 2D Exergame platforms. This allowed participants to visualize each platform without requiring direct physical interaction, which may have been difficult for some. As shown in Fig. 1, the game content for all three platforms is semantically very similar. However, it should be noted here again that this study does not involve or even intend to run a statistical comparison between the platforms.

3.3   Data Collection and Further Exploration

The purpose of the survey phase was to gather structured responses from participants in order to directly address the research questions. This included specific inquiries aimed at identifying the criteria that older adults consider important when selecting between VR, Exercube, and 2D Exergames (RQ1), as well as their perceived effectiveness in fulfilling their individual needs and preferences (RQ2).

We proceeded with 20 semi-structured interviews to obtain more detailed knowledge on the criteria and preferences highlighted in the survey responses. These interviews were conducted with a different group of older adults, ensuring a diverse viewpoint on the research questions. To facilitate a comprehensive understanding, the interviews were guided by a series of open-ended questions, as shown in Table 2, giving participants the opportunity to expand on the findings from the surveys. Depending on the context of the interview, the interviewer paraphrased the questions to ensure clarity for the participants. The order of the questions was not necessarily the same as shown in the table.

The qualitative data collected through semi-structured interviews with older adults were transcribed and subjected to thematic analysis [14]. This method of analysis involved the systematic coding of the transcripts and the identification of recurrent themes, allowing for a comprehensive understanding of participants' perspectives on exergaming platforms. The integration of survey results with relevant excerpts from the interviews further enriched the data and provided a more robust understanding of older adults' perceptions and experiences with exergaming. This approach ensures the validity and reliability of the findings, as it allows for a thorough exploration of the subject matter through the convergence and triangulation of multiple data sources.

4   Ethical Considerations

After obtaining ethical clearance from our research institution, this study was carried out in accordance with the recommended ethical guidelines for conducting research involving human subjects. Prior to their participation, informed consent was obtained from all individuals involved in the study. They were explicitly informed about the confidential and anonymous nature of their responses, as well as their right to withdraw from the study at any point. Our institutional review board thoroughly examined and approved this research protocol, which consisted of a survey and interview phase.

5   Findings

The investigation into the preferences of older adults in exergaming platforms has yielded valuable insights into the influencing factors and perceived effectiveness of each platform type. In addressing the central research inquiries, RQ1

Table 2. Interview Questions Categorized by Themes

Theme	Questions
Initial Impressions and General Perceptions	1. What were your first thoughts after being introduced to the VR, Exercube, and 2D Exergames through the video?
Technology Adoption Factors	2. Which factors do you prioritize when considering an exergame for personal use, such as physical effort, fun, or potential health benefits? 3. How does your familiarity with technology influence your openness to trying new exergaming platforms?
Accessibility and Usability	4. Could you describe any accessibility features that you think are essential for exergaming platforms targeting older adults? 5. Were there any aspects of the exergaming platforms that you found challenging to comprehend?
Safety Concerns	6. What safety concerns, if any, do you associate with the use of VR, Exercube, or 2D Exergames?
Economic Considerations	7. How does the cost factor into your decision-making process for adopting new technology or gaming platforms?
Social Engagement and Interaction	8. In what ways do you think exergaming could enhance your social interactions or provide social benefits?
Preferences and Appeal	9. Are there any specific features of the exergaming platforms that you found particularly appealing or off-putting? 10. Which exergaming platform do you feel would best suit your physical activity goals and why? 11. Reflecting on the exergaming options presented, which one are you most inclined to try, and what motivates this choice?
Recommendations and Advocacy	12. How likely are you to suggest any of these exergaming platforms to friends or family, and what are your reasons?
Suggestions for Improvement	13. What enhancements or additional features could make these exergaming platforms more attractive to you?
Comparative Experience	14. If you have previous experience with either VR, Exercube, or 2D gaming, how do those experiences compare to what you've seen of these new platforms?
Open Feedback	15. Is there any other feedback or thoughts you'd like to share about your perceptions of exergaming?

and RQ2, this study reveals a complex interplay between the desire for autonomy, safety, efficacy, and social connection, and practical considerations such as cost, accessibility, portability, and durability. Through a comprehensive survey and in-depth interviews, participants from East Asia expressed a clear inclination towards 2D exergames, citing their alignment with these key factors. The subsequent Sects. 5.1 and 5.2, provide an in-depth exploration of the identified criteria and a comparative analysis of the advantages and limitations of Virtual Reality (VR), Exercube, and 2D exergames, offering a thorough understanding of the current landscape and potential future directions for exergaming within the fields of gerontechnology and HCI.

5.1   RQ1: Criteria for Platform Selection

Independence: The desire for independence was a recurring theme among participants. Prior research shows that independence could potentially delay the process of cognitive deterioration in older adults [29]. Older adults exhibited a strong preference for platforms that allowed for autonomous use, suggesting a deeper, psychologically rooted need for self-efficacy and agency in their daily activities [38]. This independence is not solely about the physical ability to use the technology but also encompasses the cognitive assurance that they can engage with the game mechanics without constant assistance. Interviewee No. 6 (P6) and P9 believe that exergaming platforms must be *intuitive* and *empower* users, fostering an environment where older adults *feel in control* and *capable*.

Safety: Safety concerns were paramount. Participants showed an acute awareness of their physical limitations and the potential risks associated with immersive technologies. The fear of falling or sustaining injury while engaging in VR or Exercube activities was significant, which tempered their enthusiasm for these platforms. This insight calls for a design paradigm that prioritizes the creation of a secure exergaming environment. P18 says, *"Designers need to innovate new ways to ensure a safety net within the gaming experience, through the integration of real-time monitoring systems or adaptive mechanisms that respond to the user's physical state."*

Efficacy: The perceived health benefits and effectiveness of the exergaming platforms were critical in the participants' evaluation process. They sought evidence of the positive impact on their physical health, such as improved balance, strength, and cognitive function. This criterion goes beyond mere enjoyment and delves into the pragmatic assessment of the platform's value in maintaining or enhancing the users' quality of life. It suggests that while entertainment is a draw, the ultimate endorsement of any exergaming platform by older adults hinges on its efficacy as a tool for health maintenance. P19 says, *"In the path where our technology and health meet, the value of a truly good exercise game is revealed not only when it provides fun but also when it is effective as a tool to improve health."*

Accessibility: Accessibility is a multifaceted concern that encompasses the ease of use, understanding, and interaction with the technology [19,40]. Participants highlighted the need for simple interfaces and clear instructions, emphasizing that the value of an exergame is rooted in its usability. This finding emphasizes the need for *human-centered design* approaches that account for varying levels of technological literacy among older adults. It also underscores the importance of user testing in this demographic to ensure the accessibility of exergaming platforms. In this regard P7 says, *"Accessibility means creating exergames that us older adults can use as easily as our grandchildren."*

Cost: Economic considerations are a pragmatic and influential factor in the adoption of exergaming platforms. The cost-benefit analysis conducted by our participants underscores the necessity for affordable solutions. Older adults are often on fixed incomes and are therefore likely to be sensitive to the price of technology. The findings suggest a market opportunity for cost-effective exergaming options that do not compromise on quality or experience. P4 says, *"In a world where the cost of living never takes a day off, finding an exergame that doesn't ask for your wallet to do the heavy lifting is like striking gold."*

Portability: The preference for portability reflects a desire for flexibility in the context of use. P8 says, *"Keep it light, make it portable! I need it with me everywhere!"* Older adults valued the ability to use the platform in various settings, whether at home or in community centers. This suggests an overlap between the physical realm of the exergame and the social spaces in which older adults operate. Designers should consider the mobility of exergaming platforms, ensuring they can be easily transported and set up in different environments to cater to this need for portability.

Social Connection: The social aspect of exergaming was a compelling factor for our participants (also see [38]). Platforms that facilitated or enhanced social interactions were preferred, as they offer a dual benefit of engaging in physical activity while connecting with peers or family. This preference points to the potential of exergaming to act as a social catalyst, strengthening community bonds and addressing the issue of social isolation among older adults. P3 says, *"Playing these games together, it's like we're all young again, laughing and moving."*

Durability: Durability emerged as a consideration reflective of long-term thinking and investment. Older adults (especially in East Asia) are interested in sustainable options that promise longevity and resist obsolescence. This criterion is a call to action for sustainable design practices in technology development, where the lifespan of the product is extended, and considerations for maintenance and updates are integral to the design process. P20 says, *"We want things that last, not break down the moment we get the hang of it."*

5.2   RQ2: Platform Preferences and Comparisons

The analysis of factors derived from the first research question revealed a strong inclination towards the use of 2D exergames, particularly those that can be accessed through mobile devices. This preference can be attributed to their compatibility with the specified criteria. The mention of their safety, convenience, affordability, and ability to foster social interaction was consistently reiterated, indicative of a larger trend in the field of gerontechnology which values user-friendly design and seamless integration into existing technological systems.

Despite its potential for promoting health, the Exercube often faced exclusion due to concerns about its accessibility. Issues such as its large size, complexity during setup, and perceived lack of mobility were seen as significant obstacles. Nevertheless, participants believed that these barriers could be overcome, for example, by using the Exercube in a community center with assistance. This was especially true when it was used in collaboration or shared spaces. This

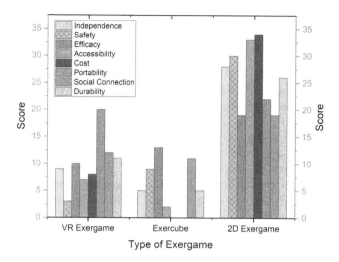

Fig. 2. Comparative performance of each exergame in specific domains based on the survey outcomes

suggests that there is a possibility for group exergaming experiences that could encourage social connections and encourage people to engage in physical activity together.

VR exergames, offering an immersive and novel experience, were met with mixed reactions. While some were intrigued by the depth of engagement it promised, apprehensions about cognitive overload and the blurring of lines between the virtual and real world were deterrents. The physical side effects, such as cybersickness, further contributed to the hesitancy. For VR to be a viable option, there needs to be a balanced approach that mitigates these concerns, potentially through gradual introduction periods, user customization options, and safety features that reassure the user of their real-world anchor.

The comparative analysis of these platforms highlights a critical point: the intersection of user experience with individual capabilities and preferences determines the success of an exergaming platform among older adults. Figure 2 depicts the comparative performance of each exergame in specific domains based on the survey outcomes.

6   Discussion

6.1   Suggestions and Implications

The pronounced preference for 2D exergames, especially mobile apps, among older adults is indicative of a broader requirement for simplicity, safety, and accessibility in technology design. These findings dovetail with existing HCI principles that advocate for user-centered design and accessibility but further emphasize the need to tailor these principles to the capabilities and preferences of older adults [21,31]. The study underscores the potential for mobile-based exergames to serve as a catalyst for physical activity and social interaction, aligning with the growing body of research that supports mobile technology as a means of enhancing the well-being of seniors.

Furthermore, the apprehension towards VR and Exercube platforms highlights a significant barrier to the adoption of more immersive and complex systems. Concerns about cognitive overload, safety, and the physical side effects, such as cybersickness, suggest that there is a critical threshold of technological complexity beyond which the perceived benefits are overshadowed by the potential risks. This revelation is crucial for HCI researchers and practitioners as it calls for the development of guidelines to moderate the complexity of interactive systems intended for older adults.

The study's outcomes also have implications for the adoption of exergaming in communal settings such as senior centers or assisted living facilities. The communal use of technology aligns with cultural factors that influence technology adoption among older adults, particularly in East Asian contexts. This insight is pivotal for HCI professionals focusing on communal technology experiences, as it suggests that collaborative and socially-oriented exergaming could enhance the adoption rates and overall engagement of older adults in physical activity.

6.2 Limitations and Future Work

While the study has provided valuable findings, it is not without limitations. The exploratory nature of the research and the focus on East Asian older adults may limit the generalizability of the results. Future work should aim to include a more diverse demographic to understand cross-cultural perspectives. Additionally, the absence of longitudinal data restricts the ability to comment on long-term engagement and adherence to exergaming platforms. Future research should consider longitudinal studies to assess the sustained use and long-term impacts of exergaming on the physical and psychological health of older adults.

There is also an opportunity for future research to investigate the balance between technological complexity and user-friendliness in exergaming platforms. Studies could experiment with varying levels of immersive experiences to find an optimal middle ground that maximizes engagement without overwhelming the user. Furthermore, the role of personalized adaptive systems that can adjust to the individual's capabilities and preferences warrants further exploration.

7   Conclusion

The rise in the older adult population underscores the importance of engaging in physical and social activities to enhance their quality of life. Exergaming, which merges exercise with interactive gaming, is emerging as a compelling avenue to encourage this demographic to remain active. However, there is a notable gap in comparative research on older adults' perspectives and preferences regarding various exergaming platforms. This study addresses this gap by investigating the views of older adults from East Asia on the adoption of different exergaming systems. We conducted a survey with 42 older adults aged 61 to 75 from China, Japan, and South Korea, aimed at understanding the factors that influence their preferences for Virtual Reality (VR), Exercube, and 2D exergames. The survey collected initial data on their perspectives, which we then explored in depth through 20 follow-up interviews. These interviews allowed us to capture a clearer picture of the older adults' preferences, building on the initial data from the survey. The assessment criteria included independence, safety, efficacy, accessibility, cost, portability, social connection, and durability. Our findings revealed a distinct preference for 2D exergames, particularly mobile apps, which older adults found safer, more accessible, cost-effective, and conducive to social engagement. While Exercubes were acknowledged for their perceived effectiveness in health promotion, they were criticized for their lack of accessibility, affordability, and portability. It was also observed that older adults preferred using Exercubes with a partner. VR exergames, despite offering an immersive experience, were met with apprehension concerning potential cognitive overload and the challenge of differentiating virtual from real-world environments. Additionally, cybersickness was reported by some users, which could hinder wider acceptance. The insights from this study highlight the key factors that are significant to older adults when selecting exergaming platforms and point toward future research directions that could improve the desirability and uptake of these interactive technologies for an aging population.

Acknowledgement. This research was supported in part by a grant from the Guangzhou Municipal Nansha District Science and Technology Bureau under Contract No.2022ZD01 and the MetaHKUST project from the Hong Kong University of Science and Technology (Guangzhou).

References

1. Avers, D.: Exercise and Physical Activity for Older Adults, p. 166-200. Elsevier (2020). https://doi.org/10.1016/b978-0-323-60912-8.00008-7
2. Bamidis, P.D.: Gains in cognition through combined cognitive and physical training: the role of training dosage and severity of neurocognitive disorder. Front. Aging Neurosci. **7** (2015). https://doi.org/10.3389/fnagi.2015.00152
3. Bamidis, P., et al.: A review of physical and cognitive interventions in aging. Neurosci. Biobehav. Rev. **44**, 206–220 (2014). https://doi.org/10.1016/j.neubiorev.2014.03.019
4. Barry, G., Galna, B., Rochester, L.: The role of exergaming in parkinson's disease rehabilitation: a systematic review of the evidence. J. NeuroEng. Rehabilit. **11**(1) (2014). https://doi.org/10.1186/1743-0003-11-33
5. Bloom, D.E., Canning, D., Lubet, A.: Global population aging: facts, challenges, solutions & perspectives. Daedalus **144**(2), 80–92 (2015)
6. Brox, E., Fernandez-Luque, L., Evertsen, G., González-Hernández, J.: Exergames for elderly: social exergames to persuade seniors to increase physical activity. In:

Proceedings of the 5th International ICST Conference on Pervasive Computing Technologies for Healthcare. PERVASIVEHEALTH. IEEE (2011). https://doi.org/10.4108/icst.pervasivehealth.2011.246049

7. Calkins, M.P.: From research to application: supportive and therapeutic environments for people living with dementia. Gerontologist **58**(suppl_1), S114-S128 (2018). https://doi.org/10.1093/geront/gnx146

8. Chao, Y.Y., Scherer, Y.K., Montgomery, C.A.: Effects of using nintendo wii™ exergames in older adults: a review of the literature. J. Aging Health **27**(3), 379–402 (2014)

9. Chau, P.H., et al.: Feasibility, acceptability, and efficacy of virtual reality training for older adults and people with disabilities: single-arm pre-post study. J. Med. Internet Res. **23**(5), e27640 (2021)

10. Chen, C.K., et al.: Acceptance of different design exergames in elders. PLoS ONE **13**(7), e0200185 (2018)

11. Chen, K., Chan, A.H.S.: Gerontechnology acceptance by elderly Hong Kong Chinese: a senior technology acceptance model (stam). Ergonomics **57**(5), 635–652 (2014). https://doi.org/10.1080/00140139.2014.895855

12. Chen, P.J., Hsu, H.F., Chen, K.M., Belcastro, F.: Vr exergame interventions among older adults living in long-term care facilities: a systematic review with meta-analysis. Ann. Phys. Rehabil. Med. **66**(3), 101702 (2023)

13. Chua, P.H., Jung, Y., Lwin, M.O., Theng, Y.L.: Let's play together: effects of videogame play on intergenerational perceptions among youth and elderly participants. Comput. Hum. Behav. **29**(6), 2303–2311 (2013)

14. Clarke, V., Braun, V.: Successful qualitative research: a practical guide for beginners. Sage publications ltd (2013)

15. Dall, T.M., Gallo, P.D., Chakrabarti, R., West, T., Semilla, A.P., Storm, M.V.: An aging population and growing disease burden will require alarge and specialized health care workforce by 2025. Health Aff. **32**(11), 2013–2020 (2013)

16. van Diest, M., Lamoth, C.J., Stegenga, J., Verkerke, G.J., Postema, K.: Exergaming for balance training of elderly: state of the art and future developments. J. Neuroeng. Rehabil. **10**(1), 101 (2013)

17. Eckstrom, E., Neukam, S., Kalin, L., Wright, J.: Physical activity and healthy aging. Clin. Geriatr. Med. **36**(4), 671–683 (2020)

18. Fratiglioni, L., Paillard-Borg, S., Winblad, B.: An active and socially integrated lifestyle in late life might protect against dementia. Lancet Neurol. **3**(6), 343–353 (2004)

19. Hadi Mogavi, R., Hoffman, J., Deng, C., Du, Y., Haq, E.U., Hui, P.: Envisioning an inclusive metaverse: Student perspectives on accessible and empowering metaverse-enabled learning. In: Proceedings of the Tenth ACM Conference on Learning @ Scale, L@S 2023, pp. 346-353. Association for Computing Machinery, New York (2023). https://doi.org/10.1145/3573051.3596185

20. Hall, A.K., Chavarria, E., Maneeratana, V., Chaney, B.H., Bernhardt, J.M.: Health benefits of digital videogames for older adults: a systematic review of the literature. Games Health J. **1**(6), 402–410 (2012)

21. Kappen, D.L., Mirza-Babaei, P., Nacke, L.E.: Older adults' physical activity and exergames: a systematic review. Inter. J. Hum.-Comput. Interact. **35**(2), 140–167 (2018). https://doi.org/10.1080/10447318.2018.1441253

22. Koon, L., Mullen, S., Rogers, W.: Self-determination through technology: understanding physical activity engagement for older adults. Innov. Aging **4**(Suppl 1), 849 (2020)

23. Kruse, L., Karaosmanoglu, S., Rings, S., Steinicke, F.: Evaluating difficulty adjustments in a vr exergame for younger and older adults: transferabilities and differences. In: Proceedings of the 2022 ACM Symposium on Spatial User Interaction, SUI 2022. Association for Computing Machinery, New York (2022). https://doi.org/10.1145/3565970.3567684

24. Larsen, L.H., Schou, L., Lund, H.H., Langberg, H.: The physical effect of exergames in healthy elderly-a systematic review. Games Health J. **2**(4), 205–212 (2013)

25. Levine, D.M., Lipsitz, S.R., Linder, J.A.: Trends in seniors' use of digital health technology in the united states, 2011–2014. JAMA **316**(5), 538 (2016)

26. Li, C., Li, J., Pham, T.P., Theng, Y.L., Chia, B.X.: Promoting healthy and active ageing through exergames: Effects of exergames on senior adults' psychosocial well-being. In: 2018 International Conference on Cyberworlds (CW). IEEE (Oct 2018). https://doi.org/10.1109/cw.2018.00059

27. Loos, E., Kaufman, D.: Positive impact of exergaming on older adults' mental and social well-being: in search of evidence. In: Zhou, J., Salvendy, G. (eds.) ITAP 2018. LNCS, vol. 10927, pp. 101–112. Springer, Cham (2018). https://doi.org/10.1007/978-3-319-92037-5_9

28. Maranesi, E., et al.: The effect of non-immersive virtual reality exergames versus traditional physiotherapy in parkinson's disease older patients: preliminary results from a randomized-controlled trial. Int. J. Environ. Res. Public Health **19**(22), 14818 (2022)

29. Mlinac, M.E., Feng, M.C.: Assessment of activities of daily living, self-care, and independence. Arch. Clin. Neuropsychol. **31**(6), 506–516 (2016)

30. Nakamura, J., Csikszentmihalyi, M., et al.: The concept of flow. Handbook Positive Psychol. **89**, 105 (2002)

31. Newcomer, N.L., Lindahl, D., Martin, K.: User centered design. In: Encyclopedia of Database Systems (2014). https://api.semanticscholar.org/CorpusID:12482810

32. Pacheco, T.B.F., de Medeiros, C.S.P., de Oliveira, V.H.B., Vieira, E.R., de Cavalcanti, F.A.C.: Effectiveness of exergames for improving mobility and balance in older adults: a systematic review and meta-analysis. Syst. Rev. **9**(1) (2020). https://doi.org/10.1186/s13643-020-01421-7

33. Pahor, M., et al.: Effect of structured physical activity on prevention of major mobility disability in older adults: the life study randomized clinical trial. JAMA **311**(23), 2387 (2014)

34. Ribas, C.G., Alves da Silva, L., Corrêa, M.R., Teive, H.G., Valderramas, S.: Effectiveness of exergaming in improving functional balance, fatigue and quality of life in parkinson's disease: a pilot randomized controlled trial. Parkinsonism Related Disorders **38**, 13-18 (2017). https://doi.org/10.1016/j.parkreldis.2017.02.006

35. Ringgenberg, N., et al.: Exerg: adapting an exergame training solution to the needs of older adults using focus group and expert interviews. J. NeuroEng. Rehabili. **19**(1) (2022). https://doi.org/10.1186/s12984-022-01063-x

36. Sharek, D., Wiebe, E.: Using flow theory to design video games as experimental stimuli. In: Proceedings of the Human Factors and Ergonomics Society Annual Meeting, vol. 55(1), pp. 1520–1524 (2011)

37. Stanmore, E.K., et al.: The effectiveness and cost-effectiveness of strength and balance exergames to reduce falls risk for people aged 55 years and older in uk assisted living facilities: a multi-centre, cluster randomised controlled trial. BMC Med. **17**(1) (2019). https://doi.org/10.1186/s12916-019-1278-9

38. Tyack, A., Mekler, E.D.: Self-determination theory in hci games research: current uses and open questions. In: Proceedings of the 2020 CHI Conference on Human

Factors in Computing Systems, CHI 2020, pp. 1-22. Association for Computing Machinery, New York (2020). https://doi.org/10.1145/3313831.3376723,

39. Vaziri, D.D., et al.: Exploring user experience and technology acceptance for a fall prevention system: results from a randomized clinical trial and a living lab. Europ. Rev. Aging Phys. Activ. **13**(1) (2016). https://doi.org/10.1186/s11556-016-0165-z

40. Venkatesh, T., Xu, X.: consumer acceptance and use of information technology: extending the unified theory of acceptance and use of technology. MIS Q. **36**(1), 157 (2012)

41. Wollersheim, D., et al.: Physical and psychosocial effects of wii video game use among older women. Inter. J. Emerging Technol. Soc. **8**(2), 85–98 (2010)

42. Wu, Z., Li, J., Theng, Y.L.: Examining the influencing factors of exercise intention among older adults: A controlled study between exergame and traditional exercise. Cyberpsychol. Behav. Soc. Netw. **18**(9), 521–527 (2015)

"I Hope There Are Beasties in the Next One": Positivity Through Interaction in Death-Themed Digital Games

Monica Evans[(⊠)]

School of Arts Humanities and Technology, The University of Texas at Dallas, Richardson, TX 75080, USA
mevans@utdallas.edu

Abstract. Death is prevalent if not near-ubiquitous in digital games. It is the most common failure state for player characters, often serves as a metaphor for growth and change, and functions as a core gameplay mechanic in numerous critically acclaimed games from *Hades* (2019) to *Elden Ring* (2022). Death in digital games is rarely permanent. Games in which the player is expected to die often, like *Celeste* (2018) and *Cuphead* (2017), often include in-game counters that track how many times they player has died, sometimes with notes of encouragement; in many others, from recent games like *The Legend of Zelda: Tears of the Kingdom* (2023) and *God of War: Ragnarok* (2022) to early games like *Metroid* (1986) and *Castlevania* (1987), the player character's death isn't considered part of the game's canon narrative, and each death simply reverts the game to a previous save state. As digital games are by definition interactive, challenging, and meant to be replayed multiple times, it is perhaps unsurprising that death is a common but unserious occurrence for the majority of gameplay experiences.

F the few games that genuinely explore concepts of death, dying, and the grieving process, one might expect them to present weightier, more solemn experiences than their counterparts above. Interestingly, many games that are thematically centered on death, such as *Spiritfarer* (2020), *I Am Dead* (2020), and *Outer Wilds* (2019), are on the whole strikingly positive and uplifting, especially those in which the game's central characters are either close to death or already dead at the game's beginning. Digital games that consider a person's entire life after it has ended can focus gameplay and content on a celebration and appreciation of that life, rather than the unknown aspects of a life intended to continue after the game's completion. This is particularly true with games that encourage or require players to interact with aspects of deceased characters' lives, as with the challenge events, often based on a character's greatest fear, and cooking/hugging interactions in *Spiritfarer;* or the excavation of memories about a deceased person from multiple people that remember them in *I Am Dead*. This paper uses a humanities-based critical methodology to explore how death-themed digital games use game mechanics, user interface design, and interaction design to create positive, uplifting, and celebratory experiences around grief, death, and dying, and how these interactive experiences can help players more fully consider death as a fundamental part of human existence.

X. Fang (Ed.): HCII 2024, LNCS 14731, pp. 177–190, 2024.
https://doi.org/10.1007/978-3-031-60695-3_12

Keywords: Digital games · game mechanics · game design · death · grieving · positivity · *I Am Dead* · *Spiritfarer* · *Outer Wilds*

1 Introduction – Death and Digital Games

At the end of *Outer Wilds* (2019), most of the game's remaining characters are coming to terms with the impending death of their universe. As the player gathers them around a campfire to await their inevitable end, the mood is surprisingly positive and uplifting. One character comments "This has been really fun. And I got to help make something pretty cool, so I've got no complaints… It's the kind of thing that makes you glad you stopped and smelled the pine trees along the way, you know?" [1]. Another notes, "The past is past, now, but that's… you know, that's okay! It's never really gone completely" [1]. A third says "Well, it worked out alright in the end… I hope there are beasties in the next one" [1]. For a game in which players are expected to wrestle with the death of themselves, their loved ones, their entire species, and every known thing in the universe, this is a notably cheerful, celebratory ending, one that might come as a surprise to the casual player but is in fact unusually common for games centered on death, dying, and grieving.

Death is a common occurrence in video games, but players often spend a great deal of time trying to prevent it. In many digital games, death is considered a failure state: something that signifies a mistake or error, is expected to occur more than once, and is intended to be overcome or avoided once the player gains enough in-game experience or skill. Fewer games consider the concept of death itself, and many that do, such as *Grim Fandango* (1998), *Death's Door* (2021), and *Hades* (2020), use death and the afterlife as a backdrop for a story about something else entirely. Of the small number of games that engage seriously with concepts of death, one might expect they would be bleak or morbid with a darker narrative tone. Instead, many games that focus on grief, death, and dying have a comforting aesthetic and positive, celebratory tone, bolstered by interactive systems that encourage players to reckon with and reflect on both the messiness of death and the joyful complexities of life. These games also commonly focus on the complete life of an individual after they have died, changing the player's focus from preventing or avoiding death to understanding a full, completed life. In other words, games that take placed after a character has already died can examine a life as a whole, and come to it with celebration, positivity, and gratitude, ultimately fostering a healthier attitude towards death in their players. Instead of focusing on pain, fear, and loss, death-themed digital games encourage players to engage with the concept of death through interactive systems that support positivity. Games like *Outer Wilds*, *Spiritfarer* (2019), and *I Am Dead* (2020) use game mechanics and interactions that focus on confronting rather than avoiding death, cozy game aesthetics, and narratives centered on lives that have already ended in order to create uplifting, celebratory experiences around grief, death, and dying. These games provide playful interactive experiences that can help players more fully consider death as a fundamental part of human existence.

2   Interacting with Death in Digital Games

2.1   Death as Failure State

Death is arguably the most common experience among players of digital games. Considering the medium as a whole, it is safe to say that many if not most digital games position the player as an embodied, often human or human-like character that can be controlled for the majority of play. Even when the player character is definitively nonhuman, as with the wolf goddess Amaterasu in *Okami* (2006), the alien slugcat in *Rainworld* (2017), or the robots Atlas and P-body in *Portal 2* (2011), characters are generally assumed to be alive, implying that death is possible. Formally, digital games are structured around challenges, goals, and obstacles that are expected to be attempted multiple times, and for which players need clear feedback when they succeed or fail. Determining conditions for victory and loss are a critical part of game design: achieving specific in-game goals are not the only reason people play, but a game's goals must "be recognized as a primary structure that shapes the game as a whole" when considering games as a formal system [2]. The death of a character gives clear, immediate, and instantly understandable feedback to the player, often simultaneously through graphics, sound, interface, and interaction, ensuring that players understand both that they have failed an objective and that they can attempt it again.

Death in digital games is both common and impermanent. When playing through *Horizon Zero Dawn* (2017), *God of War Ragnarok* (2022), or *The Legend of Zelda: Tears of the Kingdom* (2023), main characters Aloy, Kratos, and Link are expected to die multiple times during the course of their adventures, but their deaths are not considered part of the game's narrative experience: any individual death simply reverts the game to a previous save state and let the player try again. The death of a player character or non-player character (NPC) is rarely considered canon unless explicitly stated by the narrative. Famously, Aerith Gainsborough, one of the main playable characters of *Final Fantasy VII* (1997), dies permanently at the hands of antagonist Sephiroth halfway through the game in a narrative cutscene often called one of the most shocking and emotionally devastating in games history [3] – a scene that pointedly ignores how many times Aerith may have died and been revived during standard gameplay up to that point. The result is that death in digital games is easily ignored, as it rarely incurs any repercussions or serious consequences for characters, the game world, and the player.

This paradox, that death is both pervasive and easy to ignore, is rooted in principles of game design. Modern developers are familiar with the concept of loss aversion: that the pain of losing something feels demonstrably worse than the pleasure of gaining something of the same value [4]. In digital games, developers are careful to keep players feeling "good," meaning appropriately engaged and challenged without frustration, as often as possible, even in games with steep difficulty curves. For most modern games, good design generally means that "once an ability is gained, it is never lost. It may be superseded, improved, or upgraded, or negative effects may be applied, but it is not taken away from the player" [4]. Permadeath, a design structure in which a dead character is deleted or otherwise removed permanently from the game, is most often included as an option, such as "hardcore" mode in *Diablo II* (1998) and *Minecraft* (2011), and death in hardcore mode is "more akin to losing the game" than the death of an individual character [4]. In other words, digital game designers take as much sting out of death as possible, encouraging players to consider it a minor setback rather than anything with real weight.

Additionally, players expect to fail during gameplay. This may seem paradoxical in that failure is unpleasant and game playing is meant to be pleasurable, even when it is mechanically, narratively, or emotionally challenging. Jesper Juul describes the act of game playing as "pleasure spiked with pain," in which failure is "an integral element of the overall experience…a motivator, something that helps us reconsider our strategies… a clear proof that we have improved… Failure brings about something positive, but it is always potentially painful" [5]. He describes this seeming paradox as a conflict between the "moment-to-moment desire to avoid unpleasant experiences" and the "longer-term aesthetic desire in which we understand failure, tragedy, and general unpleasantness to be necessary for our experience" [5]. This expectation of failure undermines the seriousness of death, in that games are replayable experiences in which failures are intended to be overcome, including those that result in the death of a character.

2.2 Death as Core Game Experience

While most games treat character death with suspension of disbelief, some games include death as part of the game's core mechanics, narrative, or world. *Prince of Persia: The Sands of Time* (2004) adopts the narrative conceit that the titular Prince is telling the game's events as a story of his exploits after they occurred – so when the Prince-as-player-character dies, the Prince-as-narrator interrupts, saying "Wait a minute, I didn't die" or "It didn't happen like that" [6], negating the death that just occurred. *Prince of Persia: The Lost Crown* (2023) adopts a similar narrative structure, in that the game's characters are trapped in an ancient citadel in which time has shattered. Each of main character Sargon's in-game deaths are considered to be one of many variable timelines, "as if all possibilities are occurring at once" [7]. The *Dark Souls* (2011–2018) trilogy of games include death as a core mechanic: rather than reverting to a previous save state, a player character's in-game death turns them from human to "hollow," an undead-like form that incurs a variety of degenerative effects and requires the player to re-acquire their humanity to reverse it. Numerous games require the player character to return to the site of their last death, often to retrieve their corpse and its equipment, as with *Diablo II* (1998) or *World of Warcraft* (2004), or to fight their own lost body or soul to regain resources, as in *Hollow Knight* (2017).

For games in which death is a failure state, most expect the player to die more than once, to the point that some games include a "no-death" achievement, marking how unusual it is for players not to die during the standard course of the game. On the other end of the spectrum, players can expect to die more often in some genres than in others. Roguelikes, a genre marked by "procedural content generation, permadeath, and a tendency towards mechanical complexity" [8], as well as the, more accessible variant "rogue-lite," are designed with the expectation that players will not only die multiple times, but that those deaths are an integral part of the game's core experience. Roguelikes are "known for their tremendous difficulty, unpredictability, permanent character death, and the large number of methods they use to inflict that death" [9] and are one of the few genres that include permadeath as a core mechanic, often by requiring the player to create a new character that continues in the footsteps of their previous one. Some modern roguelikes incorporate character death directly into the narrative, including *Hades* (2020) in which Zagreus, the son of Hades and a functionally immortal god, dies multiple times during his escape attempts from the underworld but returns to the House of Hades each time, as all dead souls do. Likewise, *Returnal* (2021) positions its main character Selene as caught in a time loop that resets when she dies, no matter how or where she dies, resulting in a mid-game sequence where she escapes the planet Atropos, returns to Earth, lives another sixty-three years, and dies of old age – only to find herself once again trapped on Atropos as her younger self.

While roguelikes are marked by both permadeath and difficulty, other games separate the two. Neither *Heat Signature* (2017) nor *Wildermyth* (2019) are unusually challenging, but both include concepts of permadeath through a mechanic by which characters can die or retire, removing them from the game and replacing them with new playable characters. *Destroy All Humans* (2005) uses cloning to account for player deaths, in that main character Crypto-137 is presented as the one hundred thirty-seventh clone of the original Cryptosporidium, and after dying the player respawns as Crypto-138, Crypto-139, and so on. Likewise, extreme difficulty is possible without permadeath. Games considered to be "masocore" are not only punishingly difficult but subvert the player's expectations of how the game world works in order to center death as a core experience [10, 11], regardless of whether death is addressed as part of the game's narrative or not. *Celeste* (2018), both a celebration of overcoming internal struggles and a love letter to speedrunning, keeps a death count, which for some players can reach into the thousands. *Celeste* is staggeringly difficult but also empathetic, and encourages players to keep trying with in-game tips: "Be proud of your death count! The more you die, the more you're learning. Keep going!" [12]. At the other end of the spectrum, *Cuphead* (2017) openly mocks the player with its death counter, presented by a grinning pond that is all too happy to inform the player how many times they have "failed and perished" [13] during the course of their mechanically difficult adventures.

In an era where every "game over is seen as undesirable," most contemporary game design "shies away from player death" [10], such that players lose time and perhaps resources but are not penalized for death. Even survival games like *The Long Dark* (2017) and *Subnautica* (2018), in which players are expected to survive a hostile environment as long as possible, do not punish the player upon death. In. Short, most modern games use death as an immediately understandable shorthand for mechanical failure, intentionally avoiding any substantial consideration of death as a real world concept.

3 Death-Themed Games and Coziness

It is uncommon but not unusual for digital games to focus on death narratively, mechanically, and thematically. Many death-themed games use the concepts of death for aesthetic or narrative purposes without fully grappling with its wider implications. Consider *Death's Door*, a top-down action game in which the player controls a crow who works as a reaper of souls for a bureaucratically-structured afterlife. The game "finds interesting ways to make a point about the unending cycle of life and death" but "doesn't take itself too seriously" [14], and is primarily focused on strategically complex combat with multiple weapons and environmental tools, rather than the larger themes its setting implies. Likewise, *Hades* takes place entirely in the underworld but is more concerned with familial relationships among immortals than the emotional state of the afterlife's deceased denizens. *The Return of the Obra Dinn* (2018) includes a mechanic literally entitled "Memento Mori – Remember Death" that allows the player to experience a person's last seconds before death for more than sixty characters, but its gameplay is focused entirely on solving the mystery of the Obra Dinn's disappearance, as well as the moral conundrums faced by the ship's past crew and passengers. In short, even games ostensibly focused on death rarely tackle the realities of grieving and dying.

At this point, it is necessary to differentiate between various kinds of death-themed games. Writing about horror games, Bernard Perron describes what he calls the "pyramid of scary games," which makes a distinction between games in which horror is "expressed at a contextual level" through iconography or thematic content, games of "sporadic fear and horror effects," and true "scary games" in which creating fear in the player is a primary goal, achieved simultaneously through narrative, mechanics, and theme [15]. A game like *Castlevania: Symphony of the Night* (1997) uses the imagery of horror but isn't intended to scare the player on any serious level, as opposed to games like *Alien: Isolation* (2014) or *Amnesia: The Dark Descent* (2010), in which players are intended to feel fear consistently throughout. A similar argument may be made for death-themed games, in that we differentiate between games that express elements of death through aesthetic or contextual choices; games that grapple with death but aren't primarily focused on it; and games that engage in a meaningful way with concepts of death through their mechanics, aesthetics, and theme. This in no way is meant to suggest that games considering death on a primarily aesthetic level are less meaningful or important. *Grim Fandango* (1998), generally considered to be one of the most influential games ever made [16, 17], takes place in the Land of the Dead and is inspired heavily by Aztec mythology and Day of the Dead imagery, but is primarily structured as an adventure game influenced by film noir, particularly its plot structure, characters, and puzzle mechanics. Death in *Grim Fandango* is presented as bland, mundane, and non-threatening, an ordinary feature of a world that players can enjoy "without ever feeling glum about the fear of potential nothingness" [18], most clearly evidenced by the fact that main character Manny Calavera begins the game as a travel agent to the recently deceased.

Of recent games that engage with the realities of death, dying, and grieving, many of them ascribe to the cozy game aesthetic. Cozy games, a relatively recent subgenre, are marked by "how strongly a game evokes the fantasy of safety, abundance, and softness" [19] and generally center on relaxing gameplay, soft and muted color palettes, and low-stress game mechanics, narratives, and environments [20, 21]. Exemplars of the genre include the *Animal Crossing* series, most recently *Animal Crossing: New Horizons* (2020), as well as numerous independent games such as *Unpacking* (2021), *Carto* (2020), *A Short Hike* (2019), and *Stardew Valley* (2016). Notably, most cozy games do not include a way for the player character to die. Instead, they present low stakes, low stress experiences that emphasize reflection over mechanical difficulty, and are therefore ideally suited for games that consider the realities of death, often more so than games in which death is included primarily as a failure state to be repeated, learned from, and ultimately avoided.

Cozy games are interestingly well suited to heavy or difficult topics [21, 22]. *GRIS* (2018), a platform adventure game that follows a young woman through animated representations of the five stages of grief, begins with nearly no mechanics or interactive options, only allowing the player to slowly walk left. As the character gains more abilities, for example turning into a protective stone block that prevents them from being blown back into the fetal position by overwhelming winds, the game gets more mechanically complex but never difficult; by contrast, the game world becomes substantially easier to move through, as well as more colorful, detailed, and aesthetically pleasing. *GRIS*'s mechanics and narrative are expressly designed to helps players "navigate feelings related to grief and depression in a supportive, safe and cozy game environment," to the point that they can potentially "help heal emotional and psychological wounds" in players [22]. Ultimately, games that emphasize comfort, safety, a relaxed pace, and a focus on narrative reflection are well suited to handle difficult, emotionally challenging topics with empathy and care, including death, grieving, and dying.

4 Death-Themed Games and Positivity Through Mechanics

Death in modern Western society is often obfuscated, to the point that "societal understandings of death [are] found primarily by metaphor or adjacency…We consume and understand death by proxy" [23]. Digital games, through interactive systems, offer a means by which players can grapple with death more directly, often in a playful, recreational, or otherwise positive way. *I Am Dead*, *Spiritfarer*, and *Outer Wilds* approach death with dramatically different interactive systems and narratives, but all three focus their experiences on curiosity, compassion, gratitude, and understanding. They do so by creating mechanics that treat death as more than a simple failure state; by adopting the safety and empathy of cozy game aesthetics; and by considering characters whose lives are already over, placing the focus on appreciation rather than survival. These games create positive, uplifting, and celebratory experiences around grief, death, and dying through playful systems of interaction.

4.1 *I Am Dead*: Interacting with Memory Through Objects

Despite its morbid title, *I Am Dead* (2020) is a charming, whimsical game in which the player controls Morris Sheldon, the recently deceased curator of the tiny local museum on Shelmerston Island. The game begins as Morris reunites with his beloved dog Sparky, also deceased, and sets out to find a new caretaker for Shelmerston as the current caretaker, a deceased Bronze Age woman named Aggi, has been doing the job for nearly three millennia and can no longer keep the dormant volcano at Shelmerston's center from erupting [24]. While the volcano is a pressing concern, "starting out dead does take a lot of the pressure off" [25] and the game encourages a leisurely, curious pace, focused on getting to know the island and its residents in detail.

Mechanically, *I Am Dead* is focused heavily on objects. As Morris, the player reconstructs the spirits of other deceased residents of Shelmerston by locating mementos that were important to them, such as a tiny Buddha statue for a yoga instructor, a bronze sousaphone mouthpiece for a musician, or a lifesize concrete owl for a bird-obsessed campsite supervisor [24]. Locating each object requires digging into the memories of people or animals that remember the deceased, revealing them as complex, not always likeable people who are seen very differently by different survivors. Beloved yoga instructor Pete Noach, for example, has a tragic military background, revealed by a medal for bravery he secretly throws away; and Valerie Outram, the local Laird's independent and neglected daughter, is remembered very differently by her grieving father, members of his artist's colony, her childhood friend, and the garden fox that steals her camel-grooming gloves. Gradually, each spirit is revealed as a whole and complex person, first narratively through the memories of survivors, then mechanically once enough mementoes have been found for Sparky to reassemble each spirit. Through these piecemeal reconstructions, *I Am Dead* celebrates the messy complexities of its characters and the lives they lived by focusing on small remembered details that express the uniqueness of each individual person.

To maintain this focus on memory, *I Am Dead* puts interaction with objects and people in the environment at the center of its systems. The game's core mechanic is the cutaway, a process by which Morris focuses on an object and then slices away at the outside to peer into the inside: looking through the door of a closed fridge, for example, "you might see all the vegetables in the bottom drawer. And then you can go and look inside the vegetables, and in the heart of a lettuce you might find a little worm, monching [sic] away" [25]. This cutaway mechanic applies to nearly every object in the game, meaning that players can discover and investigate a great many details, truths, and secrets about the residents of Shelmerston: "the sailors are all smugglers, the toilet might have a lobster in it, and the lighthouse is full of mismatched pairs of Crocs" [25]. Similarly, once Morris has identified a person with a memory of a deceased spirit, he can look into their head and interact with their thoughts by spinning a series of images until they come into focus, revealing the memory in total. As a ghost, Morris – and by extension, the player – is peering into objects, into people's heads, and into the past in order to fully understand each deceased person, a powerful expression of how the dead come to be defined by the objects, memories, and people they leave behind.

While *I Am Dead* qualifies as a cozy game, both through its whimsical aesthetic and its safe, rewarding game mechanics, it doesn't shy away from the complexities of life and death. Shelmerston Island is gradually revealed as existing in a world only partially like our own, one that includes sentient robot gardeners, birds that serve as ship captains, a colony of non-binary fishfolk that live and work alongside Shelmerston's human residents, and a strong belief that camels are mythical creatures [24]. The whimsy of the world belies surprisingly nuanced and realistic characters, particularly the deeply unpopular and strident Greg Litherland; the sweet but complicated romance between Blythe Tonikan, a bird, and Samphire the fishfolk harbormaster, now deceased; and even the Bronze Age struggles of Aggi and her political differences with her daughter Ibni. *I Am Dead* may not include failure states, but neither is it a particularly safe game, in that many of the secrets and small details about the lives of Shelmerston's residents are surprisingly sharp-edged. The game's core mechanic of slicing into objects and seeing inside them is a fitting metaphor for how Morris and the player explore the island and its characters: *I Am Dead* is "obsessed with the details and history of things" [26], both individual people and the wider history of Shelmerston itself. To this end, it is fitting that Morris is a museum curator, particularly one with a narrow, local focus, as it affords him "the unique opportunity to see how much of a difference *he* has made as the island's lone curator, particularly in the way in which his work has helped shaped the *memory* of the island itself" [27]. Ultimately, the game's core mechanics encourages players to interact with a myriad of small objects in order to appreciate the people who left them behind, reinforcing gratitude and understanding as key aspects of grieving, death, and dying.

4.2 *Spiritfarer*: Interacting with Characters Through Care

Spiritfarer (2020) can be an unusually difficult game to play. Mechanically, the game is simple, with no failure state, no strategically or mechanically challenging sections, and a focus on relaxing, forgiving resource management. Emotionally, on the other hand, *Spiritfarer* is a "cozy management game about dying" [28], one that the developers designed explicitly to explore and confront death by "interacting with systems and experiencing them firsthand…facing the concept of passing away head-on, of actually losing something" in a "wholesome and kind way" [29]. Players control Stella, the most recently appointed Spiritfarer who along with her cat Daffodil is responsible for ferrying the souls or spirits of the recently deceased to the afterlife. As souls only pass through the Everdoor when they are truly ready, Stella and Daffodil spend a great deal of their time tending to the souls in their care. The majority of gameplay is focused on building and managing Stella's increasingly large boat, which includes individualized cabins for each spirit; functional spaces including a kitchen, a foundry, a loom, gardens and orchards, and a windmill; and spaces in which Stella can care for animals including a chicken coop, cow stalls, and a sheep corral. Players also attend to the wants and needs of each individual spirit, who are represented as anthropomorphic animals like a stag, a frog, and a snake, but are heavily implied to be humans that Stella cared for in the real world, where she was a palliative care nurse. Ultimately, Stella helps each spirit pass out of this world and into the next through gentle game mechanics that reward "paying attention and trying to be kind" [29].

As with *I Am Dead*, the characters of *Spiritfarer* are complicated, nuanced, and not necessarily nice people: "None are…purely good or bad; some are people leaving a mess behind for others to grapple with. Sometimes they're angry – at Stella or others on the ship" [30]. *Spiritfarer*'s characters are realistically challenging, especially as most of them are painfully aware that they are dying. Appropriately, Stella's interactions with her passengers emphasize care. Stella and Daffodil, and by extension the player, are encouraged to keep their passengers as happy and comfortable as possible, which they achieve through interactive systems that include cooking each passenger's favorite foods, which must be deduced through contextual clues; building each passenger their own personalized cabin on the ship; and hugging them to lift their spirits. The game provides no substantial mechanical reward for these actions: instead, "your thousand acts of labour are done entirely for, on the face of it, nothing. Or at least not for your own material gain. It's all given away" [31]. The game's core mechanics encourage the player to build strong connections with its characters through interactive, intertwined systems, many of which take hours to come to fruition.

These connections are particularly important when each of *Spiritfarer's* characters inevitably dies, moments that are intentionally emotionally difficult. Nicolas Guérin, the game's creative director and lead writer, notes that "death is unfortunately central to our existences" and that most people "spend an inordinate amount of time actively avoiding it" [29]; consequently, the characters in *Spiritfarer* were designed to connect with a broad range of players, such that "every player has one spirit whose death really gets to them" [31]. In this way, *Spiritfarer* causes players to confront the realities of death, dying, and the grieving process in a safe environment. Additionally, the focus on interactive care prevents a feeling of helplessness: the player's "acts of caring [don't] fix the spirit's current or past problems…But they do help the spirits come to terms with their deaths, and ease them into the afterlife as they work through their own grief, anger, and confusion," a process that "makes the repetition of management and care feel so rewarding" [30]. After their deaths, each passenger's personalized cabin remains on the boat, and Stella can choose to sit in each empty cabin and contemplate the night sky, which gradually fills with constellations representing each sprit. This contemplation has no mechanical benefit but instead encourages quiet reflection in the player, demonstrating how *Spiritfarer* encourages engaging with the complex processes of death and grieving through mechanics.

Fittingly, *Spiritfarer* ends with Stella's death from a long-term terminal illness, which she learns to accept after a series of conversations with Hades, a spirit owl heavily implied to be the avatar of Death itself. In one of their last conversations, Hades tells Stella, "You have opened your heart to the suffering of others. And, in return, their spark warms your heart and shapes your fate" [28]. Stella's journey of caring is replicated by the player's carefully constructed suite of interactive actions, in that taking care of the game's suite of digital characters causes players to mourn them when they pass, feel gratitude for the time and experiences they shared, and appreciate them after they are gone: an experience that encourages players to wrestle with complex, even contradictory issues of grieving and death.

4.3 *Outer Wilds:* Interacting with the Universe Through Curiosity

Unlike *Spiritfarer* or *I Am Dead*, *Outer Wilds* doesn't immediately present as a game that asks players to wrestle with death. Instead, the player is initially focused on curiosity-driven exploration as they control an unnamed Hearthian researcher across the six planets of a tiny solar system, learning about the extinct Nomai civilization. It soon becomes clear that the solar system is trapped in a twenty-two-minute time loop that resets every time its sun goes supernova, and that the main player character has only recently gained the ability to retain their memories of previous loops. Eventually, the player realizes that, regardless of the time loop, the universe of *Outer Wilds* is coming to a natural end, and the player's main task is not to save it but to come to terms with the death of everything, including themselves.

In a previous article, I argued that *Outer Wilds* is both bleak and surprisingly positive due in part to its time loop mechanics, which encourage players to approach the game with curiosity, optimism, and a sense that the game world is in the best possible place due to the player's repeated interactions with it [32]. As a time loop game, *Outer Wilds* allows players to experience hope, regardless of the apparent futility of their actions, and focuses the game experience on appreciating and celebrating the world even though it cannot be saved. This is best exemplified by the game's ending, in which all remaining characters express their own appreciation for their lives, as well as hope that the mysterious entity called the Eye of the Universe will start a new world from the ashes of their own. The mood is appreciative, hopeful, and grateful, even though the characters will never know what comes next, a sentiment best exemplified by the Nomai character Solanum, who says "This song is new to me, but I am honored to be a part of it" and "I'm glad you remembered me" [1]. Rather than examining the lives of individual characters after their passing, *Outer Wilds* centers on understanding a dead civilization. Players must understand the Nomai and their curious, determined, and science-positive society in order to solve many of the game's environmental puzzles, which also encourages players to appreciate that society and the final writings and remembrances of many of its individuals.

In terms of fostering curiosity, *Outer Wilds'* game mechanics support both a central narrative mystery and a structure for enthusiastic exploration and discovery. Much of the player's time is spent exploring large areas that change over time, solving environmental puzzles, and examining Nomai writing and other context clues, all in twenty-two minute chunks of time. The exact length of the time loop, extended from eighteen minutes in earlier version [33], is tuned precisely to encourage players to explore without feeling rushed or stuck, especially as the only thing that persists between time loops is gathered information. This repeating game structure focuses the player on appreciating rather than speeding through the game world, secure in the knowledge that nothing can be permanently broken and everything they do will be reset: "You might only have twenty-two minutes to save the world, but you have that twenty-two minutes as many times as you need. There is never enough time, yet there is always more" [34]. In other words, there are no negative ramifications for the players' actions as they piece the world's puzzles together. The game "unfolds as a seemingly natural consequence of [the player's] own curiosity" [33], and that curiosity is always rewarded.

Narratively, *Outer Wilds'* initial bleakness is tempered by a cozy aesthetic. The beginning of the game, and the beginning of every new loop, is set at a campfire in the woods, at which the player can roast as many marshmallows as they like. This action has no mechanical benefit but plenty of emotional resonance, and is in fact the touchstone of the game's emotional tone. Alex Beachum, the game's creative director, notes that "the whole game is all about things like nature, forces, and things falling apart beyond your control" and that the marshmallow represents "this one small moment you can control" [35]. Likewise, the campfire itself is "this one little beacon of light. One little place of safety and coziness in the middle of the big dark forest" [35]. *Outer Wilds* ends where it begins: around exactly the same campfire, now populated by the rest of the game's characters, in a scene that is simultaneously melancholy and celebratory. From an emotional standpoint, *Outer Wilds* can be a difficult game to finish, particularly as its mechanics encourage players to confront the "tension between practicality and contemplation. Your exploration rarely feels heroic... [and] it becomes clear that there are no easy answers" when it is revealed that the universe is dying naturally and cannot be saved [33]. The game leaves players with a heavy moment of reflection on what it means to appreciate a life or an experience that is drawing to a close. Ultimately, *Outer Wilds* inspires an appreciation of the universe and every individual in it: all lives inevitably will end, and the player's job is to accept, understand, and ultimately celebrate the fact that they had a chance to experience it before it was gone.

5 Conclusion

Digital games that grapple seriously with concepts of death often approach those concepts with positivity, reflected in their mechanics, narrative, and themes. From a mechanical perspective, death-themed games do not treat the mechanics of death as a simple failure state, or as something to be avoided or prevented by players as their skill increases. Instead, death-themed games create interactive systems and mechanics that encourage players to reflect on and consider death, dying, and grieving in a positive, empathetic light. From a narrative and thematic standpoint, death-themed games also tend to adopt aspects of the cozy game aesthetic, as cozy games create feelings of safety, comfort, and empathy in players and are therefore well suited to games that tackle emotionally difficult topics. Lastly, death-themed games often take place after the game's characters have already lived a full life, allowing these games to focus not on survival but on the celebration of and gratitude for a life already lived, which can be explored and appreciated through interactive mechanics. The positivity of death-themed games may have future implications for their use as therapeutic tools [22, 29], but importantly allow current players to consider death, dying, and grieving in new ways. Rather than ignoring death, or removing its sting through failure-state-based game mechanics, death-themed games encourage players to interact with death in playful ways, and ultimately come to terms with one of the hardest aspects of human existence.

References

1. Outer Wilds. Mobius Digital, Annapurna Interactive (2019)
2. Salen, K., Zimmerman, E.: Rules of Play: Game Design Fundamentals. The MIT Press, Cambridge (2003)
3. Purslow, M.: Resurrecting Aerith: The Final Fantasy 7 Fans Who Re-Wrote Fate, IGN (2023). https://www.ign.com/articles/resurrecting-aerith-the-final-fantasy-7-fans-who-re-wrote-fate. Accessed 12 Feb 2024
4. Engelstein, G.: Achievement Relocked: Loss Aversion and Game Design. The MIT Press, Cambridge (2020)
5. Juul, J.: The Art of Failure: An Essay on the Pain of Playing Video Games. Playful Thinking, Mass. MIT Press, Cambridge (2013)
6. Prince of Persia: The Sands of Time. Ubisoft Montreal, Ubisoft (2004)
7. Prince of Persia: The Lost Crown. Ubisoft Montpelier, Ubisoft (2023)
8. Parker, R.: The culture of permadeath: roguelikes and terror management theory. J. Gaming Virtual Worlds 9(2), 123–141 (2017)
9. Harris, J. *Exploring Roguelike Games*. CRC Press, 2020
10. Anthropy, A.: Masocore games, Aunte Pixelante (2010). http://www.auntiepixelante.com/?p=11. Accessed 2 Feb 2024
11. Wilson, D., Sicart, M.: Now it's personal: on abusive game design. In: Proceedings of the International Academic Conference on the Future of Game Design and Technology, pp. 40–47 (2010)

12. Celeste: Maddy Makes Games, Maddy Makes Games (2018)
13. Cuphead: Studio MDHR, Studio MDHR (2017)
14. Barbosa, A.: Death's Door review – A murder of crows, Gamespot (2021). https://www.gam espot.com/reviews/deaths-door-review-a-murder-of-crows/1900-6417699/. Accessed 2 Feb 2024
15. Perron, B.: The World of Scary Video Games: A Study in Videoludic Horror, Bloomsbury (2018)
16. Matulef, J.: Retrospective: Grim Fandango: Dead can dance, Eurogamer.com (2015). https://www.eurogamer.net/retrospective-grim-fandango. Accessed 14 Feb 2024
17. Savage, P.: Museum of Modern Art to Install 14 Games, Including EVE, Dwarf Fortress and Portal, PC Gamer (2014). https://www.pcgamer.com/museum-of-modern-art-to-install-14-games. Accessed 14 Feb 2024
18. Troughton, J.: Grim Fandango isn't afraid of death, it laughs in the face of it, TheGamer (2022). https://www.thegamer.com/grim-fandango-death-depiction/. Accessed 2 Feb 2024
19. Cook, D.: Cozy games, LOSTGARDEN (2018). https://lostgarden.home.blog/2018/01/24/cozy-games/. Accessed 02 Feb 2024
20. Meiners, R.: Coziness in games: an exploration of safety, softness, and satisfied needs. Project Horseshoe (2018). https://www.projecthorseshoe.com/reports/featured/ph17r3.htm. Accessed 02 Feb 2024
21. Waszkiewicz, A., Bakun, M.: Towards the aesthetics of cozy video games. J. Gaming Virtual Worlds **12**(3), 225–240 (2020)
22. Baker, M.: The visual and narrative rhetoric of mental health in Gris. J. Gaming Virtual Worlds **14**(3), 249–266 (2022)
23. Coward-Gibbs, M.: Introduction: death≠ failure. Death, Culture & Leisure: Playing Dead, pp. 1–7. Emerald Publishing Limited (2020)
24. I Am Dead. Hollow Ponds, Annapurna Interactive (2020)
25. Bell, A.: I am dead: ghosts of summer holidays past. Rock Paper Shotgun (2020). https://www.rockpapershotgun.com/i-am-dead-review. Accessed 14 Feb 2024
26. Webster, A.: I am dead is a playful exploration of death and memories. The Verge (2020). https://www.theverge.com/21506636/i-am-dead-review-pc-nintendo-switch. Accessed 17 Feb 2024
27. Fitzpatrick, A.: The archaeology of memories and mementoes, animal archaeology (2021). https://animalarchaeology.com/2021/10/14/the-archaeology-of-memories-and-mem entos-an-archaeologists-review-of-i-am-dead/. Accessed 24 Feb 2024
28. Spiritfarer: Thunder Lotus Games, Thunder Lotus Games (2020)
29. Couture, J.: Inside the Thoughtful Design of Thunder Lotus' Spiritfarer, Game Developer (2020). https://www.gamedeveloper.com/design/inside-the-thoughtful-design-of-thunder-lotus-i-spiritfarer-i. Accessed 20 Feb 2024
30. Carpenter, N.: Video games revel in death, Spiritfarer focuses on what happens next, Polygon (2020). https://www.polygon.com/reviews/2020/8/18/21373518/spiritfarer-review-release-date-switch-pc-ps4-xbox-one-thunder-lotus. Accessed 24 Feb 2024
31. Bell, A.: Spiritfarer review: death becomes her. Rock Paper Shotgun (2020). https://www.roc kpapershotgun.com/spiritfarer-review. Accessed 24 Feb 2024
32. Evans, M.: "Should my best prove insufficient, we will find another way": time loop mechanics as expressions of hope in digital games. In: Fang, X. (ed.) HCI in Games: 5th International Conference, HCI-Games 2023, Held as Part of the 25th HCI International Conference, HCII 2023, Copenhagen, Denmark, July 23–28, 2023, Proceedings, Part II, pp. 198–209. Springer Nature Switzerland, Cham (2023). https://doi.org/10.1007/978-3-031-35979-8_16
33. Campbell, C.: Outer Wilds became a GOTY contender by trusting the player, Polygon (2019). https://www.polygon.com/interviews/2019/7/23/20706307/outer-wilds-game-of-the-year-interview. Accessed 24 Feb 2024

34. Walker, A.: 'Outer Wilds' is a captivating sci-fi mystery about the end of the world, Vice (2019). https://www.vice.com/en/article/mb8p7y/outer-wilds-is-a-captivating-sci-fi-mystery-about-the-end-of-the-world. Accessed 24 Feb 2024
35. Diaz, A.: How roasting marshmallows became the 'emotional core' of outer wilds, polygon (2022). https://www.polygon.com/23166164/outer-wilds-space-roasting-marshmallows-interview. Accessed 24 Feb 2024

Prototyping a Virtual Reality Therapeutic Video Game to Support the Social Reinsertion of Burned Children

Pablo Gutiérrez[1], Matías Orellana Silva[2], Maria Gabriela Hidalgo[3], Jorge A. Gutiérrez[3], and Francisco J. Gutierrez[1]([✉])

[1] Department of Computer Science, University of Chile, Beauchef 851, North Building, Santiago, Chile
{pgutierr,frgutier}@dcc.uchile.cl
[2] Instituto Teletón de Santiago, Av. Libertador Bernardo O'Higgins, 4620 Santiago, Estación Central, Chile
morellana@teleton.cl
[3] Corporación de Ayuda al Niño Quemado – COANIQUEM, Av. San Francisco, 8586, Pudahuel Santiago, Chile
{ghidalgo,jgutierrez}@coaniquem.org

Abstract. Treating burned children is a complex and multidisciplinary endeavor that goes beyond physical recovery and wound healing. In the later stages of this process, the patient has to regain their emotional and social tools to cope with the potentially adverse conditions they might face once they become—once again—active members of society. Building upon successful and effective advances in the development of therapeutic video games, in this paper we report the design of a virtual reality (VR) immersive and ludic simulation to increasingly support patients in their social reinsertion while completing their physical rehabilitation programs. This piece of software, which works as a complement to traditional controlled exposure therapy facilitated by a clinical psychologist, aims to bridge the playful, immersive, and flow experiences that are naturally embedded in VR-mediated video games as a way to ease patient adoption and increase the effectiveness of the social reinsertion program. Our preliminary results show that the conceived application was perceived as highly valuable by multidisciplinary specialists working in burn recovery programs, highlighting the rehabilitation and social reinsertion possibilities that a VR-mediated video game can support as well as how it effectively integrates alongside conventional controlled exposure therapy programs.

Keywords: Video game · Therapeutic game · Virtual reality · Rehabilitation · Burned children

1 Introduction

Recovering from a burn injury is a complex process, given that, in most cases, it involves surgery, wound healing, and other kinds of medical care that may be

X. Fang (Ed.): HCII 2024, LNCS 14731, pp. 191–202, 2024.
https://doi.org/10.1007/978-3-031-60695-3_13

overwhelming for the patient. These procedures also require addressing psychological concerns during and after the physical recovery. Among these, the social reinsertion of burned patients aims to assist them in overcoming the trauma and potential emotional consequences that might arise from being exposed to usually long treatments, such as coping with visible scars and pain that might limit the independent execution of daily living activities.

The Burned Aid Children Corporation (COANIQUEM)[1] is a Chilean not-for-profit organization that provides support for burned children in Latin America and the Caribbean. As part of their recovery program, a team of experts works closely with every child patient, not only during the physical recovery from burn injuries but also in equipping them with emotional and psychological tools to cope with the potentially adverse conditions that they might face once they complete their treatment. In the particular case of social reinsertion, the preferred ways to go rely on role-playing games and psychological projection exercises through controlled therapeutic exposure. However, once the child is discharged from their recovery program, experience has shown that their transition is prone to emotional distress and anxiety, despite the best efforts of the medical team to assist them in their social reinsertion.

This situation opens up a space for human-centered design opportunities. In particular, extended (XR) and virtual reality technology (VR) have been increasingly finding their place in the mass market due to reduced costs and increased software usability and hardware affordability. Therefore, it is not surprising that domains such as specialized work training, education, and health care have turned their eyes to conceiving novel ways for simulation and controlled exposure in an immersive virtual or augmented space.

For instance, virtual reality exposure therapy (VRET) allows for an individualized, gradual, controlled, and immersive exposure that is easy for therapists to implement and often more acceptable to patients than in vivo or imaginal exposure [2]. Likewise, play therapy represents an alternative form of treatment based on the playful, immersive, interactive, and flow experiences that are facilitated by games. This approach is particularly suitable among preschool and school-age children, showing favorable results in decreasing negative emotions, as demonstrated by numerous research works [13].

In this paper, we explore how to provide a meaningful and playful experience aiming to increase the effectiveness of the social reinsertion program currently developed at COANIQUEM. To do so, we prototyped a VR-controlled therapeutic video game, grounded in self-determination theory principles, simulating interpersonal interaction in a classroom as a way to bridge the reintegration of a burned child who has completed their recovery treatment, in a social context that is suitable and relatable for them. In particular, our solution does not intend to replace the professional assistance provided by a psychologist but rather as a complement to a controlled exposure therapy program.

According to related literature, the proposed approach is promising. In fact, virtual reality has shown favorable results when used in rehabilitation programs.

---

[1] https://coaniquem.cl/en/.

For instance, according to Lindner et al. [15], VR has evolved as an approachable and potentially effective alternative in medical and psychological treatments, not only in conducting exposure therapy to treat anxiety disorders but also in a range of other disorder types. Following this line of reasoning, the preliminary results of our prototype video game are highly promising. In that respect, a group of domain experts from COANIQUEM evaluated the software's perceived usability and usefulness, highlighting the rehabilitation and social reinsertion possibilities that emerge from integrating therapeutic and VR game elements to support and complement the exposure therapy program.

The rest of this paper is structured as follows. Section 2 reviews and discusses prior work. Section 3 presents the VR-mediated therapeutic video game prototype designed to support the social reinsertion of burned children in the final stages of their recovery process. Section 4 presents the empirical setup and results of a proof-of-concept study aiming to assess the perceived usefulness and perceived usefulness of the proposed approach by a multidisciplinary team of domain experts actively working in burn recovery programs. Finally, Sect. 5 concludes and provides perspectives on future work.

2   Related Work

VR technology has successfully opened a new path in supporting and complementing medical treatments (e.g., [1,6,9]). For example, a team of researchers in Brazil [27] explored the effectiveness of using interactive VR simulations, such as riding a roller coaster or exploring the depths of the ocean, when healing the wounds of burned children. Likewise, Maani et al. [16] deployed a set of immersive VR-controlled simulations to help recover pain. These results show that VR interventions may complement conventional treatments (in this case, healing active wounds), where patients could be otherwise affected or be in discomfort.

In the case of mental health treatments, VRET has proven as a valuable and effective asset to complement more traditional approaches as well as supporting patients when controlled exposure is difficult to achieve in practice [2,7,20,21,28]. In a typical VRET software application, the user navigates through a 3D immersive environment without having to be exposed to the aversive stimulus physically. For instance, Rothbaum and Schwartz [25] found that controlled exposure therapies effectively alleviate the symptoms related to emotional distress, while Parsons and Rizzo [22] identified the psychotherapeutic opportunities leveraged by introducing VR in the treatment of anxiety and phobias. The evolution of VR as a feasible, plausible, and effective alternative to support medical and psychological treatments has steadily increased [15]. Therefore, VR software designers and developers may count on specialized domain-expert knowledge to favor the proliferation of novel, engaging, immersive, and interactive tools.

Besides the technical aspects of VR software design and development, the self-determination theory (SDT) [5,26] has gained terrain in media and game design research [11,23] to understand how individuals may benefit from being motivated and increase their engagement when using a specific piece of software. The key constructs of SDT, namely (1) autonomy, (2) competence, and (3) relatedness, all tribute to the development of an individual's intrinsic motivation in fulfilling their psychological needs [10]. In particular, recent research [8] has provided empirical evidence on its effectiveness when mapping SDT constructs to the interaction mediated in VR environments. On the one hand, autonomy in a VR environment refers to the ability of a user to freely interact with their surroundings, make informed and rational decisions, and have control over the situations and effects that happen in the scenario. On the other hand, competence in a VR environment refers to the user's ability to manage a satisfactory performance when interacting with their surroundings, i.e., being capable of controlling and navigating effectively. Finally, relatedness in a VR environment refers to the sense of presence, connection, and immersion a user builds with the different elements configuring the interactive setting. These constructs jointly shape a user's motivation, particularly when the interactivity is supported as a (serious) video game [14,19].

3   Video Game Design

Following a user-centered design approach, we designed and developed a prototype video game to assist psychologists in mediating and promoting tailored cues to promote social reinsertion among children recovering from burn injuries. The design process was informed and iteratively validated by a team of domain experts specialized in the treatment of burn injuries in children. The software was optimized to run in the Oculus Quest family of head-mounted displays due to their mass-market availability.

In the developed prototype, the player (i.e., patient) is immersed in a virtual classroom where several interpersonal exchanges are sustained: (1) interacting one-on-one with other classmates, (2) being directly addressed by the class teacher, and (3) interacting with the whole class. These scenarios have been decided jointly with a team of psychologists specialized in controlled exposure therapy and having broad experience in promoting the social reinsertion of burned children once they have completed their rehabilitation programs. The developed video game is intended to be used under the supervision of a psychologist, who also leads the social reinsertion and transition procedure.

The interactive role play is structured around three scenarios: a tutorial (Fig. 1), a safe zone (Fig. 2), and a classroom for providing context to the intended interpersonal interaction (Fig. 3). The tutorial was designed to provide an initial exposure to the player for learning how to navigate, use the VR controls, and get a grasp of the key interaction mechanics in the game. Likewise, the safe zone is a particular environment where the player can feel at ease, unwind, and let go of any negative emotion and/or feeling that may emerge during their interaction in the classroom. As such, the safe zone is modeled as a forest and can interact with the therapist to require assistance and engage in a one-on-one conversation.

Fig. 1. Tutorial

Fig. 2. Safe zone

Fig. 3. Interpersonal scenario

Regarding the interaction itself, it consists of several explicit and implicit mechanics [12,18] which all aim to sustain player immersion, involvement, and presence [24]. In particular, the key interaction states are modeled as follows: (1) the player is welcomed by their teacher and is then introduced to their classmates; (2) a classmate asks the player to lend them a pencil; (3) the class takes a break and all classmates interact with each other. Several implicit interaction stimuli, both visual and auditory, are also modeled throughout the simulation. Figures 4 and 5 depict the state-transition diagrams that sustain the core interaction in the application.

In the case of the teacher (Fig. 4), she may perform several actions to interact with the classroom (i.e., walk, speak, sit, stand, and leave). The condition If Recess indicates that the contextual situation changes from being a class to students freely interacting during a break.

In the case of the students, all are modeled after the same script. The patient, being also a student, has one additional action: Asking, which will prompt the interaction with other students in the class (i.e., borrowing an eraser from a classmate). Given that the contextual scenario is a classroom, all students are initially Sitting. Then, when the teacher points to a specific student, they change their state to Looking and after some time, will resume the Sitting state. If the Asking action is launched, then the patient model will be idle until another student lends them their eraser (and then resumes the Sitting state). After some time, the Recess Action is activated, which prompts both the teacher and students to change their interaction mode.

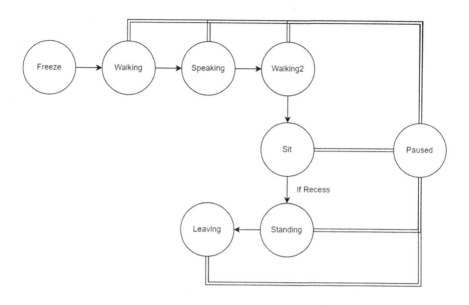

Fig. 4. State-transition: Teacher

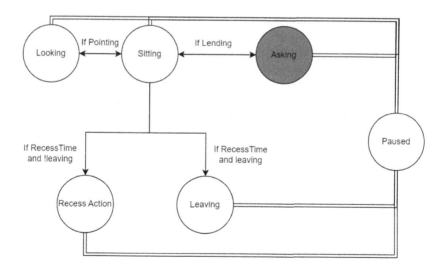

Fig. 5. State-transition: Classroom

4   Proof of Concept

To evaluate the pertinence and adoption potential of the developed prototype, we conducted a proof of concept study in two stages. On the one hand, we ran a software inspection with domain experts (i.e., physical therapists, psychologists, and physiatrists working closely to recover burned children). On the other hand, we ran a formative user study designed to understand the player experience and specific VR measures regarding immersion, presence, and involvement. Participants were asked to interact with the developed prototype using an Oculus Quest 2 headset in both stages. This study was approved on ethical grounds by the Institutional Review Board at the University of Chile.

4.1   Focus Group with Domain Experts

In this stage, domain experts ($N = 8$) were asked to conduct a software inspection and assess the solution's perceived usefulness and adoption potential. In particular, they were asked to evaluate the safe zone scene, given the impact that it may have from a psychological point of view in the context of social reinsertion and VR-controlled exposure therapy.

Each participant was allowed to interact with the prototype during the focus group session. Then, they had to complete predefined tasks to assess the offered functionality, facilitated by the first author. Participants had to follow the thinking-aloud technique to identify possible usability concerns and the perceived usefulness of the developed prototype. At the end of the session, all participants were asked to provide open comments, emphasizing the adoption potential of the video game, both from a medical and technical point of view.

The collected evidence was transcribed, coded, and analyzed following a thematic analysis approach [3]. All in all, domain experts praised the overall design, look-and-feel, and interactivity of the produced prototype. They highlighted the rehabilitation and social reinsertion possibilities that the video game can mediate and how it can effectively be inserted into conventional controlled exposure therapy programs. The safe zone was praised for opening the opportunity to enhance the therapist-patient relationship without compromising the effectiveness of the immersion, involvement, and presence throughout the VR session.

4.2   Formative User Study

In this stage, a sample of potential users ($N = 25$) were asked to interact with the produced prototype, covering the execution of a complete play session. We aimed to assess game usability, player experience, player immersion, involvement, and presence when interacting in a VR environment. These measures were captured at the end of the game session through a questionnaire modeled after the Multimodal Presence Scale for VR Environments [17] and the Core Elements of the Gaming Experience inventory [4]. Scores ranged from 0 (totally disagree) to 6 (totally agree), as depicted in Figs. 6, 7 and 8.

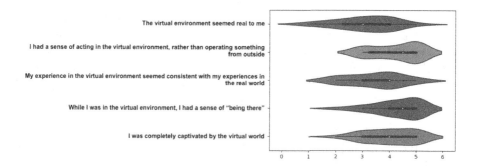

Fig. 6. Results: Physical Presence

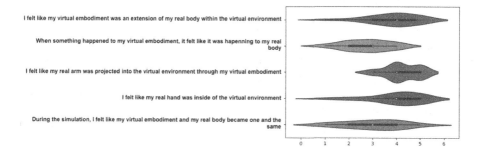

Fig. 7. Results: Self-Presence

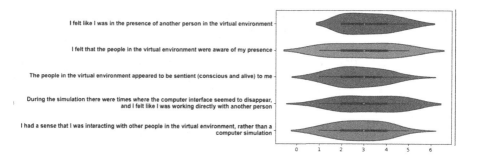

Fig. 8. Results: Social Presence

Physical presence refers to concepts such as physical realness, i.e., the capability to accurately and precisely represent the virtual environment's interaction objects and scenarios. It also implies enabling an immersive interaction, where the virtual surroundings overcome the physical surroundings. According to the study results, participants displayed a favorable view regarding physical presence. Therefore, the developed simulation was able to be perceived as immersive. Regarding self-presence, i.e., pursuing immersion not by the contextual surroundings but by the user's sense of embodiment, we observe that the study results yield neutral views. In particular, the simulation could improve by relating the simulated experience with the potential physical—embodied—experience in a better way. Finally, regarding social presence, the median value for all items is neutral, which indicates that the application's social presence aspect was not completely translated into the experience. In particular, this could be improved in the next iteration by working with more realistic textures, facial expressions, and fluid movements to design the 3D models representing the simulation actors.

5   Conclusion and Future Work

In this paper, we presented the design of a prototype therapeutic video game, controlled in VR, to complement the social reinsertion therapy to burned children provided by COANIQUEM. This process is traditionally undertaken by a multidisciplinary team, facing several challenges and barriers, yielding a broad range of success. Therefore, the consideration of emerging technologies (such as VR), and the demonstrated success of VR exposure-controlled therapies in other domains, justify a design opportunity to explore the acceptance and potential usefulness of this approach. We developed an interactive simulation of a classroom, which is a natural environment for the recovering children and is one of the critical social contexts that they will experience once discharged. This simulation works as a complement to traditional controlled exposure therapy practices, which are led by a clinical psychologist.

The produced prototype was evaluated as a proof-of-concept in two stages. On the one hand, we conducted a software inspection led by a team of multidisciplinary domain experts, specialized in treating burned children. These experts praised the potential usefulness of the therapeutic video game, particularly highlighting the rehabilitation and social reinsertion possibilities that a VR-mediated interactive simulation can provide for this kind of treatment. On the other hand, we ran a user study with a sample of potential users with a particular interest in assessing the VR interactivity of the software, i.e., immersion, presence, and involvement. The obtained results show that the simulation was considered as immersive but there is also space for further improvement, particularly in embodiment and social aspects of presence.

References

1. Baradwan, S., et al.: The effect of virtual reality on pain and anxiety management during outpatient hysteroscopy: a systematic review and meta-analysis of randomized controlled trials. Arch. Gynecol. Obstet. (2024). https://doi.org/10.1007/s00404-023-07319-8

2. Boeldt, D., McMahon, E., McFaul, M., Greenleaf, W.: Using virtual reality exposure therapy to enhance treatment of anxiety disorders: Identifying areas of clinical adoption and potential obstacles. Front. Psych. **10** (2019). https://doi.org/10.3389/fpsyt.2019.00773

3. Braun, V., Clarke, V.: Using thematic analysis in psychology. Qual. Res. Psychol. **3**(2), 77–101 (2006)

4. Calvillo-Gamez, E.H., Cairns, P., Cox, A.L.: Assessing the Core Elements of the Gaming Experience, pp. 37–62. Cham (2015)

5. Deci, E.L., Ryan, R.M.: The "what" and "why" of goal pursuits: Human needs and the self-determination of behavior. Psychol. Inq. **11**(4), 227–268 (2000). https://doi.org/10.1207/S15327965PLI1104

6. du Plessis, J., Jordaan, J.: The impact of virtual reality on the psychological well-being of hospitalised patients: a critical review. Heliyon **10**(2), e24831 (2024). https://doi.org/10.1016/j.heliyon.2024.e24831

7. Fodor, L.A., Coteţ, C.D., Cuijpers, P., Szamoskozi., David, D., Cristea, I.A.: The effectiveness of virtual reality based interventions for symptoms of anxiety and depression: a meta-analysis. Sc. Rep. **8** (2018). https://doi.org/10.1038/s41598-018-28113-6

8. Grasse, K.M., Kreminski, M., Wardrip-Fruin, N., Mateas, M., Melcer, E.F.: Using self-determination theory to explore enjoyment of educational interactive narrative games: A case study of academical. Front. Virt. Real. **3** (2022). https://doi.org/10.3389/frvir.2022.847120

9. Guan, H., Xu, Y., Zhao, D.: Application of virtual reality technology in clinical practice, teaching, and research in complementary and alternative medicine. Evi.-Based Complem. Alternat. Med. (2022). https://doi.org/10.1155/2022/1373170

10. Huang, Y.C., Backman, S.J., Backman, K.F., McGuire, F.A., Moore, D.: An investigation of motivation and experience in virtual learning environments: a self-determination theory. Educ. Inf. Technol. **24**(1), 591–611 (2019). https://doi.org/10.1007/s10639-018-9784-5

11. Jinhee Yoo, S.L., Ohu, E.A.: A cross-cultural analysis of vr gaming psychological needs and motivations: a self-determination theory approach. Managing Sport Leisure, 1–21 (2022). https://doi.org/10.1080/23750472.2022.2046490

12. Ju, W.: The Theory and Framework for Implicit Interaction, pp. 7–20. Springer International Publishing, Cham (2015)

13. Koukourikos, K., et al.: An overview of play therapy. Materia Socio-Medica **33**(4) (2021). https://doi.org/10.5455/msm.2021.33.293-297

14. Lau, H.M., Smit, J.H., Fleming, T.M., Riper, H.: Serious games for mental health: are they accessible, feasible, and effective? a systematic review and meta-analysis. Fron. Psych. **7**, 59–75.https://doi.org/10.3389/fpsyt.2016.00209

15. Lindner, P., et al.: Attitudes toward and familiarity with virtual reality therapy among practicing cognitive behavior therapists: A cross-sectional survey study in the era of consumer vr platforms. Front. Psychol. **10** (2019). https://doi.org/10.3389/fpsyg.2019.00176

16. Maani, C.V., et al.: Virtual reality pain control during burn wound debridement of combat-related burn injuries using robot-like arm mounted vr goggles. J. Trauma: Injury, Infection Critical Care **71**(1), 125–130 (2011). https://doi.org/10.1097/TA. 0b013e31822192e2

17. Makransky, G., Lilleholt, L., Anders, A.: Development and validation of the multi-modal presence scale for virtual reality environments: a confirmatory factor analysis and item response theory approach. Comput. Hum. Behav. **72**, 276–285 (2017)

18. Maldonado, C., Gutierrez, F.J., Fajnzylber, V.: Implicit interaction mechanisms in vr-controlled interactive visual novels. In: Fang, X. (ed.) HCI in Games, pp. 605–617. Springer International Publishing, Cham (2022). https://doi.org/10.1007/978-3-031-05637-6_39

19. Mandryk, R.L., Birk, M.V.: Toward game-based digital mental health interventions: player habits and preferences. J. Med. Internet Res. **19**(4), e128 (2017). https://doi.org/10.2196/jmir.6906

20. Omar Hawajri, J.L., Suominen, S.: Virtual reality exposure therapy as a treatment method against anxiety disorders and depression-a structured literature review. Issues Mental Health Nursing **44**(4), 245–269 (2023). https://doi.org/10.1080/01612840.2023.2190051

21. Park, M.J., Kim, D.J., Lee, U., Na, E.J., Jeon, H.J.: A literature overview of virtual reality (vr) in treatment of psychiatric disorders: recent advances and limitations. Front. Psychiat. **10** (2019). https://doi.org/10.3389/fpsyt.2019.00505

22. Parsons, T.D., Rizzo, A.A.: Affective outcomes of virtual reality exposure therapy for anxiety and specific phobias: a meta-analysis. J. Behav. Ther. Exp. Psych. **39**(3), 250–261 (2008). https://doi.org/10.1016/j.jbtep.2007.07.007

23. Reer, F., Wehden, L.O., Janzik, R., Tang, W.Y., Quandt, T.: Virtual reality technology and game enjoyment: the contributions of natural mapping and need satisfaction. Comput. Hum. Behav. **132**, 107242 (2022). https://doi.org/10.1016/j.chb.2022.107242

24. Rivera, F., Gutierrez, F.J.: A metamodel for immersive gaming experiences in virtual reality. In: Fang, X. (ed.) HCI in Games, pp. 315–326. Springer Nature Switzerland, Cham (2023). https://doi.org/10.1007/978-3-031-35979-8_25

25. Rothbaum, B.O., Schwartz, A.C.: Exposure therapy for posttraumatic stress disorder. Am. J. Psychother. **56**(1), 59–75 (2002). https://doi.org/10.1176/appi.psychotherapy.2002.56.1.59

26. Ryan, R.M., Deci, E.L.: Self-determination theory and the facilitation of intrinsic motivation, social development, and well-being. Am. Psychol. **55**(1), 68–78 (2000). https://doi.org/10.1037/0003-066X.55.1.68

27. ScapinMaria, S.Q., Echevarría-Guanilo, E., Fuculo, P.R.B., Martins, J.C., da Ventura Barbosa, M., Pereima, M.J.L.: Use of virtual reality for treating burned children: case reports. Revista Brasileira de Enfermagem **70**(6) (2017). https://doi.org/10.1590/0034-7167-2016-0575

28. Schröder, D., Wrona, K.J., Müller, F., Heinemann, S., Fischer, F., Dockweiler, C.: Impact of virtual reality applications in the treatment of anxiety disorders: a systematic review and meta-analysis of randomized-controlled trials. J. Behav. Therapy Exper. Psych. **81**, 101893 (2023). https://doi.org/10.1016/j.jbtep.2023.101893

How StarCraft II Players Cope with Toxicity: Insights from Player Interviews

Samuli Laato[1]($\boxtimes$) , Bastian Kordyaka[2] , Velvet Spors[1] ,
and Juho Hamari[1]

[1] Gamification Group, Tampere University, Tampere, Finland
{samuli.laato,velvet.spors,juho.hamari}@tuni.fi
[2] University of Bremen, Bremen, Germany
kordyaka@uni-bremen.de

Abstract. Toxicity in the context of online interactions is understood as an umbrella term describing negativity-inducing and harmful behaviours. Despite multiple efforts, user's toxic behaviour remains rampant particularly in multiplayer online games with real-time high fidelity social affordances. In this work, we conducted player interviews among StarCraft II players to understand how they cope with toxicity that they experience while playing. We approached the data inductively, and discovered both emotion-focused and problem-focused coping strategies. We sorted the discovered forms of coping into eight categories (such as functional detachment and affective detachment). Our findings offer new empirical perspectives on coping in multiplayer online games. This work sheds light on the strategies that players opt for managing stressors arising from toxicity, and can help in the design of measures that better enable players to shield themselves from harmful interactions.

Keywords: Toxicity · toxic behavior · multiplayer online games · online gaming · coping

1 Introduction

Multiplayer online gaming has become a hugely popular pastime activity. According to Statista, the global video game market value is growing steadily, with overall sales increasing from 155.89 billion USD in 2020 to 217.07 billion USD in 2023, and a projected growth to 268.81 billion USD by 2025 [42]. The share of online gaming from this market is substantial, with the majority of sales coming from digital purchases (with a growing trend), and hundreds of million people playing multiplayer games online each month [5]. Today, multiplayer online gaming also covers forms such as AR and VR gaming [25,28,29] and is an enjoyable meaningful pastime for many [19,23,24,27]. However, this rapid growth has not come without issues. Competitive online gaming in particular has been prone to gamer toxicity i.e., an umbrella term describing players' behaving

X. Fang (Ed.): HCII 2024, LNCS 14731, pp. 203–219, 2024.
https://doi.org/10.1007/978-3-031-60695-3_14

in ways that induce negative sentiment in their fellow players [7,21,22,39,40,46]. In this work we adopt the definition for toxicity from Frommel and Mandryk who define toxicity as: *"disruptive behaviors that are perceived as harmful by others."* [16].

Previous research has argued that multiplayer online gaming spaces have on average worse behavior than offline interactions due to phenomena such as the online disinhibition effect, which relates to players having no social responsibility over their actions due to anonymity [18]. Other drivers for toxicity may include factors such as anger and frustration [20,43], as well as personal and cultural factors [22]. Toxicity can manifest differently depending on the social affordances of games in question. For example, Clash Royale [44] (from Supercell) and Hearthstone [2] from (Activision-Blizzard) allow players to communicate with each other during matches only through emotes and gameplay. By contrast, games like StarCraft II [1] and League of Legends [17] include options to communicate through written text, and games such as Apex Legends [12] and Counter Strike: Global Offensive [10], and League of Legends [17] as well, have built in voice-chat functions. The different competitive environments and in-game cultures coupled with different interaction affordances give birth to widely different forms of expected and accepted behaviours, and also reflects on the different forms of toxicity that appear in the games [19,38].

Due to the prominence of toxicity in multiplayer online gaming, players are forced to come up with ways to cope (i.e., employ processes that help them manage) with the negative behavior they are prone to face [3,7,46]. This may include muting toxic players, disengaging from the situations [46] and employing emotion-regulation processes [7]. The extant academic corpus on coping with toxicity is currently limited to only looking at the phenomena in the context of a few game genres, primarily multiplayer online battle arena games. Furthermore, the empirical research has drawn from relatively small samples of players (see e.g., [47]). Furthermore, there is a lack of an explicit categorization of available and possible coping mechanisms in the context of multiplayer online games. To begin addressing these research gaps, we interviewed players of the real-time strategy (RTS) game StarCraft II [1], approached the data inductively, and analyzed the coping behaviours from the viewpoint of Lazarus and Folkman [32]. To guide the interviews and subsequent analysis we propose the following research question (RQ):

RQ: *How do StarCraft II players cope with toxic behaviours that they encounter while playing the game online?*

By answering this RQ, we make research contributions to the HCI literature on coping with toxicity [7,46] through the data-driven elucidation and categorization of players' coping strategies in the context of the Real-Time Strategy (RTS) game StarCraft II (see Fig. 1 for a screenshot of the game). Our work enables scholars as well as practitioners to better understand some of the strategies that players select for dealing with and shielding themselves from toxicity. Therefore, this research builds towards a future where gamers can enjoy high fidelity interactions while playing without compromising their mental health and enjoyment through rampant unchecked toxicity.

Fig. 1. A screenshot from the game StarCraft II taken by the authors showing Terran units entering a Zerg base.

2 Background

2.1 Theoretical Perspective: The Coping Theory of Lazarus and Folkman

Lazarus and Folkman offered a conceptualization of coping in their seminal book *"Stress, appraisal, and coping"* as a process for managing and dealing with stress [32]. In this coping theory, the causes/instigators that people "are coping with" are called *stressors*. According to the authors, coping can take the form of cognitive or behavioral efforts, leading to two high order categories of coping: (1) problem-focused coping; and (2) emotion-focused coping [30,31]. *Problem-focused coping* strategies aim to change the source of the stress, e.g., by organizing one's life in a new way so the stressor has less effect, working to neutralize the stressor or studying it to better understand how to deal with it. *Emotion-focused coping* approaches, by contrast, are about managing one's emotions to mitigate the negative effects caused by the stressor.

In the context of video gaming, there has been research on coping from two main perspectives. The first is the use of video games as a means to cope with stressors that originate outside gaming [14,37]: Here, gaming itself can be described as a coping measure or tool for relaxation. The second stream of research relates to coping with events and stressors that originate within gaming [7]. In this context, stressors relate to gameplay events in the game, and also potentially harmful players' behaviours. It can be that players cope with real-world stressors by gaming (e.g., via escapism [28] or using games as self-care [41]). However, where players may meet, people are always at risk of encountering toxicity; even when playing for their own purposes. Therefore, gaming-to-cope behaviours themselves can lead to new stressors (e.g., problematic video game playing [33], or gender-based harassment in gaming communities [34]), which then require further coping strategies. It becomes clear that coping in, with or through games is not an easy undertaking, and closely situated to toxicity—which reflects the complexity of human behaviour in this domain.

2.2 Previous Research on Coping with Toxicity in Multiplayer Online Games

There have been both qualitative (e.g., [3,46]) and quantitative studies (e.g., [9]) on coping with toxicity in video games. Coping is generally framed as an important process for regulating emotions, enabling players to perform well particularly in competitive games [7]. A rather rich and in-depth discussion of coping with toxicity in video games is presented in the work of Türkay et al. [46], who discovered that players employ a wide variety of coping measures to deal with toxicity that they encounter while playing [46]. These could include problem-focused approaches such as disengagement from situations through muting chats as well as emotion-focused approaches such as psychological maneuvering (e.g., dismissing toxicity as irrelevant). This highlights the importance of games offering players measures to shield themselves from toxic actions [39]. In certain contexts players may accept of what might be considered toxicity as valid criticism and try to change their behaviour to provoke less toxic actions in the future [46]. Players could also intervene in toxic behaviours of others, rescuing victims of toxicity [46]. Here, coping is less personal and could even be framed and studied as a social phenomenon. An important element is also how to cope and deal with players' own frustrations, where players are forced to manage and cope with their own urges to behave in toxic fashion [3]. Recent research has considered the role of bystanders in instances of toxicity in team games, and shown that toxicity exhibited by teammates significantly increases the chances of bystanders to become targets of toxicity, or engage in toxic behaviour themselves [19], which ultimately requires stakeholders to engage in a wide variety of coping behaviours.

Players can build resilience against toxicity through the mechanism of positive reappraisal [9], which can be considered as a more long-term coping strategy, and links to the normalization of toxicity discussed in the work of Beres et al. [6]. Perhaps the most complete and rigorous categorization of mechanisms in gaming for coping with toxicity come from the work of Passmore and Mandryk who discovered seven categories of coping: (1) Endure/ignore, (2) modify the digital self, (3) modify the digital environment, (4) modify the experience, (5) modify/dismiss self, (6) social support-seeking, and (7) direct confrontation [36]. These categories were inductively derived from the responses of 230 gamers. As such, these coping approaches are rather general and cover the entire spectrum of gaming as opposed to any specific genres or types of games. However, there are two gaps remaining after this extensive work: first, the sample was obtained from the crowdsourcing website MTurk and further study is needed to assess the external validity of the findings with other samples and related contexts [36]. Second, the data was based on open responses to an online survey as opposed to more in-depth data such as player interviews that allow researchers to ask follow-up questions and understand more holistically the coping measures and the situations in which they are applied. In order to address these research gaps we continue to our study context, which is the RTS game StarCraft II. Studying this game enables us to obtain insights from a well-defined context and can help researchers draw between-genres connections in evaluating players' coping strategies.

2.3   Study Context: The RTS Game StarCraft II

StarCraft II [1] is the currently most popular multiplayer online RTS game, a popular esport title that regularly reaches thousands of concurrent viewers on platforms such as Twitch.tv, and has a competitive ranked *ladder*, where players encounter each other continuously in settings [45]; most commonly *1v1*, but there are casual and team modes as well. In terms of gameplay, Starcraft II requires players to mine resources in order to build up an army of units, to attack their opponents with. The game offers three different races, each with their own unique (counter-)abilities and affordances. (Zerg, Protoss and Terran). In such a competitive environment frustration is not uncommon, and players are given multiple affordances for expressing their frustration [1]. For example, StarCraft II allows players can type messages to each other. There is an optional language filter, but besides that, players have free reign to type whatever they wish to their opponents in-game. Players can also intentionally prolong games, use technical cheats, taunt and/or provoke the opponent among other things [26].

The presence of a highly competitive environment coupled with various affordances to express frustration makes StarCraft II an ideal study target when thinking about how players cope with toxicity in RTS games. In Fig. 2 we display an interaction between two players during a match. It provides an example of the types of verbal interactions that players might have with each other while playing. In addition to toxicity occurring within individual StarCraft II matches, players may send each other messages after games and in shared chat channels. Due to the broad landscape of where toxicity can occur in StarCraft II, we opted to gather rich qualitative data instead of quantitative data. Next we present our materials and methods for our research.

3   Materials and Methods

3.1   Data Collection

We formulated an interview guide based on previous research on coping with toxicity [3, 46] as well as the authors' own knowledge and experience of the study

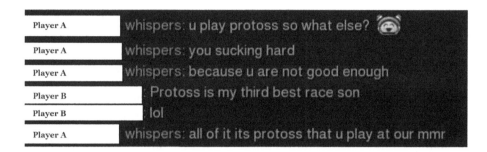

Fig. 2. An exchange between two anonymized players in the game StarCraft II. Player A is suggesting that Player B only won the match because they played Protoss, one of the three races that players can choose from when they play StarCraft II. The screenshot is taken by one of the authors.

context. We included questions about the game, toxicity, and asked specifically about how the players cope with toxicity in the various circumstances where they encounter it. Using the authors' extended networks we contacted StarCraft II players in two European countries: Germany and Finland in the summer of 2023. Altogether 12 people agreed to join the interviews and gave their permission to use their responses anonymously for research. All interviews were recorded and transcribed. The interviews lasted from half an hour up to almost one and half hours depending on how verbose the participant was. The list of participants is given in Table 1.

Table 1. Demographic information of the interview participants ($N = 12$). We also provide an estimate of the number of games played, which league the players play at (ranging from the lowest, Bronze, all the way to the highest, Grandmaster) and an estimate of the players' experience of multiplayer games in general and how important role gaming has in their daily life (casual/hardcore).

ID	Games played	Approx. Rank	Playing activity	Age	Occupation
1	23,000	Master	Hardcore	31	Postman
2	20,000	Grandmaster	Hardcore	28	Harbor worker
3	4,000	Diamond	Casual	31	Audio system architect
4	3,500	Diamond	Casual	34	Content creator
5	1,300	Gold	Casual	25	Programmer
6	1000	Gold	Hardcore	37	Researcher
7	800	Gold	Hardcore	26	Programmer
8	700	Silver	Casual	26	Student
9	500	Silver	Hardcore	25	Student
10	400	Silver	Hardcore	34	Mathematician
11	200	Bronze	Hardcore	33	Researcher
12	100	Bronze	Casual	31	Licensed therapist

3.2   Analysis

We approached the data inductively, first identifying all unique coping mechanisms mentioned in the data, and then employing a reflexive analysis approach
to bring further nuance to the discovered coping mechanisms. The advantage
of reflecting the data against the researchers existing knowledge regarding the
study context is that it allows for the discovery of emergent phenomena and
aspects that are perhaps not self-evident in the material [4,8,15,35]. In our case,
this approach enabled us to understand how the coping approaches tied to the
in-game affordances, and the circumstances in which specific coping mechanisms
are prudent. As is typical with qualitative analyses, the sense-making process
occurred in a non-linear fashion and we performed multiple iterations around the
themes. All authors participated in commenting on, and refining, the categories
of coping.

After finalizing the categories of forms of coping, we revisited the data
through the lens of Lazarus and Folkman [31,32] to distinguish emotion-focused
and problem-focused mechanisms in the discovered coping strategies. We understood problem-focused strategies as such which related to behavioural actions
that the players took to influence the source of coping, and emotion-focused
strategies as such which involved techniques to manage the effects of toxicity
internally.

4   Findings

Through our analysis we arrived at eight categories of coping with toxicity as
mentioned by our StarCraft II player informants. These are listed in Table 2.
Both the forms of toxicity experienced by players as well as the coping mechanisms were connected to the in-game affordances, whereby players' behaviors
were tied to, and mediated by, game and system design. For example, the participants (e.g. P1, P3, P4, P6, P7) reported to regularly make use of options
to hide interactions or block players. All except one of the mentioned forms
of coping could be classified as problem-focused coping, two of the problem-
focused approaches also contained emotion-focused elements in them. However,
the authors suspected that perhaps the participants were engaged in emotion-
focused coping more than they disclosed in the interviews, as the replies were
often practice-oriented and focused on actions that players took to manage toxic
instances, as opposed to engaging with internal processes. The authors further
suspect that players may be less capable in general to articulate emotion-focused
approaches as opposed to problem-focused approaches.

4.1   Reciprocal Reactance

Reciprocal reactance related to responding to toxicity with toxicity. A common
example would be to verbally respond to the opponent's provocations during
a match. When discussing this form of coping participants often mentioned to

Table 2. Forms of coping discovered in the data. We sorted the mechanisms to emotion-focused (EF) and problem-focused (PF) coping as explained in Sect. 3.2.

Form of coping	Description	PF	EF
Reciprocal reactance	Responding to toxicity with toxicity	X	
Psychological maneuvering	Approaching the toxic player as if they were inferior and treating them accordingly	X	X
Social silencing	Muting the chat, blocking the perpetrator or otherwise using in-game functionalities to disable interactions with the perpetrator	X	
Functional detachment	Disengaging from the situation by moving away from it. The most severe form of this is to leave the match and uninstall the game	X	
Affective detachment	Ignoring the perpetrator and emotionally withdrawing from the situation		X
Interpersonal bargaining	Making peace with the perpetrator or reasoning with them	X	
Crisis signaling	Reporting the perpetrator to the admins or asking help from other players	X	
Eroding trust	Conceding trying to play the game seriously, declining experience of meaningfulness of playing	X	X

change modality or form of the toxicity as they responded. E.g., P10 mentioned that if a perpetrator engaged in toxic behaviour such as pause buffering (pausing, unpausing and pausing again during a match), they might respond back verbally calling the opponent names. However, reciprocal reactance at the core appeared to be linked to frustration and losing one's temper. Even those participants who admitted to engaging in such behaviour were not proud of it, and suggested that they know they should not engage in reciprocal behaviour when faced with toxicity. The following quote illuminates this perspective:

"Well it's toxic [to verbally assault someone who behaves in a toxic way] so I don't do it that often" (P1)

"It would be better to just ignore them [instead of reacting with toxicity]" (P8)

A few participants (P3, P9) also noted that responding to toxicity with toxicity could add fuel to the fire and make the situation worse for all parties involved. While reciprocal reactance could offer momentary satisfaction, it was thus not seen as a good strategy for coping. The following two quotes showcase this line of thinking:

"It's always good not to add gasoline into the fire" (P3)

"I try not to [respond to toxicity with toxicity] since it usually escalates the situation." (P9)

4.2   Psychological Maneuvering

Psychological maneuvering was linked to re-positioning oneself as the superior in the toxic situation. P9 discussed this as an effective strategy he uses, imagining the perpetrator as a hopeless person in need of help. While this strategy primarily relates to emotion-focused coping, as it all about re-framing one's thinking, psychological maneuvering often related to action. For example, P9 gave examples of asking the perpetrator "is everything alright at home? who hurt you?". Relatedly, P1 mentioned he was dismissive of some of the negative remarks he receives, and said he does not take most of them seriously. The following quote from P1 (presented with a tongue in cheek tone during the interviews) highlights this:

"When someone provokes me and says get out, I often don't exactly' do as they say." (P1)

Psychological maneuvering could also take other forms, such as making fun of the opponent or trying to find funny aspects in the perpetrator's behaviour. This was common e.g., in the interviews with P1, P2, P9 and P10 who all offered examples of how they found some toxic behaviours rather funny. For example, certain rage quits and balance rages were seen as comical particularly when they were not targeted towards any person. However, sometimes the participants admitted to taking a superior stance and even intentionally provoking the aggressor a little. P10 offered an example of this kind of behaviour, which he argued was a way of making the situation more humorous while maintaining control over the events:

"If someone rages I let them rage. I like to provoke them to rage more. They can rage all they want and if they step over the line they get a report." (P10)

4.3   Social Silencing

Social silencing was inherently linked to the interaction affordances. In StarCraft II players have options to filter bad words, and to mute and block players. The participants saw these features as critically important for maintaining control over the types of behaviours they could be exposed to. The participants also ubiquitously reported to use the muting and blocking functions, and many viewed them as the main methods for coping with toxicity. The following two quotes illustrate this:

"I [block people] a lot, it's a clear way to put an end to to the interaction. Sometimes I say a final word and then block them" (P1)

"It is the usual way to cope for toxicity" (P11)

Social silencing was a form of conflict avoidance, and could sometimes be used pre-emptively e.g., in situations where the participants felt they were tilted. P2 mentioned that he was sometimes in the mood where he did not wish to read comments or any provocations or anything, and just wanted to play the game. P5 brought forward that sometimes it is rude if another player is not responding, suggesting that perhaps this form of coping, especially if proactively used, can feel as unfriendly to opponents. Regardless, social silencing remained a critically important feature in supporting players' coping, and was mentioned as one of the most used feature by a majority of the participants.

4.4   Functional Detachment

Functional detachment differs from social silencing in that it is about disengaging from toxic situations behaviourally within the game as opposed to disabling interactions completely. For example, avoiding behaviours that trigger teammates or walking away from toxic circumstances could be seen as forms of functional detachment. This form of coping could be seen as a natural response in trying to get a way from the source of stress, in this case, toxicity. In case players were unable to do so within the game, they could close the game. This was given as a concrete example by P4:

"When I'm tilted, the opponent is annoying, winning and abusing, or something, (...), I leave the game." (P4)

StarCraft II contains both 1v1 games as well as team games. Leaving a 1v1 game was considered a resignation, while leaving was more problematic in team vs team matches. Yet, many participants (e.g., P1, P2, P3) reported to occasionally do this. P6 mentioned that he even uninstalls the game sometimes when he is particularly upset with the events that occurred in the game. The importance of functional detachment for players highlights that in addition to social silencing, players need to be supported in disengaging from behavioural toxicity as well.

4.5   Affective Detachment

As opposed to functional detachment, affective detachment is predominately a form of emotion-focused coping related to emotionally withdrawing from the toxicity stressors. This could be achieved through multiple means such as reflecting on one's thoughts to maintain a positive mindset or working towards ignoring the toxicity and instead focusing on the game. For example, P2 mentioned the following:

"If someone rages and spams, it's better to ignore them and just play your game" (P2).

While affective detachment was an important method for leveling up the mental state, some participants noted that this option was not always enough. Sometimes the stressors from toxicity required multiple coping strategies and simply attempting to emotionally detach oneself from the situation was inadequate. For example, P11 argued as follows:

"I see [affective detachment] is an option when the case is not bad" (P11)

4.6   Interpersonal Bargaining

Interpersonal bargaining relates to trying to make peace with the perpetrator e.g., by telling them to calm down or apologising for whatever triggered the perpetrator to behave in a toxic fashion. This appeared as a context-dependent approach whereby factors such as who was the perpetrator and how serious the offence was impacted players' willingness to engage in interpersonal bargaining to defuse the situation.

We also found differences between the participants in their approaches, such as P12 expressing that she did not care about the game enough to negotiate with toxic players if she encountered hostile behavior, but in case she knew the perpetrator, then she would feel the urge for confrontation. In contrast, P2 and P10 felt that toxic players should not be allowed to "get away" with their insults, and should be taught their place. Finally, P1 noted that sometimes confronting the perpetrator developed into a friendly and productive conversation, and viewed such instances as empowering and encouraging. The following quote highlights this:

"My strategy is that I might reason and say that yea that can feel a bit unfair. This often calms the situation down. I've had positive outcomes through this quite often. Perpetrators have even apologised after." (P1)

4.7 Crisis Signaling

Crisis signaling relates to things such as calling friends for help or reporting the perpetrator. Calling for friends to help generally was available only in team vs team games while reporting functions were available at all times, although in the context of StarCraft II according to the players it was unclear if reports were handled and acted upon. Some participants felt that reports still were a key functionality for coping with toxicity, and filing reports of perpetrators was something they regularly engaged in. For example, P11 commented the following:

"In the game you will report the bad cases" (P11)

Calling friends for help could bring players some peace of mind, as they felt they were not alone in the toxic situation. The social support was an important coping measure for many, and some participants expressed that teammates not only had a duty to protect their allies against toxicity from the opponents, but also in calming teammates if they behaved in a toxic fashion. This was explained in the following quote from P3:

"The playing partners especially should help calm down their friends. It is difficult to get a tilted guy to acknowledge that what they are doing is unacceptable." (P3)

4.8 Eroding Trust

As the final category of coping that emerged from the interviews is eroding trust. Eroding trust linked to players' losing their willingness to play the game, and view events within the game as meaningful and important. This form of coping was perhaps the least well defined of the discovered categories, since it contained elements of both problem-focused and emotion-focused coping, and was simultaneously a coping mechanism and an outcome of experiencing toxicity over lengthy periods of time. This form of coping was also linked to a few other categories, primarily affective detachment (i.e., emotionally withdrawing from thinking the game and events within are important) and functional detachment (being less often engaged with the game). The reason this category emerged as a standalone category linked to the unique role of trust and meaning as defining factors. For example, the following quote from P3 highlights the outcomes or toxicity and negative mood on his trust and willingness to engage in playing:

"In my own playing friend circles I've felt that the negative mood spreads to me, and I have not felt good playing in those friend circles. That's one of the reasons I've mostly quit playing competitive [team] games [such as StarCraft II]." (P3)

Eroding trust appeared as a coping mechanism for broader issues faced while playing, such as continued as sustained toxicity that was never corrected by admins. By viewing the game and matches as less important, players would draw distance between events in the game and their well-being. Linking back to the category of psychological maneuvering, players could position themselves as people in the realm world as opposed to characters in the game, effectively detaching themselves from toxicity they experience. Eroding trust also had other drivers besides stressors such as toxicity, highlighting it as a behavioural response with other functions besides coping.

5   Discussion

5.1   Key Findings

The main finding of this work is the inductive discovery of eight categories of coping measures that players employ when faced with toxicity in StarCraft II. These are enumerated in Table 2 and were discussed in more detail in the Findings section. With this we managed to provide a data-driven view on coping with toxicity, similar to what was presented in the work of Passmore and Mandryk [36], but did this specifically for the RTS genre.

Second, we explored the connection of the inductively derived forms of coping to the coping theory of Lazarus and Folkman [32]. With our interview approach we discovered that while five categories of coping were exclusively problem-focused and one exclusively emotion-focused, there were two categories that were both problem-focused and emotion-focused forms of coping. These were psychological maneuvering and eroding trust. We discussed the interplay between emotion-focused and problem-focused coping, and how the two influence each other.

Third, we demonstrated that players employ multiple forms of coping when dealing with toxicity, and do this by and large intuitively without thinking or rationalizing their behaviour. In addition to coping with toxicity specifically, players also cope with their own emotions such as frustrations related to losing matches. Similarly to what was argued in the work of Frommel and Mandryk [16], our work suggests that it is critically important to empower players to control and manage the toxicity that they are exposed to.

5.2   Theoretical and Practical Contributions

As mentioned, this study answers recent calls to address toxicity through giving players more control over what kinds of behaviours they are exposed to [16].

It provides an overview of the current coping mechanisms that players have, which can be useful for designers looking to come up with features for players to better shield themselves from toxicity. Our work also suggests that players' eroding trust in the game, which is linked to discontinuance of playing, is directly connected to coping with toxicity. Eroding trust may be a missing link between toxicity and long-term discontinuance. Indeed, based on our findings we encourage the quantitative line of work on toxicity [19,20,22] to investigate eroding trust as an outcome of exposure to toxicity and as an antecedent for discontinuance.

On the level of practice our work can be useful for players as well as developers. The conceptualization of coping mechanisms can help players become more mindful of the strategies they have at their disposal for dealing with toxicity, and developers may also wish to inform and guide players much more specifically in how they can and should shield themselves from toxicity. For example, are some coping mechanisms (e.g., reciprocal reactance) discourage while others (crisis signaling) encouraged?

Through the identification of eight distinct coping strategies employed by players in response to toxic behavior, we also noted that participants employed multiple of these mechanisms at the same time, and revealed coping as a multi-faceted process involving both emotion-focused and problem-focused approaches [30,32]. As an important outcome of coping, this work suggests that a single act of toxicity can trigger multiple coping behaviors, influencing both individual responses and the broader game culture over time. For example, if players are constantly triggered to emotionally detach from the game events, or unintentionally learn reciprocal reactance, these can have dramatic consequences on the playerbase and the popularity of the game. Recognizing this complexity is essential for fostering sustainable player communities in multiplayer live service games over longer periods of time.

5.3   Limitations and Future Work

This work supports future studies on coping with toxicity by introducing eight distinct approaches that can be further probed and understood. However, the study has limitations which require discussing. First, while we appeared to reach saturation already at 12 participants, we acknowledge that the sample size is smaller than what is typical in other similar research.

Second, the participant pool is fairly homogeneous—particularly in regards to gender identity. Here, previous research has also pinpointed gender as a critical aspect in both coping with toxicity and experiencing it [11,13,23]. For example, women might opt for gender-neutral names to avoid drawing unwanted, sexist attention to themselves during gaming [11,46]. Similarly, other identity aspects inform how players are perceived, and in turn, shape the toxicity they may receive: As toxicity can borrow from current oppressive structures (e.g., racism, sexism, or homophobia), (already) marginalised players therefore are at risk of encountering an additional layer of vitriol. These aspects shape how players can cope, and they are important to highlight. However, they did not feature in our participants' responses, which is a limitation since we did not go into detail regarding e.g., the content of verbal abuse that players reported to have been coping with.

Third, the interview guide undoubtedly guided the participants' responses, which might explain why the inductively derived forms of coping were mostly related to problem-focused coping. Thus, we encourage future research to in particular engage in analysis of emotion-focused coping mechanisms in gaming. Regarding future research in this domain, we encourage more detailed analysis of coping mechanisms to understand when they occur, how they occur and how they shape players' thinking. This might require employing longitudinal research methods such as player diaries, experiments testing how players behave under controlled scenarios or combining telemetry data analysis with player interviews. However, we feel that it is critically important to understand the effects of toxicity on players also from the perspective of shaping the player's behaviours through promoting them to engage in various coping behaviours. We also encourage quantitative research on the effects of coping mechanisms, particularly those connected to play discontinuance in our interviews such as eroding trust and the more radical forms of functional detachment.

6 Conclusion

In this work we looked at players' perspectives on coping with toxicity in the popular RTS multiplayer online game StarCraft II. Through player interviews we inductively discovered eight categories of coping, and found that players had diverse and varied views on when and under what circumstances these approaches were suitable, and in some cases, acceptable. Players also showed evidence of individual differences in applying these strategies, and showed varied levels of tolerance for toxicity. Participants primarily referred to problem-focused coping strategies and were much less vocal about emotion-focused approaches. This work illuminates players' coping strategies, and can help practitioners design systems that better support coping with toxicity in multiplayer online games.

References

1. Activision-Blizzard: *StarCraft II*. Game [PC/OS-X], blizzard Entertainment, Irvine, California, USA, July 2010
2. Activision-Blizzard: *Hearthstone*. Game [PC/OS-X/iOS/Android], blizzard Entertainment, Irvine, California, USA (2014)
3. Adinolf, S., Turkay, S.: Toxic behaviors in esports games: player perceptions and coping strategies. In: Proceedings of the 2018 Annual Symposium on Computer-Human Interaction in Play Companion Extended Abstracts, pp. 365–372 (2018). https://doi.org/10.1145/3270316.3271545
4. Altarriba Bertran, F., Buruk, O., Hamari, J.: From-the-wild: towards co-designing for and from nature. In: CHI Conference on Human Factors in Computing Systems Extended Abstracts, pp. 1–7 (2022)

5. Anubha, Islam, J.U.: Unveiling key gratifications and stimuli to engage generation z with multiplayer online games. J. Internet Commer., 1–29 (2022). https://doi.org/10.1080/15332861.2022.2088037
6. Beres, N.A., Frommel, J., Reid, E., Mandryk, R.L., Klarkowski, M.: Don't you know that you're toxic: normalization of toxicity in online gaming. In: Proceedings of the 2021 CHI Conference on Human Factors in Computing Systems, pp. 1–15 (2021)
7. Beres, N.A., Klarkowski, M., Mandryk, R.L.: Playing with emotions: a systematic review examining emotions and emotion regulation in esports performance. In: Proceedings of the ACM on Human-Computer Interaction (CHI PLAY), vol. 7, pp. 558–587 (2023). https://doi.org/10.1145/3611041
8. Braun, V., Clarke, V.: Reflecting on reflexive thematic analysis. Qual. Res. Sport Exerc. Health. 11(4), 589–597 (2019). https://doi.org/10.1080/2159676X.2019.1628806
9. Chang, K., Uhm, J.P., Kim, S., Lee, H.W.: Paradoxical relationship between esports toxicity and toxicity tolerance: moderated mediation by gender and positive reappraisal coping. Int. J. Sports Mark. Spons. 24, 737–752 (2023)
10. Valve Corporation and Nexon and Gamania Digital and Vivendi: Counter Strike: Global Offensive. Game [PC] (2000)
11. Cote, A.C.: "I can defend myself" women's strategies for coping with harassment while gaming online. Games Cult. 12(2), 136–155 (2017)
12. Respawn Entertainment and Panic Button Games: Apex Legends. Game [PC/OS-X/Switch/PS4/PS5/XBOXOne] (2019)
13. Fox, J., Tang, W.Y.: Women's experiences with general and sexual harassment in online video games: rumination, organizational responsiveness, withdrawal, and coping strategies. New Media Soc. 19(8), 1290–1307 (2017)
14. Frommel, J., Johnson, D., Mandryk, R.L.: How perceived toxicity of gaming communities is associated with social capital, satisfaction of relatedness, and loneliness. Comput. Hum. Behav. Rep. 10, 100302 (2023)
15. Frommel, J., Klarkowski, M., Mandryk, R.L.: The struggle is spiel: on failure and success in games. In: Proceedings of the 16th International Conference on the Foundations of Digital Games, pp. 1–12 (2021)
16. Frommel, J., Mandryk, R.L.: Individual control over exposure to combat toxicity in games. ACM Games Res. Pract. 1(4), 1–3 (2023). https://doi.org/10.1145/3633768
17. Riot Games: League of Legends. Game [PC/OS-X] (2009)
18. Kordyaka, B., Kruse, B.: Curing toxicity-developing design principles to buffer toxic behaviour in massive multiplayer online games. Safer Communities 20(3), 133–149 (2021)
19. Kordyaka, B., Laato, S., Jahn, K., Hamari, J., Niehaves, B.: The cycle of toxicity: exploring relationships between personality and player roles in toxic behavior in multiplayer online battle arena games. In: Proceedings of the ACM on Human-Computer Interaction(CHI PLAY), vol. 7, pp. 611–641 (2023). https://doi.org/10.1145/3611043
20. Kordyaka, B., Laato, S., Niehaves, B.: A toxic triad: aggression anger and authoritarianism - a study with multiplaye ronline battle arena game players. In: Proceedings of the 8th Annual International GamiFIN Conference 2024 (2024)
21. Kordyaka, B., Laato, S., Weber, S., Niehaves, B.: What constitutes victims of toxicity-identifying drivers of toxic victimhood in multiplayer online battle arena games. Front. Psychol. 14, 1193172 (2023). https://doi.org/10.3389/fpsyg.2023.1193172

22. Kordyaka, B., Park, S., Krath, J., Laato, S.: Exploring the relationship between offline cultural environments and toxic behavior tendencies in multiplayer online games. ACM Trans. Soc. Comput. **6**, 1–20 (2023). https://doi.org/10.1145/3580346
23. Kordyaka, B., Pumplun, L., Brunnhofer, M., Kruse, B., Laato, S.: Gender disparities in esports-an explanatory mixed-methods approach. Comput. Hum. Behav. **149**, 107956 (2023). https://doi.org/10.1016/j.chb.2023.107956
24. Laato, S., Fernández Galeote, D., Altarriba Bertran, F., Papangelis, K., Hamari, J.: How location-based games incentivize moving about: a study in the context of nature-going. In: Proceedings of the ACM on Human-Computer Interaction (CHI PLAY), vol. 7, pp. 642–664 (2023). https://doi.org/10.1145/3611044
25. Laato, S., Kordyaka, B., Hamari, J.: A review of studies on location-based live-service games during the Covid-19 pandemic: players' behavior and reluctance to return to the pre-pandemic state. In: Gaming and Gamers in Times of Pandemic, p. 155 (2024)
26. Laato, S., Kordyaka, B., Hamari, J.: Traumatizing or just annoying? Unveiling the spectrum of gamer toxicity in the starcraft II community. In: Proceedings of the 2024 CHI Conference on Human Factors in Computing Systems. ACM (2024). https://doi.org/10.1145/3613904.3642137
27. Laato, S., Rauti, S., Hamari, J.: Resemblance of religion and pervasive games: a study among church employees and gamers. In: Proceedings of the 2023 CHI Conference on Human Factors in Computing Systems, pp. 1–15 (2023). https://doi.org/10.1145/3544548.3581056
28. Laato, S., Rauti, S., Islam, A.N., Sutinen, E.: Why playing augmented reality games feels meaningful to players? The roles of imagination and social experience. Comput. Hum. Behav. **121**, 106816 (2021)
29. Laato, S., Xi, N., Spors, V., Thibault, M., Hamari, J.: Making sense of reality: a mapping of terminology related to virtual reality, augmented reality, mixed reality, XR and the metaverse. In: Proceedings of the 57th Hawaii International Conference on System Sciences (HICSS) (2024)
30. Lazarus, R.S.: Coping theory and research: past, present, and future. Psychosom. Med. **55**(3), 234–247 (1993)
31. Lazarus, R.S.: Toward better research on stress and coping. Am. Psychol. (2000). https://doi.org/10.1037/0003-066X.55.6.665
32. Lazarus, R.S., Folkman, S.: Stress, Appraisal, and Coping. Springer, New York (1984). https://doi.org/10.1007/978-1-4419-1005-9_215
33. Maroney, N., Williams, B.J., Thomas, A., Skues, J., Moulding, R.: A stress-coping model of problem online video game use. Int. J. Ment. Heal. Addict. **17**, 845–858 (2019)
34. McLean, L., Griffiths, M.D.: Female gamers' experience of online harassment and social support in online gaming: a qualitative study. Int. J. Ment. Heal. Addict. **17**, 970–994 (2019)
35. Passmore, C.J., Mandryk, R.: An about face: diverse representation in games. In: Proceedings of the 2018 Annual Symposium on Computer-Human Interaction in Play, pp. 365–380 (2018)
36. Passmore, C.J., Mandryk, R.L.: A taxonomy of coping strategies and discriminatory stressors in digital gaming. Front. Comput. Sci. **2**, 40 (2020)
37. Plante, C.N., Gentile, D.A., Groves, C.L., Modlin, A., Blanco-Herrera, J.: Video games as coping mechanisms in the etiology of video game addiction. Psychol. Pop. Media Cult. **8**(4), 385 (2019)

38. Poeller, S., Dechant, M.J., Klarkowski, M., Mandryk, R.L.: Suspecting sarcasm: how league of legends players dismiss positive communication in toxic environments. In: Proceedings of the ACM on Human-Computer Interaction (CHI PLAY), vol. 7, pp. 1–26 (2023). https://doi.org/10.1145/3611020
39. Reid, E., Mandryk, R.L., Beres, N.A., Klarkowski, M., Frommel, J.: Feeling good and in control: in-game tools to support targets of toxicity. In: Proceedings of the ACM on Human-Computer Interaction (CHI PLAY), vol. 6, pp. 1–27 (2022). https://doi.org/10.1145/3549498
40. Reid, E., Mandryk, R.L., Beres, N.A., Klarkowski, M., Frommel, J.: "Bad vibrations": sensing toxicity from in-game audio features. IEEE Trans. Games **14**(4), 558–568 (2022). https://doi.org/10.1109/TG.2022.3176849
41. Spors, V., Kaufman, I.: Respawn, reload, relate: exploring the self-care possibilities for mental health in games through a humanistic lens. In: Proceedings of the ACM on Human-Computer Interaction (CHI PLAY), vol. 5, pp. 1–31 (2021)
42. Statista: Global video game market value from 2020 to 2025 (2023). https://www.statista.com/statistics/292056/video-game-market-value-worldwide/
43. Suler, J.: The online disinhibition effect. Cyberpsychol. Behav. **7**(3), 321–326 (2004)
44. Supercell: Clash Royale. Game [Android/iOS] (2016)
45. Thompson, J.J., Leung, B.H., Blair, M.R., Taboada, M.: Sentiment analysis of player chat messaging in the video game StarCraft 2: extending a lexicon-based model. Knowl.-Based Syst. **137**, 149–162 (2017)
46. Türkay, S., Formosa, J., Adinolf, S., Cuthbert, R., Altizer, R.: See no evil, hear no evil, speak no evil: how collegiate players define, experience and cope with toxicity. In: Proceedings of the 2020 CHI Conference on Human Factors in Computing Systems, pp. 1–13. ACM (2020). https://doi.org/10.1145/3313831.3376191
47. Wijkstra, M., Rogers, K., Mandryk, R.L., Veltkamp, R.C., Frommel, J.: Help, my game is toxic! First insights from a systematic literature review on intervention systems for toxic behaviors in online video games. In: Companion Proceedings of the Annual Symposium on Computer-Human Interaction in Play, pp. 3–9 (2023)

Human Use of Vintage Beings: How to Harness the Shock of the Old

Nicolas LaLone[1](✉)🆔 and Phoebe O Toups Dugas[2]🆔

[1] Rochester Institute of Technology, Rochester, NY, USA
njligm@rit.edu
[2] Monash University, Melbourne, Australia
Phoebe.ToupsDugas@monash.edu

Abstract. At present, there is a paradoxical space wherein consumers and how they communicate is under constant change. Emergency managers (EM), who need special connections to those communication tools, are not considered. Instead, EM professionals are often accused of being a profession disconnected from the current technological reality. This issue is a paradox because it is a problem of technology–old is abandoned for new. In a similar way, tabletop role-playing games (TTRPGs) have been disconnected from game studies for decades though recent work has adjusted this oversight [1]. For researchers, TTRPGs provide context for how to consider systems, data-driven communication, and the role of data, all mental models from computational spaces in an original, or vintage, form. We call those who still play, design, or discuss TTRPGs vintage beings. The present research explores how vintage beings can use the shock of the old to connect younger learners to old tech and older learners to new tech.

Keywords: Vintage Computing · Tabletop Games · Human Use of Human Beings · Norbert Wiener · Computer Science Education · CSEd

1 Introduction

There is a paradoxical space between two groups of people that will define the coming era of climate-driven global change. One group is the general public, who are *consumers* that are sold new tools for communication constantly (e.g., ubiquitous smart technologies, social media, smart phones, wearables...). The other group helps consumers when a hazard event (e.g., an earthquake) occurs – *emergency managers* – who receive no capacity to use these same tools for public safety and are, by-and-large, of a generation that has relied upon established technologies [42,43,52]. There is a need to connect our technological history to our technological present to best prepare emergency management for the future. As part of this need, learners from all backgrounds must either be brought into current technological developments or we must unearth perspectives on how older technology functioned.

ⓒ The Author(s), under exclusive license to Springer Nature Switzerland AG 2024
X. Fang (Ed.): HCII 2024, LNCS 14731, pp. 220–246, 2024.
https://doi.org/10.1007/978-3-031-60695-3_15

While current modes of computer science education may not be effective in either of these scenarios [37], tabletop role playing games (TTRPGs) offer a bridge. From the perspective of emergency managers, TTRPGs are much like the simulation exercises emergency management professionals engage with regularly and rooted in vintage experiences such folks grew up with. At the same time, TTRPGs are enormously popular and are constantly incorporating new technologies.[1] We expect that TTRPGs offer a promising vector to create new socio-technical approaches to education for older or existing information technology in addition to informing design processes for future technologies. The present work takes a step toward this – we interview a range of TTRPG enthusiasts to understand the how and why of play and begin to apply it to educational and design process goals in support of emergency management.

This work speaks across domains, disciplines, practices, and fandoms to a topic that is difficult to describe. Each of the researchers here belong to a place disconnected from each other whether they be student, teacher, practitioner, researcher, designer, or fan. At the core is a desire to understand how to help get older learners not only understand information communication technology, but how programming and design works within the tenets of computer science.

While the present research is targeted at older learners, the domain it rests in is that of the practice of emergency management (EM). EM, much to the disappointment of crisis informatics, has eschewed almost everything related to computers for reasons relating to their stability in the midst of disaster [52]. While this did not really matter for many decades, recent shifts in consumer use of information communication technology (ICT) relevant to how people use their mobile devices, has left a large, unbridgeable gap for those currently under duress trying to get help using everything but the phone portion of their telephone [41,43].

To wit, we are grasping at something, anything, we can do to begin to address this gap without using the lessons and knowledge of computer science education (CSEd) [26,28]. This is because extant CSEd is founded in higher education, yet our learners and intended classes are used to a very specific type of education that is disconnected from higher education in nearly every way. The tricks and understanding of CSEd simply cannot be used for this group. So, we turn to TTRPGs, to games like *Dungeons & Dragons* (*D&D*) (1974), to help inform avenues of learning that may have been partially obfuscated by history. We do this because the domain of EM is intimately connected to role-playing and tabletop exercises and, as such, their use in CSEd is of paramount importance.

The present research contributes the notion of *vintage*, or history, in the space of computation while concurrently providing nuance and overlap in TTRPGs. By speaking to people who identify as tabletop role-players, we show that TTRPGs and CSEd share not only common ancestry, but tools educators can use as the wave of vintage technology, of nostalgia, of retro markets, and of the old school renaissance, can provide CSEd with an opportunity to re-consider and re-deploy

---

[1] This is a nascent area of inquiry but products include Tabletop Simulator, Roll20, Fantasy Grounds, MapTool, and Gametable [48].

what it has learned in the past several decades. Concurrently, we provide a rich and useful description of the connectivity between digital and analog games and suggest that their being united as equals not only strengthens the study of games in general, but elevates their similarities to useful spaces in specific. Much of this begins with Norbert Wiener and his thoughts on entropy in relation to the computer.

Wiener in *The Human Use of Human Beings* wrote, "It is my thesis that the physical functioning of the living individual and the operation of some of the new communication machines are precisely parallel in their analogous attempts to control entropy through feedback." [70]. Yet, when he wrote this, the prevailing thought was that only a few computers were actually needed in the world. What Wiener, nor the quotes that reflect the sentiment in the previous sentence from Thomas Watson [58], Sir Charles Darwin, Douglas Hartree, or Howard Aiken took into account was the sheer number of uses that computation would eventually provide to the everyday consumer.

Entropy, or the propensity of all things to descend into chaos, is avoided in computation because while the machinery itself may degrade and cease to work, the function of a computer is itself an anti-entropic engine [70]. This anti-entropy was so strong that Wiener goes on to note that, "We have modified our environment so radically that we must now modify ourselves in order to exist in this new environment." [70]. In essence, we created a machine that can stabilize humanity as long as it re-organizes itself around it. And it has, the computer is now so ubiquitous that it is harder to get away from the computer than it is to use [38, 40].

Yet, if the computer essentially negates entropy, then it is partially responsible for the relative lack of chaos we have had since Wiener's book was published in 1950. Unfortunately, as should be evident from current events, politics throughout the world, and the growing number of disasters that while the computer may have staved off entropy, staved off chaos, there is something happening now that needs to be addressed. It would seem that over the last century that while we created a machine to stave off entropy, it has found new ways to manifest [38].

We are now at the precipice of entropy, descending into chaos, as the sheer volume of software removes that once stabilizing force. Yet, within that new form of potential entropy is situated a different kind of entropy halting thing, vintage use or old school products or re-formulations of the original spaces surrounding computation. Within this vintage space is a relative lack of potential aside from entropy in the form of cataloging history. History rarely has a use because of the philosophies surrounding: programming, labor in computation, and the basic epistemology of software in that replacement is easier than editing [56].

But vintage has a use, vintage allows us to circumvent that which is far off in the future and caged within the present. The human use of those being who maintain vintage things can allow us to not only learn from the past, but negate the new entropy we are seeing all around us. These vintage beings, if used by humans themselves, provide not only ways to re-think the past as a future, but to stave off entropy. Through that re-consideration, we can state that the human use of vintage beings is now becoming more important than the future technology is seeking to provide.

The paper is organized by first briefly describing the current state of scenes and systems in TTRPGs and their connection to computation. After discussing and naming terms, we then briefly describe the background of the relationship between computer-mediated role-playing games, tabletop role-playing games, and computer science education. Next, we provide a discussion of our interview-based study. After describing our data, we then move to initial results. Once we have sufficiently covered our results, we then discuss their meaning and provide any concluding remarks that computer science educators may be interested in carrying away from our discussion.

2   Current Art Worlds and Terms of Importance in TTRPGs

Since this work focuses on differences between similar spaces, we use the Howard Becker term "art worlds" to group them together. In this case, an "art world" is a space within which there are conventions among people who may not interact with each other directly that are mutually understood [4]. While TTRPG is itself a broad heading, there are a number of smaller spaces under that heading that are identifiable by the differences among their shared norms.

The TTRPG space is mostly defined by the earliest game systems that players engaged with. So, we can say that TTRPGs first appeared in 1974 with the publication of *D&D* (1974). While *D&D* (1974) was the first published game, it was preceded by a number of games played by a club in the Twin Cities of Minneapolis-St. Paul throughout the mid-to-late 1960s [39,65]. Since their publication, the TTRPG scene has surged, dwindled, re-appeared, collapsed, gone indie, and is now back to a popularity the TTRPG space has not seen since the early 1980s when they were the most popular form of game in the world [71]. Throughout that history, it has influenced and been influenced by software and games [39,65].

Presently, there are three roughly equal communities of players. The first community is that of the "old-school renaissance" or OSR. This community is sometimes also referred to as "traditional games" and also includes the current iteration (5th edition) of *D&D* (1974). As *D&D* (1974) was the first game created, it has served as an introductory space for gamers for over four decades. It was appended with the terms, "old school" and "renaissance" as to indicate that, while these were the original games in the space, they should be re-considered and re-designed in the present in order to best represent the lessons learned since their creation. These games tend to be defined as "heavy" in terms of their use of variables and procedures to mediate play.

The second community is sometimes referred to as "story games" or "narrative games". Wherein the OSR sees characters as numbers, as agents of a system they are using to define player actions, story gamers carefully craft their character's backstory and each of their sessions tend to use character motivations as a space of play. These games are typically seen as "medium" in terms of their system weight often favoring to remove rules to accommodate player choice rather than using the system as an adversary necessary to overcome.

Finally, our third scene is mostly congealed under the affordances and categorization of the website Itch.io[2]. Many of these games are under 10 pages with a large proportion of them being 1–2 pages at most. This is in comparison with OSR and *D&D* (1974), which typically comprise a few hundred to a few thousand pages of rules and explanations spread out among the core rulebooks, supplements, and various online spaces. These games more directly reflect the approach of an improv troop rather than a standard TTRPG. As a result, these games are typically seen as "light" in terms of their system weight in that they often have a handful of variables to be calculated or tested against at any given time.

We discuss these art worlds in terms of the philosophical approach of phenomenology. Under this term, we seek to understand how disparate subjective experiences like playing a TTRPG reflect the spaces from which those players come from [66]. Play, in this case, is engaging a system or design with the intent of figuring out how it works [9] (or in this case making a character and seeing how the system and player intent agree and disagree). That these disparate art worlds themselves represent a variety of unique experiences that, once defined, can provide useful discovery that practice or the art of techniques found under the term technology can use in their designs.

3   Background

In order to best contextualize how players relate to different kinds of TTRPGs, it is necessary to take a few logical steps. First, we will discuss early TTRPGs. This will allow us to show that computation, war games, and TTRPGs all share a common ancestor. Next, we will discuss early video games that came out of these first intersections of wargames, TTRPGs, and computer systems. Specifically, this will allow us to show why TTRPGs and video games needed each other in order to establish their presence as an industry. Finally, we will briefly touch on computer science education (CSEd) and enthusiast self-teaching. In doing this, we can show that if wargames, computation, and TTRPGs share ancestry, their relationship affords them a unique opportunity for teaching, learning, and development.

3.1   Early Enthusiast Computing & the Shift from the Parlor to an Industry

When computation first became available to people not in the military or in research labs devoted to developing new military intelligence capabilities [62],

---

[2] The games in question for this art world can be found under the tag, "tabletop-rpg" at https://itch.io/physical-games/tag-tabletop-rpg.

these first enthusiast programmers did not develop new tools, new programs, or other types of software that their predecessors did. Instead, they developed video games [13,18]. These were not parlor games, toys, card games, or physics simulators like their predecessors, they were games based on what was considered the most popular game at the time, *D&D* (1974) [39,71].

D&D (1974) is a tabletop role-playing game (TTRPG) that consists of a system meant to mediate a group's imagination by representing each individual character, monster, and choice as a check against pre-defined variables like strength, intelligence, charisma, dexterity, wisdom, and constitution with modifiers like skills (e.g., "I am good at swordplay so when I am using my sword, my dice rolls get to add +3 to their results") [45,67]. Games like *Pedit5*, *dnd*, and *Oubliette* would provide players of the PLATO system[3] inspiration to develop other games resulting in foundational games like *Wizardry* which would form the basis of the computer-role-playing game industry [18].

Other developers outside of PLATO's short-lived scene would create games like *Rogue*, *Colossal Cave Adventure*, and *Akalabeth*, a predecessor to the *Ultima* series [13,14,27]. Each of these creators all shared the common experience, *D&D* (1974). Even games like *John Madden Football*, today one of the largest game franchises in the world, began through the spaces that inspired *D&D* (1974), that of war games like *Strat-o-Matic Baseball* [15], another variable-driven, nearly computer mediated game from the period of time where the computer was still too new to bring home.

Those initial games would form the basis of the modern computer game industry and set a precedent for enthusiast programmers learning how to write computer programs based on their experiences with TTRPGs [13,18,39]. While the period between the 1950s and 1980s would see enthusiast programmers inspired by their fantasy-driven exploits, the relationship between the tabletop, computer programming, and the potential of the relationship between these two has remained not only important, but almost a requirement to learn programming for some new programmers [39]. Despite its importance, this relationship is under-explored.

3.2   Early Role-Playing Games

Over the course of the 18th and 19th centuries, relationships to human space began to shift [39]. While somewhat obtuse, this relationship had an impact on military strategy, training, and especially logistics. This slow move to thinking of space as an asset meant to be enhanced by maps, cartography, and careful gathering of information about battlefields. The paragon of this new way of thinking, Napoleon Bonaparte, nearly conquered the world. While his failure is typically the one that is often discussed, his successes, particularly at the Battle

---

[3] PLATO was a computer system based on the mainframe model that evolved from the ENIAC machine developed at the University of Illinois at Urbana Champaign. This system was the origin point of Massively Multiplayer Online Games, Chatrooms, Email, and a host of other computational products [18].

of Jena-Auerstedt, changed not only military strategy forever, but set in motion the chain of events that would culminate in the creation of the computer [24,62].

One product that came out of this success was a method of training new officers and troops to understand Napoleon's new conceptualization of war. That product, called a war game, was named *Kriegspiel* (1812). This game consisted of two players feeding commands to a third person, an umpire, or what could be considered a mental model of a computer processor [24]. Fed commands by each player, the umpire would move pieces around according to pre-defined rules. It is this game, this style of play, that began to spread around the world.

After several wars, the American version of this wargame, *Strategos* [63] was discovered by David Wesely in the Twin Cities of Minneapolis-Saint Paul [54]. This game indicated that an umpire should officiate play (a rule forgotten after the second World War wherein players simply interfaced with systems). Wesely rewrote *Strategos* (1880) as *Strategos N* (1968), adjusting for new military tactics and understandings of the world [54]. He then further augmented the game into a freeform simulation of play wherein each player, rather than controlling groups of soldiers, took on a role of a resident of a town called Braunstein.

It is here that the TTRPG emerged. Wherein games like *Kriegspiel* (1812) were labeled and criticized by people like Clausewitz that they robbed their players of the emotion of war [24], this form of play by Wesely did away with these criticisms by joining the logic of war strategy, the logic that would become the logic of computation, with the emotion of war by placing the player within a single person, an avatar or character. This small shift afforded by the development of systemic thinking [29] allowed computation and emotion to exist in concurrence. By 1974 under the name of *D&D* (1974), this style of play would become the most popular game in the world.

3.3   Early Video Games

The creation of a new era of creativity in the mid-1970s resulted in an explosion of computer-mediated games. Much of this early exploration of the potential of computation was not written down and is only recently being cataloged as a part of oral history. The game *D&D* (1974) was the most popular game in the world concurrent with the spread of systems thinking and the popularity of wargames. This was later joined by the first moments that civilians could access the first computers. The PLATO system or the Programmed Logic for Automatic Teaching Operations system embodied the concepts of B.F. Skinner's behaviorism [18].

It was conceptualized as a teaching device but as a mainframe system it afforded users an ability to send programs to the mainframe and receive their results in real time. The TUTOR programming language at the University of Illinois at Urbana-Champaign allowed early enthusiasts to create email, chat rooms, massively multiplayer games, first person shooters, and the computer RPG for the PLATO system [18]. These early video games were almost entirely based on *D&D* (1974).

Among these games were a game called *pedit5*, which afforded players an ability to wander around a dungeon. This game was created in the Population and Energy Group memory space of the PLATO system by Rusty Rutherford, an avid *D&D* (1974) player. It was constantly deleted as, at the time, games were forbidden. Two players of *pedit5* (1974), Gary Whisenhunt and Ray Wood, were increasingly frustrated with the game. This frustration, paired with a lot of *D&D* (1974) dungeon crawls, inspired them to not only learn how TUTOR worked, but to replicate the game they enjoyed. This resulted in the game *dnd* (1975) on the PLATO systems [18,39]. These two games inspired dozens of copycats, incremental improvements, and distinct developments. The result was the formation of the modern computer role-playing game industry, and the video game industry more generally [13,18,64,65].

While TUTOR was one particular scene, this use of *D&D* (1974) was present in nearly all computer-centered design scenes at the time [18,39]. For example, Lord British or Richard Garriott created his first computer roleplaying game (CRPG) called Akalabeth which had been called "*DND*" and relied heavily on his local *D&D* (1974) campaign. And even earlier, *Adventure*, later called *Colossal Cave Adventure* was based on two things: Mammoth Cave and his local *D&D* (1974) campaign [34]. We also see games like *Return to Apple Manor* (1978) which began wiht the inspiration from a local *D&D* (1974) campaign [46]. And Rogue, the game from which Roguelikes [31] take their name, additionally relied on how *D&D* (1974) worked to present a player with tension and adventure [13]. Even sports games like *Madden Football* relied not specifically on *D&D* (1974) but those games *D&D* (1974) pulled from, wargames [57]. While the source code of these original games exist, the labor that went into them, the conversations, the learning, and its components –all essential components of the first communities of practice [30]–is lost. In its place has been inserted an artificial space called CSEd.

3.4 Computer-Science Education or Computing Education Research

CSEd (e.g., computing education) is primarily concerned with how people learn what a computer can do and how to best approach that learning [28]. This domain appeared in conjunction with the term computer science [3,18,35]. One concept that has been of primary interest has been what language to use in the action-oriented work that takes place after this. With little to no programming or even technology exploration done by Emergency Managers [41], we know that we are working at a deficit. That said, some of the work around the first computer languages notes that graphical computer languages seem to enhance grades and through better grades, more enjoyment [12]. This is important for two reasons.

First, Guzdial [28] notes that students use enjoyment as a stand-in for liking programming. If students use enjoyment in this way, then maximizing enjoyment seems to be of paramount importance. If this is true, then the additional note of Chen et al. [12] wherein they saw that students whose first language was graphical tended to have higher grades than those who learn text-based languages first. For Chen et al. [12], this was correlated to adolescent engagement with programming and has been repeated a number of times [49]. This finding stands in juxtaposition to adult learners who primarily learn text-based languages first [36,49]. Additionally, there is the problem of childhood wherein girls are pushed away from learning programming whereas boys are not [11]. And even further, there exists a variety of stereotypes that the "dungeons and dragons" type of persons are the only ones who learn programming [44]. We begin with this concept and postulate that the confinement of TTRPGs to this type of person is a misnomer in need of unpacking.

One approach that saw useful results was in DiSalvo and Bruckman's [20] work on the place of video games in stoking the interest in computer science. To learn about this concept, the researchers polled 1872 undergraduate students in 2007 about the use of games with relation to learning programming. While the results of the survey were a such that it was an extremely small impact, they note that further variables must be influencing learning. We suggest that it is not programming that is interesting about games persae, but how game states are manifested. The results of this work are repeated in different ways with similar results [19,21,22].

Another approach for CSEd that is of interest for the current research is that of CS Unplugged. In CS Unplugged, students create knowledge for themselves by working within constraints. This is a constructivist approach that seeks to students from their own interests. In doing so, instructors can harness that interest to further complicate the problems they are solving [5,6,55,60]. While this approach is focused on learners in compulsory ed in the United States, many of the lessons here could be useful with vintage beings.

Where the work continually reaches a frustrating conclusion is that it rarely seeks to explicate the influence of other media that programmatic concepts can come from. For example, one of the most formative aspects of this work was a discussion point from Brian Dorn, a researcher at the University of Nebraska at Omaha, who noted, "I think we're afraid to go outside of computer science at times" [26]. And so, looking at the current state of CSEd and the current debates around the relationship around digital and analog games, we felt it was time to promote not only an outside perspective, but one so unlike anything currently existing in CSEd as to be a new approach.

Despite being present since the beginning of computing, much of computer science education or computing education research is still nascent in relation to other education-focused domains. Instead of focusing on assembling important lessons, computer science education tends to focus on how students feel about learning computer science, the mistakes they make, and the different ways that they learn [59]. What is needed is more integration, more elucidation, of how students learn to do things they want to do, like make games, and how the way they do these things might be used elsewhere. And this is where our contribution as the TTRPG is a space where systems thinking, computational thinking, emotion, and explorations of humanity converge.

4   Data

We chose to interview known figures in the TTRPG world in order to glimpse how prevalent computing was in their lives. We did this because, if TTRPGs can provide an avenue to teach, then we need to understand where the hooks from TTRPGs to learn programming and technology are situated. We decided to use semi-structured interviews paired with topics that are general to not only RPGs, but the phenomenon of play [8]. We did this because how and what TTRPGs are lend themselves to the exploration of programmatic concepts and by discussing their actual play, the phenomenological aspects of play, we can tease out the relationship between the types of systems TTRPGs use and computer-mediated games, development environments, even online community technologies like Google+, Facebook, Roll20[4], and DNDBeyond[5].

4.1   Targeted Recruitment

Because the first author is a known figure in the TTRPG industry and various scenes, they relied heavily on their status to recruit central figures in each of the stated scenes. We recruited figures central to each of the scenes. For OSR, we recruited not only well-known players and GMs based on their blog and/or forum participation, but designers who often have their names attached to books players buy. For itchio, we recruited via Twitter and our existing social networks and targeted makers who were well-followed. For story games, we targeted folks we have played with, authors and designers of popular story game TTRPGs, and other kinds of figures like researchers and historians in the space. While this was our initial recruitment criteria, we then began snowball sampling by asking each initial respondent for the names of 2–3 more.

4.2   Method

While each of the researchers involved with this study could fall under the auspices of being "well-played" [17], there is a need to dig further into the concepts in and around TTRPGs that negate that potential. More than simply engaging in thematic analysis of a series of transcripts, there is a need for the researchers to engage these data as novices, as naive researchers attempting to understand a space as an insider. Ethnography is the wrong approach for this style as we are not in the field, we are not at the table with these individuals watching them play, or playing with them. What is needed for studies like these is a method that affords the researchers the capability to learn.

---

[4] A digital platform to mediate TTRPG play that includes digital twins of counters, figures, dice, maps, and includes camera and audio components which can be found at: https://roll20.net/.

[5] DNDBeyond is the publisher of *D&D's* (1974) digital platform where players can purchase digital copies of the handbooks, make characters, and maintain the logistics of a campaign. It can be found at https://www.dndbeyond.com/.

That method, Qualitative Media Analysis [2], puts researcher understanding of their object of inquiry as central to generating the meaning that arises out of interacting with stakeholders and respondents. As the meaning, as the understanding of the space grows, protocols, data collection measures, and other forms of data gathering will change. For example, our instrument which is described in the next section originally ended with what we called the "lightning round." In this lightning round, we asked respondents to define terms for us as we still do; however, the terms assigned for respondents to define were generated by each of the scenes we were interested in.

What this did was infuriate our respondents as they struggled to define potentially nebulous and politically charged terms. Confirmation bias began to become a pivotal aspect of each interview as respondents would either tell us never to ask anyone that question or they would apologize for failing us as researchers. In both cases, we were not generating the information we sought and so we discussed this with a few respondents and as researchers. The result was that we mapped out common terms that appear across scenes and instead limited the list to 10 terms. The results of this new approach, retroactively gathered from the respondents who did not answer them provided some incredible information. Through standard approaches to semi-structured interviews, this would not have been possible.

After our interviews were completed, we loaded them into a transcription service run by an artificial intelligence, otter.ai. This service, for a minimal fee, produces usable transcripts that require minimal editing. Once those transcripts were available, the first author sat down with them and looked at what interesting items came out of them. While Qualitative Media Analysis offers guidance for how to interpret and understand the data once it is collected, we sought to understand these data in terms of traces. This method of analysis most closely reflects thematic analysis [7,10]. The resulting themes are assembled and present in the discussion of the present research. To get to these themes, we took five distinct steps.

First, we familiarized ourselves with the data by reading each transcript and noted items of interest. Next, we generated a number of categories or codes that interested us. After these initial categories were created, we searched for how much information they generated. We then went back with what we had learned and looked at our data again Finally, we renamed the categories to what you see in the discussion now [8,10].

4.3   Instrument

Because we are deploying Qualitative Media Analysis, the researchers understand that their initial attempts to understand the space that they belong to will be incomplete [2]. It is important to note that the focal point of this paper was not specifically sought for in this instrument. We did this as we wanted to understand traces to technical knowledge and because TTRPGs are so heavily reliant on computer-rpgs and vice versa, this was not something we needed to pursue as it was going to emerge from the data anyway. Our interviews focused on a number of phenomenological themes that were identified by the primary researchers. These themes include: gaming identity, gaming affiliations, and phenomenological explorations.

Within gaming identity, the interviewer facilitates respondent exploration of how they were introduced to role-playing games, what games they played, and what sort of groups they were involved with. After this, the interviewer probes the respondent to explore how their experiences evolved over time and what gaming affiliations they identify with. Because the researchers are experts and well-played [39,64,65] in this space, they felt that they understand much of the community. While they were able to consolidate many of the communities down to their bare minimum in order to better focus the respondent, this test would allow the researchers to see if they were correct.

Each respondent is asked recall a memorable role-playing experience and reflect upon what happened in that particular instance. Finally, the respondent is provided a series of words that they are asked to define that we call, "The lighting round" as a means through which to understand how different communities would identify them. Initially, the interview concluded with a "lightning round" consisting of 29 TTRPG-related terms meant to be explored. However, this list was cumbersome and contained too many terms specific to some scenes and not present in others. This lightning round was replaced by a set of 10 terms focused on TTRPG concepts that are used across communities.

5   Analysis

Each transcript was explored for themes within themselves, and then compared to each other. Adjustments to our instrument, follow-up questions, and spaces of agreement then afforded the researchers an ability to connect disparate individual experience in favor of general qualities related to getting into TTRPGs and their overlap with other forms of games. The interview transcripts were reviewed and evaluated by two researchers with a third being brought in to mitigate disagreements and difference. This resulted in 4 items of interest that will be highlighted in the discussion.

5.1   Respondent Backgrounds

One thing about TTRPGs that is important to note is that they are not a diverse space. Whereas video games are not diverse in their representation [16], audience [11], or development team [50], TTRPGs make the video game industry look far more diverse than it is. If we are meant to examine the vintage being, we need then, to examine the middle-aged white male. And we have gathered 11 respondents who mostly fit that description. While this is just our initial gathering of respondents, our sample will diversify as we move from vintage beings to more recent types of TTRPG players.

Our respondents primarily identify as cis-gendered, white men with an average age of 47. Many of our respondents either have a PhD or are ABD. This is due to our initial recruitment of prominent members of various TTRPG scenes. The nature of TTRPGs and their creation is as such that they (stereotypically) attract curious people who enjoy seeking to learn. Or, you can just call them nerds. And so, the purposeful nature of our sample is shown here. We sampled stereotype first and will expand as this project continues. Everyone lived in North America.

So while this sample is discouraging, it is not without purpose. By highlighting the lack of diversity, we additionally highlight that not only is this approach needed, but vitally important for a variety of diversity issues. By approaching the past both in how it was and what it looked like, not only can we re-frame, re-consider, and re-form that past in as much as those retro products do. Next, we discussed gaming identity.

5.2 Gaming Identity

This set of questions focused on a number of very important concepts. First, we asked about how the respondent got into TTRPGs. Next, we asked about game preference and the type of people that they tend to play with. After this, we engage in understanding if there are any labels associated with their gaming identity. This question of labels are those as such as we have already described. OSR tends to focus on the promise of TTRPGs as they were intended. Story gamers tend to focus on their character's development and place within a narrative or story.

Toward the end of this section, we begin to ask questions related to "additional" content related to games in general. Itchio gamers tend to focus on new ideas with TTRPGs or those fringe elements that often permeate the edges of communities. This could be a single-page TTRPG or TTRPGs that are essentially crowdsourced poetry. Within each of these spaces, we expected a different relationship to technology yet as we discussed this with respondents, we did not end up seeing one. Instead, what we did see was push back against labels and community membership writ large. This tended to be shaped by the way our respondents got into TTRPGs and where inspiration came from.

5.3 Affiliations and Scene Participation

This section of the interview expands on how and where people play, what communities they belong to, and other sorts of scenes. This collection of questions is meant to tease apart those who might reject labels based on the 3 big communities above. While a gamer may claim to not be part of a community, there are only so many places online and in-person where gamers like TTRPG players gather and talk.

Answers to these questions tended to solidify the initial thoughts we had about the disparate communities out there. Whereas folks tended to identify strongly with the communities in question, the personal feelings about who they were in relation to those communities was even stronger. The strongest aspect of this discussion had to do with 2 specific items. First, respondents consistently noted that they did not *only* play TTRPGs. The concept of, "the trifecta gamer" emerged where players felt that in order to understand TTRPGs, one needed to play war games, video games, and TTRPGs. Only in this way could one enjoy this type of game completely. Second, we received not only more information than we anticipated about scene participation, we were offered a number of descriptions and thoughts about what TTRPGs are meant to do. What do we mean, for example, when we consider vintage beings? These will be discussed in the next section.

5.4   Actual Play

After demographics, identity, and affiliation are discussed, we move into what we call, "phenomenological explorations." This is a theory-driven name meant to call upon phenomenology which has been used by several of the researchers attached to this project [45,68]. What this section provides is a way for the researchers to understand how players think about their given community and identity in the midst of a session.

Answers to this question tended to focus on the role of actual play in discourse. What the purpose of play was, what podcasts and things related to actual play tended to be the results of this question. So while this section did not offer much in the way of trace data to examine, it did provide useful discourse on what this aspect of play is for. We will discuss this in the next section.

5.5   Word Association

Finally, we asked respondents to answer a number of questions related to terms common to all aspects of TTRPGs. Those terms were:

- Adventure - this term comes from the physical books that contain story and encounters for players to engage.
- Balance - this term refers to how much balance rests between game master and player within the system that game uses.
- Character - refers to the player's avatar in-game.
- Crunch - tends to refer to how much detail and how many rules exist.
- Immersion or Flow [47] is often referred to as the goal of TTRPGs in the form that player and character boundaries disappear.
- Randomness or the prevalence of random number generation in games.
- Safety tend to refer to recent developments in TTRPGs concerning player psychology.[6]
- Story is that thing that emerges during play.
- System is the thing that mediates play.
- World is where the adventure or story takes place.

---

[6] Safety tools in rpgs have been a controversial aspect of play in recent events. These are contracts and artifacts meant to provide the game master a number of ways to avoid triggering players. For a longer discussion of these tools, see [69].

Or particular interest here are the items system, crunch, balance, and immersion. Each of these items and the ways that people refer to and define them will note how prevalent they are will provide useful knowledge for our trace analysis here. While we will not discuss this directly in the next section, it will appear throughout each section. Having described the intent and general findings gathered from this section, we next move to discuss what we found and what it can mean to the concept of human uses of vintage beings.

6   Discussion

For the 11 interviews, we noticed some similarities and moments of overlap that are worth teasing apart. First, we want to talk about the path to playing TTRPGs. Next, we discuss the mono-gamer (those who play one game) versus the tri-fecta gamer. Next, we discuss the impact of Youtube and Twitch "actual play" shows. Finally, we discuss the word vintage. This word has a meaning that is hard to pin down because of how it tends to manifest in the respective spaces it appears in.

6.1   Paths to Role-Playing and Their Potential Uses

For vintage beings, the paths to computation, to systems, to the passion that focuses the vintage being are often moments in time that cannot be repeated. This is due to the fact that each person has a unique story of their introduction. In addition, each of our respondents, with an average age of 47, came to learn about TTRPGs at a time when the computer was not prevalent. In some cases, this path matched that of the birth of computer role-playing games. One respondent noted that: *"dnd* (1975) was my first encounter with *Dungeons & Dragons* (1974) and it was a computer program... I realized that what I wanted was *Dungeons & Dragons* (1974)...dnd (1975) = *Dungeons & Dragons* (1974). I'd never even known *dnd* (1975) stood for that."

While this was one path to playing TTRPGs, it is often repeated though the particulars often change. For example, the path to the birth of the video game industry tends to go from war game to TTRPG to video game. Or to be more specific, from *Strategos* (1880) to *Dungeons and Dragons* (1974) to *Wizardry: Proving Grounds of the Mad Overlord* (1980) or the PLATO game *Oubliette* (1977) [39]. This relationship is very prominent when talking to TTRPG fans though the inverse is not always true. For example, one respondent noted that:

> ...So for me, it was originally *Phantasy Star* (1987) which was a role-playing game for the Sega Master System. *Phastasy Star* (1979) was kind of like the Final Fantasy of the Sega line so the console JRPGs and then later just any computer role-playing game I could get my hands on...not actual D&D (1974) ...I was avoiding it because I was gonna get possessed by the devil...

There are multiple items of interest in this quote. First while the computer role-playing game originated in the United States, they became far more complicated than they needed to be very quickly [53]. While this was fine with the gamers who enjoyed these complex games, it did not result in a healthy industry. As such, there was ample room for not only improvement but different interpretations that could result in a more welcoming, more accessible space.

This is a way to consider the vintage being. The closer to the release of *D&D* (1974) that a video game is, the more closely it resembles that original system. And by resembling that original system, there was far more cross-pollination of these media. While this is present apocryphally as members of these communities, it is moved from apocrypha to actual history through the accounts of our respondents. But the problem with this is that there is an issue wherein engaging a TTRPG system can be done, learning how to make adventures, to make stories, to make characters was not. For example, one respondent noted:

> ...Like one was just like military fantasy, you know, and the other one was like, fantasy sword and sorcery. They both told me here's a box that I could have elements I can pull from to then make my own stories to play around in the forest, in the woods, with my friends, in a way that was cohesive and understandable. The actual role-playing; like i'm sitting at a table rolling dice, yeah, that came later...

And this is where the CRPG and TTRPG tend to differ slightly. TTRPGs often are released as a rulebook or trio of rulebooks (*Dungeon Master's Guide, Player's Handbook*, and *Monster Manual*). Rarely do these rulebooks contain material that players could engage easily. Instead, they are often given examples of what actual play looks like. And interested players are offered some tips and tricks on how to engage with players.

It would not be until much later in this respondent's life that they would actually begin playing the game. They noted further that, "And so it was a real struggle for me, you know, to just figure out like, what is this? You know, like, how do I put together a world with the characters can walk around and up to that point, *D&D* (1974), we were just running the pre-published adventures, you know, so we're just we're playing *Castle Caldwell and Beyond* (1985), okay, now we're gonna play through, you know, whatever." As time continued and new editions were released, they would contain these pre-published adventures. Yet, much of the introduction in more recent times relies on those adventures, on those running the games to teach them the entirety of this complex game. One respondent noted:

> ...I did a game design course and part of that game design class was like, playing D&D (1974). So I played D&D 3.5 edition (2003), in school and then didn't really play much for a few years in between but I was doing like chat RPs in that between time with like friends. And then I started playing D&D (1974) again, when I got to college...

Here we see a repeat of the above quote referencing military fantasy. This respondent was taught to play in class in high school and yet, they did not understand what it meant. It took some time for this respondent to not only find the game interesting, but something that could be played. Elsewhere in their interview, they note that: "But um, yeah, when I came back to *D&D* (1974), I was like, really excited. I hadn't played on in a long time, I had been playing like video games, that let me do that kind of character creation, like Bioware stuff, like I'd played *Neverwinter Nights* (2002). And I just hadn't had a group that was interested in it."

And this speaks to a difficult issue that needs to be overcome for vintage beings. Wherein this respondent notes that they played in high school and did not play again until college, they also note that video games filled the void between TTRPGs. And this speaks to the issue of friendships, numbers of friends, and other kinds of things that we lose from childhood to adulthood. Next, we consider another layer of this vintage being, the "tri-fecta" gamer.

6.2   The Mono Gamer and the Tri-Fecta Gamer

One theme that came out of our interviews that was a surprise was a term, "trifecta gamer." While initially meant as a bit of an insult to other kinds of gamers, the term has a use from the perspective of trying to understand the vintage being. This term, as defined in the interview was "I play role-playing games, I play role playing games, and I play war games." This is the trifecta gamer.

Within fandoms right now, there are constant references to purity. The easiest way to refer to this idea of purity is Mary Douglas' *Purity and Danger: An analysis of concepts of pollution and taboo* [23]. In that text, Douglas describes the place of the clean, unclean, and sacred. Douglas notes that what is considered clean, unclean, or sacred changes over time and that anything not clean is pollution of these types of things. When attached to fandom, those things that do not neatly fit a particular telling is considered profane.

An aspect of fandom then, is that those who belong to a community have an idea of what belongs to their collective identity and what does not. Those things that are sacred to that community are pure whereas those things that are not are either unclean or profane. In the case of vintage beings, the connection between wargames, TTRPGs, and video games are as such that they belong together contextually, historically, and literally. Yet the fandoms around each of those things are not as connected as their focus of fandom.

For the vintage being, these things are connected to them from their childhood and follow up through adulthood. As an example, consider this respondent's tale:

And we play war games, you know, Avalon Hill and SPI board games. *Third Reich* (1974) remember playing a lot of Third Reich, and somebody gives to squad leader as well as some of the Sci Fi SPI games that were coming out at the time, though those not as much I remember, one was kind of like a post apocalyptic. You know, it's the US and US is divided up into factions and each of the factions fight each other. And I remember feeling like ganged up on, but then one, one day, I guess, you know, he brought in that as Adam brought in, like the blue Holmes book.

While slightly older, this respondent began by playing some of the original wargames. In this way, this person's connection to TTRPGs is from their original inspiration. Once that connection is made, it can be called on to teach other things. In this way, the human use of vintage being is another way to consider the past of those around a particular activity. This continues as a cycle though it gets polluted and more difficult to discern over time. Consider this respondent:

> as a kid, we played a lot of *Legend of Zelda* (1986). And one of the things that we started to do with *Legend of Zelda* (1986) is we started to draw dungeons ourselves. And we started to come up with ways for us to be able to be challenged while we were going around those. And I was showing one of these to a friend of mine who said, hey, you know, this is a lot like *Dungeons and Dragons* (1974). Why don't you? Why don't I show you what that's like? And then maybe we can play some and I was like, Oh, what's this? I don't know what that is. And that was kind of my introduction to *Dungeons and Dragons* (1974).

This respondent did not learn to play TTRPGs via wargames but from the thing that TTRPGs inspired, video games. Here, a video game inspired by the movie *Legend* (1986) which sees a boy of the forest introducing a princess to Unicorns and then having to battle the devil to rescue her, serves as an introduction to TTRPGs. While the game itself is not a direct inspiration from TTRPGs, it has all of the trappings: dungeons, adventure, treasure, danger, and a character. Each of these things lends itself to the basic nature of TTRPGs. And so the relationship among disparate media, systems, and procedures can be glimpsed. Even more recent gamers repeat this path:

> ...But um, yeah, when I came back to *D&D* (1974), I was like, really excited. I hadn't played on in a long time, I had been playing like video games, that let me do that kind of character creation, like Bioware stuff, like I'd played *Neverwinter Nights* (2002). And I just hadn't had a group that was interested in it...

Here, we see a connection to TTRPGs in the form of more recent games. For example, Bioware, now a subsidiary of Electronic Arts (EA), used to make games that used the d20 system, an open source version of the 3rd edition of *D&D* (1974) as the system that undergirded its games. Games like *Mass Effect* (2007), *Jade Empire* (2005), and others all used this system. As such, people who played these games were being introduced to how TTRPGs worked. As such, it is perhaps no mistake that this relationship correlates to the rise of TTRPGs to recent, unheard of popularity. Another aspect of this popularity is the rise of what is often called "actual play."

6.3   The Role of Actual Play

Actual Play is best encapsulated by the intellectual properties surrounding the company Critical Role. In this space, actual play consists of a collection of friends and voice actors sitting around a table filled with a number of cameras performing their character's roles, voicing them, and using their knowledge of production to maintain high production value. Critical Role and shows like it offer interested fans ways to see how people play *D&D* (1974) and other games. While these shows provide useful ways to show how games are played, they are not universally loved. Much of the disagreement seems to be one of age and generation. For example, one respondent noted when asked about if they view these shows that:

> ...Oh yeah. Love it. Okay, that culture, like it's far different from my experiences, I don't enjoy it. But also there's like, there's a whole younger generation, and that's their connection. If I don't at least participate that in some way, I'm going to not be able to run games effectively for folks...[in my] under 20 crew that I run some games for...and they're amazing...

So for this respondent, the shows offer a way to connet to the ways that newer players will understand TTRPGs. For those who are used to streaming culture, these shows offer tremendous value, entertainment, and can fill the void between sessions. Yet, these things have a lot of buy in. Some episodes go for a number of hours and so this requires spending a huge amount of time listening.

> ...once I stopped driving as much because of the pandemic it just kind of became really hard to keep up with. I haven't really engaged in a lot of actual play. Besides that, like friends, the table has been the one that I really enjoyed. I've listened to some that my friends have done. But that's about it. I haven't listened to like a series like that in a sustained way. And a long time...

With so much effort required to view and digest these shows, it is little wonder that fans of them are so willing to keep going. They offer a massive amount of content to digest and it informs the way that they anticipate playing. While this may be something to seek for new players, this is often the source of the frustration from those who do not. Vintage beings seem to see actual play as an anathema that creates false hopes for how *D&D* (1974) can or should be played. For example, one respondent noted that:

> In one sense, oh I just worry that I know a lot of people enjoy it I think that's great but I worry that it's giving people a false impression of how polished and coherent any given session of role playing game actually is and they'll be disappointed when they sit down and try to play it themselves.

Yet, stream is not necessarily a new idea. Mixtape culture [25], participatory culture [33], online culture [61], these ways of streaming one's life has been part of a variety of research trends. As such, we can say that these records of actual play are not necessarily new. What is new is the quality of production, the talent these actors contain, and the connectivity between the creators of *D&D* (1974) and the show itself. As example, we see a particularly prescient memory from a respondent who notes:

> ...I'm trying to think like the first time I bought like a non TSR role playing game because I think that's when like role playing itself became interesting to me... I was struggling to understand like, what is this game like it's this game engine, I get that and learning these new rules. But it never had the cohesive element of *D&D* (1974) where like, you know, I understood fantasy I had read Tolkien, you know, and all that. So I understood a fantasy world look like, and try to make sense of what a game a world looked like, was difficult for me... we were just running the pre-published adventures, you know, so we're just we're playing *Castle Caldwell and Beyond* (1985). Okay, now we're gonna play through, you know, whatever... I think it was in high school that I kind of started to have this understanding of like, the systems and rules behind the games...

And so, we see that while Actual Play is more of a recently named entity, the connectivity of TTRPGs is as such that it can provide a useful concept to dig into. It is useful because TTRPGs are spaces of convergence. Again, hearkening back to the tri-fecta gamer, we can say that understanding and being a good TTRPG player requires not only a variety of media exposures. What actual play provides is a way for players to see the performative aspects of TTRPGs at the professional level. While professional play is often derogatory to play in general [32], it does provide useful ways to teach others that a TTRPG space of play is relaxed, fun, and welcoming. While the vintage beings we interviewed are as such that they mostly did not engage them now, as children and younger players they used their exposure to pop culture to inform their play. Yet, this gets to what might be the most important aspect of this piece, what exactly do we mean when we say the word vintage and how does it fit with CSEd?

6.4 What Do We Mean When We Say Vintage?

Perhaps the most important aspect of this piece is what vintage actually means to the TTRPG players we interviewed. Vintage, if we used a dictionary and scroll past all of the definitions that refer to win, means something like, "Characteristic of the best period of a person's work, etc.; classic" [51]. In this way, we can say that vintage for TTRPG players refers back to the creation of *D&D* (1974) and that this is the classic we all seek to reflect on. And so with this knowledge, we found a number of ways that our respondents defined vintage in similar ways. For example, one respondent called on this definition of vintage by saying.

> Well, the way I explain it to people is that I think of it in historical terms in the sense that in 2008, in 2009, Gary Gygax and Dave Arneson died.

And with my anthropology background, I know that one of the things that happens when the founders of movements die is that there's things called revitalization movements, about going back to the basics of back to the old ways. And so I think that like the OSR, kind of fits that pattern really well, because that's around when it gets started started is around when they, they die.

Here, we see a discussion of what vintage means from the concept of his education. In this case, the respondent calls upon the best two individuals did, Gary Gygax and Dave Arneson. These two created *D&D* (1974) with the help of a number of other individuals like David Wesely, David Megarry, and others referred to as the Twin Cities gamers at times [54]. In this sense, he is being literal about the vintage concept. Yet, there are other ways to consider what vintage means. For example, this respondent shifts the meaning slightly when they say:

> "So most of my gaming stuff is done. Old school, not for your aesthetic value, because like, My eyes hurt at the end of the day. To work up with paper and machines that are moving way slower than my laptop is. It's a luxury that I you know, I probably leverage my privilege there to have that luxury to be able to slow down and not have my livelihood depend upon cranking out zines."

That respondent connects vintage and old school to physically doing things and not digitizing them. They also connect to older ways of doing things. This is another definition of vintage that the *Oxford English Dictionary* provides. This definition states, "Denoting an old style or model of something" [51]. So this respondent treats vintage as ways of doing before computation gained the ubiquity it has now. And so with these two definitions, how do we approach using this concept. We postulate that the human use of vintage beings is closer to what this respondent notes when they say:

> "And they had a friend who stopped by who used to play with them a lot. And he brought this stack of old stuff and he said, anybody that wants it can have it. So I took, like three or four things... among the things I took was a copy of the blue book, because hey, there's that book that I saw back way back when, you know. And in that, in the back, you know, there's the sample dungeon, which is one of the greatest things ever...I didn't know a lot, you know, history. At that time. Maybe back in the early days, those statistics really were more used for things like saving throws. And so I started to think was there a game that kind of plays on that, and I stumbled on castles and crusades. And so that was sort of my entry drug back into gaming after after we bought the house and I moved out here where I still am actually."

For this respondent, we see him re-connecting to something from his childhood. This connection is so strong that even if we are referring to it 30, 40 years later, it has the same wonder that it did as a child. In this case, *D&D* (1974) has been through 6 or 7 editions though only 5 have are called editions. Each of these are more and more treated as computer software, thus replacing older editions as though patched. Yet vintage here, means going to previous editions and exploring them with new eyes. This approach is exemplified by this final quote when the respondent notes: "And then that was when some sort of the light went on because someone said, well, why can't you just, why don't you play the old *D&D* (1974)? Wow, you could do that. So I just sort of dusted off all of my old books and started looking at them again."

There are a number of definitions of vintage being used in this quote. Each definition lends itself quite readily to using for educational purposes. Where the tricks lie, the trick to deploying these concepts seems to be, is within the ability for TTRPGs to travel across media. Thus, we would offer that a TTRPG can be used to bring learners into the uses of pseudocode and then be used as scaffolding for programming that everyone in class must interpret on their own. While this concept of vintage is itself vintage and old, it is most useful for older learners or at least those individuals so hesitant to learn technology as to fail before beginning.

7 Conclusion

In the present research, we discuss the initial interpretation of a data gathering effort meant to help understand how TTRPG players differ in an effort to find new approaches to a wicked problem in *emergency management*. Because of the way TTRPGs developed, their connection and uses in other media, we felt, could lend themselves to teaching often unavailable learners: adult learners, elderly learners, and the technophobe or hesitant learner. From our trace data in these semi-structured interviews, we found that there were a number of similarities among the different types of people we talked to.

First, the path to TTRPGs is often something that will fuel that later nostalgia. From *D&D* (1974) to even something like *TMNT* (1985) or other kids media, the vintage beings we talked to presented a nearly universal path to TTRPGs. This path is perhaps best exemplified as the "tri-fecta" gamer wherein exposure might not have been to TTRPGs first, but the style of play emerged from other media and eventually found itself being applied to TTRPGs. The ways that media connect seem to reflect the way they have been connected historically in the form of wargames, TTRPGs, and video games are essentially a path of development. That our respondents still identify with those aspects of their youth is something worth considering in future work.

This tri-fecta approach seems to have gained new ground with high quality shows devoted to showing TTRPGs as actual play. While these shows are varied in how much they are enjoyed or not-enjoyed, the connections between current actual play and imaginary play generated by old Saturday Morning Cartoons seems to indicate that this is a model of exposure that has been active since the original wargames. Addressing this development not as a new technology but as an evolution of existing communities and the past will inevitably help inform future work in CSEd. Finally, we discussed what vintage actually means.

Vintage, in the cases of our respondents tend to reflect the meanings attached to the best works of someone or older ways of doing things. In this way, we can state that old ways of doing are those things we can pull on to teach new ideas, these are the human use of vintage beings. Through these vintage beings, new types of entropy created by the vast and complex eco-system of apps, software, hardware, programming, algorithms, and everything else connected to computation can be stymied if not stopped completely. While it is readily available, vintage, retro, and classic ideas can be overdone, overused, and could be otherwise over-saturated. As such, we promote the idea of using this phenomenon to a useful degree but additionally suggest that it should not be used in name, but in spirit.

By spirit, we mean to say that something like PICO-8[7], a fantasy console that uses an extremely limited version of lua is a re-imagining of old ways of doing. This product offers new programmers very limited ways of writing code, limited space for memory, and other forms of limitations that reflect old ways of doing things. This new interpretation of old limits has added valuable knowledge from its inspirational future in that it adds ways to share code, share sprites, share cartridges, and discuss the code of games. It takes that vintage idea and re-imagines that in the present. This is where the spirit of vintage gains its power. Old things contain ideas that were perhaps never met, old potentials never realized. And so by maintaining the spirit of vintage, we acknowledge that those potentials could never be realized the way that those things were but can be re-imagined and used to foster new ways of doing vintage things.

While we gained a lot of insight from our 11 interviews, this work is still nascent and its capacity to be applied to EM is of particular interest as more insider knowledge of things like the Homeland Security Exercise and Evaluation Program will be required to move forward. We will continue interviewing respondents and discussing TTRPGs with them until we are satisfied with the results. Additionally, we will begin talking to exercise planners and will take the Master Exercise Practitioner Program certification course in an effort to find new approaches to the concepts this work has provided. New information, new concepts, new uses for vintage ideas will no doubt emerge from these content. Though we do not anticipate any new information shaking this core understanding that our respondents seemed to universally pull on. While each respondent was different, the spirit of their answers were not. And so that similarity within difference points to something that can be used to engage CSEd in new, old ways.

Acknowledgements. We want to thank the TTRPG creators that took the time to talk to us, to answer follow-up questions, and help us understand their perspective.

---

[7] From the PICO-8 website: https://www.lexaloffle.com/pico-8.php the creators note that "PICO-8 is a fantasy console for making, sharing and playing tiny games and other computer programs.".

This work would not have been possible without you. Additionally, we would like to thank Nick Mizer and Bill White for the initial discussion and interviews. This material is based upon work supported by the National Science Foundation under Grant Nos: IIS-1651532, IIS-2105069, and IIS-2106402.

References

1. Aarseth, E.: Just games. Game Stud. **17**(1), 10 (2017)
2. Altheide, D.L., Schneider, C.J.: Qualitative media analysis, vol. 38. Sage Publications, Los Angeles, CA, USA (2012)
3. Atchison, W.F.: Computer science as a new discipline. Int. J. Electr. Eng. Educ. **9**(2), 130–135 (1971)
4. Becker, H.S.: Art worlds: updated and expanded. University of California Press, Berkeley, CA, USA (2008)
5. Bell, T.: Cs unplugged or coding classes? Commun. ACM **64**(5), 25–27 (2021)
6. Bell, T., Vahrenhold, J.: CS unplugged—how is it used, and does it work? In: Böckenhauer, H.-J., Komm, D., Unger, W. (eds.) Adventures Between Lower Bounds and Higher Altitudes. LNCS, vol. 11011, pp. 497–521. Springer, Cham (2018). https://doi.org/10.1007/978-3-319-98355-4_29
7. Blandford, A., Furniss, D., Makri, S.: Qualitative hci research: going behind the scenes. Synth. Lect. Hum.-Centered Inform. **9**(1), 1–115 (2016)
8. Blandford, A.E.: Semi-structured qualitative studies. In: The Encyclopedia of Human-Computer Interaction, 2nd Ed. Interaction Design Foundation, Denmark (2013)
9. Bogost, I.: Play anything: The pleasure of limits, the uses of boredom, and the secret of games. Basic Books, New York, NY (2016)
10. Braun, V., Clarke, V.: Thematic analysis. APA Handbook Res. Methods Psychol. **2**, 57–71 (2012)
11. Cassell, J., et al.: Genderizing hci. In: The Handbook of Human–Computer Interaction, pp. 402–411. L. Erlbaum Associates Inc., Broadway Hillsdale, NJ, USA (2002)
12. Chen, C., Haduong, P., Brennan, K., Sonnert, G., Sadler, P.: The effects of first programming language on college students' computing attitude and achievement: a comparison of graphical and textual languages. Comput. Sci. Educ. **29**(1), 23–48 (2019)
13. Craddock, D.L.: Dungeon Hacks: How NetHack, Angband, and Other Roguelikes Changed the Course of Video Games. Press Start Press, Canton, Ohio, USA (2015)
14. Craddock, D.L.: Stay Awhile and Listen: How Two Blizzards Unleashed Diablo and Forged an Empire: Book 1. Digital Monument Press, Canton, Ohio, USA (2017)
15. Criblez, A.: Games about the game: A history of tabletop baseball. NINE: J. Baseball History Culture **29**(1), 125–141 (2020)
16. Daniels, J., LaLone, N.: Racism in video gaming: connecting extremist and mainstream expressions of white supremacy. Social exclusion, power, and video game play: new research in digital media and technology, pp. 85–99 (2012)
17. Davidson, D.: Well played: interpreting prince of persia: the sands of time. Games Culture **3**(3–4), 356–386 (2008)
18. Dear, B.: The Friendly Orange Glow: The Untold Story of the Rise of Cyberculture. Vintage, New York City, USA (2017)

19. DiSalvo, B., Bruckman, A.: Race and gender in play practices: young African American males. In: Proceedings of the fifth International Conference on the Foundations of Digital Games, pp. 56–63. Association for Computing Machinery, New York (2010)
20. DiSalvo, B.J., Bruckman, A.: Questioning video games' influence on cs interest. In: Proceedings of the 4th International Conference on Foundations of Digital Games, pp. 272–278. Association for Computing Machinery, New York (2009)
21. DiSalvo, B.J., Crowley, K., Norwood, R.: Learning in context: digital games and young black men. Games Culture **3**(2), 131–141 (2008)
22. DiSalvo, E.B.: Glitch game testers: the design and study of a learning environment for computational production with young African American males. Georgia Institute of Technology, Atlanta, GA, USA (2012)
23. Douglas, M.: Purity and danger: An analysis of concepts of pollution and taboo. Routledge, Oxfordshire, England, UK (2003)
24. Engberg-Pederson, A.: Empire of Chance: The Napoleonic Wars and the Disorder of Things. Harvard University Press, Cambridge, MA, USA (2015)
25. Fenby-Hulse, K.: Rethinking the digital playlist: mixtapes, nostalgia and emotionally durable design. In: Networked Music Cultures, pp. 171–188. Palgrave Macmillan, London (2016)
26. Fincher, S.A., Robins, A.V.: The Cambridge handbook of computing education research. Cambridge University Press, Cambridge, MA, USA (2019)
27. Fine, G.A.: Shared fantasy: Role playing games as social worlds. University of Chicago Press, Chicago, USA (2002)
28. Guzdial, M.: Learner-centered design of computing education: research on computing for everyone. Synthesis Lect. Hum.-Centered Inform. **8**(6), 1–165 (2015)
29. Heyck, H.: Age of system: Understanding the development of modern social science. JHU Press, Baltimore, MD, USA (2015)
30. Hinkelmann, K., Holzweißig, K., Magenheim, J., Probst, F., Reinhardt, W.: Linking communities of practice with learning communities in computer science education. In: Kumar, D., Turner, J. (eds.) Education for the 21st Century — Impact of ICT and Digital Resources. IIFIP, vol. 210, pp. 83–92. Springer, Boston, MA (2006). https://doi.org/10.1007/978-0-387-34731-8_10
31. Ho, X., Carter, M.: Roguelike ancestry network visualisation: insights from the roguelike community. In: Proceedings of the 14th International Conference on the Foundations of Digital Games, pp. 1–9 (2019)
32. Huizinga, J.: Homo Ludens: Routledge & Kegan Paul Ltd. MA, USA, Boston (1954)
33. Jenkins, H.: Fans, bloggers, and gamers: Exploring participatory culture. nyu Press, New York (2006)
34. Jerz, D.G.: Somewhere nearby is colossal cave: Examining will crowther's original "adventure" in code and in kentucky. Digital Humanities Q. **1**(2) (2007)
35. Kay, A., Goldberg, A.: Personal dynamic media. Computer **10**(3), 31–41 (1977)
36. Krafft, M., Fraser, G., Walkinshaw, N.: Motivating adult learners by introducing programming concepts with scratch. In: Proceedings of the 4th European Conference on Software Engineering Education, pp. 22–26. Association for Computing Machinery, New York (2020)
37. Kulik, C.L.C., Kulik, J.A., Shwalb, B.J.: The effectiveness of computer-based adult education: a meta-analysis. J. Educ. Comput. Res. **2**(2), 235–252 (1986)
38. Lalone, N.: Association Mapping: Social Network Analysis with Humans and Non-Humans. Ph.D. thesis, The Pennsylvania State University (2018)

39. LaLone, N.: A tale of dungeons & dragons and the origins of the game platform. Analog Game Stud. **3**(6) (2019)

40. LaLone, N.: Gameplay as network: understanding the consequences of automation on play and use. In: Fang, X. (ed.) HCII 2021. LNCS, vol. 12789, pp. 293–313. Springer, Cham (2021). https://doi.org/10.1007/978-3-030-77277-2_23

41. LaLone, N., Dugas, P.O.T., Semaan, B.: The crisis of designing for disaster: how to help emergency management during the technology crisis we created. In: Proceedings of the International ISCRAM Conference (2023)

42. LaLone, N., Toups Dugas, P.O., Papangelis, K.: Practical considerations on applications of the popularity of games: The case of location-based games and disaster. In: International Conference on Human-Computer Interaction, pp. 213–233. Springer (2022). https://doi.org/10.1007/978-3-031-05637-6_13

43. Lalone, N., Toups Dugas, P.O., Semaan, B.: The technology crisis in US-based emergency management: Toward a well-connected future. In: Proceedings of the 56th Hawaii International Conference on System Sciences (2023)

44. Miller, O.A.: HipHopathy. A Socio-Curricular Study of Introductory Computer Science. University of California, Berkeley, Berkeley, CA, USA (2015)

45. Mizer, N.J.: The Greatest Unreality: Tabletop Role-Playing Games and the Experience of Imagined Worlds. Ph.D. thesis, Texas A&M University (2015)

46. Moss, R.: The Secret History of Mac Gaming. Unbound, London, UK (2018)

47. Nakamura, J., Csikszentmihalyi, M.: The concept of flow. In: Flow and the Foundations of Positive Psychology, pp. 239–263. Springer, Dordrecht, Netherlands (2014)

48. Niarchos, A., Petousi, D., Katifori, A., Sakellariadis, P., Ioannidis, Y.: Bridging the gap between the physical and the virtual in tabletop role playing games: exploring immersive vr tabletops. In: International Conference on Interactive Digital Storytelling, pp. 489–503. Springer (2023). https://doi.org/10.1007/978-3-031-47655-6_30

49. Noone, M., Mooney, A.: Visual and textual programming languages: a systematic review of the literature. J. Comput. Educ. **5**(2), 149–174 (2018)

50. O'Donnell, C.: Developer's dilemma: The secret world of videogame creators. MIT press (2014)

51. Online, O.: Vintage. In: The Oxford English Dictionary. Oxford University Press, Oxford, UK (2022). https://www.oed.com/

52. Palen, L., Anderson, K.M.: Crisis informatics-new data for extraordinary times. Science **353**(6296), 224–225 (2016)

53. Pepe, F.: The CRPG Book Project: Sharing the History of Computer Role-Playing Games. Bitmap Books, Bath, England (February (2019)

54. Peterson, J.: Playing at the World: A History of Simulating Wars, People and Fantastic Adventures, from Chess to Role-Playing Games. Unreason Press, San Diego, USA (2012)

55. Rodriguez, B., Kennicutt, S., Rader, C., Camp, T.: Assessing computational thinking in cs unplugged activities. In: Proceedings of the 2017 ACM SIGCSE Technical Symposium on Computer Science Education, pp. 501–506. Association for Computing Machinery, New York (2017)

56. Schatzberg, E.: " technik" comes to America: Changing meanings of" technology" before 1930. Technol. Cult. **47**(3), 486–512 (2006)

57. Stein, A.: Playing the game on television. In: Sports Videogames, pp. 115–137. Routledge, London, UK (2013)

58. Strohmeyer, R.: The 7 worst tech predictions of all time (2008), PC World

59. Szabo, C., et al.: Review and use of learning theories within computer science education research: primer for researchers and practitioners. In: Proceedings of the Working Group Reports on Innovation and Technology in Computer Science Education, pp. 89–109. Association for Computing Machinery, New York (2019)
60. Taub, R., Ben-Ari, M., Armoni, M.: The effect of cs unplugged on middle-school students' views of cs. ACM SIGCSE Bull. **41**(3), 99–103 (2009)
61. Taylor, T.L.: Play between worlds: Exploring online game culture. MIT Press, Cambridge, MA, USA (2009)
62. Thomas, W.: Rational action: The sciences of policy in Britain and America, 1940–1960. MIT Press, Baltimore, MD, USA (2015)
63. Totten, C.A.L.: Strategos: A Series of American Games of War, Based Upon Military Principles and Designed for the Assistance Both of Beginners and Advanced Students in Prosecuting the Whole Study of Tactics, Grand Tactics, Strategy, Military History, and the Various Operations of War, vol. 1. D. Appleton, New York (1880)
64. Toups Dugas, P.O., Lalone, N., Alharthi, S.A., Sharma, H.N., Webb, A.M.: Making maps available for play: Analyzing the design of game cartography interfaces. ACM Trans. Comput.-Hum. Interact. **26**(5) (2019). https://doi.org/10.1145/3336144
65. Toups Dugas, P.O., LaLone, N., Spiel, K., Hamilton, B.: Paper to pixels: a chronicle of map interfaces in games. In: Proceedings of the 2020 ACM Designing Interactive Systems Conference, DIS 2020, pp. 1433-1451. Association for Computing Machinery, New York (2020).https://doi.org/10.1145/3357236.3395502
66. Turgut, Y., İrgin, P.: Young learners' language learning via computer games. Procedia. Soc. Behav. Sci. **1**(1), 760–764 (2009)
67. White, W.J.: Player-character is what you are in the dark: the phenomenology of immersion in dungeons & dragons. In: Dungeons & Dragons and Philosophy: Read and Gain Advantage on All Wisdom Checks, pp. 82–92. Wiley Blackwell, Chichester, West Sussex, UK (2014)
68. White, W.J.: Actual play at the forge: a rhetorical approach. Inter. J. Role-Playing **7**, 36–39 (2016)
69. White, W.J.: The discourse of player safety in the forge diaspora, 2003–2013. Japanese J. Analog Role-Playing Game Stud. **1**, 35–47 (2020)
70. Wiener, N.: The Human Use of Human Beings: Cybernetics and Society. Da Capo Press, Boston, Massachusetts, USA (1988)
71. Witwer, M.: Empire of Imagination: Gary Gygax and the Birth of Dungeons & Dragons. Bloomsbury, New York, USA (2015)

Towards Attainable Game Experiences

Adam Palmquist, Izabella Jedel, and Ole Goethe[(✉)]

Nord University, Bodø, Norway
{adam.palmquist,izabella.a.jedel,ole.goethe}@nord.no

Abstract. The expanding global engagement in gaming across a wide range of demographics highlights that video games transcend their traditional perception as mere entertainment for children and adolescents. They fulfil diverse roles for various societal groups. Creating universally designed games goes beyond simply featuring a diverse array of characters. These games are intrinsically designed to be accessible to all players, integrating inclusive mechanics, options, and user experiences from their inception. Researchers describe universally designed artefacts as proactively embracing and welcoming participants from diverse backgrounds. A profound and genuine connection between players and a video game markedly boosts engagement with the game's content. Conversely, obstacles such as physical inaccessibility or the absence of relatable characters can create a sense of exclusion and prevent players from accessing meaningful learning and collaborative experiences. This article explores the concept of Universal Design in video games by introducing the AGE (Attainable Game Experience) framework. It outlines four comprehensive heuristics aimed at maximizing the impact of games by ensuring they are accessible, empowering and representative of all players.

Keywords: Game accessibility · Interaction design of games · Accessibility · Attainability · Player Experiences · Game Experiences · Playability · Gameplay · Video Game Usability · Universal Design

1 Introduction

The COVID-19 pandemic has starkly underscored the crucial role of digital inclusivity in contemporary society. This period has borne the reality that essential services are predominantly delivered online, necessitating their accessibility to all individuals, irrespective of their diverse abilities. Fulfilling digital inclusivity is not merely a matter of convenience; it is imperative for full societal participation and independent living, ultimately contributing to a more inclusive and empathetic world.

In video game development, considerations of accessibility and inclusivity are often relegated to peripheral concerns, particularly at the project's inception. These seemingly tangential aspects typically gain prominence only when unforeseen challenges arise. This reactive approach, however, can lead to significantly increased resource expenditure post-launch, as opposed to proactive integration during the development phase. The oversight of accessibility in game design is not merely a missed opportunity but can also

X. Fang (Ed.): HCII 2024, LNCS 14731, pp. 247–261, 2024.
https://doi.org/10.1007/978-3-031-60695-3_16

have financial implications. For instance, stringent accessibility legislation, such as the European Accessibility Act [1], poses legal risks for game companies and studios that fail to comply.

By focusing on accessibility and attainable gameplay, developers avoid legal risks and invite a diverse spectrum of players into their virtual realms. This inclusivity fosters a broader and more varied community, enriching player interactions and exchanges. Prioritizing attainable gameplay is not only a statement of ethical values - a domain in which the gaming industry has historically shown deficiencies - but also aligns with pragmatic business considerations. For example, approximately one in four adult Europeans live with a disability [2] that could impede their access to digital services. By addressing these barriers, developers can potentially expand their player base, thereby increasing revenue and enhancing the longevity of their game products in a highly competitive market.

This paper aims to enhance the discussion on Universal Design in video games and provide insights for practitioners, educators, and scholars to improve gaming experiences for all. It utilizes a typological approach, as outlined by Jaakkola [3], to categories conceptual variations and design heuristics for attainable game experiences. By combining different constructs, this paper seeks to clarify the nature of Universal design in Video Games and offer a detailed understanding of the phenomenon, highlighting key dimensions that define its variants, following Jaakkola's [3] process for explicative typologies. Through this paper, our objective is twofold: firstly, to elevate the discourse on Universal Design within the context of video games and secondly, to equip practitioners, educators, and scholars with the necessary insights to pursue an enhanced gaming experience for all users.

2 Universal Design in Video Games – Towards a Definition?

Universal design is an approach in which products and services are designed to be used by people with all abilities to the greatest possible extent without adaptation [4]. The approach acknowledges that people who interact with products have diverse abilities and needs [5] and that designers should strive to incorporate adjustable features that enable use for a broad set of the population [6, 7]. Even though designers and researchers have previously addressed the importance of accessibility in video game design, the discussion has focused chiefly on adding accessibility options for people with specific disabilities [8, 9] rather than adopting a universal approach of designing for all. Universally accessible video games have previously been defined as games proactively designed to be simultaneously accessible to people of diverse requirements [10]. However, this definition is somewhat limited as the design landscape differs significantly for video games compared to other products.

Accessibility in games should not only be centered around being able to control the game but also overcoming the challenges presented and accessing the intended player experience [11]. Compared to other products, the central focus of video games is the hedonic (enjoyable) as opposed to utilitarian (useful) attributes of the experience [12]. Originating from consumer psychology [13, 14], hedonic and utilitarian dimensions represent two fundamental motivations and functions of interacting with technological artefacts [15, 16]. Even though hedonic attributes have been the primary focus of video game design, in the context of accessibility, we argue that both utilitarian dimensions and hedonic dimensions should be considered. The utilitarian dimension represents players' functional needs that allow them to interact with the game, adhering to the first two stages of accessibility presented by Power et al. [11] of being able to control the game and partake in challenges. This could, for example, entail having intuitive layouts and straightforward navigation that allows the player to perform the functional tasks in the game. The hedonic dimension represents the experiential needs of players that keep them engaged in the gameplay. This dimension represents the game experience, corresponding to the third stage of an accessible game experience [11]. Striving for Universal Design in video games, therefore, requires that designers adopt a balance between considering both the hedonic and utilitarian attributes of the experience of interacting with the game *(see* Fig. 1*)*.

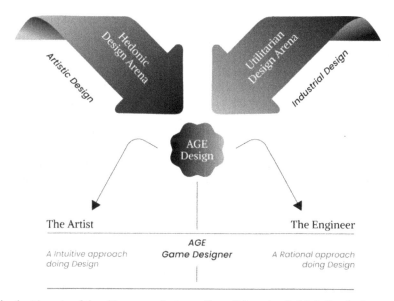

Fig. 1. The role of the video game designer (from Palmquist, Jedel & Goethe in press)

Like the distinction between hedonic and utilitarian attributes, the design of games differs from that of other products in terms of not only needing to consider the user experience (UX) but also the player experience (PX). The distinct player experience of video games was recognized merely for 10–15 years [17, 18]. UX is centered around the utilization of a system [19], whereas PX zeroes in on the emotional, social, and cognitive facets of the interaction between players and games [20]. Compared to PX, UX design focuses on usability, functionality, ease of use, or other impressionistic indicators of an individual's experience [21]. PX design instead revolves around the experience of play—how a game caters to the sensation a player seeks when participating in gameplay [22] for a comprehensive list of variables influencing PX.

Together, UX and PX refer to the overall experience of a person interacting with a system. They share many principles but are distinct in the context in which they are applied and their ultimate goals (Table 1). UX is broader and applies to any user interaction interface. PX is specific to games and often involves more emotional and narrative considerations. Assessing a video game's playability differs from evaluating players' nuanced experiences within that game's environment [23].

At the same time, evaluating games entails both a UX and PX dimension. UX evaluations investigate barriers to gameplay, while PX evaluations explore obstacles to the sought sensation(s) and delve into the nature of player-game interactions. Traditional UX testing metrics fall short in video game evaluation, e.g., task completion for effectiveness or error rates for efficiency [22]. However, the distinction has also raised awareness of the importance of UX analysis in the game interface while staying consistent with traditional criteria for video game playtesting studies [22].

Table 1. Differences between the **User eXperience** and **Player eXperience**

Elements	UX	PX
Scope	UX encompasses all user interactions with a product or service. Typically includes websites, apps, software, and, to some extent, physical products	PX is a subset of UX specific to video games and interactive entertainment. While UX can be applied to any product or service, PX is concerned with the playability and game experience
Goal	The primary aim of UX is to ensure that users can achieve their objectives as efficiently, effectively, and enjoyable as possible. Entangles create intuitive, accessible, and user-friendly interfaces	PX often seeks to evoke specific emotions, immerse the player, and ensure they are entertained and engaged. Enjoyment, challenge, frustration, and immersion can all be intentional parts of the PX
Components	UX involves multiple components, including usability, accessibility, information architecture, visual design, content strategy, and more	PX involves game mechanics, narrative design, audio design, game aesthetics, player agency, and more, in addition to traditional UX components
Feedback & Metrics	In UX, success is often measured by metrics like task completion rate, time on task, user satisfaction surveys, net promoter score, etc.	PX might be measured by player retention, time played, in-game achievements, and player satisfaction, among other metrics

The distinction between utilitarian and hedonic dimensions and between PX and UX in games highlight the importance of considering the game experience when addressing Universal Design in video games. Instead of focusing on making the game itself accessible, we argue that the central concern for Universal Design in video games is to make the game experience attainable. This entails focusing on the utilitarian and UX dimensions and the gameplay's hedonic and PX dimensions. Based on the definition of Universal Design and the unique characteristics of video games, we have therefore extended the definition by Grammenos et al. [10] on universally accessible games and defined Universal Design in video games as: *"games that are proactively designed so that the game experience is concurrently attainable by people with all abilities, to the greatest extent possible, without adaptation when possible, and with adaptation when necessary"* [24].

3 Achieving an Attainable Game Experience

Incorporating Universal Design in video games includes several important steps to consider. Firstly, designers need a comprehensive understanding of the diverse conditions influencing players' abilities concerning in-game interactions. From a Universal Design perspective, accessibility problems arise in designing environments that do not consider the full range of human capabilities [25].

Four main conditions are commonly discussed in the context of making video games accessible: visual conditions, which affect players' sight; auditory conditions, which affect players' hearing; mobility conditions, which affect players' sensation, coordination, and movement; and cognitive conditions which affect players' mental and social functioning [9, 26]. A Universal Design approach in video games does not solely focus on designing for people with specifically defined disabilities. It adopts the notion that people with defined disabilities are a diverse group of individuals [27], that disabilities emerge in the interaction between the person and the environment [28], and that disability can arise for any person depending on situational factors [29, 30]. Understanding the conditions that affect players' interaction with a game provides a broader market reach and can improve the experience for all players. For example, adding subtitles to a game can enable players with limited hearing access. However, it can also allow players in noisy environments or with technical sound problems to engage in a game.

Secondly, the design process should actively involve the perspectives of players and other stakeholders with a range of attributes and abilities. This inclusion is vital for appreciating and addressing players' individualized experiences and needs in the design and development stages. Including people with disabilities or high awareness of disabilities can be valuable in prioritizing accessibility in game design and development process [31], ensuring a more attainable experience for all. To incorporate diverse perspectives, game designers can employ participatory design and open development methods. Participatory design is a user-centered approach that involves relevant stakeholders in the design process [32].

Compared to the traditional approach to game development, which has primarily neglected stakeholder participation in the game design process [33], participatory design entails actively incorporating design opinions from stakeholders into the design journey. Open development is an approach that incorporates player feedback at various stages of development, cultivating a reciprocal relationship between the player and the game development team [34]. This can, for example, include providing early access to games [35], adding in-game feedback options [36] and live streaming development work [37].

Thirdly, aligning with the Universal Design perspective [6, 7], the design solution should integrate features as seamlessly as possible, enabling the broadest possible participation without compromising the overall player experience. In video games, the traditional approach to accessibility has been integrating assistive technologies or developing specific games for people with disabilities [10]. These approaches are often insufficient as players face various conditions [8] and often perceive specialized solutions as not addressing their specific needs or being too expensive [38]. Universal design in video games moves beyond creating specific solutions for individual disabilities. Instead, it should offer multiple options and modes of interaction, catering to various needs and preferences. Moreover, the gaming experience, transcending mere considerations of disability, should be central to universally designed video games. The goal is to provide an accessible, engaging gaming experience attainable for as many people as possible, ensuring inclusivity and broader enjoyment.

To complement Universal Design's video game design process, several guidelines exist for incorporating accessibility features into video games [39, 40]. These guidelines are a valuable resource for developers in creating higher awareness of accessibility and identifying current accessibility issues with their games [8]. At the same time, the guidelines are insufficient in terms of addressing the in-game experience [11] and integrating accessibility options with different gameplay variations [41]. Lacking in previous literature is an overarching framework for addressing Universal Design in video games, considering the centrality of the player experience, players' various abilities and preferences, and the need for seamlessly integrated and adaptable features. To address these issues, the upcoming section presents the attainable game experience (AGE) framework. The AGE framework is synthesized from the principles for Universal Design [4], previous accessibility guidelines and insights from inclusive design. The framework provides a lens through which game designers can critically reflect on and communicate how to facilitate a more universal approach to their video games.

4   A Framework for Attainable Game Experience

Based on the definition of Universal Design in video games, we propose a framework and several design implications and processes for an attainable game experience (AGE). The AGE framework presents four design heuristics that can be used to design and evaluate video games from a universal design lens (see Fig. 2).

The AGE framework and its design heuristics primarily focus on enhancing the attainability of overall game experiences and gameplay features. However, it is crucial to note that the AGE framework does not delve deeply into the specifics of a particular game or its gameplay elements. Digital game design is an intricate, multidisciplinary craft with nuances and complexities that go beyond the surface. It intersects with various disciplines such as programming, narrative design, art direction, sound design, and systems design. Each of these disciplines significantly contributes to players' meaningful experiences with a video game. The involvement and focus of the AGE framework and its heuristics lie more at the macro level of granularity than the micro level. To fulfil the AGE framework's goal of making video game experiences more attainable for a diverse audience, regardless of their conditions and circumstances, efforts should concentrate on

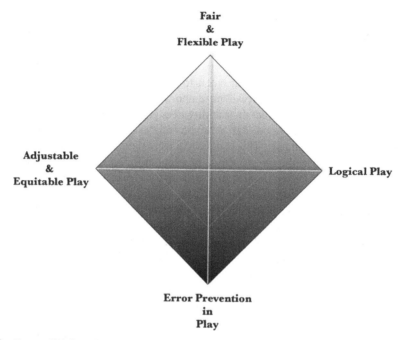

Fig. 2. Four radial lines interconnect each of the four design heuristics of the AGE Framework centered around a thin mainline in the matrix's core (from Palmquist, Jedel & Goethe in press).

the game's 'interaction interfaces'—the points of contact between players and the video game experience. By contemplating how to create robust and inviting interaction interfaces, we can discuss attainability without delving too deeply into the distinct aspects that often arise in a video game project. Our goal is rather to provide a broader approach that can shape the perception and direction of game design. This assists creators in laying the groundwork for in-depth, game-specific design considerations without micromanaging or interfering with the game development team's goals and desires. Adopting this interface-centric approach, we believe we can maintain the scope and focus of our design heuristics. This ensures their applicability across various gaming contexts without overly intruding on the design space and process. The following subsections describe the four heuristics of the AGE framework.

Heuristics I: Fair and Flexible Play. The heuristic Fair and Flexible Play is the first of our proposed cornerstones in the AGE framework for a broader audience of participants, irrespective of their unique conditions and abilities. The heuristic strives toward making the game accessible, that is, allowing as many people as possible to play the game [42], even those functioning under limiting conditions [40]. The gameplay is perceived as "Fair" in that people are not hindered from playing the game due to their individual abilities by integrating higher "Flexibility" when interacting with the game.

At its core, this heuristic prioritises players by recognising their varied conditions, contexts, and circumstances and the disabilities that could arise during gameplay. It involves designing multimodal software interfaces and game controllers to facilitate interaction between players and the video game. The "Fair and Flexible Play" heuristic considers and integrates various interaction modalities, such as visual, audio, and motor, to ensure seamless information transfer between the video game and its participants. Consequently, reducing the visual, auditory, motor, and cognitive barriers that can arise during gameplay [9, 26]. This heuristic caters to players from diverse backgrounds, considering the needs of those with permanent, temporary, situational, or evolving conditions or circumstances that might affect their ability to engage with the game.

AGE Fair and Flexible Play design heuristic emphasises examining, evaluating, and refining the gameplay elements. This is done to ensure their adjustability, enhancing the game's accessibility. Meeting these criteria is essential for crafting gaming experiences that invite participation and enjoyment from a diverse and expansive spectrum of players. To realise the Fair and Flexible Play heuristic, game developers should incorporate interfaces that provide adjustable settings, alternative controls, and other accessibility options to meet various players' capabilities. Including these adjustable settings and assistive features should allow players with broad abilities to participate in the game. For example, features for higher visual accessibility could include adjustable options for colour schemes, text, fonts and zooming in and out, as well as adding auditory interaction options [41, 43]. Such design features might be necessary for players with visual conditions but also benefit those who wish to adjust these parameters due to technological constraints or personal preferences.

Similarly, design features that provide the option for audio cues and subtitles have a broad reach [41, 43]. These features accommodate players with hearing conditions and enable non-native speakers by offering clarity to game narratives presented in a foreign language or aiding those trying to distinguish between various audio sources in their multiplayer gaming experience. For players who experience reduced motor abilities, video game designers can, for example, include options for users to remap controllers and allow players to utilise only one hand [41]. These options can also allow players with temporary impairments, such as a broken arm, to participate in the game, allowing for a more comfortable and adaptable game experience. To overcome cognitive accessibility barriers, game designers could include more lenient challenge levels and provide more time to deal with threats [41]. These options are also valuable for players of different ages and with various gaming experiences to participate in the game. These options present some current features that can be incorporated into video games to make them fairer and more flexible. However, it should also be noted that further options are likely to emerge with the evolving technological landscape.

The Fair and Flexible Play heuristic also encompasses a game design that ensures the gameplay experience can be modified and adapted to better align with a player's preconditions for participation, thereby providing the possibility of enjoyment for a more diverse spectrum of players. Accomplishing this suggests a heightened focus on various game features, exploring how to make them customisable to enhance their inclusivity and versatility, thereby accommodating a more comprehensive range of player preferences. In the "Fair and Flexible Design" heuristic, game developers are urged to delve deep into the longstanding philosophical debate on "fairness". Rather than just presenting every player with the same conditions and calling it a day, developers should actively engage with the disability community and its advocates. The aim is to craft games that ensure equality of outcome, not just equality of opportunity. The real challenge for game developers in adhering to the heuristic of Fair and Flexible Play lies in designing accessibility options that cater to differently abled gamers without compromising on the game challenge. The gameplay experience should be as engaging and rigorous for a person with a disability as it is for a fully non-disabled player. It is imperative to understand that the ongoing discussions about introducing "easy" or "narrative" modes are not mere debates between commercial and creative goals. Gamers with impairments can possess the same, if not more, fervour as any other player, challenging the conventional notions of what a "core" gamer should be. Disability arises from the characteristics of an environment, which makes it crucial to understand each player's experience. This heuristic recognises and underscores that every player deserves a fulfilling and fair gaming experience.

Apart from considering the physical accessibility space of the game, it is also vital to consider inclusivity in terms of how players experience the communicative aspects of the game. This includes aspects such as the content and terminology used throughout the game so that certain players do not experience stigmatisation or exclusion. When adding lenient challenge levels, for example, such options must not be introduced in patronising ways [41]. Achieving this type of inclusivity necessitates becoming and remaining informed and actively engaging with various strands within the gaming community.

The inclusivity aspect of the Fair and Flexible Play also encourages being mindful of the game's localisation. This includes adapting the game's content for new regions, which involves more than mere language translation. It considers associated imagery and cultural elements that influence how the game, and its content will be perceived. Depending on the type of game, several different game elements warrant consideration. For instance, this could include interaction interface information such as player stats, location names, item names, map names, and the names of non-player characters (NPCs). Subtitles for in-game dialogue and cutscenes also fall into this category. Furthermore, attention should be given to in-game dialogue between characters, prompts from NPCs, and quest-related text, which steer players through the virtual world.

Heuristics II Adjustable and Equitable Play. The Adjustable and Equitable Play heuristic underscores that a game should provide features enabling players to tailor and personalise the gameplay experience to their preferences and needs. The heuristic strives to increase the game's usability, reaching higher satisfaction with the game [44] and a more attainable game experience. The objective is to ensure every player has an equitable chance to enjoy, compete in, and complete the game. This may be reflected in features such as adjustable difficulty settings, input controllers, or game elements that adapt to different playstyles. Adjustable and Equitable Play focuses on devising games that accommodate various individual preferences and abilities. Compared to the Fair and Flexible Play heuristic, the Adjustable and Equitable Play heuristic goes beyond being able to access the game and feeling a sense of inclusion and involves satisfaction with the game and being able to reach the game experience intended.

This principle highlights the need to offer multiple ways to customise the gaming experience. Key considerations include support for different input devices, the capacity for remappable controls, and the availability of adjustable gameplay parameters. Developers should provide options for players to adjust game controls, audio and visual settings, difficulty levels, and supportive features designed to cater to differing player tastes and skill sets. Adaptability is central to Adjustable and Equitable Play, with game designers facilitating customisable features that let players modify the game experience as per their needs.

Adjustable and Equitable Play mandates the game developer to provide various means of interaction and access. For instance, support for diverse input devices like mouse, keyboards, gamepads, touch controls, or eye-tracking technology empowers your players to select what input device best suits them. Design features providing the option of remapping gamepad/keyboard controls and the option to invert the Y-axis cater not only to those with mobility challenges but also to left-handed individuals and those who have grown accustomed to such control setups, having encountered them as default options in their initial gaming experiences. Incorporating a variety of control options and input methods into your game design is beneficial. Doing this empowers players to choose their interaction and play style that best aligns with their priorities and preferences. This aligns with both the Fair and Flexible heuristic, allowing players to access the game, and with the Adjustable and Equitable heuristic, allowing players to experience a satisfying game experience.

Incorporating the Adjustable and Equitable design heuristic in the gameplay settings and assistive features into your game design opens the experience to players of diverse skill levels and those contending with fluctuating conditions for game participation. These conditions range from temporal and spatial constraints to differing equipment, such as hardware or software. The concept of "situational disabilities," [29], is also covered under this premise. Situational disabilities refer to circumstances or temporary conditions that may impact and impede a player's ability to engage and interact with a game. For instance, a player engrossed in a game on a handheld device during a night-time flight may deem voice commands unsuitable for guiding their avatar, given the environment. Instead, they may opt for a more discreet and contextually appropriate interaction method, such as touchscreen commands. This choice reflects a trade-off between maintaining the game's immersive quality and the practicality of playing under specific conditions, demonstrating the player's adaptability to their situational constraints.

Recognising these variable conditions and incorporating adaptable gameplay options into game design are vital strategies to enhance usability and game experience. This approach assures a more inclusive and enjoyable gaming experience tailored to a broad spectrum of players, thus taking into consideration their distinct needs and diverse circumstances. Moreover, by implementing such design features, designers can allow players to enjoy the game at a pace and under conditions uniquely suited to their preferences and participation constraints. This level of customisation allows for a more personal, adaptable gaming experience, acknowledging the situational factors that influence game engagement. As such, these considerations contribute to creating an accessible, immersive, and inclusive gaming environment that respects and values player diversity. Using this design strategy not only expands the game's reach and accessibility but also enhances player engagement and satisfaction. It acknowledges that many factors shape every participant's prospect to play and seeks to create an equitable and adaptable gaming environment. In this way, players can enjoy the game on their terms, contributing to a more personalised, inclusive, and, ultimately, enjoyable gaming experience.

Heuristics III Logical Play. The Logical Play heuristic for game design emphasizes crafting comprehensible, intuitive, and logical games that make sense and appear meaningful to interact with. This approach places great importance on a player's experience, considering the diverse range of players' skill levels, prior experience, and knowledge. First and foremost, developers are encouraged to create intuitive interfaces that align closely with players' expectations and experiences. Whether a navigation menu or a control layout, every interface should be as intuitive as possible, minimizing the learning curve and allowing players to dive into the gameplay swiftly and effortlessly. Moreover, clear, easily digestible game tutorials providing player onboarding are a cornerstone in the Logical Play game design heuristic. These tutorials should walk players through the game's mechanics step-by-step, allowing them to understand the basics and acquire the necessary skills at their own pace.

The Logical Play heuristic advises developers to strive for a streamlined game interface, avoiding unnecessary complexity. This also goes for game mechanics; while complex mechanics can add depth to a game, they should not be at the expense of the overall game logic. Simplicity and complexity must coexist harmoniously in a well-designed game, providing an experience that is easy to pick up and difficult to master. The heuristic strongly advocates that designers and developers place resources forming logical in-game direction, tooltips, and context-aware assistance. This asset can be a game-changer for participants, helping them overcome hurdles, grasp challenging concepts, and master the game mechanics. These tools are not mere add-ons but integral to a supportive and immersive gaming environment. In integrating clear and intuitive game mechanics into the design, developers must ensure that players can quickly and effortlessly understand the game's rules, controls, and objectives. This requires thoughtful design and consistent feedback, ensuring players can navigate and comprehend the game, regardless of their prior expertise or abilities.

The interaction interface and PX are cornerstones of the Logical Play heuristic. The interaction interface encompasses all the on-screen elements that players interact with, including menus, buttons, icons, health bars, maps, inventory systems, and even the in-game cursor. It is the medium through which players interact with the game world; therefore, it should be clean, instinctive, and responsive. Navigation between different parts of the interaction interfaces, such as going from the game world to the inventory menu or settings, should be seamless and logical. Additionally, feedback through the interface, such as highlighting a button when it is clicked or showing damage points when a player hits an enemy, can enhance the sense of interaction and responsiveness. Not all players have the same abilities, so accessibility options such as text size adjustment, color-blind modes, or subtitles should be considered during interaction interface design. The PX is a broader concept that covers all aspects of a player's interaction with the game. It begins from the game's launch to the player's progression through its content. It includes how satisfying the game controls feel, the pacing of the gameplay, the difficulty curve, the balance between challenge and reward, and the emotional engagement elicited by the game's narrative and aesthetics. Respectable interaction interface design makes a game enjoyable and memorable. It ensures that players feel a sense of accomplishment as they progress, that challenges are fair and surmountable with skill and strategy, and that the game world is immersive and consistent. For example, in a role-playing game, interaction interface design would ensure that the Quest log structure is functional, understandable, emotionally fitting, and connected to the other design elements. Good PX in game design aims to make playing the game a pleasant, intuitive, and rewarding experience. It requires understanding the players' needs, desires, and potential frustrations. This is often achieved through design best practices, playtesting, player feedback, and iterative design.

The Logical Play heuristic emphasizes that consistency and adherence to established standards should be considered fundamental building blocks in crafting a logical game design. This perspective encourages designers and developers to deliver an intuitive gaming experience that is engaging and satisfying for the player, minimizing confusion, and enhancing overall immersion. Like any interactive medium, players must not be confused, wondering if diverse terms, situations, or actions signify the same outcome. Aligning with platform conventions can also enhance clarity, fostering a more immersive gaming experience. For instance, each gaming console carries a set of ingrained player expectations shaped by years of gameplay on similar platforms. Over time, the gaming industry has cultivated a series of design conventions akin to web and app design, which would the player's interaction with the game. These expectations, formed and reinforced over time, become instinctive, entwining with the player's muscle memory. Any deviation from conventional control mappings can noticeably affect the gameplay experience. Players must invest additional time and mental effort to comprehend and adjust to a new control scheme. Simultaneously, they must resist the urge to revert to familiar button presses, increasing the likelihood of in-game errors.

By adhering to industry standards and upholding control consistency, game developers can expedite the player's learning process, encourage more intuitive gameplay, and ensure a seamless and immersive gaming experience. The primary objective is to lessen the cognitive burden on the player, enabling them to immerse themselves in the game world rather than grapple with control mechanics.

Heuristics IV Error Prevention in Play. Error Prevention in Play encourages developers to look beyond immediate game elements and mechanics and consider the broader interaction between the game system and the player. Borrowing principles from interaction design, this heuristic advocates for implementing mechanisms that prevent players from committing easily avoidable mistakes, thus enhancing the gaming experience.

The Seven Principles for Universal Design [4] recommend a design approach that is lenient towards user errors. These established principles advise that errors, when they occur, should be communicated to the users gracefully, in an actionable manner, and with utmost clarity. This approach mitigates user frustration and confusion, thus enhancing the overall UX. However, the Error Prevention in Play heuristic suggests taking the perspective further, stressing the importance of proactive error prevention rather than mere error management. From our viewpoint, it is far more beneficial to construct a design that precludes players from making errors in the first place, which relates to the Error Prevention in Play with Logical Play game design heuristics.

The Error Prevention in Play heuristic draws from the synthesized guidelines and the Seven Principles of Universal Design - especially Principle 5: Tolerance for Error. The heuristic aligns with Nielsen's [45] usability heuristics for interface design, emphasizing the need to preemptively identify potential pitfalls and implement safeguards that minimize the chance of participants' errors. Rather than downplaying the importance of clear and actionable error messages, we suggest a recalibration of the design focus: shifting the paradigm towards preventing unnecessary player errors before they materialize in the interaction interface.

5 Conclusion

This paper has discussed Universal Design in video gaming, emphasizing the necessity of creating universally attainable gaming experiences. By integrating the AGE (Attainable Game Experience) framework and its associated heuristics, we have outlined a comprehensive approach towards enhancing game accessibility, engagement, and representation for a diverse audience. Our discourse underscores the imperative of adopting a proactive stance in game design, which aligns with ethical imperatives and serves pragmatic business interests by broadening the potential user base. The insights presented herein aim to catalyze a paradigm shift in the gaming industry towards more inclusive and empathetic practices, fostering a community underscoring accessibility to all, regardless of individual abilities or circumstances. This endeavor towards inclusivity enriches the gaming landscape and mirrors broader societal shifts towards embracing diversity and inclusivity.

As explored in this discourse, the integration of Universal Design principles advocates for a more inclusive gaming environment where accessibility, engagement, and representation is paramount. Future research should delve deeper into the empirical validation of the AGE framework, exploring its applicability across diverse gaming genres and platforms. The real-world impact of AGE-guided design on player experiences should be investigated, especially among traditionally underrepresented groups. The inquiry could yield insightful data to refine and further enhance the framework. Moreover, interdisciplinary studies combining HCI principles with cognitive psychology, sociology, and assistive technology could provide a holistic understanding of user experiences, informing more empathetic and inclusive design strategies.

Additionally, exploring the economic implications of Universal Design in gaming, in terms of market expansion and user retention, could provide compelling evidence for its broader adoption within the industry. Pursuing inclusivity in gaming, as championed by this paper, is a matter of ethical consideration and a strategic imperative for the evolution of interactive digital media. The AGE framework serves as a foundational step towards this goal, inviting a collaborative effort among researchers, designers, and stakeholders to reimagine the boundaries of accessible and engaging gaming experiences.

References

1. European Union: European Accessibility Act (2024). https://ec.europa.eu/social/main.jsp?catId=1202&langId=en
2. European Union: Disability in the EU: facts and figures. Europa (2024). https://europa.eu/!FXWJBh

3. Jaakkola, E.: Designing conceptual articles: four approaches. AMS Rev. **10**(1–2), 18–26 (2020)
4. Center for Universal Design: The principles of universal design (Version 2.0). North Carolina State University (1997). https://design.ncsu.edu/research/center-for-universal-design/
5. Iwarsson, S., Ståhl, A.: Accessibility, usability, and universal design—positioning and definition of concepts describing person-environment relationships. Disabil. Rehabil. **25**(2), 57–66 (2003)
6. Holloway, C.: Disability interaction (DIX) a manifesto. Interactions **26**(2), 44–49 (2019)
7. Story, M.F.: Maximizing usability: the principles of universal design. Assist. Technol. **10**(1), 4–12 (1998)
8. Cairns, P., Power, C., Barlet, M., Haynes, G., Kaufman, C., Beeston, J.: Enabled players: the value of accessible digital games. Games Cult. **16**(2), 262–282 (2021)
9. Aguado-Delgado, J., Gutierrez-Martinez, J.M., Hilera, J.R., de-Marcos, L., Otón, S.: Accessibility in video games: a systematic review. Universal Access Inf. Soc. **19**, 169–193 (2020)
10. Grammenos, D., Savidis, A., Stephanidis, C.: Designing universally accessible games. Comput. Entertainment (CIE) **7**(1) (2009). Article 1
11. Power, C., Cairns, P., Barlet, M.: Inclusion in the third wave: access to experience. In: Filimowicz, M., Tzankova, V. (eds.) New Directions in Third Wave Human-Computer Interaction: Volume 1-Technologies, pp. 163–181. Springer, Cham (2018). https://doi.org/10.1007/978-3-319-73356-2_10
12. Hamari, J., Keronen, L.: Why do people play games? A meta-analysis. Int. J. Inf. Manage. **37**(3), 125–141 (2017)
13. Batra, R., Ahtola, O.T.: Measuring the hedonic and utilitarian sources of consumer attitudes. Market. Lett. **2**, 159–170 (1991). https://doi.org/10.1007/BF00436035
14. Holbrook, M.B., Hirschman, E.C.: The experiential aspects of consumption: consumer fantasies, feelings, and fun. J. Consum. Res. **9**(2), 132–140 (1982). https://doi.org/10.1086/208906
15. Palmquist, A.: Plug & play? Stakeholders' co-meaningmaking of gamification implementations in workplace learning environments. Dissertation, University of Gothenburg Department of Applied Information Technology (2023)
16. van der Heijden, H.: User acceptance of hedonic information systems. MIS Q. **28**(4), 695 (2004). https://doi.org/10.2307/25148660
17. Nacke, L.: From playability to a hierarchical game usability model. In: Proceedings of Future Play 2010, pp. 11–12. ACM (2010)
18. Nacke, L.: Games user research and physiological game evaluation. In: Bernhaupt, R. (ed.) Game User Experience Evaluation, pp. 63–86. Springer, Cham (2015). https://doi.org/10.1007/978-3-319-15985-0_4
19. Lazzaro, N.: The four fun keys. In: Isbister, K., Schaffer, N. (eds.) Game Usability: Advancing the Player Experience, pp. 315–344 (2008)
20. Nacke, L.E., Drachen, A.: Towards a framework of player experience research. In: Proceedings of the Second International Workshop on Evaluating Player Experience in Games at FDG 2011. ACM (2011)
21. Scapin, D.L., Senach, B., Trousse, B., et al.: User experience: buzzword or new paradigm? In ACHI 2012: The Fifth International Conference on Advances in Computer-Human Interaction, pp. 336–341. Valencia, Spain (2012). https://hal.inria.fr/hal-00769619
22. Wiemeyer, J., Nacke, L., Moser, C., Mueller, F.: Player experience. In: Dörner et al. (eds.) Serious Games (Chapter 9) (2016). https://doi.org/10.1007/978-3-319-40612-1_9
23. Engl, S., Nacke, L.: Contextual influences on mobile player experience—a game user experience model. Entertainment Comput. **4**(1), 83–91 (2013)

24. Palmquist, A., Jedel, I., Goethe, O.: Universal Design in Video Games: Active Participation Through Accessible Play. Human–Computer Interaction Series. Springer, Cham (2024). https://doi.org/10.1007/978-3-031-30595-5. ISBN 978-3-031-30597-9

25. Clarkson, P.J., Coleman, R.: History of inclusive design in the UK. Appl. Ergon. **46**, 235–247 (2015)

26. Bierre, K., Chetwynd, J., Ellis, B., Hinn, D.M., Ludi, S., Westin, T.: Game not over: accessibility issues in video games. In: Proceedings of the 3rd International Conference on Universal Access in Human-Computer Interaction, pp. 22–27 (2005)

27. World Health Organization: Global report on health equity for persons with disabilities (2022)

28. Lid, I.M.: Developing the theoretical content in universal design. Scand. J. Disabil. Res. **15**(3), 203–215 (2013)

29. Heilemann, F., Zimmermann, G., Münster, P.: Accessibility guidelines for VR games—a comparison and synthesis of a comprehensive set. Front. Virtual Reality **2**, 697504 (2021)

30. Sears, A., Lin, M., Jacko, J., Xiao, Y.: When computers fade: pervasive computing and situationally induced impairments and disabilities. In: HCI International, vol. 2, no. 3, pp. 1298–1302 (2003)

31. Porter, J.R., Kientz, J.A.: An empirical study of issues and barriers to mainstream video game accessibility. In: Proceedings of the 15th International ACM SIGACCESS Conference on Computers and Accessibility, pp. 1–8 (2013)

32. Simonsen, J., Robertson, T. (eds.): Routledge International Handbook of Participatory Design. Routledge (2012)

33. Thominet, L.: Open video game development and participatory design. Tech. Commun. Q. **30**(4), 359–374 (2021). https://doi.org/10.1080/10572252.2020.1866679

34. Spock, J.: Bringing the community into the dev team: a look into open development. In: GDC Vault. GDC Next 2014 (2014). http://www.gdcvault.com/play/1021475/Bringing-the-Community-into-the

35. Lin, D., Bezemer, C.-P., Hassan, A.E.: An empirical study of early access games on the Steam Platform. Empir. Softw. Eng. **23**(2), 771–799 (2018). https://doi.org/10.1007/s10664-017-9531-3

36. Jeremy, H.: Subnautica feedback system. In: GDC Vault. Game Developers Conference (2015). http://www.gdcvault.com/play/1022284/Tech

37. Ismail, R.: Nuclear throne: performative game development in hindsight. In: GDC Vault. GDC Europe 2016 (2016). http://www.gdcvault.com/play/1023774/-Nuclear-Throne-Performative-Game

38. Baltzar, P., Hassan, L., Turunen, M.: Assistive technology in gaming: a survey of gamers with disabilities. In: Proceedings of the 7th International GamiFIN Conference, GamiFIN 2023. CEUR-WS (2023)

39. Barlet, M.C., Spohn, S.D.: Includification: A Practical Guide to Game Accessibility. The Ablegamers Foundation (2012)

40. IGDA: Accessibility in games: motivations and approaches. In: White Paper. International Game Developers Association (2004)

41. Brown, M., Anderson, S.L.: Designing for disability: evaluating the state of accessibility design in video games. Games Cult. **16**(6), 702–718 (2021)

42. ISO 9241-210: Ergonomics of human-system interaction. Part 210: Human-centered design for interactive systems (2019)

43. Yuan, B., Folmer, E., Harris, F.C.: Game accessibility: a survey. Univ. Access Inf. Soc. **10**, 81–100 (2011)

44. Federoff, M.A.: Heuristics and usability guidelines for the creation and evaluation of fun in video games. Master's thesis, Indiana University (2002)

45. Nielsen, J.: Ten usability heuristics (2005)

Empathic Characters for Digital Games: A Prototype Proposal

Tânia Ribeiro[1]([✉]) [iD], Ana Isabel Veloso[1] [iD], and Peter Brinson[2] [iD]

[1] DigiMedia, University of Aveiro, Aveiro, Portugal
ribeirotania@ua.pt
[2] USC Games, University of Southern California, Los Angeles, USA

Abstract. This paper seeks to introduce a toolkit designed for game designers and creative professionals, providing resources to facilitate the development of characters for empathy communication. This research project is conducted according to the principles of grounded theory and describes the process of converting a research hypothesis into an instrument.

A survey was developed and carried out in gamers' communities to identify potential correlations between gamer's attributes and playable Characters' characteristics, yet in the survey analyses, no correlations were identified between variables. Notwithstanding, the character mentioned as the most Emphatic one was Character 2B from the digital game NieR: Automata. Further analysis of 2B's story within the game world led to the following hypothesis: Empathy is information, and the better the character's network of information is communicated, the more Empathy the Player will feel.

This toolkit is an analog instrument composed of a set of cards with instructions divided into four topics: the character's personality (15 cards), the character's life foundation (16 cards), the character's physical appearance (6 cards), and the character path and conflict (14 cards). The toolkit was evaluated in the classroom context, proving to be a good creative tool for character creation, yet the instructional design guidance needs to be addressed.

According to the theory proposed in this paper, if all the cards are completed and their information is introduced into the design of a playable character for a digital game, we will have a character who can communicate empathy to the gamers.

Keywords: Game Design · Character Design · Empathy · Creativity

1 Introduction

In the realm of digital game development, characters transcend mere visual representations: they embody the essence of connecting gaming audiences with immersive narratives [1, 2]. While a visually appealing character can enhance player enjoyment, a character brought to life through a compelling personality and narrative has the potential to transform players into active participants within the game world. A well-drawn character can help a player enjoy the game, but a convincing personality and story can deeply immerse a player in the game [3, 4].

X. Fang (Ed.): HCII 2024, LNCS 14731, pp. 262–274, 2024.
https://doi.org/10.1007/978-3-031-60695-3_17

When a Player is immersed in a digital game, the narrative premise, the visual rendering of the character and its surroundings, played through the character's perspective, may cause the player to feel sympathy for the character. After a while, they are distressed and may feel good or bad for themselves, depending on their challenges or the circumstances they may find themselves in; after knowing the character for a while, a conflict or personal distress occurs within the player: they feel a sense of responsibility and agency for the character's actions and fate, and the player feels empathy [5–7].

This paper begins with a discussion of empathy and character creation and presents the methodology and procedures applied to the research in the second section. The third section is dedicated to the instructions to create empathic characters – the developed toolkit and its evolution. In the fourth section, the discussion of the research output is carried out. The paper outlines the expected impact, imitations, and future work perspectives.

1.1 Empathy

Empathy, a fundamental aspect of human interaction, entails the emotional understanding of the motives behind expressions of joy, sorrow, aspirations, and resignations, compelling individuals to comprehend the sentiments of others as if they were their own [8]. This phenomenon has garnered significant attention within social, philosophical, and psychological academic discourse, primarily due to its intrinsic connection to the social nature of human beings, exemplified by the capacity to engage with others in a social context [9].

Empathy encompasses a range of sentiments, such as sympathy, compassion, or tenderness, conveyed through various means of communication, fostering emotional contagion in the empathetic subject. The emotive facet of empathy acts as a motivational force, compelling individuals to alleviate the suffering of those to whom empathy is communicated. These include understanding another person's internal state, adopting the posture or matching neural responses of an observed other, coming to feel as another person feels, intuiting or projecting oneself into another's situation, imagining how another is thinking and feeling, imagining how one would think and feel in the other's place, feeling distressed at witnessing another person's suffering and feeling for another person who is suffering. A concern for others is a factor of remarkable evolution in human evolution concerning social health maintenance and the development and fulfillment of social and moral norms [6, 10].

Concern for others is an essential feature of healthy social functioning; Empathic concern plays a crucial role in facilitating prosocial behavior with altruistic motivations toward others and is implicated in developing morality [11].

1.2 Character Creation

The creation of a character begins with an idea, which can come out of nowhere or, more frequently, from creativity sessions where some method is used to generate ideas. Despite the acknowledged importance of characters as one of the main engagement factors for audiences [16, 17], existing literature lacks models or frameworks to offer guidance on crafting digital game characters [1, 3].

Several design techniques have supported character creation [12]. Among the frequently used are brainstorming, mind mapping, or lists. The most used technique for groups may be brainstorming, a well-known and creative technique that can also be used individually, where they explore spontaneous ideas and write them down. It is suitable for generating many ideas very freely and quickly. Mind mapping is a more structured version of the brainstorming technique, working very well when participants arrive at a core concept and want to explore it in greater depth, consisting of writing down the core idea in the middle of a paper, sheet, or screen and then following principles of brainstorming. The use of lists is also a common technique, similar to mind mapping but with the ideas ordered in an organized sequence [12]. These techniques are widespread and used, but they can end up in chaos and confusion for less experienced content creators. This can happen because some key aspects might be forgotten or delayed, breaking the creation flow process [13].

Creating a character for digital games or other mediums can be challenging. The designer must remember the previously cited concepts and use a method that provides enough freedom to align with creativity [4, 14].

This paper describes the journey of conceptualizing an instrument – a toolkit – that game designers and creatives could follow to create Empathic characters.

2   Method and Materials

The foundational principle inherent in grounded theory methodology asserts that the outcome of research is the inductive development of a theory derived systematically from data collected across various phases of the research process. Grounded theory involves formulating hypotheses and theories through systematically collecting and analyzing data: a predefined set of tasks is established for data collection, with subsequent analysis aimed at identifying patterns indicative of relationships between variables [15, 16]. By methodically executing these stipulated tasks, the research process adheres to a principle directly aligned with the observed phenomena [17].

This research explores the following research question: What should be the characteristics of a toolkit for game designers to craft empathic characters in digital games? Firstly, a survey was designed, validated, and distributed in gaming communitie [18]. Then the results of the survey were analyzed, taking into account the relationships between the survey variables and an analysis of the digital game Nier Automata [19]. Correlating the two tasks, a hypothesis is postulated, leading to the conceptualization of a toolkit designed for crafting empathic characters. The aim of this toolkit is to transform the prompted hypothesis into a practical and usable instrument.

2.1   Survey: Exploring the Variables of Empathy in Gamers

To understand the possible patterns of the empathic relationship between the gamer and the playable character, a survey was designed, validated, and distributed in private networks of gamers [18]. The survey assessed players' favorite playable characters from whom they felt an emotional, empathic connection. The survey collected 301 valid responses (236 from male players, 55 from female players, and ten from non-binary players) from 48 countries. The survey showed that gamers are mostly young white boys from the middle class. Their political inclination is toward Left-wing ideologies; on average, they tend to be Atheists. They like to explore the game world instead of enrolling in violent activities [20] which matches their agreeableness score (a construct related to prosocial behavior). Regarding their personality, they tend to be introverted but open-minded. The majority spent between 5 and 24 h playing per week [21].

Regarding the patterns in data regarding the picked character, the results show that these gamers tend to have more meaningful gaming experiences with fictional characters whose bodies are presented on the screen (third-person view). Those bodies tend to be human and male, with a bias for female babyface features and mature male faces [22].

Besides these data patterns, no correlations were identified between variables related to respondents' characteristics and picked characters in the survey analyses.

Notwithstanding, the character mentioned as the most Emphatic one was the "YoRHa No. 2 Type B" (2B) from the digital game "Nier Automata.

2.2 2B Empathic

"NieR:Automata," set in a dystopian future with alien machine invasions, is a 37-h action-adventure Role-Playing Game (RPG) requiring players to complete the main story three times for the full game completion. Achieving full completion, including digital game objectives, achievements, and side quests, significantly extends the time required [23]. The narrative complexity is notable due to multiple endings and branching storylines, contributing to an intricate narrative architecture [24, 25].

Regarding the gameplay, "NieR:Automata" features a mix of action-based combat and RPG elements [2]. Gamers engage in fast-paced battles against various machine enemies using a combination of melee and ranged attacks.

2B is the main protagonist of the digital game. She is a fictional character [26] with a human-like aesthetic, a babyface [1, 22], and a hyper-sexualized body and clothes [1, 3].

Around the Internet forums of debate [19, 23–25, 27–29], "Nier: Automata" is known for its deep and philosophical narrative [29], exploring existential questions, the nature of consciousness, and the consequences of war. The game challenges players with thought-provoking scenarios and moral dilemmas, with 2B at the center of these challenges [28].

2B is a military android designed to be emotionless [30]. However, she undergoes transformative growth when she has to watch her android companion 9S dying multiple times (Fig. 1), giving the character an emotional background. This fact highlights her internal conflict between her duty as a soldier and her emerging human-like feelings. The game explores the conflict between her duty and emotions, providing an emotional landscape as she grapples with forming attachments in the face of her programmed purpose in her path [23, 29].

2B and 9S bond goes beyond cooperation, evolving into a meaningful friendship. This emotional connection becomes a central point of internal conflict for her, as her duties often involve making decisions that impact both, adding layers of emotional depth to her character [19].

The overarching narrative involves a repetitive cycle of life, death, and memory wipes, leading to an existential dilemma from which we can empathize: *"Who am I, and What am I doing Here? What is the meaning of life?"* The narrative exposes these themes in a network of explanations about the characters' path and conflicts: why they behave the way they do; everything is explained, giving humanity to the character.

Fig. 1. "Nier Automata" screenshot, 2B companion dying. Retrieved from [19]

The theme of memory plays a significant role in the game. Androids undergo memory wipes, leading to questions about the continuity of identity and the impact of losing or altering memories. This raises philosophical questions about the relationship between memory, identity, and the sense of self embedded in the game narrative.

The multiple endings of "Nier: Automata" contribute significantly to exploring the possibility of life's meaning, wherein each conclusion offers distinct outcomes that inform the player about various aspects of 2B's journey. The acts and consequences of the player's actions are elucidated based on the character's life choices, with each decision consistently justified within the narrative framework. This complex interplay of options and outcomes adds depth to the existential exploration presented in the game.

2.3 The Information Hypothesis

The survey designed to understand the empathic relationships between gamers and playable characters in video games yielded 301 valid responses from 48 countries, primarily from young white males with left-wing political leanings and an inclination towards atheism. Gamers, identified as introverted, open-minded, and agreeable (a factor associated with empathy), tend to play 5 to 24 h per week [21]. The survey revealed a preference for fictional characters presented in a third-person view, with human male bodies, and a bias towards female babyface features and mature male faces [22]. No correlations were found between respondents' characteristics and chosen characters, except for the character identified as the most empathic, "2B".

The narrative complexity of "Nier: Automata" involves a 37-h RPG with multiple endings and branching storylines. The game explores deep philosophical themes, particularly through character 2B, a military android facing existential dilemmas and emotional conflicts as she grapples with her evolving human-like feelings and attachments. The overarching narrative revolves around experiences and their emotional meaning, posing existential questions. The game challenges players with moral dilemmas, exploring the role of memory in identity and the sense of the self.

Joining these two outputs – the lack of a concrete correlation between survey variables and the analyses of the 2B path in the "Nier Automata" – it seems that the gamer can feel Empathic connections with a character that communicates empathy to them, which means that the concern on the research should be on the character and the information that the character conveys.

This conclusion led to the hypothesis that empathy is information, and the better the character's network of information is communicated in the digital game, the more empathy the gamer will feel.

3   Instructions to Create Empathic Characters

Following the methodology described at the beginning of the previous chapter, in interpreting the hypothesis [31] and translating it into an instrument feasible for further testing and validation, a structured toolkit was designed to exemplify and ascertain the validity of the prompted hypothesis.

This section explains the toolkit design and its first evaluation, a case study [31]. This first evaluation aims to find the instrument's usability problems.

3.1   Toolkit Design

This instrument adopts the form of an analog brainstorming tool, comprising a series of instructional cards systematically organized into four distinct categories: (A) Personality (15 instruction cards), (B) Life Foundation (16 cards), (C) Appearance, (6 cards) and (D) Path and Conflict (14 cards), Fig. 2.

(A) Personality: It delineates the character's intellect, level of consciousness, extroversion, neuroticism, and agreeableness across 15 instructional cards. The toolkit introduces colored cards, each presenting a facet on one side and corresponding characteristics on the other. Users are prompted to make choices pertaining to each facet, with examples including extroversion choices such as "Outgoing, sociable" or "Reserved, not very social," and dominance choices such as "Is dominant, acts as a leader" or "Is subordinate, prefers to be ordered."

(B) Life Foundation: This category imparts instructions concerning the character's background. It includes directives to assign an age and a name to the character while also urging consideration of the character's hopes, dreams, room, and home.

(C) Appearance: This category, printed on translucent paper, encourages a tactile element with scratching prompts. Beyond instructing users to "Describe how the Character looks", it also prompts them to "Set up the Character's special weapon" and "Describe the Character's distinctive visual feature", among other directives related to the character's visual attributes.

(D) Path and conflict: This category integrates the preceding components and establishes a connection between the character's personal narrative and the game itself. It provides instructions related to conflict, such as "Identify the Character's enemies", "Describe how the Character feels when the conflict is solved", and "Name the one to whom the Character is most loyal". This category effectively ties the character's personal story to the overarching game narrative.

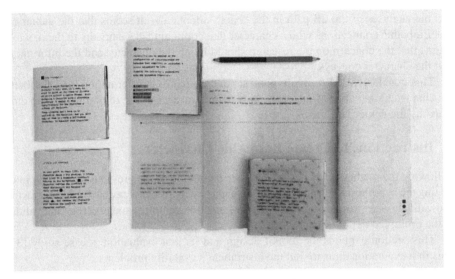

Fig. 2. Toolkit to create emphatic characters

3.2   Toolkit Testing: A Case Study

To test the toolkit developed in terms of usability, a case study involved the participation of sixteen students in interactive media course, lectured by one instructor and an external researcher. The objective was to evaluate the produced toolkit flow unfolded across four distinct phases (Fig. 3):

Phase 1 (P1) Workshop. The Professor, who carried on the activity, began with a 10-min presentation introducing the instrument, followed by addressing questions raised by the 16 students. Subsequently, the students were divided into four groups, each comprising four members, and were assigned to create a character within one hour using the tool. The activity took place at the University of Southern California;

Phase 2 (P2) Instrument Usability. Utilized survey methodologies, wherein character creation usability data were gathered from both students and the Professor. The students were surveyed through a qualitative questionnaire, which comprised six questions. These questions were non-mandatory and covered two main aspects: (i) sample personal characterization and (ii) an assessment of the instrument, which included two open-ended questions (Table 1);

Phase 3 (P3) Task Assignment. The sixteen students were organized into pairs. Each pair was assigned to produce and present a short film based, but non-mandatory, on the characters they had previously created in Phase 1 (P1). This meant that every character produced in Phase 1 was further developed into two separate short films;

Phase 4 (P4) Instrument Effectiveness Evaluation. The students presented the eight short films resulting from the assignment in Phase 3 (P3). The evaluation of these short films was conducted jointly by the Professor and an external researcher, focusing on three main aspects: (i) the degree of resemblance between the characters created using the toolkit and the characters featured in the films, (ii) the quality of the characters themselves, and (iii) the overall coherence of the message conveyed.

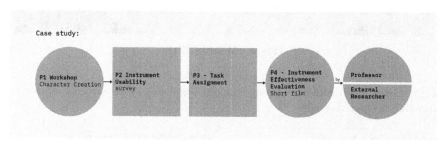

Fig. 3. Experimental proof of concept: Case-study design

3.3 Toolkit Testing: A Case Study Results

A total of 16 students participated (Fig. 4) in the case study regarding the instrument, and the Professor guided the tool implementation.

Although the experiment was conducted in at University of Southern California, most of the student participants (N = 16) were from China (9/16), followed by Americans (4/16), with one student from Columbia and another from Spain, ages from 21 to 35 years. The Professor has 20 years of game design teaching experience.

Regarding P1, the students seem to understand the task and engage in the activity, as reported in the report on P2. The most problematic issue reported was the lack of guidelines for the toolkit use. Table 1 systematizes some positive and negative aspects.

At P3, the students were organized in pairs during Phase 3 of the case study, P3 - Task Assignment (Fig. 3). Each pair was assigned to produce and present a short film based, but non-mandatory, on the characters they had previously created in Phase 1 (P1), (Fig. 4). This meant that every character produced in Phase 1 was further developed into two separate short films.

During **P4 - Instrument Effectiveness Evaluation** (Table 1), the students presented the eight short films resulting from the assignment in Phase 3 (P3). The evaluation of these short films was conducted jointly by the Professor and the external researcher, focusing on three main aspects: (i) the degree of resemblance between the characters created using the "Creating Empathetic Characters – A Method Prototype 1" tool and the

Fig. 4. Workshop (P1)

Table 1. List of the negative and positive aspects mentioned by the students regarding the instrument's design and usability, P2:

Reported Positive Aspects	Reported Negative Aspects
Quality of the method: 7 mentions	Repeated instructions: 7 mentions
Personality Instructions: 6 mentions	User instructions: 4 mentions
Design: 6 mentions	Undo impossibility: 2 mentions
Usability: 5 mentions	Obligation to draw: 2 mentions
Paper texture: 2 mentions	Time-consuming: 2 mentions
Card explanation: 2 mentions	Graphics lack: 1 mention
Pencil: 1 mention	Limited: 1 mention
Character appearance Instructions: 1 mention	Absolute: 2 mentions
Character Life Foundation Instructions: 1	Lack of Examples: 1 mention
mention	Character Personality Guidance Design: 1
Character Life curve card: 1 mention	occurrence
Character type: 1 mention	Sections Guidance: 1 occurrence
	Follow-up questions: 1 occurrence

characters featured in the films; (ii) the quality of the characters themselves, which means the depth and logical connection in the character behavior; (iii) the overall coherence of the message conveyed. The analysis revealed that students who remained faithful to the characters created through the abovementioned method tend to exhibit a more coherence in the character created, as summarized in Table 2.

Table 2. Professor and an external researcher evaluation regarding (i) the character resemblance between the one created with the tool and the film feature, (ii) the quality of the characters (ii) the coherence of the message:

		(i) character resemblance	(ii) the quality of the characters	(iii) the coherence of the message
Character A	Film A1	identical	good
	Film A2	alike	acceptable
Character B	Film B1	unlike	acceptable
	Film B2	unlike	poor
Character C	Film C1	alike	poor
	Film C2	alike	poor
Character D	Film D1	identical	good
	Film D2	identical	good

4   Discussion and Research Future Directions

In the survey analyses, no correlations were identified between variables related to respondents' characteristics and picked characters. Notwithstanding, the character mentioned as the most Emphatic one was 2B from the digital game "NieR: Automata" [12]. Further analysis of 2B's story within the game world led to the following hypothesis: Empathy is information, and the better the character network of information communicated, the more Empathy the Player will feel.

A toolkit was conceptualized to test this hypothesis, serving as a creative instrument, theoretically enabling the creation of characters capable of conveying empathy to the gamer. The toolkit developed was not tested for character empathy but for its usability with a group of 16 students supervised by a Professor observed by an external researcher. It is pertinent to note that the students were not using the toolkit for character creation in digital games as it was designed, but for film, the empathic connection between the character developed and its audience was not accessed.

The findings from this usability evaluation highlighted notable issues, prominently featuring challenges such as "repeated instructions", the "inability to undo actions", a perceived "obligation to draw", reported time inefficiency, and concerns regarding the "lack of graphics" and "insufficient examples". These issues were consistently associated with ineffective instructional design guidance in toolkit usage (Table 1).

Conversely, the students underscored the positive aspects of the toolkit, emphasizing the "quality of the tool", its well-conceived design, and the effectiveness of the character personality segment. These insights contribute valuable information for refining its design and functionality, addressing identified challenges, and optimizing its potential application in creating empathic characters for digital games. The Professor highlighted the practicality of the tool to teach character creation.

In the future, the issues reported by the students had to be addressed to pursue the hypothesis test. With the toolkit's second version, a second evaluation should be conducted, this time with experts in character design-related fields, to discuss the hypothesis in coordination with the toolkit.

5 Conclusion, Limitations, and Future Work

Empathy is a fundamental aspect of human interaction that enables humans to understand each other. It is a factor linked to prosocial behavior that can lead to collective well-being, where individuals are more likely to engage in actions that benefit others. This includes acts of kindness, altruism, and cooperation [6, 32].

Studying, teaching, and making character design for digital games bridges multiple disciplines, including psychology, sociology, literature, and game design. It encourages collaboration between researchers from various fields, contributing to a holistic understanding of human emotions, behavior, and creativity [1–4].

This paper presents a study conducted within the grounded theory framework [15–17] focusing on transforming a theoretical concept into a practical toolkit for testing a hypothesis. The central hypothesis posits that empathy within the realm of digital games is information, and the better the character's network of information is communicated in the digital game, the more empathy the gamer will feel.

The foundation of this hypothesis is substantiated by an examination of 301 valid responses gathered from participants in 48 countries [18]. Yet, the most cited character as emphatic is the character "2B" from the digital game "Nier Automata," whose narrative explores existential questions about the nature of consciousness in a network of explanations about the characters' paths and conflicts [19, 29].

Regarding the answer to the research question – What should be the characteristics of a toolkit for game designers to craft empathic characters in digital games?

In pursuit of converting this hypothesis into a framework usable for the character creators, a group of student future game designers tested the designed toolkit, showing that students stuck to the character created with the toolkit had more coherence than those who gave up on the originally created character. This observation is substantiated by the analysis of "Nier Automata," underscoring the criticality of character coherence and narrative structure for empathy (Table 2).

The findings highlight the efficacy of the analogic toolkit, which is categorized into four distinct sections: (A) Personality (15 instruction cards), (B) Life Foundation, (C) Appearance, and (D) Path and Conflict (Fig. 2). The toolkit's analogic nature, coupled with the instructional guidance provided by the cards, adds significant value to the character-creation process.

As future work, the issues reported by the students need to be addressed. The forthcoming phase involves the development of the toolkit's second version, for which a comprehensive evaluation process is recommended. This evaluation should commence with scrutiny by experts specializing in character design-related fields to ensure the toolkit's efficacy and alignment with industry standards. Subsequently, an empirical application of the toolkit is proposed by employing it to fabricate Emphatic characters within the realm of digital games, aligning with the initial design objectives. This application phase is crucial for validating the toolkit's practical utility and assessing its performance in real-world scenarios. The outcomes derived from this second evaluation will not only contribute to refining the toolkit further but also to test the proposed hypothesis. This future work proposal is inked with the research imitations: the toolkit developed was only tested on a small scale, in a classroom context, and further evaluations are needed.

The successful development of a toolkit to create empathic characters for digital games holds promising implications for academia and the digital game industry. This comprehensive approach to character creation can revolutionize how educators teach and students learn about the intricate art of game design. Furthermore, game developers will benefit from a streamlined methodology that creates empathic, resonant characters that can be a powerful instrument to address critical societal issues.

Acknowledgments. The study reported in this publication was supported by FCT – Foundation for Science and Technology (Fundação para a Ciência e Tecnologia), I.P. nr. SFRH/BD/143863/2019 and DigiMedia Research Center, under the UIDB/05460/2020 project. The authors want to acknowledge Jiaqi Shu's help and support in the toolkit evaluation process.

References

1. Ribeiro, T., Ribeiro, G., Veloso, A.I.: Playable characters attributes: an empirical analysis based on the theoretical proposal from Katherine Isbister and Ernest Adams. In: Fang, X. (ed.) HCI in Games. HCII 2022. LNCS, vol. 13334, pp. 84–100. Springer, Cham (2022). https://doi.org/10.1007/978-3-031-05637-6_6
2. Adams, E.: Fundamentals of Game Design, 2nd edn. New Riders (2013)
3. Isbister, K.: Better Game Characters by Design: A Psychological Approach. Elsevier/Morgan Kaufmann (2006)
4. Lemarchand, R.: A Playful Production Process for Game Designers (and Everyone). Massachusetts Institute of Technology, Massachusetts (2021)
5. de Waal, F.B.M.: Empathy, the umbrella term. Neurosci. Biobehav. Rev. **129**, 180–181 (2021). https://doi.org/10.1016/j.neubiorev.2021.07.034
6. Preston, S.D., de Waal, F.B.M.: Empathy: its ultimate and proximate bases. Behav. Brain Sci. **25**, 1–20 (2002). https://doi.org/10.1017/S0140525X02000018
7. Holland, A.C., O'Connell, G., Dziobek, I.: Facial mimicry, empathy, and emotion recognition: a meta-analysis of correlations **35**, 150–168 (2020). https://doi.org/10.1080/02699931.2020.1815655
8. Stein, E.: On the Problem of Empathy, 1st edn. Springer, Heidelberg (1964). https://doi.org/10.1007/978-94-009-1051-5
9. Stueber, K.: Empathy. In: Zalta, E.N. (ed.) Stanford Encyclopedia of Philosophy. Stanford University, Stanford (2013)
10. Rae Westbury, H., Neumann, D.L.: Empathy-related responses to moving film stimuli depicting human and non-human animal targets in negative circumstances. Biol. Psychol. **78**, 66–74 (2008). https://doi.org/10.1016/J.BIOPSYCHO.2007.12.009
11. Matsumoto, D.: The Cambridge Dictionary of Psychology. Cambridge University Press, San Francisco (2009)
12. Lemarchand, R.: A Playful Production Process: For Game Designers (and Everyone). The MIT Press (2021)
13. Fullerton, T.: Game Design Workshop: A Playcentric Approach to Creating Innovative Games, 2nd edn. (2008)

14. Flanagan, M.: Playful aesthetics: toward a ludic language. In: Walz, S.P., Deterding, S. (eds.) The Gameful World: Approaches, Issues, Applications, 1st edn., pp 249–271. MIT Press (2014)
15. Walker, D., Myrick, F.: Grounded theory: an exploration of process and procedure. Qual. Health Res. **16**, 547–559 (2006). https://doi.org/10.1177/1049732305285972
16. Charmaz, K., Thornberg, R.: The pursuit of quality in grounded theory **18**, 305–327 (2020). https://doi.org/10.1080/14780887.2020.1780357
17. Corbin, J.M., Strauss, A.: Grounded theory research: procedures, canons, and evaluative criteria. Qual. Sociol. **13**, 3–21 (1990). https://doi.org/10.1007/BF00988593
18. Ribeiro, T., Veloso, A.I., Brinson, P.: Exploring the variables of empathy in gamers: a survey validation (2024)
19. Nishimura, E., Saito, Y., Taro, Y.: Nier Automata (2017)
20. Bartle, R., Muse, L.: Hearts, clubs, diamonds, spades: players who suit MUDs. J. MUD Res. **6**, 39 (1996). https://doi.org/10.1007/s00256-004-0875-6
21. Ribeiro, T., Veloso, A.I., Brinson, P.: Be a gamer: a psycho-social characterization of the player. In: Fang, X. (ed.) HCI in Games. HCII 2023. LNCS, vol. 14047, pp. 301–314. Springer, Cham (2023). https://doi.org/10.1007/978-3-031-35979-8_24
22. Ribeiro, T., Mendes, R., Veloso, A.I.: Playable characters in digital games: aesthetics and gender identity in digital game player's preferences. In: Fang, X. (ed.) HCI in Games. HCII 2023. LNCS, vol. 14047, pp. 285–300. Springer, Cham (2023). https://doi.org/10.1007/978-3-031-35979-8_23
23. Lugo, J.J., Joeapseyoo, M., et al.: NieR Automata Guide: Walkthrough. In: IGN (2018). https://www.ign.com/wikis/nier-automata/Walkthrough. Accessed 9 Feb 2024
24. Stalberg, A.: Nier automata: how to get all endings. In: GameRant (2022). https://gamerant.com/nier-automata-how-to-get-all-endings/. Accessed 2 Feb 2024
25. Mumrah: Chapter Select and triggering Side Quests - How does it work? In: NieR: Automata > General Discussions > Topic Details (2021). https://steamcommunity.com/app/524220/discussions/0/3109142236144611718/. Accessed 9 Feb 2024
26. Ribeiro, T., Veloso, A.I.: Playable characters in digital games: a genre taxonomy proposal. In: 23rd International Conference on Intelligent Games and Simulation, GAME-ON 2022, pp. 32–37. EUROSIS (2022)
27. r/NieR (2024). https://www.reddit.com/. https://www.reddit.com/r/nier/. Accessed 9 Feb 2024
28. Waifutriss: The philosophy of Nier automata is astounding. reddit.com/r/Nier (2022). https://www.reddit.com/r/nier/comments/vy19pr/the_philosophy_of_nier_automata_is_astounding/. Accessed 9 Feb 2024
29. canigetawarmblanket: What is your philosophical take on NieR Automata. r/NieR (2024). https://www.reddit.com/r/nier/comments/15xf2li/what_is_your_philosophical_take_on_nier_automata/. Accessed 9 Feb 2024
30. NieR Wiki: YoRHa No. 2 Type B. Fandom (2024). https://nier.fandom.com/wiki/YoRHa_No.2_Type_B. Accessed 9 Feb 2024
31. Gray, D.E.: Doing Research in the Real World, 2nd edn. SAGE Publications, Chennai, India (2012)
32. Håkansson Eklund, J., Summer Meranius, M.: Toward a consensus on the nature of empathy: a review of reviews. Patient Educ. Couns. **104**, 300–307 (2021). https://doi.org/10.1016/j.pec.2020.08.022

Meaning in Digital Games: A Mixed Methods Investigation

Owen Schaffer[✉] [iD]

Computer Science and Information Systems, Elmhurst University, 190 Prospect Avenue, Elmhurst, IL 60126, USA
Owen.Schaffer@Elmhurst.edu

Abstract. Understanding what leads to meaningful experiences in digital games can help researchers and practitioners create more meaningful games and other interactive experiences. Literature on meaning is reviewed from the fields of Positive Psychology, Existential Psychology, and Human-Computer Interaction. An interview and survey mixed-methods study is proposed to identify the factors that contribute to meaningful experiences in digital games. Purposive sampling will be used to recruit participants who have had a meaningful or important experience playing a digital game in the last month. Participants will be interviewed and then fill out the Enjoyment Questionnaire (EQ) and Sources of Enjoyment Questionnaire (SoEQ) to assess that recent meaningful experience. Interviews will be transcribed, and the qualitative data will be analyzed with thematic analysis. This research will advance the study of positive player experiences by helping identify sources of meaning when people play digital games.

Keywords: Enjoyment · Meaning · Task Significance · Narrative Framing · Character Upgrades · Eudemonia · Controlled Experiment · Flow · Task Engagement · Intrinsic Motivation · Digital Games · Computer Games · Video Games

1 Introduction

The Positive Psychologists Peterson, Park, and Seligman identified three paths to human happiness, which they called orientations to happiness: pleasure, engagement and meaning [1]. The pleasure path to happiness is experiences that please the five senses, such as beautiful audio-visuals, haptic feedback, tangible interfaces, or pleasurable smells. The engagement path to happiness is about optimal challenge, having an optimal level of difficulty that gets people into what Csikszentmihalyi [2–6] called a flow state of "getting in the zone" while overcoming those challenges. Digital games can be designed with dynamic difficulty adjustment or adaptive difficulty to maintain an optimal level of challenge [7–10], which involves continuously monitoring player performance and adjusting the difficulty level of the game to match the performance of the player.

The meaning path to happiness is about what makes life worth living. There is extensive literature on meaning in life, from Aristotle's eudemonia [11] to Viktor Frankl's logotherapy [12].

© The Author(s), under exclusive license to Springer Nature Switzerland AG 2024
X. Fang (Ed.): HCII 2024, LNCS 14731, pp. 275–283, 2024.
https://doi.org/10.1007/978-3-031-60695-3_18

Meaning, as we define it here, is the sense that what you are doing contributes to a life well lived, or a life that you will perceive more positively in retrospect at the end of your life. Task significance, as we define it here, is the extent to which what you are doing feels important or meaningful. Enjoyment, as we define it here, is the extent to which an experience is perceived as positive. People may be motivated to pursue meaningful experiences because they perceive the experience as important whether the experience is enjoyable or not.

Schaffer and Fang conducted a card sorting study that identified 34 categories of the sources of computer game enjoyment [13, 14]. One of those categories was "Significance, Meaning, Purpose, and Legacy", which was described in part as "Knowing why your actions are important, significant, or meaningful" [14]. Schaffer built on these enjoyment sources to develop the *Enjoyment Questionnaire* and the *Sources of Enjoyment Questionnaire* [15]. One factor in the Sources of Enjoyment Questionnaire was Task Significance, which was defined as "feeling that what you are doing is important or meaningful" [15].

More research is needed to better understand what motivates people to play digital games, and what leads to meaning and task significance in digital games. Knowing what leads to meaningful experiences in digital games is important not only for video and computer game designers, but also for Gamification and Serious Games as well. Gamification is "the use of game design elements in non-game contexts" [16], such as to make non-game systems more game-like and enjoyable. Serious games are "full-fledged games for non-entertainment purposes" [16], such as education, research, exercise, or persuasion.

To reliably create meaningful experiences, practitioners need empirical research exploring what leads to meaningful experiences digital games. The main research question guiding this study is: what leads to experiences in digital games that players feel are meaningful or important? To address this question, an online interview and survey mixed-methods study is proposed to identify the factors that contribute to meaningful experiences in digital games.

2   Related Work

For those who wish to design and develop positive interactive experiences, Positive Psychology is a useful field from which to draw ideas. Positive Psychology is the empirical study of what makes life worth living, or each of the factors that lead to a positive evaluation of one's life. Peterson, Park, and Seligman [1] identified three paths to happiness, which they called orientations to happiness: engagement, pleasure and meaning. Meaning is perhaps the least well understood of these three, especially in terms of how to design meaningful interactive experiences.

There may be many paths to a life of meaning. One path to a life of meaning explored by Positive Psychologists has its roots in the ethics of Aristotle [11]. According to Aristotle, voluntarily taking virtuous actions until virtuous actions become a habit leads to virtuous character, which in turn leads to a life well lived, or *eudaimonia. Eudaimonia* or a life of meaning is, as we define it, a life that is evaluated positively in retrospect at the end of life. Peterson and Seligman [17] developed the Values in Action Classification of Character Strengths and Virtues (CSV) as Positive Psychology's response to Clinical Psychology's *Diagnostic and Statistical Manual of Mental Disorders* (DSM) [18]. The CSV presents 24 character strengths categorized into 6 virtues: Wisdom and Knowledge, Courage, Humanity, Justice, Temperance, and Transcendence [17]. While each kind of virtuous action may be a fulfilling source of meaning in life or enjoyment, character strengths focus on the traits of the individual rather than on qualities of an experience or a task.

Another path to a life of meaning may be the combination of meaning and another path to happiness, flow. Vital engagement is a concept proposed by Nakamura and Csikszentmihalyi, which they defined as "a relationship to the world that is characterized both by experiences of flow (enjoyed absorption) and by meaning (subjective significance)" [19]. Nakamura and Csikszentmihalyi interviewed artists and scientists and found that meaning can grow out of sustained interest in an activity that provides flow and enjoyment. They called this emergent meaning. They found that vital engagement involves a strong connection between the self and the object being engaged with, regardless of what or who the object is [19].

So, Positive Psychologists focus on virtuous action and vital engagement as paths to a meaningful life. Virtuous action has as its aim virtuous habits that become character strengths. Vital engagement has as its aim engagement with interesting activities that provide a flow state over long enough time that meaning emerges from the sustained interest. Now we turn to Existential Psychology.

In *Man's Search for Meaning*, Viktor Frankl developed a psychotherapy approach focused on helping people find meaning in their lives that he called logotherapy [12]. Frankl described his experience surviving Nazi concentration camps, and what he learned from that experience about finding meaning in life. Frankl quoted Nietzsche [20], "He who has a *why* to live for can bear almost any *how*," and adds that "in the Nazi concentration camps…those who knew that there was a task waiting for them to fulfill were most apt to survive" [12]. This suggests that a sense of purpose may be an important component of meaning in life.

For Frankl, responsible action is the path to meaning in life, regardless of what, to what, or to whom one decides to be responsible. Frankl wrote that the aim of logotherapy is to make people "fully aware of their own responsibleness; therefore, it must leave to [them] the option for what, to what, or to whom [they] understand [themselves] to be responsible" [12].

Frankl emphasized that this responsibility must be directed to something or someone other than oneself, that self-actualization is only possible "as a side-effect of self-transcendence" [12]. Frankl describes self-transcendence as forgetting oneself or giving oneself to a cause or another person [12]. So, Frankl's proposed path to meaning in life is self-transcendence, deciding what or whom one will be responsible for, and taking responsible action.

Inspired by Frankl's work, Wong [21] developed the PURE model of meaning for meaning therapy, consisting of Purpose, Understanding, Responsible Action, and Evaluation. Purpose is the motivational component of the PURE model and includes goals, values, and aspirations; Understanding is the cognitive component and focuses on making sense of one's situation and identity; Responsible action is the behavioral component and focuses on taking actions that are congruent with one's values; Evaluation is the affective component and includes assessing the extent of one's satisfaction with life, making adjustments if needed, and then re-evaluating [21].

McDonald, Wong, and Gringas [22] developed a Personal Meaning Profile consisting of seven sources of meaning: Achievement, Relationship, Religion, Self-transcendence, Self-acceptance, Intimacy, and Fair treatment. Edwards [23] combined several existing measures of meaning in life and used exploratory factor analysis to identify 10 factors: Achievement, Framework/Purpose, Religion, Death Acceptance, Interpersonal Satisfaction, Fulfillment/Excitement, Giving to the World, Existential Vacuum, Intimacy, and Control.

George and Park [24, 25] created the *Multidimensional Existential Meaning Scale*, a measure of existential meaning in life with three dimensions: Comprehension, Purpose, and Mattering. George and Park [26] defined existential mattering as "the degree to which individuals feel that their lives are of value and significance in the world".

Costin and Vignoles [27] tested the impact of coherence, purpose, and mattering on meaning in life judgements and found across three online, large-sample survey studies that mattering was consistently a significant predictor of meaning in life judgements while purpose and coherence were not. Their study included longitudinal data showing mattering had a significant impact on meaning in life judgements over a 1-month time lag.

Much of the research on meaning from Psychology has focused on people assessing meaning in their lives, which is a broad assessment. The research from the Human-Computer Interaction field on meaning focuses on people's assessments of experiences, such as an experience using an interactive system or playing a digital game.

Mekler and Hornbæk [28] distinguished between meaning in life and the experience of meaning, and presented a framework for the experience of meaning in HCI. This is distinction between the broader evaluation of meaning in one's life and the meaningfulness of an experience is important for games HCI researchers and practitioners who focus on improving player experiences. Mekler and Hornbæk's framework consisted of five components of meaning: Connectedness, Purpose, Coherence, Resonance, and Significance. They defined significance as "the sense that our experiences and actions at a given moment feel important and worthwhile, yet also consequential and enduring" [28]. Mekler and Hornbæk noted that significance has also been called value, mattering, and the affective or evaluative component of meaning.

Abeele et al. [29] created a *Player Experience Inventory* measure that included a meaning subscale. Rather than focusing on the more detailed subscale level, they combined their ten subscale factors into two high-level factors, which they called functional and psychosocial consequences, and tested how those high-level factors impacted enjoyment.

Schaffer and Fang conducted a card sorting study to develop a model of the sources of computer game enjoyment [13, 14]. In their study, sixty participants sorted 167 sources of digital game enjoyment drawn from the literature into categories, and the cards and categories were refined after every ten participants to iteratively develop the categories. Through this process, 34 categories of enjoyment sources were identified. One of those categories was "Significance, Meaning, Purpose, and Legacy", which was described in part as "Knowing why your actions are important, significant, or meaningful" [14]. Schaffer built on these enjoyment sources to develop the *Enjoyment Questionnaire* and the *Sources of Enjoyment Questionnaire* [15]. One factor in the *Sources of Enjoyment Questionnaire* was Task Significance, which was defined as "the extent to which you perceive what you are doing as important or meaningful" [15].

In a recent study, Schaffer conducted an online controlled experiment with 391 participants and a 4 × 4 factorial design using 16 versions of a custom research game to explore the impact of narrative framing and character upgrade mechanisms on task significance [30]. A prosocial narrative framing that framed player action as helping people in need had a significant positive effect on task significance, social responsibility, clear task purpose, and honor subscales of the *Sources of Enjoyment Questionnaire*, but did not have a significant impact on enjoyment as measured with the *Enjoyment Questionnaire*. Upgrade mechanisms had a significant but smaller effect on task significance and a significant effect on enjoyment. Although this was just one study, these results suggest that factors related to meaning such as task significance and social responsibility may not always increase enjoyment but may be valued intrinsically or have other positive effects. Schaffer suggested that it may be better to treat task significance and all the positive experiences in the *Sources of Enjoyment Questionnaire* as intrinsically valued dependent variables rather than only as means to the end of enjoyment [30].

While there has been extensive research on sensory pleasure and flow in digital games, there has been little research on task significance in digital games. The present research aims to fill that gap in the literature.

3 The Significance of Task Significance and the Sources of Meaning in Digital Games

The present research aims to explore and identify the factors that contribute to meaningful experiences in digital games. As the literature review above shows, meaning is a broad concept. Several models of meaning have been proposed. This section discusses how task significance fits into this literature on meaning, the importance of task significance, and the reason meaningful experiences were chosen as the focus of the present study rather than task significance to identify the factors that lead to meaning in digital games.

Costin and Vignoles's [27] research described above found that mattering was consistently a significant predictor of meaning in life judgements while the other two components of meaning that they tested, purpose and coherence, were not. This suggests that mattering, or what Mekler and Hornbæk [28] called significance, plays an important role in people's judgements of their meaning in life. In particular, their longitudinal data suggests that mattering or significance has a larger and longer-lasting impact on peoples' judgements of meaning in life.

Task Significance is "the extent to which you perceive what you are doing as important or meaningful" [15]. This concept is intended to take the broader concepts of mattering or significance, which are at the level of evaluating one's life, and narrow it to the more specific level of a specific experience doing a specific task. There is a long history of task analysis in HCI [31, 32]. Tasks can be decomposed into recursive hierarchies of subtasks. Significance at the task level rather than at the broad level of evaluating one's whole life is intended to be concrete and specific enough to be useful for design of interactive systems. Understanding what makes a task important or meaningful may be the key to understanding what motivates people to do those tasks.

The present research focuses on the last time the participant had a meaningful or important experience playing a digital game. Focusing on an experience rather than a task is intended to be broad enough to capture any sources of meaning that may be contributing to the meaningful experience even if they are not related to the task they are doing. For example, if a participant says that playing the game was meaningful because they were playing it with a family member, then that would be a valid source of meaning even if it is not related to the task. This study is intended to be exploratory and focused on discovering sources of meaning in digital games according to the experiences the participants share and the themes that emerge through qualitative data analysis.

4 Method

An online interview and survey mixed-methods study is proposed to investigate the factors that contribute to meaning in digital games.

4.1 Participants

Sample size will be based on saturation of data after a minimum of 10 interviews. Saturation will be defined as the point during data collection and analysis at which two consecutive interviews reveal no new second-level categories. This stopping criterion is similar to the stopping criterion used by Coenen, et al. [33] for qualitative research. Saturation is when no new qualitative insights are being found with additional interviews [34]. Hennink and Kaiser reviewed 17 interview studies and concluded that saturation was reached with 9–17 interviews [35]. This inspired us to require a minimum sample size of ten for this study in addition to the stopping criterion.

4.2 Procedure

Participants will be recruited with Amazon Mechanical Turk and Cloud Research. Purposive sampling will be used to recruit participants who have had an experience they felt was meaningful or important while playing a digital game in the last month. Purposive sampling involves recruiting participants who are well-informed about the phenomenon of interest [36].

Participants will be presented with an information sheet about informed consent. They will be presented with this definition of a digital game: A digital game is any game that you play on a computerized device, like a video game console, Personal Computer (PC), smartphone, or on the Internet. Screening questions will be asked to screen out those who have not had an experience they felt was meaningful or important while playing a digital game in the last month.

Participants will be asked to name the digital game they were playing the last time they had a meaningful or important experience playing a digital game. They will then participate in a qualitative interview for about 45 min conducted online with audio-video conference software focused on that meaningful gameplay experience. Video is optional so the interviews may be audio-only if the participant so chooses. This will be followed by a short survey focused on evaluating the same recent meaningful gameplay experience using the measures described below. The game name that they typed in at the beginning of the study as the name of the game they were playing when they had the target meaningful experience will be piped or inserted into the questionnaire to make it clear that is the experience the questionnaire is focused on. Finally, participants will provide demographic information and information about their gameplay experience and habits.

4.3 Measures

Participants will respond to the short versions of the *Enjoyment Questionnaire* (EQ) and the *Sources of Enjoyment Questionnaire* (SoEQ) [15] about their experience playing the game they reported as meaningful to assess how much they experienced enjoyment and 39 positive experiences including task significance, using 7-point Likert scales of agreement with each scale point labeled.

4.4 Plan for Analysis

Recordings of the interviews will be transcribed, and the qualitative data will be analyzed with thematic analysis [37, 38]. This means the transcripts will be coded, and then the codes will be combined to identify categories or themes supported by quotes from participants. The survey data will be analyzed to add context to the qualitative findings.

References

1. Peterson, C., Park, N., Seligman, M.E.: Orientations to happiness and life satisfaction: the full life versus the empty life. J. Happiness Stud. **6**, 25–41 (2005)
2. Csikszentmihalyi, M.: Flow: The Psychology of Optimal Experience. Harper Perennial Modern Classics, New York (2008)
3. Csikszentmihalyi, M.: Finding Flow: The Psychology of Engagement with Everyday Life. Basic Books, New York, NY (1998)
4. Csikszentmihalyi, M., Csikszentmihalyi, I.S. (eds.): Optimal Experience: Psychological Studies of Flow in Consciousness. Cambridge University Press, Cambridge, New York (1988)
5. Csikszentmihalyi, M., Nakamura, J.: Effortless attention in everyday life: a systematic phenomenology. In: Effortless Attention: A New Perspective in the Cognitive Science of Attention and Action, pp. 179–189 (2010)
6. Csikszentmihalyi, M., LeFevre, J.: Optimal experience in work and leisure. J. Pers. Soc. Psychol. **56**, 815–822 (1989). https://doi.org/10.1037/0022-3514.56.5.815
7. Keller, J., Bless, H.: Flow and regulatory compatibility: an experimental approach to the flow model of intrinsic motivation. Pers. Soc. Psychol. Bull. **34**, 196–209 (2008)
8. Hunicke, R.: The case for dynamic difficulty adjustment in games. In: Proceedings of the 2005 ACM SIGCHI International Conference on Advances in Computer Entertainment Technology, pp. 429–433. ACM, New York, NY, USA (2005). https://doi.org/10.1145/1178477.1178573

9. Moller, A.C., Meier, B.P., Wall, R.D.: Developing an experimental induction of flow: effortless action in the lab. In: Effortless Attention: A New Perspective in the Cognitive Science of Attention and Action, pp. 191–204 (2010)

10. Abuhamdeh, S., Csikszentmihalyi, M.: The importance of challenge for the enjoyment of intrinsically motivated, goal-directed activities. Pers. Soc. Psychol. Bull. **38**, 317–330 (2012)

11. Aristotle: Nicomachean Ethics. Hackett Publishing Company, Inc., Indianapolis (2019)

12. Frankl, V.E.: Man's Search for Meaning. Simon and Schuster (1985)

13. Schaffer, O., Fang, X.: Sources of computer game enjoyment: card sorting to develop a new model. In: Kurosu, M. (ed.) Human–Computer Interaction. Interaction Contexts. LNCS, vol. 10272, pp. 99–108. Springer, Cham (2017). https://doi.org/10.1007/978-3-319-58077-7_9

14. Schaffer, O., Fang, X.: What makes games fun? Card sort reveals 34 sources of computer game enjoyment. Presented at the Americas Conference on Information Systems (AMCIS) 2018, New Orleans (2018)

15. Schaffer, O.: Development and preliminary validation of the enjoyment questionnaire and the sources of enjoyment questionnaire. In: Extended Abstracts of the 2022 CHI Conference on Human Factors in Computing Systems, pp. 1–7. Association for Computing Machinery, New York, NY, USA (2022). https://doi.org/10.1145/3491101.3519819

16. Deterding, S., Dixon, D., Khaled, R., Nacke, L.: From game design elements to gamefulness: defining gamification. In: Proceedings of the 15th International Academic MindTrek Conference: Envisioning Future Media Environments, pp. 9–15. ACM (2011)

17. Peterson, C., Seligman, M.E.: Character Strengths and Virtues: A Handbook and Classification. Oxford University Press (2004)

18. Association, A.P.: Diagnostic and Statistical Manual of Mental Disorders (DSM-5®). American Psychiatric Pub (2013)

19. Nakamura, J., Csikszentmihalyi, M.: The construction of meaning through vital engagement. In: Flourishing: Positive Psychology and the Life Well-Lived, pp. 83–104. American Psychological Association, Washington, DC, US (2003). https://doi.org/10.1037/10594-004

20. Nietzsche, F.: Twilight of the Idols. CreateSpace Independent Publishing Platform (2012)

21. Wong, P.T.P.: Meaning therapy: an integrative and positive existential psychotherapy. J. Contemp. Psychother. **40**, 85–93 (2010). https://doi.org/10.1007/s10879-009-9132-6

22. McDonald, M.J., Wong, P.T., Gingras, D.T.: Meaning-in-life measures and development of a brief version of the personal meaning profile. In: The Human Quest for Meaning: Theories, Research, and Applications, vol. 2 (2012)

23. Edwards, M.J.: The Dimensionality and Construct Valid Measurement of Life Meaning (2007)

24. George, L., Park, C.: Meaning in Life as Comprehension, Purpose, and Mattering: Toward Integration and New Research Questions. Review of General Psychology, vol. 20 (2016). https://doi.org/10.1037/gpr0000077

25. George, L.S., Park, C.L.: The multidimensional existential meaning scale: a tripartite approach to measuring meaning in life. J. Posit. Psychol. **12**, 613–627 (2017)

26. George, L.S., Park, C.L.: Existential mattering: bringing attention to a neglected but central aspect of meaning? In: Batthyany, A., Russo-Netzer, P. (eds.) Meaning in Positive and Existential Psychology, pp. 39–51. Springer, New York (2014). https://doi.org/10.1007/978-1-4939-0308-5_3

27. Costin, V., Vignoles, V.L.: Meaning is about mattering: evaluating coherence, purpose, and existential mattering as precursors of meaning in life judgments. J. Pers. Soc. Psychol. **118**, 864–884 (2020). https://doi.org/10.1037/pspp0000225

28. Mekler, E.D., Hornbæk, K.: A framework for the experience of meaning in human-computer interaction. In: Proceedings of the 2019 CHI Conference on Human Factors in Computing Systems, pp. 1–15. Association for Computing Machinery, New York, NY, USA (2019). https://doi.org/10.1145/3290605.3300455

29. Abeele, V.V., Spiel, K., Nacke, L., Johnson, D., Gerling, K.: Development and validation of the player experience inventory: a scale to measure player experiences at the level of functional and psychosocial consequences. Int. J. Hum. Comput. Stud. **135**, 102370 (2020). https://doi.org/10.1016/j.ijhcs.2019.102370

30. Schaffer, O.: Task significance in digital games: controlled experiment shows impact of narrative framing and upgrades on player experience. In: Fang, X. (ed.) HCI in Games, vol. 14047, pp. 327–340. Springer, Cham (2023). https://doi.org/10.1007/978-3-031-35979-8_26

31. Crystal, A., Ellington, B.: Task analysis and human-computer interaction: approaches, techniques, and levels of analysis. In: AMCIS 2004 Proceedings, vol. 391 (2004)

32. Diaper, D., Stanton, N.: The Handbook of Task Analysis for Human-Computer Interaction (2003)

33. Coenen, M., Stamm, T.A., Stucki, G., Cieza, A.: Individual interviews and focus groups in patients with rheumatoid arthritis: a comparison of two qualitative methods. Qual. Life Res. **21**, 359–370 (2012). https://doi.org/10.1007/s11136-011-9943-2

34. Corbin, J., Strauss, A.: Basics of Qualitative Research: Techniques and Procedures for Developing Grounded Theory. Sage Publications (2014)

35. Hennink, M., Kaiser, B.N.: Sample sizes for saturation in qualitative research: a systematic review of empirical tests. Soc. Sci. Med. **292**, 114523 (2022). https://doi.org/10.1016/j.socscimed.2021.114523

36. Etikan, I., Musa, S.A., Alkassim, R.S.: Comparison of convenience sampling and purposive sampling. Am. J. Theor. Appl. Stat. **5**, 1–4 (2016)

37. Braun, V., Clarke, V.: Thematic analysis. In: APA Handbook of Research Methods in Psychology. Research Designs: Quantitative, Qualitative, Neuropsychological, and Biological, vol. 2, pp. 57–71. American Psychological Association, Washington, DC, US (2012). https://doi.org/10.1037/13620-004

38. Clarke, V., Braun, V., Hayfield, N.: Thematic analysis. In: Qualitative Psychology: A Practical Guide to Research Methods, vol. 222, p. 248 (2015)

Can We Gamify Computer Hardware Education?

Fan Zhao(✉), Gene Hoyt, and Rebeca Muniz

Florida Gulf Coast University, Fort Myers, FL 33965, USA
fzhao@fgcu.edu

Abstract. Given the intricate and abstract nature of computer hardware, instructing computer science students on the functioning of hardware devices is frequently a challenging endeavor, demanding significant dedication from both instructors and students. While the delivery of theoretical lessons and exercises is a crucial aspect of the teaching process, the most pivotal element in hardware-based courses is hands-on exercises. These practical engagements play a vital role in awakening or sustaining the curiosity of computer science students for hardware courses. This paper seeks to assess the efficacy of two teaching methods, namely practice and lecture, with the aim of determining the more effective approach in enhancing students' learning outcomes in computer hardware. The results did not align with our initial hypothesis, and potential reasons for this discrepancy were discussed. Additionally, future study plans were outlined to further investigate and address the observed outcomes.

Keywords: Computer education · Simulation · Gamified education

1 Introduction

As an integral pillar of Information Systems foundational knowledge, understanding computer hardware is a crucial element in the curriculum. Immersing themselves in hardware knowledge empowers students to grasp the operational intricacies of computers. This comprehension not only allows them to conceptualize the fundamental principles of computer hardware but also enhances their ability to discern the intricate relationship between computer hardware and Information Systems. This, in turn, contributes significantly to advancements in the field of Information Systems. According to Xie et al. [1], despite their best efforts and the students' commitment, only a few students in the class could effectively translate the content of computer hardware knowledge into practical applications because it appeared overly abstract and challenging to grasp. Students generally do not find hardware concepts particularly engaging [2]. Generating interest among students for hardware knowledge poses a significant challenge. Hence, it becomes imperative to explore alternative approaches to traditional teaching methods in computer hardware education to enhance students' learning outcomes [3]. This paper endeavors to identify an alternative teaching method, comparing it with the traditional lecture approach, with the aim of presenting a more effective strategy to enhance students' learning outcomes in the computer hardware education.

© The Author(s), under exclusive license to Springer Nature Switzerland AG 2024
X. Fang (Ed.): HCII 2024, LNCS 14731, pp. 284–293, 2024.
https://doi.org/10.1007/978-3-031-60695-3_19

2   Literature Review

2.1   Simulation

Simulation learning has come a long way in its implementation in the classroom. They are used as an accompaniment to a lesson to enrich the learning of the students. It allows for better retention because a simulation can provide context for an abstract concept in a lesson [4]. Simulations are an imitation of a real-world process over time. Students are used to this type of example when they practice a fire drill at school. The student learns that when it sounds, they are to leave the classroom and go to a designated evacuation zone. They practice this periodically during the school year to reenforce the lesson. If this were to happen in real life, the student is better prepared for the emergency.

The same concept is applied when doing a computer simulation. Computer simulations allow an abstract concept to be represented for the student and they can interact with it to view potential choices and consequences from those decisions. They can make the learner the active agent controlling their knowledge [5]. A computer can manipulate variables, create visualizations, and test out experiments. This boosts the student's engagement and knowledge by having them oversee the way they are learning. Students have different types of learning styles. Learning style is the method a learner prefers and prioritize in their learning process. People have differences in how they make decisions and problem solve. Some learners may learn better by listening to a lecture while others may like the information presented visually. A simulation can touch on all those aspects. There is a lot of trial and error that can be tested during a simulation which can have the learner understand why a certain situation can be correct instead of another. Simulations greatly improve the learning of visual, kinesthetic, and auditory learners. Almasri [5] claims that kinesthesis learners have a relatively higher influence on student engagement as compared to their satisfaction. Simulations improved their learning because it promotes intrinsic motivation to enhance curiosity. This can be something to consider if a teacher were able to assess their classroom and see of there are a higher proportion of the three learning styles mentioned.

Simulations have been proven to help with learning when accompanied with spoken text. Liu et al. [6] found that participants that learned with animations and spoken text tested better on the intermediate and delayed posttest than participants that learned with a simulation with written text. There were similar results for simulations that included spoken test. This improved learning and did not have any effect on the cognitive load of the task. The advantages of simulation learning are that a simulation can speed up or slow down periods of time for a learner to see changes. This is useful for automation systems to view if implementation new machines would increase efficiency in a factory like in the minerals industry. Models can be made to view how different purchases could potentially improve a company working. The company can choose what is best for them that is financially realistic.

Simulations are also useful for situations that have many what if questions. The mineral and mining industry poses many questions on what the right reaction to specific scenario is. In those types of industries, accidents caused by poor training are the root causes of fatal and non-fatal injuries. A study conducted by Bergamo et al. [7] found that even though regular training was satisfactory, the simulation revealed that there were flaws in the training. The decisions that some employees made did not correlate with what they were taught in the training session. They discovered where there needed to be improvements to reduce the number of accidents to the workers. The simulation also determined that age and process work experience are better indicators of performance than academic experience. This brings up another benefit that it can find unexpected problems in a system from a simulation. The study previously mentioned revealed flaws in the training. They determined that having people learn the training in the class was not enough to ensure that they understood what they learned. The new employees needed more experience in the field. This information was not the point of the simulation but was discovered because of the simulation. This could have been ignored if the company continued to train their employees the traditional way.

The drawbacks to simulation learning can be that there needs to be a considerable amount of information to be collected to have an accurate simulation. Simulations can become outdated very quickly. There are many science concepts that develop every year and if the simulation wants to be maintained there would have to be regular updates to the newest findings. This can end up becoming very costly for a school since there is likely not enough money in their budget to keep up with these updates. The simulation would be less effective since there isn't a need for this knowledge. Students would use it less and eventually the software would be removed from computers because it is no longer relevant. Another drawback would be that with new technology there is a learning curve when it comes to its implementation in the classroom. Teachers would need to be trained in how to run simulations properly which results in figuring out how to put in the time. Teachers do not have a lot of time to learn new software during the school year so it would have to be done during their summer vacation. This would be difficult to execute as some teachers leave for the summer to vacation or like to use it to rest after a difficult year. The financial portion would need to be considered because a school would need trainers to teach the staff how to use it and they may not have the funding. The final drawback to simulation is if the modeler creating the simulation is not properly trained, then the quality of the model will lead incorrect analysis. The data collected for a model could not be accurate so when a user tries to make decisions the results may not make sense. The model becomes inaccurate, and the results interpreted are skewed. This would not be useful in a classroom since they rely on this information to learn difficult concepts.

Overall simulations are best used for automation-based training, performance calculations, and systems thinking. They are best to analyze different scenarios and visualize what the effects of multiple situations could be. It is cost effective for a company to use since they would not experience any physical losses from a decision. Simulations have paved the way for the newest simulation-based technologies like augmented reality and virtual reality.

2.2 Augmented Reality

Augmented reality is a technology that combines real and virtual objects in the environment and real time to run in a 3-D space. This sounds like virtual reality, but the main difference is in how the objects are presented to the user. Virtual reality completely replaces a user's vision with the use of a headset and handheld device. Augmented reality only appears on the device the system is running on. An example of this would be a game called "State Change of Water" [8] where students can control the water flow and try to save as much water as possible until the water reaches the desired location. The student can change the state of the water as they view it flowing down a river. This type of reality follows the model that is proposed in a study by Alrashidi et al. [5] where there are three main components: the view, the model, and the controller. The view is the visual presentation that appears on the display system. This consists of camera view, main page, AR view, and login view. The model is how the data is saved and represented by the system. This can be object data, learner profile, learning progress, and learning activity content. The controller is the bridge between the view and the model. It acts as the main center to send requests/commands from the view to change the presentation in the model. The way the cycle works is by having the model update the view which is seen by the user. The user can interact with the controller to manipulate the model to whatever simulation they would like to view.

Augmented reality games are very useful in teaching science topics. It was found that adventure and simulation games are playing a major role in science learning [8]. Many of these games are single player so the student can learn at their own pace. The gamification of the concept makes the topic seem applicable to real life because they are viewing the effects of a simulation in real life. These types of occurrences happen and seeing it in a practical view makes it easier to understand. Another advantage of augmented reality is that it has been proven to show positive results in achievement of students in the classroom. According to Bal & Bicen [3] in their study about augmented reality and QR code integration the achievement it was found that in the experimental group was significantly higher than in the control group. Augmented reality works well with other technologies contributing to the education lesson. This results in positive views of the course that will motivate students to continue learning. A disadvantage is that there have been studies that there has been links to overloading the mental workload and weakening the learning effect from augmented reality. When a learner finds a game to be too difficult to learn than the intellectual workload increases [8]. This negatively affects gameplay and will not continue playing. The student will not learn the intended lesson from the game.

The benefits of augmented reality outweigh many of the drawbacks from the research given. The biggest drawback of overworking the cognitive load can be improved upon to make it a more effective learning tool in the classroom.

2.3 Virtual Reality

Virtual reality is a computer-based simulation of a 3-D image or environment that can be interacted with in a realistic way. The user can experience simulations, perform actions, and view the effects of decisions in the environment. This can be very useful when it comes to game development. This type of experience increases user satisfaction using the self-determination theory. There are drawbacks with this technology because it is still developing. There are going to be further enhancements in the future to accommodate the needs of the users.

There are two popular devices on the market: the Oculus Rift and the HTC VIVE. These systems are mainly used for gaming entertainment. These are the two affordable virtual reality systems that the public can use. They both use a set of goggles and have some sort of handheld device that the user can hold to move through the environment. The introduction of these systems into the public market allowed for virtual reality to be accessible to the everyday person. It was previously too expensive to use commercially since the technology was hard to develop [9]. Virtual reality is proven to positively influence the gaming experience but the factors that aide in its enjoyment are overlooked. According to Reer et al. [10] natural mapping and needs satisfaction were the main factors of game enjoyment. These two psychological factors allowed the game to satisfy the player's motivation to continue playing. This produces an almost addictive association to playing the game.

The technology is very useful in training students or workers a new skill or use of a technology. It was found that virtual learning makes up the weaknesses of traditional experimental teaching [9]. The reason being that the virtual learning provided feedback for why a specific decision was incorrect. This provided instant correction in a non-judgmental way, so the person was able to fulling recognize the issue. They can learn from it safely and not feel like their low knowledge was exposed to others. Another advantage is that the virtual reality has been shown to improve the mood of the player. The amount of immersion that the player can experience in the can allows them to feel like their issues that are currently happening in real life are not real. The new world that they entered is in their control [9].

This is one of the negative features of virtual reality since this can cause a person to draw out of society to stay immersed in the game. The game satisfies some innate desires in a person that can be just as realistic to experiencing it in everyday life. The game is easier to experience since there is a level of player control in the experience. The game gets better as the user gets better which motivates the user to improve themselves. Another drawback to virtual reality is that virtual reality technology can be improved in its naturalness of the experience [10]. The design of interface needs to be naturally mapped to how a person would logically use items. Incomplete natural mapping captures the natural movement of the user through a controller. Another type of natural mapping used in virtual reality is kinesics which record the natural movement of a user and project them into the virtual environment. This allows the user to roam around the environment in real time combined with incomplete mapping it provides a realistic experience. The technology is still in development so it is not working as perfectly as it could. There is some lagging or movements that don't match exactly to what the user is doing. This frustrates some users because it ruins the effect of the immersion in the game.

Teaching the intricacies of computer hardware requires engaging, hands-on exercises where the instructor's active involvement is paramount [2]. The teaching method plays a crucial role in maintaining control over students' curiosity about hardware, as a loss of this curiosity can lead to student disinterest. In such cases, students may focus solely on passing the course rather than truly absorbing the knowledge. As we discussed above, while various methodologies and approaches exist for instructing students on hardware, the most crucial component remains practical work on real hardware [11]. In this study, we are trying to offer a practical in-class exercise for students to learn computer hardware and compare it with the traditional lecture approach.

3   Research Method

According to our literature review, computer hardware practice has a potential advantage over other methods. Thus, we propose the following hypothesis:

Hypothesis: In-class computer hardware practice proves to be a more effective approach for enhancing students' learning outcomes compared to the traditional lecture method.

To assess our hypothesis and compare the effectiveness of two teaching methods, we conducted an experiment in an Introduction to Information Systems course for juniors (practice group) and a capstone course for seniors (lecture group) at a university in the US. We employed convenience sampling for this study. In both courses, students were tasked with a pre-test and a post-test containing identical 10 questions related to computer hardware. In the Introduction to Information Systems course, students engaged in a hands-on activity, disassembling and reassembling a desktop computer, while simultaneously receiving basic knowledge about computer hardware from the instructor. Conversely, in the capstone course, students received a traditional lecture on computer hardware between the pre-test and post-test. The same instructor taught both courses, covering identical content. Subsequently, all students were required to complete a survey about their experience with learning computer hardware.

A total of 32 students participated in the experiment from the Introduction to Information Systems course, while 23 students completed their quizzes and attended the lecture in the capstone course.

4   Results and Discussion

The collected data was analyzed using one-way ANOVA. Descriptive statistics results are presented in Table 1, indicating similar post-test score means of 7.5 for the practice group and 7.87 for the lecture group. A comparison of pre-test scores in Table 2 reveals that the practice group had a lower pre-test score of 5.16 compared to the lecture group's score of 6.04. Interestingly, despite the practice group's lower average pre-test score, their learning outcomes appear to be comparable to the lecture group, which achieved a higher average pre-test score.

Table 1. Descriptive Statistics

Group	Mean	Std. Deviation	N
1	7.5000	1.88372	32
2	7.8696	2.09554	23
Total	7.6545	1.96467	55

Table 2. Average Score

Methods	PreTest	PostTest
Practice	5.16	7.50
Lecture	6.04	7.87

Table 3 presents the outcomes of the Paired-Samples T test for each group. Notably, both test results demonstrate statistical significance, indicating that both the practice and traditional lecture methods effectively enhance students' learning outcomes. Furthermore, a One-Way ANOVA test was executed to contrast the outcomes of the two groups (see Table 4). The comparative analysis revealed no significant difference between the two groups. Consequently, this study does not provide support for our hypothesis suggesting that the practice method could be more effective in enhancing students' learning outcomes in computer hardware education.

Table 3. Paired-Samples T test

| | Paired Differences | | | | | | | Significance | |
	Mean	Std. Deviatio	Std. Error	95% Confidence Lower	Upper	t	df	One-Sided p	Two-Sided p
Practice	-2.34375	1.84232	0.32568	-3.00798	-1.67952	-7.196	31	0.000	0.000
Lecture	-1.82609	1.64184	0.34235	-2.53607	-1.11610	-5.334	22	0.000	0.000

One plausible explanation is that all students in the lecture group are seniors who have completed all the necessary core courses in Information Systems. They have previously acquired knowledge about computer hardware through these courses, establishing a strong foundation. The lecture session served as a means for them to recall and review the information they had learned earlier. Consequently, although the lecture may not have significantly enhanced their learning outcomes, the students still achieved improved scores in the post-test, benefiting from the reinforcement and revision of their existing solid knowledge base.

Therefore, in our future study, we plan to exclusively gather data from junior students to mitigate the potential concern identified in this research. Additional method that we plan to try to improve learning is to implement blended learning. The way to structure the learning environment is by offering students a mixture of classroom teaching, virtual labs, and websites to help them understand lessons [1]. A classroom lesson introduces the topic to the students, answer preliminary questions, and take notes. Websites can be used as additional sources of information the students can turn to if the teacher does not know the answer to niche questions. Virtual labs are the more hands-on approach to the lesson that can cement the knowledge learned because they are able to view the real-life applications.

Table 4. ANOVA

Source	Type III Sum of Squares	df	Mean Square	F	Sig.	Partial Eta Squared
Corrected Model	63.593[a]	2	31.797	11.415	<.001	.305
Intercept	74.538	1	74.538	26.760	<.001	.340
Pre	61.766	1	61.766	22.174	<.001	.299
Group	.488	1	.488	.175	.677	.003
Error	144.843	52	2.785			
Total	3431.000	55				
Corrected Total	208.436	54				

a. R Squared = .305 (Adjusted R Squared = .278).

There is a general assumption that students come into a lesson with poor background knowledge. Xie et al. [1] developed a curriculum teaching student about computer hardware and software. They had a website allowed student to learn at their own pace in an asynchronous manner. It was accessible outside of school. The data from these sites can be saved on a cloud platform so that it doesn't take up a lot of space on a personal computer [12]. There was also a virtual lab that allowed them to design computer components to test the signal flow. The results of this curriculum determined all twenty students thought it was better than a traditional classroom setting. Virtual labs can be beneficial in providing resources to all student using less physical classroom supplies. Having a cloud platform to spread the resources and distribute any special equipment to them virtually [12]. This lessons the space used in class while not sacrificing a students education by not having enough physical equipment to go around to the students.

Virtual labs are some of the hardest things to do since they are mainly done on their own. The amount of effort that student must do can overwhelm them. Students sometimes felt that a lab was due too close to when the topic was introduced [2]. They did not have the proper time to digest the information. A change to this could be to wait a week after introducing a topic to have a virtual lab due. Another way to make sure virtual labs stay effective is to make lab due during class time so that there are not similar results from other students. The labs are online, and the answers could be shared by other students. Having the labs due during class makes the students stay productive and force them to prepare for the labs. There could also be a minimum score that the students must achieve on the labs. This would make a student care about the content because they will have to at least understand half of it to get any credit for the assignment.

5   Conclusions

Over the years, the classroom has become a hub of technology with it now becoming easily accessible to give a student a computer or tablet. This change in method of teaching can be met with opposition from either side, student, or faculty. Change is difficult to become accustomed to, but it has been found that there are some willing to learn.

A challenge when it comes to computer hardware learning is the fact that educators find it difficult to manage a classroom, class materials, and the devices associated with computer science instruction. There are too many things to juggle when their main objective is to have the students learn the concept. They may not want to raise the effort of spicing up a lesson plan with new technology. Another challenge to face is only a few students had the capability of transferring the course content to real life applications [1]. The concepts in computer hardware are difficult realize in the real world because a lot of the interaction in computer science happens invisibly to the naked eye. Computer Science implements coding as well into learning. Coding uses computational thinking to conceptualize problems to be worked through with a computer [13]. This bridges the gap between applying these abstract concepts to real world situations. The hands-on approach of writing code allows a student to understand the process of how a computer would go through displaying data on a screen.

The primary objective of this paper is to evaluate the effectiveness of two teaching methods—practice and lecture—in improving students' learning outcomes in the context of computer hardware. Unfortunately, the results did not substantiate our initial hypothesis. In light of these findings, potential reasons for the disparity were explored.

Students are ready for a change in the delivery of curriculum using a tablet or personal computer. There are many innovative ways to teach computer hardware. A method of handing out tablet kits for students to learn how to build it from scratch rather than a simulation on a computer. It was found that even though the method was foreign many of the students did not have difficulty in the transition and nearly half found it easier to work on [14]. This is an indication that students are ready for the next step in improving computer hardware learning. However, teachers still offer some resistance to the change even though they may be capable of delivering the content in a new form. A way to try and influence teachers is by compromising. They may not want to use new technology to deliver instruction in computer hardware learning, but they can scaffold their lesson to continue the interest in the subject [13]. They can deliver the instruction in chunks with an activity to demonstrate it to the students. This will not overwhelm the students and improve retention of the subject.

As we discussed in the literature review, the alternative way to improve learning is by using games. There are many instructional games accessible for teachers to implement into their curriculum. Games allow a student to challenge their misconceptions about a topic by interacting with a game and the game can provide explanations in a easy to understand format [15]. Games have a common goal for the student to achieve and this motivates them to continue repeating a level to get win. This reinforces the knowledge with the constant exposure to the material. Computer hardware is a difficult subject to learn. The constant repetition will have them using words they don't read or hear daily which helps in its learning. When a teacher chooses a game is would be beneficial to make sure that the instructions for the game are concise and clear. A student's emotional state effects the gaming experience. When a student becomes frustrated it become difficult for them to store the learning objective in their memory [15]. They should be at the level that most students in the class can understand to eliminate the added stress it could cause from being too advance for them.

References

1. Xie, J., Li, J., Geng, Y.: Blended learning in computer hardware course education. In: 2008 International Conference on Computer Science and Software Engineering, vol. 5, pp. 905–908. IEEE (2008)
2. Ackovska, N., Ristov, S.: Hands-on improvements for efficient teaching computer science students about hardware. In: 2013 IEEE Global Engineering Education Conference (EDUCON), pp. 295–302. IEEE (2013)
3. Bal, E., Bicen, H.: Computer hardware course application through augmented reality and QR code integration: achievement levels and views of students. Procedia Comput. Sci. **102**, 267–272 (2016)
4. Krüger, J.T., Höffler, T.N., Wahl, M., Knickmeier, K., Parchmann, I.: Two comparative studies of computer simulations and experiments as learning tools in school and out-of-school education. Instr. Sci. **50**(2), 169–197 (2022)
5. Alrashidi, M., Callaghan, V., Gardner, M., Elliott, J.B.: The pedagogical virtual machine: supporting learning computer hardware and software via augmented reality. In: Proceedings of the 3rd European Immersive Education Summit, pp. 28–29, November 2013
6. Liu, T.C., Lin, Y.C., Hsu, C.Y., Hsu, C.Y., Paas, F.: Learning from animations and computer simulations: modality and reverse modality effects. Br. J. Edu. Technol. **52**(1), 304–317 (2021)
7. Bergamo, P.A.D.S., Streng, E.S., de Carvalho, M.A., Rosenkranz, J., Ghorbani, Y.: Simulation-based training and learning: a review on technology-enhanced education for the minerals industry. Miner. Eng. **175**, 107272 (2022)
8. Ullah, M., et al.: Serious games in science education. A systematic literature review. Virtual Reality Intell. Hardware **4**(3), 189–209 (2022)
9. Sun, S., Xu, T., Zhou, J.: The design and implementation of computer hardware assembling virtual laboratory in the VR environment. In: MATEC Web of Conferences, vol. 232, p. 01051. EDP Sciences (2018)
10. Reer, F., Wehden, L.O., Janzik, R., Tang, W.Y., Quandt, T.: Virtual reality technology and game enjoyment: the contributions of natural mapping and need satisfaction. Comput. Hum. Behav. **132**, 107242 (2022)
11. Kehagias, D., Grivas, M.: Software-oriented approaches for teaching computer architecture to computer science students. J. Commun. Comput. **6**(12), 1–9 (2009)
12. Chengbin, Q., Yongqiang, C., Shanshan, L., Youjian, Z.: Exploration of the computer hardware experiment teaching method based on the cloud platform. In: 2016 IEEE Frontiers in Education Conference (FIE), pp. 1–5. IEEE (2016)
13. Lee, S.J., Francom, G.M., Nuatomue, J.: Computer science education and K-12 students' computational thinking: a systematic review. Int. J. Educ. Res. **114**, 102008 (2022)
14. Raven, J., Qalawee, M., Atroshi, H.: Learning computer hardware by doing: are tablets better than desktops? Int. J. Res. Educ. Sci. **2**(1), 55–64 (2016)
15. Magana, A.J., Hwang, J., Feng, S., Rebello, S., Zu, T., Kao, D.: Emotional and cognitive effects of learning with computer simulations and computer videogames. J. Comput. Assist. Learn.earn. **38**(3), 875–891 (2022)

Author Index

© The Editor(s) (if applicable) and The Author(s), under exclusive license
to Springer Nature Switzerland AG 2024
X. Fang (Ed.): HCII 2024, LNCS 14731, pp. 295–296, 2024.
https://doi.org/10.1007/978-3-031-60695-3

Printed in the United States
by Baker & Taylor Publisher Services